Michael Hone's

MICHAEL HONE

HIS WORLD, HIS LOVES

Cover picture: Picture of me, *chez* Mammy, during the Student
Revolts of May '68 in Paris

At the end of Marco Polo's book he wrote,
''I never told the half of what I saw.''
My narration is infinitely more modest, but I can still say the same: I've
told only half.

Revised and Footnoted 2020 Edition

DEDICATION

This book is dedicated to Suzy, Sylvain, Bertrand, Vincent, Mireille and Christiane, all of whom made it possible.

This 2020 revised edition is also dedicated to Pete Buttigieg who brought the love of men into the light of day, as did Tim Cook, President of Apple, who declared that his homosexuality was the greatest gift granted him by God, both men worthy descendants of our hallowed ancestors in ancient Thebes, where it was declared illegal to maintain that sex between men was *not* beautiful.

My books include:
Cellini; Caravaggio; Cesare Borgia; Renaissance Murders; TROY; Greek Homosexuality; ARGO; Alcibiades the Schoolboy; RENT BOYS; Roman Homosexuality; Renaissance Homosexuality; Homoerotic Art [in full color]; Sailors and Homosexuality; The Essence of Being Gay; John [Jack] Nicholson; THE SACRED BAND; German Homosexuality; Gay Genius; SPARTA; Charles XII of Sweden; Mediterranean Homosexual Pleasure; CAPRI; Boarding School Homosexuality; American Homosexual Giants; HUSTLERS; Omnisexuality, the Death of Gay and Straight Sex; YMCA Homosexual Haven; All-Boy Porn Stars; Sebastian and *Christ has his John, I have my George: The History of British Homosexuality*. I live in the South of France.

BOOK I

CHAPTER ONE

A Dad and his Boy

The wind snatched a lone grain and carried it low over bent waves of matted brown and red salt grass. The wind blew in short gusts, holding the grain aloft, then died down, leaving it entrapped in the wet, trembling blades. Borne anew by the chilled air, the grain was swept over the raw, rippling marsh water until coming to rest in the hollow of the dike.

The boy sitting on the dike followed the movement of the grain, then shifted his attention to the brackish waters from which the dike was being dredged. He was aware of the sound of splashing in the heart of the dike as eddies wound their way through the tunnels of sod. The jelled wind stung his face, and the late afternoon sun began to decline beyond distant black hills. Overhead wispy red clouds hung motionless in a sky of frigid blue. He knew the light would soon fade; he had long since felt the waning of its meager heat. Now a chill gripped him, and the frozen, barbed earth stung into his buttocks.

Behind the sliding glass doors of a mechanical shovel, a bulky figure rhythmically pulled and released levers. The bucket dipped into the swamp, rose as water gushed from the seams, and dropped its load over the other loads of slippery silver mud and chunks of bent water grass. The repetition wearied the boy and he yawned for want of sleep and because of the cold. Sometimes his father searched him out and smiled broadly. The boy would see the white teeth against the blur of his father's autumn-tanned face, his eyes becoming watery from staring into the smudged whiteness. He parted his lips as widely as possible, hoping his teeth would reflect his own contentment. He forgot the cold, concentrating the whole of his energy on smiling, even long after his father had returned his attention to the dike.

His father had forbidden him to approach the machine. It was on his mother's orders. In his entire four years of life he had never been left alone with his father. So today was a great occasion, even if he felt uncomfortable because his neck itched from his first haircut, and because he was unsure of his mother's reaction to it, and if his father would take his part. From the barber's they had driven to the Duck Club where they had set off in the narrow metal marsh boat to empty the traps. They had paddled through tulles to small mounds of built-up earth. A stake had been driven into the mound with a chain that disappeared under the black surface. Pulling up the chain revealed iron jaws clamped on a muskrat, usually drowned, but if not his father dangled it over the side of the boat and struck it on the snout with a club. Back at the shed he had been sat on a pile of the corpses. Warmed by the yellow heat from the cast-iron stove, he watched water fleas shaped like minuscule shrimps jump from the wet, slicked-down fur. At the worktable, bathed in flickering light from the mica door of the stove, his father skinned the rats, throwing the pink, skeletal remains into a wheelbarrow. The pelts were stretched inside out over wooden frames before his father skinned away the fat and hung them up on an overhead wire to dry.

Later that afternoon his father wedged him between clods of earth while he constructed the dike. The child made himself small in his coat, searching within himself the most warmth. He hadn't liked the freezing wind or the acrid smell of the marshes, and the water from the dewy grass was wetting his feet and the seat of his trousers. Yet he instinctively felt that it was a momentous occasion, training for a role shared with all others of his father's sex. So he remained motionless, hovering in the grass like a nestling duck, wishing his father would nod for him to come to his side in the huge, noisy machine.

And in time his father did give the nod. ''Come on, Boyd, come on son.'' The child stood and brushed the cold and damp from his trouser seat. Through the cabin door he followed his father's smile, white and beckoning. He approached the machine, and it seemed almost inevitable that he should slip on the frost-glazed clods of freshly turned swamp grass and rupture his head upon the iron tracks of the armored monster before whom he had quivered.

The night of that day, he remembered too. His mother had pulled him along the sidewalk of a street not far from the sound of shunting train cars and the dense smell of sheep and cows. Dim signs over the entrances to the buildings announced names like The Dakota, Phil's and Coors' Best. Inside the air smelled cool and sweetly vinous. The places were all dark and country music played. The hospital had put something on his head which drew the men's stares as he and his mother entered. No one knew where his father was.

Later that night the boy had been awoken by the usual shouting. At first he drew the blankets over his head, but when the noise became unbearable, he stumbled down the stairs, one at a time, drowsily. At the kitchen door he saw that his father had swiped the dishes from the kitchen table. His mother, her back to him, was picking up the broken pieces. He feared his father's glassy-eyed, doe-crazed look. His mother was given orders to leave the wreckage where it was, but when she continued the cleaning, he hammered on her bent form with his fists. The boy's screams made him turn on his son, seemingly maddened by the bandages. As he approached, the boy saw the glassy-eyed stare and smelled the stench of alcohol and vomit. The man began slapping and hitting, then slugging until his nose gave way like the shell of an egg.

Blood splattered his face and dripped over the upper lip and into his mouth. The more the boy and his mother cried, the more intense became the blows, adding the child's blood to the walls streaked from the remnants of the shattered dinner.

.

Yet fate did not entirely conspire against him. In its mercy it took from memory the following several years, years in which he came to need his mother for sheltering him from the fears and conflicts he was too young to face. Twelve stitches had been needed to sew up the wound from the fall against the iron tracks. Too few to save the boy from a couple who had married too young. Too few to put him back together again.

CHAPTER TWO

Doug and Al

On the other side of the white duplex on Washington Street where I grew up, lived a woman, Mrs. Graham, and her three children, Wendy and Al, aged thirteen and fourteen, and little Douglas, my age, nine. Wendy, a freckled redhead, and Al, blond with the ducktail haircut of the period, were often away in reform school. All three were spoiled by Mrs. Graham, but it was Douglas, as the last born, who received the most affection. It was for him that Mrs. Graham bought a fist-size fishbowl of guppies, the kind won at amusement parks by throwing rings over the circular tops. As Doug had not returned home in several days to care for them, she decided they should go to me. So on a late summer afternoon she summoned me to her part of the duplex. It was a day darkened by rain clouds. Outside the shared yard, weeds lay trampled in brown mud. Mrs. Graham was at her oven when I came in, bent over a tray of oatmeal cookies. During the three years that we were neighbors, I would know that room well: the stairs going to the upper floor taken by Wendy and Nick, Al's buddy, she sometimes in bra and panties, he in shorts; the old sofa in front of the coffee table where Al spent most of his day; the door leading down to the basement, Doug's and my hide-out. Mrs. Graham closed the oven door and turned to me. Through my eyes she was an old woman, small and wrinkled, who had had her children very late. I had never seen a man around the house, and when Al and Wendy spoke of a father, it was always as the man they were going to visit when they learned his address.

I knew a lot about the guppies on the bare tabletop. At home I had half a dozen books on fish. I could tell that there were two males and a female, and that the female was pregnant. I took the bowl up with thanks and tiny hands and carried it home, begging God that He'd keep the water from spilling and the guppies from jumping out.

At home my mother went into hysterics. She hated our neighbors for the influence they had on me. If gifts were to be made it was she who would do the making. I was sent back with the guppies, blinded by tears, sobbing my heart out at the injustice that deprived me of their solace. For if there was a word that characterized the seemingly endless days and summers of my youth, it was solitude. Seated on the cot in my room I played with toy cavalry officers and wagon trains, and built and rebuilt the fort the Apaches ceaselessly attacked.

I was not disturbed.

There was never anyone coming around yelling to my mommy for permission to let me out. I was shielded from the Scouts with a protective "He's not in" to the recruiting patrol master. Not until puberty was I deemed old enough to take a bus by myself. I subscribed gladly to my mother's initiatives; I felt I was being protected. Why then the need, later, for vengeance, the need to destroy those I felt lurking in shadows, threatening? Who was to blame? A father who despised me, a mother too sheltering? I felt remorse, but remorse for what? Hadn't I strived to be the perfect boy? When and why did the balance tip to the side of evil?

Although my life seemed normal to me--given that I had known no other--there was a phenomenon that clearly surpassed the everyday. At age eight, the year they sent up Sputnik, I had begun a collection of posters, not of cars or sports heroes or the usual skull forbidding entrance to a boy's room, although the gargoyles on the ceiling, upon which I closed his eyes each night, were every bit as formidable--no, my posters were singular. On one wall I had a huge map of the Paris metro, one I knew so well I could have led the way for Sylvain, the first time we took it. On another was the aerial view of la Cité, at whose center was the Cathedral of Notre Dame. From its towers hovered the immense gargoyles I'd placarded on my ceiling. On the third wall was a map of Paris, each district in a different color, each building, street, avenue and boulevard accurately rendered.

In later years I became curious as to the genesis of my collection. Only the mysterious disappearance of an aunt, followed by my grandfather vanishing into thin air (my mom's dad whom she accused of simply ducking out of his paternal responsibilities after fathering six daughters and my beloved Uncle Bob), only these mysterious events, my child's mind fantasized, could explain my devotion to Paris, the City of Lights, a mystical connection from a long-forgotten, long-buried, certainly Medieval past, a past that would beckon me back to my true native soil as it had my aunt and grandfather. I took French as soon as it was offered, which, alas, at that isolationist time, was only on the university level.

In school I was bullied because I refused to mix with the other boys, or defend myself when I was set upon. Beaten by my father, my infant mind assumed it was that kind of pain I would be subject to should the boys lay hands on him. I spent hours thinking up how to escape the gangs of classmates waiting at the exits. By three o'clock the fear was so intense I was paralyzed with anxiety. Sometimes, like Odysseus strapped to the underbelly of a sheep, I tried to get out by losing myself in the middle of the mobs that burst through the doors at the first bell. Or the opposite, I remained in late, trying to outstay the kids lying in ambush. Other times I would make a dash from one of the ground-floor windows into the nearby bushes. Or I would leave school in the early afternoons, under the pretext of being ill, or get permission to go to the toilets and not come back. Once I brought a change of clothing as a disguise.

In imitation of his brother and sister, Doug was in and out of reform school. During one of his stays at home he and I took up together. Doug was shorter than me, and was a boy whose temerity led to self-sufficiency in ways I could not help but admire. He was a handsome child with curly hair and a ferret's cunning for unearthing the forbidden. I served as Doug's public and applause while Doug brought out the worst in me, compensation to one so withdrawn and overly well behaved. We cut school together, stole junk-jewelry from department stores that we sold house-to-house, and made up a secret society so exclusive no one but the two of us was qualified to be a member.

One day during recess, in an attempt to throw off a gang of troublemakers chasing us through the schoolyard, we hid in a thicket of bushes and exchanged clothes. Doug's were warm jeans and an old gray sweater, mine dirt-sown corduroys and a felt shirt smelling of damp earth. We scrambled up trees and through hedges, sharing the same hollows and branches. We laid foot-high rope trips for the hordes we imagined on our trail. Later, when we were caught entering class late and the exasperated teacher asked for an excuse, someone squealed on our having changed clothes. My flushed face hovered inches over the stenchy initial-carved desk tabletop. Outside it was very dark, and the room had the yellowish cast of lamplight. Breathlessly I awaited the punishment that when it eventually came did nothing to dispel the pride I felt when Doug owned up to having originated the exchange; more, to having given me the clothes.

In church I came across the story of David and Jonathan. From the moment David brought back Goliath's head, Jonathan developed a love for him to which all else was excluded, except the presence of their God whom they evoked to seal their friendship. They exchanged their clothing, an oriental custom symbolizing the gift of personality.

Thanks to the experience Doug gleaned during his stays in reformatories, his intimacy with me advanced as we neared adolescence. Our secret society developed its secret rites. Together day in and day out, conscious of the mysteries hidden in the whispers and gestures of those who had entered the ways of the world, we too, like Al and Nick and

Wendy, attempted entrance into the forbidden universe. One in front of the other, each a mirror image of the other, we sought to bring forth the miraculous nirvana the gods had bestowed on mortals, a wonder greater than fire. Inflamed by the passion of the prohibited, panting from exertion, we strove for the threshold our bodies were still too young to achieve. Our needs were certainly multiple at that callow age, but the common denominator was the necessity to find the magic Grail which, as with David and Jonathan, would bind us irrevocably together. Only then would we find the force to overcome the maddening problems at home, school and church. Together, I was convinced, we would create our own world of two; separate, we would founder like a rudderless boat on an uncaring ocean.

Douglas was again shipped off to a reformatory for burglary and I began knocking around with Al who had just come out of the same institution. My ticket into Al's gang was a basketball Al and his friend Neck would come over to borrow. Little by little I was accepted as their mascot, a step up for an eleven-year-old who had been alone as much as I. Al and Nick had a secret society too, one that, I had a hunch, worked better than Doug's and mine. Then Wendy got out of reform school, and she and Nick set up housekeeping during the day at Washington Street while Mrs. Graham was working as laundress at the nearby hospital.

My mother tried to keep me in but she was too wary of her neighbor's potential for violence to put on more pressure than the minimum needed to keep me out of reform school. I found myself suspended in a bubble of oxygen. Mother was forced to ally herself with my father, and for a short period they began getting along. Now I found myself out of dead center, no longer slapped around by him while sticking up for her.

Al also became more friendly. One day he was outside sitting on porch stoop. He called me over. Very slowly he ran his hand over a bulge in his levis that ran towards his knee. He told me to take over the stroking. "Huge, isn't it?" he grinned. Boy, was it. He wouldn't let me see it, but he would spend the better part of a day keeping it up by kneading it through the thick fabric with his fingers, or he'd wedge it between his thighs as he lay on the sofa at Mrs. Graham's, rubbing one muscular leg against the other. At times Al would cup my fly while letting me stroke the cylinder. One hot August afternoon I entered his house in the middle of a football match Al was watching, his hand absently fondling himself through the extended fabric. My eye caught Nick leaning into the kitchen sink, his hand at the fly of his open levis. At first I thought he was taking a leak, but then I saw his prick out, steel hard. "What's he doing?" I murmured to Al. "Beaten' off," came the unruffled answer. "I've told you about it a dozen times, numb nuts." As I neared the kitchen, Nick turned to give me a better view, totally at ease. The top buttons of Nick's shirt were open, and while he manipulated himself with his right hand, his left was rotating over his nipples. Eventually he turned back to the basin, heaving sighs while his buttocks pushed his rod in and out of his hand, and his chest heaved out like a swimmer swimming the butterfly. Momentarily he'd pause to rub a viscous substance, secreted by the piss hole, over the head. The operation brought on even deeper moans. At times he'd stop, as if to catch his breath, then he'd start up again, then stop, then begin again until he suddenly fell forward like a puppet cut from its strings, while jet after jet of a white substance pulsed into the basin and onto the wall beyond. I stepped back in surprise, while Al whooped from his place on the sofa. Although I was rock-hard myself, there was no question of exposing my boyhood to be compared to Nick's incredible tool. So I ran home to try out the experience on myself, to its blissful and natural end for the first time.

The discovery was easily the most important of my life. I had found pleasure in its purest form; a spring of which I was the source. An inexhaustible pleasure, the gift of my body to myself, an infallible solace against the terrors of solitude. And this pleasure, this unadulterated joy, had been offered by another. Never again, even in the deepest throes of distress, would I be entirely alone; always would I have this gift and the image of the boy who had given it. I knew then that Doug and I had been justified in our belief that the supreme mystery was the crystallization of two beings into one.

Sadly, it was not with Doug that I was destined to share my new knowledge. Doug came back from reformatory as enlightened as I, but changed. Soon he was occupied elsewhere with every pretty girl in the neighborhood. My sex life had begun at age twelve, and at age twelve it came to a sudden halt, and not for another ten years, until I found myself in the Salles des Vases grecs in the Louvre, would I ever know intimacy with another human soul.

Al, too, chose other pursuits which, the following summer, brought his downfall. Driving on a mountain road of serpentine curves he, his girlfriend, Nick and Wendy played chicken. Al was at the wheel. It was agreed they would turn away from the embankment overlooking a cliff-steep fall when someone yelled chicken. Skidding from one hairpin turn into another, one of them had always given in in time to keep the car from hurtling into oblivion. Curve after curve was rounded until they all took the decision at the last fatal moment to let someone else chicken out. Over the embankment and into the valley below they plunged. Only Al came out of the wreckage alive. After a year's plastic surgery and rehabilitation, he entered the army. During a permission he returned to the town. He got drunk. At one in the morning he staggered off the sidewalk into Main Street where he was struck down and killed by a motorist.

CHAPTER THREE

Bob

My father worked as caretaker of the City Duck Club, and at the age of thirteen I was taken on part-time. My job was to wade through knee-deep mud along Bill Grant Lake and make floating rafts of greenish-yellow cattails I scythed at the roots buried in the mud. Sometimes my Uncle Bob gave a hand. We would move through the high stalks, cutting them while ducking the cobwebs and caterpillars that stuck to our faces or dropped down our shirt collars. Later, in Jamaica, I would watch the cane cutters as they made their way through the fields they had burned in order to remove the useless leaves from the stalks and kill as many centipedes and other insists as possible. Bob and I turned our heads to avoid the discharges from the pockets of vile-smelling swamp gas our feet freed as we sludged along. Hip boots protected us from water leeches and our shirts kept off swarms of mosquitoes and the scorching sun.

Bob and I set out for the Club early in the morning, just as the sun rose red over the Wasatch Range. Bob would pick me up in his old jalopy. Conversation those sleepy mornings was air thin. I'd doze off again and again as we went past the dark towers of the city and out through the quiet dawn-blue suburbs.

As a child, Bob, although only four years older, had shepherded me and other kids in the family to the theater on weekends. Leaving the sun-drenched streets for the dark interior, the seats of red velvet, the huge crimson curtains minutes away from ascending, was one of the most glorious memories of my young life. The cartoons, at times over a dozen, and the two feature films, were a kind of paradise on earth.

My father would meet us at the clubhouse. He left home well before sunup to prepare things. We dumped boots, scythes and our lunches on the truck bed and drove to the nearby channel for two metal flat-bottomed marsh boats we heaved in the truck over the tailgate. My father went off with whatever cattails remained from the day before to build blinds.

The few years that separated Bob and me were critical. I was still pubescent when Bob was doing to girls what Bob's sisters' husbands were doing to them. I turned fifteen the same year Bob joined the army. But at the University I caught up: Bob's four years in Korea and a broken marriage helped me graduate well before he did.

Father was very fond of Bob. At the age of eight Bob was already wandering the swamplands hunting rabbits with Father's twenty-two that was as close to an heirloom as our family every got. The gun was supposed to come down to me, but it was pretty clear to whom Father would have preferred it to go. I started hunting when I was twelve and despised every second of it. Getting up in the cold at four; driving over that bumpy, God-forsaken landscape; spending hours slumped down behind the yellowing, desiccated cattails that chafed against the two-by-fours like dry skin on bones; and if--God forbid--my father was ever sober enough to down anything, wading out in the freezing lake to retrieve a meat-impoverished duck carcass.

One hot September weekend Father, Bob and I went to Bill Grant Lake to do some carp spearing. Both Bob and I had rusty old pitchforks. On the embankment we stripped down to our shorts as we often did. This time my father told us to go in naked so as not to soil our underwear in the muddy water. Bob didn't mind but I felt my father's eyes on me and I knew he would be comparing the two of us. It was humiliating to accept but impossible to refuse. Bob was already up to his thighs, shrieking with laughter at the cool current and the mud oozing through his toes. His full black pubic bush was an eloquent badge of manhood. I watched from the water's edge, still dressed, my father's eyes burning into my neck.

Still too young to even contemplate disobedience, I shucked my shorts and waded in after Bob. Under normal conditions this would have been the occasion for the granting of one of my deepest dreams. For although I had not yet come to terms with my sexuality--and would not until a later night at a trailer court--I nonetheless harbored the most pressing wish to see my uncle unclothed. Like any new arrival to adolescence, whose mind is sent galloping at the sight of a bared shoulder or the outline of a breast, I had studied my uncle to discover the secret to his assertive, heady masculinity.

Yet now I tried not to look; this mud hole was no temple for the worship of a god. I tried, too, to keep away from my father's prying gaze. I turned my back to them both, and with spear in hand waded through the slime. I concentrated on the murky waters for the telltale sign of a slowly cruising dorsal fin. Nearly immediately I saw one slithering out of the cattails, a carp two feet in length, coming straight for my legs. I raised the pitchfork over my head and plunged it into the back of the mud-sucking monster. The violence of its reaction took me unaware. The carp lurched in retreat, flipping the pole against my forehead. Blood shot out everywhere, completely blinding me. It ran over my face and into my mouth, salty and warm. The last sight I saw before going under was Bob coming towards him, his pendulous sex heavy in that bush of hallowed beauty, the final permanence in a life seeping irrevocably away.

I awoke in Doctor Munk's office. The doctor was bending over me, putting in the last stitches along my brow. The day had unexpectedly ended in victory. For although tears welled from my eyes as the needle went in and out of the skin, I did not emit a sound. Was I at last toughening up for what was to follow?

CHAPTER FOUR

Bud's

During high school I got a part-time job at a grocery called Bud's. The white aprons the store's namesake perpetually wore would have drowned Friar Tuck. Puffy varicose-veined cheeks, gold spectacles, hair cut short and slicked back like a statesman's, Bud was a paternalistic tyrant, a Mormon with a Jewish sense of humor, a gruff walrus who could occasionally bite. The grocery was a squat single-story structure with two bay windows framed in green tiles and roofed in zinc. Built in the twenties and eclipsed in the fifties by supermarkets, it was now benefiting from a resurgence of nostalgia. There were two checkout booths, aisles of century-old wood slats covered with sawdust, a rack of vegetables the youthful personnel had to spray every half-hour or else, windowed wall lockers with cold beer, and behind Bud's counter a glass case of the world's best chocolate chip cookies.

The hidden side of that microcosm was the basement. Once I graduated from sacker to display filler, I spent hours there. Winding stone steps, each worn to a basin, led down to a kingdom that was exclusively my own. Cool year round, the packed dirt floor supported piles of goods that rose to the ceiling. Half a dozen naked bulbs gave off a feeble light. There was a large and a small room, both smelling of dusty jars, bottles, cans and cartons. My job was to fill a hand basket with depleted merchandise for upstairs. I'd spin each ten-minute trip into a good hour. I'd lie around on the boxes, thinking and dreaming, sometimes staring so hard into the black soot overhead that the plaster broke away into madly rushing atoms. I did everything there. I ate lunches of baloney sandwiches and Dr Pepper. I took catnaps. I sampled from the tops of the best jarred delicacies. I pissed in the shadowy spider-infested corners and impregnated the floor when my fantasies got the best of me. Only Clark, Bud's half-brother, would rarely invade the domain, scaring me witless until I saw it was only Clark. In my four years at the grocery I never discovered what Clark's job was. I never saw him carrying anything, sacking anything, spraying anything, boxing anything or checking anything out. Saturday evenings when the personnel slunk to the back room to have our pay counted out for us, Clark was there at his place at the head of the line, and he left the table behind which Bud was studiously counting out the next guy's dole with a bundle that would choke a horse.

Clark knew boys well. He knew what they did and what they thought. He knew what they stole, and how they lied. He knew the secrets behind their gestures, and the meaning of their foxy grins. But he never reprimanded them, nor did he speak about himself or about why he obviously hated Bud's son Bill's guts. And beyond that, he was generous.

He would loan money when asked for it--always an awesome gesture to an adolescent. He came to our rescue if Bud went into one of his thunderbolt-launching furies, even taking the blame on occasion. Best of all, he handed out the chocolate chip cookies when Bud was away.

Bud was authoritative, often unjust in his accusations and punishments, but in general he put up with a lot before blowing his top. He had seen too many boys come and go to be friendly with them, but he came close with me. One day when I had been advanced to cash register No. 2--the highest one could go in that place since Bud's own was No. 1--we got into a conversation about my Uncle Bob who had worked there years before.

"You once said that Bob was the best employee you ever had," I reminded him.

"Well, he was..." Bud said, "until you came along."

The favorable comparison to Bob inspired me to pay back every maraschino cherry, pickle and bottle of Dr Pepper I had ever pilfered. At the cash register I was never short even a penny. I was never over, either, because that made Bud just as mad.

At the back of the story was Bill the butcher's domain. Bill had piglet eyes astray in a bloated bulldog mug. His cheeks were the color of Jewish meat, strangled and choleric. His mean streak was hidden behind a Jolly Green Giant horselaugh, but no one in his right mind tried to cross him. He was stupid and dirty, he beat his mousy wife and drank like a fish except when on duty, which was twelve hours a day. It was his work that retarded his ultimate demise from cirrhosis.

The rest of the menagerie was made up of a handsome greengrocer, Rudy, a cunning kid who couldn't keep his hand away from his fly, cupping it, caressing it, pinching the folds. His fingertips, two per testicle, hefted, nuzzled and weighed them in. A wicked grin played through fields of acne as he nudged, stroked, groped, his eyes challenging me mockingly to look down, an inner reflex forbidding me from doing so. The more he fondled himself the more I had to pretend nothing was going on, the broader was the grin, the more difficult the twitch in my eye to hide.

Another boy was Bart. He was already Bill's height and half his girth--an accomplishment of sorts at his callow age--blond, crew cut, ugly as sin, and as witless as Rudy was sharp. They stole the place blind. Late one Saturday night, a few hours after pay time, Bart drove his pickup through the narrow alley adjoining the store to the back grange where merchandise was stored before being sent down the shoot into the basement. Rudy had the key. There, under a full moon, in front of God and the hidden presence of Bud and Bill, they filled up the truck with cases of beer. When they were caught they bawled, pleaded and begged. Bud decided to give them a second chance; Bill slunk away in disgust. The next night the kids tried exactly the same thing, Rudy knowing that no one would suspect another attempt so soon. But Clark knew. This time the police were brought in and I, the only one untainted, went through a week of ass-kissing--mine for a change.

Bill went into paroxysms of righteous glee. He took it upon himself to interview the replacements. The result was a gaggle of finger-thin wimpish kids of loathsome obsequiousness. Without Rudy the place suddenly took on a sinister cast. I was surprised to discover that in the absence of that adolescent delicately fingering his fly and kneading his balls through the faded fabric, the charm was gone. I was not long in following suit.

CHAPTER FIVE

Unshackled

In the meantime there were physical and religious jolts, both dealing with the same subject. Rummaging around the grocery attic I came upon a 1910 medical journal. I looked up my favorite topic. There I read that my pastime was going to make me madder than a hatter. I went home in a daze (2). Now I knew the cause of my ill-temper, my fits of despair, my parental disobedience. Everything fell neatly into place. I was evil because I was going insane. I was going insane because my brain was rotting. My brain was rotting because I gave myself pleasure. My hobby had been too good to be true. At home I confessed to my mother that I now knew why I was not the best little boy in the world--without going into details, of course, what boy could?--and promised to shape up.

The solution--oh so simple--consisted of keeping my hands out of the vicinity of the troubling area. Three nights after promising Mother and God I would never do it again, I had only to rub--minutely, *à peine*, just the tiniest little bit--the extended pouch of his jockeys five harmless times again the bed sheets to bring on a heavenly bliss with full angelic and choral accompaniment. The resulting mess would not have pleased my mother who found me the cleanest of lads, but if this was madness, I was ready for the asylum. The discovery of this innocent stroking of cotton against cotton as-if-so-help-me-God-I-didn't-know-what's-going-on was, as the French say, *le pied*, the foot, their expression for ecstasy.

If incipient insanity was bad, offending God was worse still. As though one misfortune can't face life without another, the next Sunday a church speaker lowered the boom.

During my post-puberty years I had sought to alleviate my solitude by turning to religion. Every morning I went to seminary before school started. On Saturday I worked at the church welfare farm when not at

Bud's. Sundays I lived in church: Sunday school, I've-seen-the-light confessionals, blessing the bread and water as well as baptisms-- responsibilities I assumed as I climbed the church hierarchy--evening firesides. When I rose to give a sermon, it was I mothers pointed out to their children to emulate. I felt admired and wanted and useful, the member of a team centered about God and myself; my ascension appeared irrepressible: I was making myself inevitable.

At home all hell broke out on Sundays. My parents were what people sneeringly called jack-Mormons--smokers, coffee and beer drinkers. Religion was the way to their soft underbelly, and I exploited it to the hilt. My father was glad to escape his boy's nettling righteousness by setting out for the Duck Club, and my mother went to visit her twin sister for the length of a one-pack Pall Mall afternoon.

But the crest of the wave I rode was lonesome, although I did finally join the Scouts, eventually becoming Scout Master. I carefully hid the feelings of love I felt for the boys under me, restricting myself to mere cordiality. Yet instinctively the Scouts sensed an inner tenderness and concern for them. I drove the boys into the Uintas in an old black Chevy my father had given me when I passed my driver's test at fifteen and a half. I had designed and pricked my fingers bloody sewing an insignia for each of the Scout's shirts. We reveled in bonfires and camp lore, O'Henry stories and the candlelight ceremonies forbidden by the church due to the Catholic connotation. Later on many of the boys would outgrow the church as one outgrows the tooth fairy, but the passion which was our unspoken link would remain like the acrid sent of campfire smoke forever in the recesses of our senses--a nostalgia for those highly-charged, star-spun nights when we wanted for nothing beyond what we could offer each other.

At Christmas a few received model boats I saved up months to buy. Their fluster was manifest; I shrugged off the gifts as nothing, inwardly deeply moved by the confusion I had sown. When they turned away from my front porch how I yearned to follow them; how I hated the sterility behind the door I closed on their backs. I was fifteen going on sixteen and they twelve, an impassable bridge. I tried to make a father in loco parentis of the bishop, cycling to his house on any pretext, even when it was only to have my tie tied, but there were too many others in greater need of the bishop for him to single me out.

Among boys my age I was treated as if leprous, and I reciprocated. I looked like the others, I behaved outwardly as they did, but I could not be one of them. I was white, middle-class, healthy and Mormon as they were, yet we shared little else in common. I did not care for their games or jokes, I hated to be in constant competition with them. Their mutterings and gestures struck me as vulgar; their incessant need to affirm their virility excessive. They were extroversive, uninhibited and ostensibly at home in a world that was to me forbidding and hostile. They gained force from their rebellion against authority; I sought parental love and security, those two fragile bonds which alluded me. At the same time, I totally rejected the domain of the opposite sex. There was never any question of my taking to dolls, sewing or playing mommy and daddy. My existence was apart. I could be compared to neither one nor the other sex. And I was not attuned enough to those of my ilk to be able to recognize them, but if I had, I would have spurned them in order not to accentuate still more my difference. At my age I wanted only to belong. Originality was worse than the plagues of Egypt.

On the Sunday in question a visiting bishop came into our all-male quorum to give us a little talk on sex, an unnerving proposition because the boys could not see what good a bishop could possibly have to say on the subject. The bishop, in his early twenties, was stooped and sparrow chested, bad form for a people whose creed was the Body is the Temple of the Spirit. If that was his temple, a gnat resided within. His face was chinless and sunfish narrow, and in his eyes burned the fire of martyrs. The way to damnation, he told us right off, passed through wicked hands. At the university, he went on, he had had a roommate who openly aroused himself on the adjoining bed. But the bishop had been there with a handy yardstick to whack the boy when the Devil got into those pouncing fingers. Bending over us like a bloodless Ichabod Crane, he spewed visions of bodies rotting in hell and brains open cesspools to death maggots. The boys shrank back as much from the ejected spit and clots of foam at the corners of his razor-thin liver-colored lips as from fear of the contagion of his own personal madness. Those boys, so bright and beautiful, wormed their backs into the plywood seats, a scorching heat burning into necks and ears, their throats so dry they had to cough to swallow. We who survived thanks to that sin, we who could stay the strain of continence because of it, who could overcome the pressures of exams, of growing up, of *being* thanks to it, we who would one day have families of our own, build our country, *die* for her, we were being warped by this shell of a human being whose inanities we swallowed. Terror was indeed catching, and we fell victim to it.

Shackled spiritually and physically, I could only turn to God for help. I prayed day in and day out. I prayed until the tears streamed down my cheeks. But all He sent was cotton shorts against cotton sheets.

That was the fissure that was to destroy my faith, the minuscule crevice through which the reservoir was to eventually burst.

Instead of keeping my promise to my mother to become the best of boys, my ill temper knew no bounds. I hated everyone. At work the wear and tear I was going through did not go unnoticed, but it went uncommented upon until a certain Friday night when my cash register was $128 short. Coming not too long after Rudy and Bart's caper, Bud went off the deep end. He clammed up with fury and dismissed me for the night with a cursory, "We'll get to the bottom of this." Then early the next morning I received a call from Bill saying I wasn't to come in. Not come in on a Saturday! Clark was going to man my machine, Bill said, and on Monday I would be told my fate.

I did not wait until then. I spent Sunday writing a letter of resignation. It was only the effort of a sixteen-year-old, but when I delivered it Monday morning at 8:00 Bud trembled so hard he had to place it on his counter to read it through. In the meantime they had found a check for $128 stuck to the back of the cash tray. Not only was I exonerated, but when I entered the shop that morning Bud had put on his most paternal smile to great his best cashier. Bill came from his meat rack and scanned the letter over Bud's shoulder. Without so much as glancing at me, he scurried away with his tail tucked between his legs.

So it was that I, Boyd Hone, left my boss puffed up like a choleric bullfrog, my resignation in Bud's thick liver-spotted hands, and stepped out of the grocery with a narrow stack of dollars in my jeans pocket.

I had begun earning money from the age of eight. I had had a paper route, I'd waded through mud with Bob, I'd sold donuts door-to-door, even the money I'd earned stealing with Doug was added to that narrow stack of greenbacks. I had no idea why I was saving or for what, but something in the back of my mind guided my hoarding with the certainty of an all-knowing genie, a genie who knew the price I'd have to pay to buy, like a veritable slave, my franchise.

CHAPTER SIX

Doctor Hawks

The summer after graduation from high school I worked at the Club to put myself through the University. I worked alone. It was an especially dry and hot summer. The dusty roads I drove over in an old Model-T turned my hair silt gray, the salt marshes parched skin the sun turned as brown as mahogany. Always on the thin side, I sweated off even more weight until my jeans hung from my hips, and my felt shirt clung windswept to my body like rags on a mummy. I came of age that summer in the sense of my body and mind coming to function as a team. My demeanor was graver and more silent still, and, like Ganymede, my eyes lost their innocence. It was a solitary passage, and incomplete. A remnant of my adolescence would always hang on, an inescapable shadow.

And I lost my battle with God that summer. My fantasies fed enough excesses of pleasure to damn a legion. The rupture with the church was not abrupt, but once it ultimately occurred I stepped from--

after all--harmless shackles. To my surprise the horizon cleared a bit, and above my eyes the veil of ignorance retreated a perceptible notch.

At the University I came across a professor who embodied all the principles I admired. Doctor Hawks was in his mid-fifties and Head of the Geography Department. A remarkably handsome man, lean, with a head of gray and black hair that blanketed his forehead, he tooled around campus in the sports car left behind by one of his sons off on a mission for the church. Doctor Hawks taught Geography I, a lowly class other heads of department left to assistant professors. His lectures were punctuated with Gees and Goshes, manifestations of enthusiasm he used as his hand roamed over the valleys and plains of the wall maps. Slides illustrated hamlets of thatched eaves and gray mud courtyards, huge beige horses with gigantic hooves, farmers so sun-rutted their sweat was entrapped in the sagging skin of their faces like water in terraced rice fields. He showed Germans in their beer halls--whole families: mother, father, son, grandmother, grandfather--standing on tables sloshing themselves from giant steins; St. Tropez littered with bodies as thickly packed as seals; slender girls jumping aboard a bus at Palais Royal, silky above-the-knee dresses molding their thighs. "Boy, if I were there now," he'd say as a picture of the empty beaches along Les Landes came on the screen. "Wow!" he'd exclaim before the endless stretches of pocketed sand dunes in the Sahara, "That was a trek!"

He exhorted his students onward. "Yup, if I were your age there's where I'd be now," he said on a score of occasions, whether talking about cities or bush tribes. It was under his spell that I decided to major in Geography. Although I was only a lowly sophomore, Doctor Hawks admitted me into a three-hour seminar, Climatology 104, a grad class. It took place on Saturday on the second floor of a World War II barracks of white wood walls and corridors of ocher linoleum. Doctor Hawks arrived with donuts and black coffee. The students each took turns giving talks on world microclimates, talks followed by a general discussion. Since I was by far the youngest, I was treated as the class mascot, making blunders no one stooped to pick up.

Doctor Hawks could be earthy. In responses to a comment made by one of his not-so-favorite grads, a lumberjack type with beard and unkempt hair in his mid-thirties, concerning whether he should go on for a doctorate or end his academic career, Doctor Hawks replied: "Well, yes, that does present a problem." He took off his glasses, rubbed wrinkles into his forehead and continued: "Perhaps you had better..." he paused... "well ... shit or get off the pot." The vulgarism was shocking in the Mormon culture of the 60s, coming from a man of irreproachable urbanity, yet it seemed to me a judicious piece of advice (1).

From time to time the gardener passed below the second-floor window that I commandeered. The brown and brawn of his naked chest and arms were truly unbelievable. He was a magnificent beast, to be compared in his force to one of Doctor Hawks' dray horses, and his superb pectorals contrasted favorably to the Palais Royal fillies. In the barrack's basement there were no-door army cubicle toilets. On the thin partitions between stalls were drawings of the gardener--big-balls virile-dick affairs--a fetishist's dream of the nirvana beneath the steel buttons of his low-slung levis. I suspected that a lot of the Rabelaisian graffiti was done by an associate professor, Doctor Waffhard, who had an idiosyncratic way of speaking. "Nit-picking" and "à propos of nothing at all" came through a half-dozen times each lesson. In his late forties, he had a long, deeply lined face of parchment-thin skin. He wore impeccable gray suits and peered over half-moon glasses through steel-blue eyes that riveted his students one at a time. He took a particular interest in me, calling me "my friend" in a booming voice and affected Southern accent. I wrote a paper for him on a nearby valley town that Doctor Waffhard claimed was stupendous. "No nit-picking there," he announced to Doctor Hawks who passed over the paper's content with prudent silence.

That I could recognize Doctor Waffhard for the sexual invert he was, was due to my increasing recognition of my own bent. The awakening had come late. As a boy I had been drawn to other boys by an incomprehensible impulsion. I admired their courage and their fearless disdain. I doted on comics showing a muscular Tarzan and on weekends when I'd been shepherded to the cinema by Bob, I had nestled in the velvet seats, entranced by the exploits of Flash Gordon. Later, in the throes of adolescence, I trembled before the stacks of magazines in the local grocery, awaiting the chance to open physical culturist revues unobserved. I sought out the dark of night when I could place myself in the warm folds of my bed and give myself up to the pleasure fired by images of the nascent virility of locker-room boys who flaunted, with neither shame nor modesty, the pride-giving evidence of their coming-of-age. The pleasure I could give myself made of me a being totally autonomous. My cock became the crystallization of more than emotional release and self-sufficiency, it was a figure of adoration, the coalescing of what was to me power and mystery. It was the essence of maleness. And from the worship of my own sex, the cult spread to the adoration of all other possessors of my sex. The mystery that was I became inextricably entangled with the mystery that was they. I listened to Bob's stories of his encounters with girls, deeply stirred by Bob's role in the affairs, and wondering when, like my uncle, I too would change cap.

Throughout high school I had dated the same girl. Issued from a very strict Mormon family, her parents could only concur with the respect I showed for their little baby. Never did the parents come upon us petting or kissing or, for that matter, even holding hands. Not that I hadn't tried. A year after we were virtually going steady, I took her to an outdoor movie where I imitated the guys in the other cars as far as, for the first time, putting my arm around her shoulder. She collapsed into my chest with a sign and months of anticipation. We remained that way for three hours until I drove her home, guiding the car with my left hand, certain my right arm was permanently disabled. Having feared that if I flexed so much as a muscle she might take it as permission for outright debauch, I had stared blindly ahead at the screen, supporting her weight and excruciating pain until the cutting off of my circulation brought on blessed numbness.

Yet there were compensations. The girl had six brothers. That made ten at table when I drove by for dinner of homemade bread, garden vegetables and a chicken slaughtered in the backyard. The girl was as tall and skinny as Olive Oil, dead serious and bent on early motherhood. The boys were tall and well filled-out, as serious as their sister and as bent on early fatherhood. The last night we were together the boys invited me to go swimming at the pool in a nearby trailer court. We had been diving for an hour when suddenly it began to rain. I was underwater, slowly surfacing. From the muted gleam of the tank lamps I could clearly see the raindrops spatter on the surface, making thousands of deep craters. I stopped stroking and allowed myself to drift slowly upwards. The warmth of the pool produced a marvelous feeling of fullness. Hours seemed to pass before I broke surface. The icy raindrops startled me into a state of intense physical vigor and joy. The fusion of the two conditions, the first a passive well-being, the second an exquisite awakening, produced a moment of unequaled exaltation.

Adjoining the pool was an indoor shower installation. I went inside, whooping and howling with the brothers of the girl I was dating. There I came across a boy, fully naked, in one of the stalls. Why this sight--one of many I had witnessed--so elated me, I did not know. Yet the boy's beauty, the perfection of his body as he gyrated beneath water enfolding him in an all-inclusive embrace, made the event the uncontested summit of a perfect evening. It brought home with a force I could no longer deny the realization of what I was. My mirth vanished, my throat dried, and for me too, as with that Prince of Troy, it could be said: "Now to the son of Cronos came Ganymede, with the seriousness of the first look of youth in his childlike eyes, and the god rejoiced."

.

Doctor Hawks brought a travel log to class replete with sound track. While Tannhäuser played in the background, the seminar students were shown shots of the good doctor--then a young missionary in the late 1930s--dressed in impeccable whites, cruising up the wine-sloped Rhine Valley. Doctor Hawks had lent the film to a group of grads and it came back with bizarre cuts: one moment it jumped to a review line of half-naked chorus girls, at others there were spliced-in segments from the highly-censured Playboys of the time. The professor chuckled; the students hooted.

It was not surprising that Professor Hawks exhorted us to a destiny more vital than the somnolent backwater of an overheated army barracks. Thanks to his guidance, I knew the time had come to draw on that growing stack of dollars I had hoarded over the years. I would not buy a car as did my schoolmates, I would follow my fate to the fields of France. I would heed Doctor Hawks' counsel, as well as that of Shakespeare: At the end of my sophomore year I followed
Such wind as scatters young men through the world
To seek their fortune farther than at home,
Where small experience grows.

CHAPTER SEVEN

May '68

It was Paris who received me, as he does all his lovers, graciously, generously and with total indifference. For life to pulse there must be blood, and it was on the Left Bank of the Seine, along the arteries and through the medieval capillaries of the Latin Quarter that the beat was the most convulsive: the frenetic, throbbing quest to transform thought into act. It was among the swarms of Sorbonne students that I made my entrance into the City of Light that warm spring day of my eighteenth year. Like a foreign body dropped into a rampaging cascade I was swept up, rolled, scrubbed and polished until I emerged with a patina as uniform as theirs.

For all I knew, the sight that met me that May day in 1968 might have been part of a pubescent ritual as old as Lutetia itself. At the Luxembourg Park, halfway up the Boul' Mich', I came across the students, 15,000 strong. They were walking slowly, singing, a long white banner reading "Free Our Comrades" out in front. Their song was sung in the low male cadence of a Gregorian chant and had the force and continuance of a long beach-thirsty tidal wave.

I found myself a place against the fence of iron javelins surrounding the park gardens. The marchers walked slowly down the street--one amoebic mass--carrying a quiet dignity far older than their adolescent years. Some wore motorcycle headgear, others goggles, some had handkerchiefs loosely tied around their necks, one had flour-whitened eyes in the belief that flour was an antidote to teargas, some a dead cigarette at their lips; all wore old clothes, all sang, all advanced with solemnity. Ahead of the marchers was the buffer, young toughs whose job it was to clear the way of nonparticipating students, onlookers and motorists. Their methods were not gentle. To keep the gelatinous mass moving they had to push forward like a glacial moraine scouring out a valley, dislodging all obstacles before the slowly flowing river of ice behind. They screamed their orders to make way, and then they shoved. Anything and everything was declared impermanent to their force, subject to destruction or alteration: cars, bikes, cycles, sign posts, signal lights, fences, trees, plants and people all complied to their will. And it was perhaps that the message of their march.

I stood and waited, sharing nothing of their cause yet envious of their unity, their purpose, their hand-to-shoulder intimacy; I stood and watched, wishing to be one of them, yet unable to span the barrier that would bring me within their touch. Row after row passed by, each row one full pace behind the other, each locked in a chain that stretched across the entire width of the street. Along the periphery the helmeted security guards were linked in still another chain that encircled the advancing caterpillar like a cocoon. It was they who made sure the mass moved along in step, disciplined and correctly spaced; it was they who occasionally opened to nourish the ranks by swallowing sympathizers.

As the rows advanced, a pocket of student onlookers and I were push up against the park fence. The pressure of their passing was crushing. Cars on the curbs rocked as the wave broke around them, denting the metal; trees were scraped by shoulders and branches were heard cracking on both sides of the boulevard. Bikes were thrown over the fence or trampled under, and when the crowd opened slightly at its center to swarm around some immutable object, shop windows shattered on one or both sides. The students beside me leaped over the fence and into the bushes to escape the crushing. I stood transfixed, unprepared for the tidal force that thrust me into the iron stakes. Yet with the chant *"Viens! Avec! Nous!"* the chain--for a mere instant--parted, and I was devoured whole. An arm forcefully linked mine, I linked another, and as one we surged onward.

At the bottom of the Boul' Mich' we came to a halt. Word filtered back that the Pont au Change, the most ancient link between the two banks, had been cut off by the government's crack police force, the CRS. In addition, the iron gratings had been removed from around the base of the tree trunks, news that made no sense to me. We were therefore to turn around and back up the Boul' Mich' to the Boulevard Montparnasse. Row after row did an about-face and retraced steps already familiar. My arms, riveted to those of my companions like brittle chicken wings, began to relax. I let myself absorb the warmth and intimacy of the marchers' contact. I took a furtive glance at the boys flanking me. Their faces were impassive and cold, set like angles in marble. Even the tired lines under their eyes and the pinched creases on the sides of their nostrils seemed chipped from stone. Their skin shone with a wax-like hue in the dense light of that spring afternoon, and the leaden vault of the sky added to the gravity of the stern set of their chins and their shadowy, nascent beards.

We moved onwards. The students were now shouting *"Libérez! Nos! Camarades!"* and *"Rome! Berlin! Var-so-vie-Paris*!" At the windows people were hanging out, some throwing flowers, some applauding. Shopkeepers hurriedly locked their cafés and boutiques with all the customers trapped inside. The marchers tasted the enormous power of their movement, but channeled its potential into quiet song and a determined stride.

From the Boulevard Montparnasse we turned into the Boulevard des Invalides. Bourgeois apartments were heavily booed and government buildings scaled for their flags. Down they fluttered like autumn leaves to be lost in the heaving mob that squealed its approval as the colors disappeared under booted feet. The front ranks heaved up black and red standards, those incompatible symbols of anarchy and collectivism. Erasmus died another death on the Esplanade des Invalides, and although I was deeply ashamed of my presence there, and even moved to tears by the trodden threads underfoot, I could not exchange my emotional disapproval for the contact of those two strangers on my right and left. I stumbled on with them.

Our numbers had swelled to 50,000 by the time we reached the Pont Alexandre III, a flamboyant bridge with big buxom winged victories on the backs of flying steeds. Before us were the CRS, about 10,000. These were not the polite cops in Cardin-designed blue who flipped a full salute when you came up to ask the way to the Eiffel Tower. These were professionals hardened in mob control. They carried guns and gas masks, sticks and shields, and were backed up by troop transports with rifle-like barrels mounted on revolving turrets. The marchers halted to debate the crossing. In front was the way to the Champs-Elysées, the world's embassies, the President and First Minister's palaces, the homes of the exploiting classes, the newspapers and the Bourse, Paris' stock exchange. But because our numbers were stretched all the way back to St. Michel and therefore could not be massed for an effective frontal attack, we agreed to return to the Latin Quarter by way of tree-lined St. Germain.

But a miracle occurred: the next bridge, Pont de la Concorde, was empty. The cops had bunched all their reserves at the Pont Alexandre III, as well as in a dozen nearby alleys in order to spring ambushes should the security guard lose control of the students, unable to keep them from going on a property-breaking rampage. Sirens suddenly split the crepuscule. The CRS rushed units up to block the Concorde, but for the moment the immense bridge was ours. The marchers stopped. Our leaders debated. They wondered if it were a trap. Only when they saw the reserve units coming pell-mell, their black rubber rain coats flapping wildly, their plastic masks askance and their shields bobbing comically at their sides, did they realize the cops' blunder. The bridge stood empty, and the students rushed across. We ran in chains, each man supporting the other, sweeping girls and short boys off the pavement and carrying them suspended over the solid rock arches cut from the stones of the Bastille. The cops approached to block us, but the students were too many and moving too fast. It was the police who came to a halt, their faces distorted like an El Greco painting. The students hadn't the time to shout "*Viens Avec Nous*," but more than one of the cops was our age and felt the justice of the students' demands.

We crossed the Place de la Concorde and reached the Champs-Elysées, running, ever running. Up ahead the cops had succeeded in requisitioning coach drivers to block the wide avenue with four old World War II trolley buses. But the students kept coming and the drivers, caught in the sea of charging bodies, took it on the lamb with their vehicles, leaving hundreds of CRS without cover. They too quickly scattered. And the Champs-Elysées was ours, all ours! We had liberated the city. All the shops, buildings, windows and marquees were ablaze with light. People flocked to the sidewalks, to balconies, to display showrooms and to café entrances to get a glimpse of us. Here there was no applause. The marchers reformed their ranks, and intoning the International, we walked slowly and solemnly towards the colossal Arc de Triomphe and the eternal flame of the Unknown Soldier. Red and black banners led the way to that place where a five-story blue, white and red flag stretched from the vaulted roof to the pavement below, billowing proudly like the sail of an ancient galleon, as much a symbol as the flame itself. The crowds passed under the arches. So great was their number that many buckled upwards, clinging to the façade like cave bats. Popping flashbulbs filled the darkened vault with a white light that caught the chalky, moribund, Daumier-distorted faces as they hunched over the orange, flickering flame. Pushed by those behind, the medieval creatures pressed forward until their black shapeless forms smothered the precious fire.

Outside, the cops had regrouped and blocked off the Champs-Elysées. They had left one passage open, Avenue George V. The students regrouped too and, avoiding direct contact with the forces of order, marched into the exit afforded them. But after a few blocks we discovered that the police had blocked off George V as well. Except for the tiny alleys to the right and left, we were trapped. The student leaders went forward to parley with the Préfet. The march was over, they were told, and we were to disperse. The students' position was indeed vulnerable. The police were in front of us and to our rear, and the marchers' lines were stretched out. If we broke and ran now we would be cut off into little bunches and clubbed by the CRS. Slowly we backed up upon ourselves like an armadillo, away from the cops and their bludgeons, their gas rockets, the threat of their guns and paddy wagons. To the front ranks came the security guards, those with helmets, goggles and gloves, those armed with trash-can lid shields, those protected by handkerchiefs, powdered faces, oil-encircled eyes, in levis and padded coats. Directly behind them fluttered the red and black totems from their spearlike shafts.

Then there was quiet. A phony quiet. The police hesitated. They had received orders to attack only if provoked. The students knew of that flaw and put it to use. *They made the earth tremble.* So softly at first as to be inaudible. The cops felt the tremble beneath their feet but could not detect its source from behind the solid wall of rusty shields and massed flags. I too sought its provenance--and found it everywhere. Small groups of twenty to thirty were huddled around two or three students who had taken the iron grills from around the base of the trees and were using them as picks to pry up the paving stones. Once a breach was made and individual stones were loosened, the groups formed lines to bring the *pavés* to the front ranks where they were stacked. This was our defense. With enough accumulated stones we could keep the police away while we had time to raise barricades. But once bitten twice shy. The cops started firing. Gas rockets slammed into the mob. There were screams as the students scattered to escape the fumes. Those who stumbled were trampled. Some students were hit directly by the gas grenades, many were knocked down by the impact and left badly bruised or bleeding. One boy lost a hand. Store windows hit by the grenades splattered, sending glass into eyes and ears. Many of the marchers were overcome by the fumes and dropped to their knees blinded.

But our lines held. The security guards' gas masks, goggles, handkerchiefs and oil made them immune to the white billows. They plummeted the police with the stones, offering their comrades protection from the bludgeons. In the wake of the acrid fumes eye veins burst and skin was burned. The marchers staggered unseeing, trying to find refuge along a wall or behind a street pole. Occasionally the air would clear and we would immediately queue up, passing the *pavés* or throwing them ourselves. Then would come more salvoes of gas, and the students would again fall back. Yet bit-by-bit we became immune. We fought on more steadily and with increasing fury. Finally it was the police that broke ranks. The students rushed through into fresh air. They ran, tripping over the stones they themselves had thrown. But they were now dispersed. The police had cut into their soft underbelly, breaking them into a hundred small groups. It was then, in the moment of their undoing, that the selfsame thought came to them all: the Latin Quarter. If they had to be wounded, let them at least put up battle on their own turf, defending through instinct that which had been theirs since the Middle Ages. The words were never spoken, yet from the streets and alleys, boulevards and avenues they converged on the Left Bank. Passed smashed windows, smoking intersections, burning cars, uprooted benches, toppled kiosks and stone-strewn byways they ran: boys and girls, teachers and professors, students and workers, vandals and foreigners and curiosity seekers.

By the time we reached the Sorbonne it was already night. Barricades had been raised along the streets leading to the old University. St. Jacque, rue des Écoles and rue Soufflot had been cut off by the police. Along the Boul' Mich' six barricades were going up, each half a block behind the other. The first faced the cops at the Pont St. Michel, across from the Préfecture de Police. Entire newspaper stands went into its construction as well as benches, billboards, cinema ticket booths torn from their niches and trees toppled over by roping their branches. Here too the earth was made to tremble. Lines that stretched out as long as three blocks passed up the *pavés* which were stacked by hundreds behind the barricades. The cops waited on the other side. They stood in the unnatural darkness of a quarter cut off from its electricity, their plastic face masks, shields and raincoats reflecting the swirling red and blue light from atop police cars and ambulances. Weird-sounding sirens shrieked from everywhere. The cops were kept in abeyance by the student security guard hurtling stones. The police waited ill tempered for the command which would unleash them on their quarry. They had all been on duty nonstop for days. Only when the barricades were cleaned up and the students dispersed could they return to their homes. So when the order to storm ultimately came, they marched forward in anger, Spartan style, shield locked to shield. The students ignited the barricade. Flames leaped up five stories, leaving the police powerless to go on. Fire engines rushed across the bridge, adding their own sirens, lights and black-leathered men to the chaos.

Abandoning the first barricade, the students withdrew to the second. When building materials began to run out they went far and wide to replenish them: cars and vans were piled on, traffic lights pulled over, iron fences dug up, telephone poles cut down, and even the Mass announcement board from the local church thrown on. As the cops advanced around the edges of the smoldering first barricade, the second was lit. A nearby police station cut off from its colleagues was set ablaze by Molotov cocktails. Six police cars and two troop carriers went up in flames. From the windows over the barricades residents emptied buckets of water into the chilly night air to attenuate the effects of the police gas grenades.

At one point I found myself trapped between the CRS and the students. Had I fallen into their hands I would have been beaten senseless by the rubber bludgeons wielded by men more than fed up with our games. I made a headlong rush for the nearest barricade, literally throwing myself upon the piled-up rubble. There I clung breathless. Stones flew over my head from behind the barricade, repelling the attackers at my heels. Then invisible hands from above hoisted me up and over the wall.

I had had enough. I retreated into the clemency of the Sorbonne, a sanctuary as ancient and hallowed as Notre Dame, where the other students also withdrew, step by step, as one barricade after another was dismantled by the forces of order. I found a bench in the Amphitheatre Descartes and tried to sleep. My eyes smarted and my lungs ached. My nose drained into my handkerchief. My leg hurt where I had fallen or where I had slammed up into the barricade or where a *pavé* had caught me--I knew no longer which. Outside, the wail of ambulances went on and on. On and on. Yet that night, and during all the others that were to follow for weeks, there was not one fatal casualty to mar the simple fact that these were the hallowed children of the adults in power.

In the twilight of the next morning I snuck out. The streets were gray, wet and rock strewn. Bulldozers were shoveling away the rubble. I made my way home, unshaven, clammy and sick from having inhaled too much smoke and eaten no food. I crept into my room, shucked my shoes and sweat-soaked clothes, donned Jean's nightdress, and fell into bed. That's how Mammy found me several hours later.

CHAPTER EIGHT

Lutèce

A week before, with all the awe of a visitor from another world, I had disembarked on that legendary plot of earth, ancient Lutetia. Sylvain served as my guide. Through cobbled alleys scarcely large enough for the two of us to walk abreast, we passed under sagging facades suspended overhead like the stomach of Gargantua. Stone walls and latticed windows enclosed an eerie medieval silence. Wind-jostled shop signs depicting wares--a horse head for a *chevaline,* an old frock for a *tailleur*-- were lighted by gas lanterns, reminders that only recently had Paris become the City of Light. A century before the streets belonged to the thief, and at the dawn of each day a dozen night wanderers were found assassinated. Lamp carriers were hired to accompany theater goers to the doors of their apartment buildings; the price of the carrier's services sifted through an hourglass fastened at his waist.

Streets named the Cul-de-sac du Ha! Ha!, rue du Pas-de-la-Mule, rue des Blancs Manteaux, rue des Mauvais-Garçons, rue du Paradis, meandered through a former swampland known as the Marais.

It was there I lived, the Marais. The cobbled road fronting my seventeenth-century apartment house was called Geoffroy l'Asnier-- Geoffrey the donkey driver. The window of my room on the top story was a majestic affair, opening out with a sweep of the hands, leaving no obstruction between me and the view outside. Below, perpendicular to my street, was the rue Grenier-sur-l'eau, a short alley that ran into the rue du Pont Louis-Philippe. Above the tiled housetops was the church tower of St. Gervais which struck the hour and the half-hour.

.

Paris had its own light and smell and crispness. Mornings I walked the quarter block to the Seine and crossed the Pont Louis-Philippe to Ile St. Louis. A dawn mist enveloped buildings of gold-tinged stone, making them seem to rise directly up from the white embankments of the river. The mist blotted out all but the disk of the sun and gave to the day the solemn, bluish-gray cast of campfire smoke. There was a scent of burned wood about those mornings, a scent that was gradually swept away as the mist lifted and fresh gusts of algae-scented sea air blew up the Seine from Normandy.

It was off the coast of Normandy that my ship had cast anchor. The fishermen who came out in barks to ferry the ship passengers into Cherbourg were loud and gruff caricatures of themselves. Each had a captain's cap, and blue trousers pulled up over paunches by suspenders. One of them carted my bike ashore, carried it through customs and presented it to me on the quay where the other passengers were waiting to board the boat train to Paris. In my ignorance, I rewarded the fisherman with the largest coin I had, a French five-sous piece, not even the value of a penny. To proud for a rejoinder, the fisherman gave me a pillar-of-salt stare, turned on his heels and trotted off, pocketing the zinc piece. I wandered through Cherbourg until I came across an appropriately modest-looking hotel. From my attic room I had my first sight of a French village: the intricately windowed houses with their pointed orange-tiled dormers, the surrounding green hills spotted with black and white cows, and the incredible freshness of the air, all as Doctor Hawks had promised. I was riveted by a feeling of exquisite expectancy.

From Cherbourg I cycled to Bayeux, arriving at night outside the Hotel Lion d'Or. It was very late. I was cold and wet from a persistent drizzle the French call *crachin*--spit--and filthy from being overtaken by exhaust-spewing lorries. I took the only room available. It was large, with a baldachin bed and throw rugs. As in Cherbourg, there was no bathroom, just a porcelain basin with running cold water. Only later did I learn that few French had tubs, showers or in-the-apartment toilets. I started the apprenticeship in how to wash myself standing up with a sponge and washcloth, one limb at a time. After changing into a wrinkled sweater and clean trousers, I went down for dinner. Well-dressed guests stared at me as I entered the brightly lit, red velvet-walled dining room. I was shown to a corner table. Unlike the English upper class who ignored foreigners, the French paid one the complement of unabashed, open disapproval. By the time soup was served my nervousness and the lingering cold from the ride made my spoon tremble. I pushed my hands into the knot of my stomach to steady them. They never ceased quivering but I could at least eat. Yet later in my room a sentiment of expectancy again filled me with the burning promise that life was there waiting, and that my own small claim on it would be realized.

The following day I cycled to Rouen. Situated on the Seine, the Norman town of diamond-shaped windowpanes and tightly-clustered steep-roofed houses had changed little since the burning of Joan d'Arc. Spared the ravages of war, a Renaissance visitor would have recognized the winding streets and drinking houses where the red-faced, bulbous nosed ancestors of William the Conqueror noisily placed over-the-bar bets on horses.

The Youth Hostel was full of Parisians out of school for Easter. One of them attached himself to me, glad for the opportunity to improve his English. We roamed the city streets, going from *boulangerie* to *boulangerie* for pastries, reciting the past tenses of irregular verbs in French and English. Sylvain was polite and helpful, he had an agreeable grin and an untamable cowlick that rose above unruly flaxen hair, making him look younger still than his sixteen years. He laughed easily and was accommodating. He went right if I went right and left if I went left. We agreed we would ride our bikes to Paris together.

Sylvain disliked crowds as much as I, so we stayed away from the hostel until lights out. During one of our pointless wanderings we came to the Seine where a long bridge joined Rouen to her sister village on the other side.

At the bottom of a slope beneath the bridge were an old cabin and a shabby wooden dock. We strolled down to it just as a fleet of rowers drew up. I watched the boys crawl out of the shells and stretch their cramped limbs. One of them disengaged himself from the others and came up to me. He had jet-black hair and eyes, certainly a remarkably handsome lad, physically similar to me. His manner was very ceremonious. I looked American, the boy said, and when I confirmed the impression the boy told me about an American friend he had had the year before. Clearly my predecessor had been a worthy ambassador. The boy made an open, unabashed offer of friendship. We promised to meet in Paris where the boy would return by train. We sealed our agreement with a handshake. It was a pact solemnly made. On the top of the sunny slope I looked back. The boy was in the center of his companions. He glanced up and raised his arm in farewell. His companions followed the direction of his salute. They studied me gravely. I returned his wave, utterly convinced that the life forces which had guided me to this moment, as surely and steadfastly as a train entrapped by its rails, would see me safely through to my promised Destiny. Sylvain and I walked on.

CHAPTER NINE

Mammy

We set off before dawn the next day and made record time, getting to the Étoile at noon. It was there I had my rendezvous with the dark-haired boy at three that afternoon. We cycled down the Champs-Elysées and the quays of the Seine to the Marais where Sylvain lived. His apartment was located in a dingy narrow street of soot-blackened houses. At number twelve we pushed through a porte-cochère into a tiny court. A whiff of garbage and cooking, the dilapidated state of the windows around the court and the old wood stairway leading up to Sylvain's flat, left me with a pitiable feeling for Sylvain's obvious poverty. Only later did I learn that this was the rue de Sévigné, and the building a historical monument.

On the second floor Sylvain rang once and then opened the door with his key. We entered a badly lit vestibule of gaudy red and black that gave into a small kitchen of lacquered yellow walls. There was a worn wooden table, a gas stove, white cupboards and a larder in the wall under a high window that served as the refrigerator. Sylvain's mother, an art teacher, came through a door on the other side of the kitchen. Léa was a tall, handsome woman, nearly blond, with a bearing of Prussian correctness. Her eyes were dark blue. I noticed that her brows were identical to Sylvain's: they formed curious horns which swept upwards toward the temples. She shook my hand with comradely directness, seizing it, lifting it up, and throwing it down.

She suggested that Sylvain and I eat. I begged off, assuring her that I had a rendezvous. She said we should eat anyway, and her manner was such that I could accept without feeling contrite. I slumped over my plate, never more grateful for food. Léa stood at my back, between me and the stove, eyeing my every gesture. Years at that table under her observant guidance would see my posture improved, my elbows tucked to my sides, my sniffing curbed and my use of silverware vastly improved. But for the time being she contented herself with watching me wolf down whatever she placed in reach.

At two I prodded Sylvain into guiding me back to the Étoile. I saw Léa surreptitiously slip some money and metro tickets into Sylvain's back jeans pocket, a maneuver Sylvain took with par-for-the-course cool. At the door, Sylvain pecked Léa on both cheeks. She shook my hand and bade *au revoir*. Outside, I hurried Sylvain to the metro. We arrived at the Étoile at two-thirty. By four I had looked over the tourists hanging around the Arc de Triomphe with such intensity that they all began to resemble the boy I was to meet. At five the streets were already heavy with dusk. Sylvain told me his mother was expecting us back for dinner. I gave up; the boy's coming would really have been to good to be true.

At Léa's I was received as if Sylvain and I had merely stepped out for a walk. I was taken into the dining room which doubled as Sylvain's sisters' room. We sat on two divans, the girls' beds. Across from the divans were two giant windows, heavily draped, looking out on the court we had come through. Between the windows stood a massive table of dark oak. On the right wall was a marble chimney surmounted by a high mirror. Against the left wall stood an armoire, also of oak, reaching to the ceiling, next to which was a door the same gray color as the walls and so small it was nearly invisible. There were paintings and drawings in every available space, and two small bookcases above the beds. Léa served us drinks. She took a Marie Brizard, a syrupy licorice goo. Sylvain had a thimbleful of Cointreau and I was offered whisky because I was an American, although it was my first. If that horrible bloodless bishop, that stooped and sparrow chested Savonarola, could have seen me now, I thought to myself!

We talked about my wide travels. The conversation was constantly interrupted by the doorbell as one after another of Léa's children and their friends filed through. There was Sylvain's brother Vincent, a bear of a fellow about fifteen. He tried speaking to me in Spanish, then halting German and finally French. He was a pleasant-looking lad, perpetually smiling, the kind who would give his shirt to a bum, turn the other cheek gladly, but would fight to the death were anyone stupid enough to take him for a sucker. He started up a game of cards with the youngest brother, Bertrand, thirteen, a diffident boy who shouted questions in my face and clowned about like a court jester. Bertrand's smile was a smirk, lopsided, a comedian's barrage against an alien world. During lapses of playing the village idiot he would fall into spells of motionless silence and stare at his feet. His skin was white and pimply; thick glasses blurred milky blue eyes. But Bertrand was the family crack, a study machine never far from his books. I disliked him immediately, and it was clear that his brothers did too. Sylvain regarded him with adult disdain, and Vincent found him too sneaky for his simpler tastes. Yet Bertrand was the neighborhood Clark Kent, a boy who would one day disappear into a *cabine téléphonique* and emerge muscle-bound and minus his glasses, his eyes as azure as Zeus' own, the possessor of exquisite social tact, a surgeon, and the first of the sons to find a wife and father children as varied as Snow White's dwarves.

Christiane came home next. She was the homeliest girl with the sweetest smile I had ever seen. Verging on the edge of clinical blindness, her eyes, encompassed by immense thick glasses, were as big as tops. Her complexion was carbuncular, a combination of sores and peach fuzz. She had brownish-blond hair, what Americans might call not-*too*-dirty dishwater. It was straight to boot. But God had made her as solid as her mother whom she resembled despite her physical imperfections. Very unassumingly, she ran the family in the absence of Léa.

Mickey arrived soon afterwards. On permission from the army, in uniform and sporting close-cropped hair, this extraordinarily fine-looking kid was built like one of the many kouroi I would come to admire in Greece. And through an incredible quirk of nature, he was also Christiane's suitor. I had managed, with broken French, to communicate with the others, but this boy made me so flustered I didn't even try. Mickey and Vincent got on very well. Both were boisterous, both salt of the earth. Bertrand ceded Mickey his place at the cards table and slunk off into a corner to stare at us all owl-like.

I felt enormously elated to find myself not only the center of these people, but apparently well accepted. Whenever I could I collected words to make questions I would blurt out, sometimes sending Bertrand into spasms of exaggerated laughter. I was invited to play cards, and I learned how to say "count me in" and "it's your turn" in French. They got out the dictionary every time I needed help with vocabulary. The whiskies relaxed me, I felt at home, I felt at ease, I felt important, I felt unique, I felt I had something worthwhile to say, I felt heeded, I felt I belonged. It was *le pied*, the second real *pied* of my life, after the gift from Nick.

Dinner was delayed because the "others" hadn't arrived. In the back of my mind I never forgot that a Mister Somebody would soon make his appearance. That, I knew, would put a different coloration on everything. If Léa's husband failed to like me I would be out. Even if we managed to get along, I would have to grow up. No palsy-walsy with the boys, no pretense of familiarity with Léa.

At five Nène came in with Mammy. Nène did water colors for a living, paintings of floral arrangements, harbors and the old districts of Paris. Her cheekbones were high and prominent, covered with taut, paper-thin, wrinkleless skin powdered a healthy rouge. She wore a gray astrakhan hat and matching coat fastened at the neck with a brooch. She greeted me with a correct but distant air, and then removed her kid gloves and fur-lined boots.

Mammy was much more expansive. She took my hand with a firm patrician *Comment allez-vous, mon cher monsieur!*, her red lips pinched forward in a most engaging smile. Mammy's hair was white and fluffy; so too was her face white except for blotches of pigment applied in hit-or-miss fashion over the cheeks. Her nose was aquiline, a family trait Léa had been spared but Bertrand had inherited in its entirety.

Mammy was Léa's mother; Nène was Mammy's sister. Both were in their late seventies. Mammy's spontaneity was repeatedly quelled by Nène who barked incessant orders. "How long are you going to keep your rubbers on? Don't you see you're tracking up the floor!" "Will you remove your coat!" At such times Mammy's smile would freeze off center, redolent of someone stepping in dog manure.

Léa spent most of her time in the kitchen. Shortly Gérard, Mireille's fiancé, came. He was a tall, nice-looking, very polite boy who was studying to become a lawyer. Mireille, Léa's second daughter, was expected later.

Finally at nine-thirty the ten of us retired to the kitchen where we nudged into the few centimeters that were our due around the table. The meal consisted of a thick purée of steaming lentils with huge sausages and slices of dark-red pork. The iron pot holding it was enormous, but once about the table it all evaporated. The boys stuffed their food down with chunks of bread broken off a bicep-thick, arm length baguette, washed down with cider. Léa, Nène, Mammy and the two fiancés drank wine. Léa filled my plate from edge to edge. My hunger was such, though, that I could have downed twice as much.

The table conversation concerned the boys' studies and similarities between American and French schools. Léa kept an unceasing eye on my wants, making sure the breadbasket, mustard and cider were always in reach. Nène talked about a coming exposition, *Les Indépendants*, at the Petit Palais. I was up to my gills in French by then, and had switched off. In my mind's eye I saw the boy's face break away from the others and race towards me. "I'm sorry. I was held up." He was breathing very hard. "It's awful living in the suburbs. What's the time? 5:10! That's terrible. Come on, eveything's been arranged. You'll be staying with me. My parents have left for the weekend..." His voice trailed off as we both disappeared down the steps into the metro.

Mammy said little throughout the meal, commenting only on what Nène said. She gave out a continuous stream of misinformation. She said Léa's sister Birrie was coming on the opening morning of *Les Indépendants* when in reality she was coming in the afternoon. She said five of Nène's pictures had been chosen for the exposition, when only three had. After each faux pas Nène sucked in her breath and trembled before blurting out a disclaimer. Mammy took the corrections very badly. She puckered her lips, giving her face an emaciated shrew effect. Mostly, though, she just stared across the table at me while I ate, a smile of ecstatic beatitude lighting her face. Those beautiful eyes. "I'm terribly sorry. You have been waiting long haven't you? Gee, 5:10. Don't worry, I'll make it up to you. You'll never be kept waiting again..." How would it have been? "I'm awfully sorry. Wait till you see the house. Everything's been made ready." Deep voice. Solemn voice. "Gee..."

After dinner Léa suggested that she and I go for a walk. Thus was inaugurated the first of what were to be hundreds of late night promenades. The itinerary was invariably the same. From the rue de Sévigné we crossed the rue de Rivoli to the Église St. Paul. Then we proceeded up the rue François Miron into Geoffroy l'Asnier so that Léa could check if the lights were out at Mammy's. If they weren't, she would go up to see whether Mammy was having trouble. Often, like a tortoise turned on its back, it would take Mammy hours to locate and unsnap the clasp of the brassiere she wouldn't be caught dead not wearing. That-- added to her girdle, petticoats and slips--made her retiring as arduous as a queen's. If Mammy ate at Léa's, I would escort her home. Mammy adored Paris, and soon I knew the story of each street and house on our way to her own *maison classée*. Mammy was refined to the end of her fingertips. When climbing the stairs to her fifth-floor flat she insisted that I precede her, even though her unsteady progress upwards would have made my position behind more logical should she stumble and fall back. Yet a lady was not to allow a gentleman an excuse to admire her derrière.

From the rue Geoffroy l'Asnier Léa and I crossed the Pont Louis-Philippe to Ile St. Louis, the most exquisite section of Paris. Here the Seine rolled languidly under overhanging lanterns, catching their light and sending the beams back upwards like shooting stars. Paris was never really cold, neither in autumn nor winter, but there was usually a chill at that time of the night, and the air smelled of fresh sea grass. Beyond the cliff-tall buildings beckoned an invisible ocean. Often I had the urge to hurry there with Léa and walk barefoot on its beach. Even the drone of the faraway traffic at the Concorde added to the impression of distant breakers.

Some time in the future--light years away from this first night we spent together on Ile St. Louis--Léa and I would come across a lone stroller making his way through a strong wind blowing up the Seine. There were but a few days remaining till Christmas and Léa was asking me what gift I would like. We were holding tight to each other. I was only wearing a sports coat and sweater, and Léa was forever afraid of my coming down with the *crève*. One of Léa's arms looped my own and her hand was entwined in mine in my pocket. The boy approaching glanced up at us. Léa and I were certainly Colette-like lovers--she in her forties, I not yet twenty--and the glint in the stroller's eye suggested as much. He was dressed in the thick-wool sailor's navy-blue *caban*, a coat de rigueur for students, one that I would soon buy for myself. Around his neck was bunched a python-length wool scarf. When he was directly in front of us I said, in English, "That's what I want for Christmas, Mamma. Him." Léa had missed the meaning but the boy's eyes were crossed by a brief, disconcerted shadow. He would have blushed had his cheeks not already been winter pinched ... or perhaps not, for that too was assuredly Paris.

The intimacy which grew up between us from the outset was such that the nagging question I had concerning the origin of her children went from my mind, never to return. Léa was evidently a she-lion who had willed her cubs into existence, casting off the male when superfluous so as to fashion them with her own imprint. The place she allotted me was not uncomfortable to either of us: It gave her companionship tinged with the deeply moving albeit disavowed potential for renascent love, while providing me with what I needed most, a family, as well as the opportunity to transplant myself--roots, stem and all--to the land I loved. Yet no matter how close Léa and I became, I was always an outsider in a country where the bond of blood counted its weight in gold.

We returned home for tea before turning in. We met Mireille at the porte-cochère. Extremely pretty, Mireille too resembled her mother physically, having darker hair but the same eyes that shone with vitality. She disappeared into the girls' room where Gérard was waiting with doglike devotion.

Léa and I sat again around the pale wood table in the kitchen for tea. She had said nothing about where I would pass the night. She left me in no doubt, however, that I would be cared for. We spoke in whispers. Nène was in the adjoining room, Léa's, which they shared. We finished our tea just as the front door quietly closed. To my inquiring look Léa said that Mireille had gone to sleep at Mammy's. Christiane was already there. I would be using the girls' room.

Léa turned down the cover on one of the divans, and then folded back the sheets. I asked where the boys were. She took me through the small door next to the armoire that gave into a tiny room. The closed-in smell was fusty. Léa must have seen me wince because she opened up the single window. A narrow corridor of less than a foot separated the cots on which Sylvain and Vincent slept. Above the cots was a railed-in loggia that Bertrand had commandeered. It seemed fitting that even in this promiscuity Bertrand should have eked out a place of his own. Sylvain and Vincent were snoring. Clothes and books were flung all over. It occurred to me that Bertrand must have been driven literally up the wall by trying to keep order in this burrow. Vincent, even in sleep, seemed enormous; his blankets ballooned over him. Sylvain's head was out of sight; only his cowlick stuck up from his pillow like an Indian ceremonial feather, signaling his presence.

We closed the door. Léa politely asked me if I needed anything else. She then hastily disappeared into her room. I was left alone, too tired to think. Vaguely I remembered that I would have to find a hotel the next morning. I didn't worry about it as sleep hung far too heavy. There where I was, warm and protected, I let myself live one sweet tensionless moment.

.

The next morning Léa left for work early and I went off hotel hunting. The prices were far higher than I had estimated. Should I accept them, I would have to cut my vacation time in half. But in the back of my head I wasn't too concerned; I felt sure that Léa would somehow come through.

And she did.

A few days later, at the end of a late-night after-dinner parley between Léa, Nène and Mammy, Léa strolled out of her bedroom-cum-salon to inform me with more than a little pomp that Mammy had magnanimously consented to my taking the extra room she had at rue Geoffroy l'Asnier. The set-up would be temporary, of course. Léa spoke loudly enough for Mammy to catch her words. When Mammy came out in her turn I could see the reason. She seemed very uncertain at the prospect of taking in a boarder. Nène was nice but cool, accepting an aura of credit for the decision, but I was left with the impression that she too had acquiesced so as not to contrary Léa. A token rent of 100 francs had been decided on, a fraction of the price I would have had to pay at a cheap hotel.

After tea, I walked home with Mammy along the deserted streets of the Marais. The neighborhood was in an advanced state of decay. Many of the buildings were held in place by logs buttressing the walls, the doors and windows boarded up. On the walls I could see traces of old conflicts: À BAS L'OAS. De Gaulle had just declared *Québec libre!* and in Vietnam there was the Tet offensive. Mammy was as sweet as ever, although intermittently it would cross her mind that this time I would not be returning to Léa's, that I was there for keeps. Then she would look up at me--the stranger pulling her along the cracked pavement--and give me a skeptical Popeye-like once-over of doubt. Climbing up the stairs she twittered gaily about the building. "They tried to tear it down fifty years ago but Jean (her late husband) went to the Ville de Paris and told them we wouldn't move. That was when the whole district was full of old hotels," the French word for townhouses. She was smiling from ear to ear. "The old hotels with their original porte-cochères, the balconies of forged iron full of flowers. Jean owned a factory and the Ville de Paris," she laughed knowingly, "was obliged to listen." It took us half an hour to get to the fifth floor. Once inside, Mammy's mood changed. She said nothing, but her manner was Where does he go? Who uses the bathroom first? When do I put out the lights? To make matters easy, I immediately said goodnight, pecked her on her powdered cheeks, and went off into the room Léa had prepared during the day.

I could hear Mammy rummaging about. She came into the tiny washroom next to my room where there was a cold-water tap and a washbasin. Only a small door, the upper half a curtained window, separated us. The light there went off and on several times. She seemed to be hanging things up or taking them down. I also heard her screwing and unscrewing bottle tops. But never did she run the faucet. I quickly undressed and slipped in between the sheets. The room was a nice size. There was the very big window, a fireplace, a mahogany armoire, a table, a chair, my bed and a Persian carpet. The walls were papered in a very old motif of small faint brown clusters of leaves. In addition to the door to the washroom, there was a second door that led into Mammy's much more spacious room. Finally the light in the washroom seemed to go out definitively. I heard Mammy go into her own bedroom-salon and close the door. She moved about for a bit until at last there was silence. I lay in bed, a good distance from sleep, wondering how I was going to arrange the room and fill in the coming days. Suddenly I heard Mammy open the door to the washroom again with surprisingly determined force. There were a few faint sliding sounds as her slippers moved over the floor tiles. Then came a tap on the door and my name, tentatively tried out. I said *Entrez, Mamie!*, in as normal a voice as I could muster. The roles between intruder and host subtly altered. I felt strangely queasy.

Mammy put her head through the door. Something was clearly bothering her. She pushed the door in and followed suit hesitatingly, rather as if someone were prodding from behind. "I wanted to see if you were comfortably settled," she said, approaching my bed. Irrationally I drew the sheets up to my chin. Mammy kept mumbling something about my being well off. She reached over as though to put my sheets in order, but instead began to tug at them. Her words became jumbled, either because she wasn't paying attention to what she was saying, or because I had ceased listening. I caught Jean's name once or twice. She pulled harder and harder at the sheets, and as I was completely naked underneath, I absolutely did not want this woman to uncover me. We started a tug-a-war she was obviously intent on winning.

It was at that instant I had an absurd flashback to New York. The night before setting off for Europe I had gone to the Y where I booked one of those cubicles with iron cot, wardrobe and sink. Feeling clammy from the train trip, I went to the communal shower. I was dressed in cut-off levis and on my way back someone stopped me to comment on them. I nodded and headed back to my room. But before the self-shutting door could close, the stranger had bound inside and was pawing my bare shoulder. A split second later he was on his back under the window, his cheek red from where I'd hit him. I felt such revolting disgust that I wanted to stomp him to death. The man withdrew from the room, mumbling how sorry he was and how abject he felt. I barricaded the door with the wardrobe and the bed, and then tossed and turned through the whole sweaty night (3).

And now here was Mammy in a fluffy blue robe-de-chambre, her sagging biceps swaying as she sought to expose me. Of course I could have held out, but I didn't. Pathetically, I let myself be led to the execution block. The covers came flying back, and it was as if my body were being decapitated from my head. Mammy released the sheets as soon as she had gained possession of them, letting them fall over my stomach. She stumbled out of the room, still mumbling Jean's name. I heard her rummaging around again in the wardrobe in the washroom. When she returned it was with a nightgown, a man's, the old-fashioned kind that went over the head and dropped to the feet. I sat up while she dumped it over my head. With little pulls and tugs I got it to my knees without disturbing the covers bunched at my waist.

Satisfied, Mammy gave me a warm kiss on the cheek and left the room. In the dark, puzzled, I shucked the constraining gown and, laughing, gave myself up to the first of the many nights I would spend in that bed.

CHAPTER TEN

Léa's Room

The weeks I spent with Mammy drifted by slowly and I drifted along with them, an integral part of their movement. I pushed my bed under the high window where the light was excellent for reading, and it was in reading that I spent most of my days, in the company of Sartre, Camus, Gide and Colette, whose *Cheri* made me think of Léa. Saint-Exupéry, Montherlant and Maupassant whose two volumes in the Pléiade I reread every year, even in Jamaica. I was especially fond of plays like *Cyrano de Bergerac, La Guerre de Troie n'aura pas lieu*, Musset's *Lorenzaccio* and writers such as Molière, Labiche, Feydeau and Guitry. Seated at the round table Léa had dug up for me, a well-worn dictionary near at hand, my first book was *L'étranger*, an incredibly lucky choice as Camus wrote in a style as American as any native-born American. Gide's belief in the independence of youth, as well as a certain form of sexual liberation, was as meaningful to the generation of Léa as to mine. But she was totally ignorant of the writer's sexual persuasion. When I told her, she disbelieved me, enumerating the long list of heroines in his novels. Nène was shocked when I made a similar comment about da Vinci and Michelangelo. She gave me the same furious pout reserved for Mammy (4).

My mother had once told me that no one could find homage in my eyes. It was true that I had slammed the door on Bud and left the church, but it seemed to me that it was they who had cut me adrift. Doug, Al and certainly my father, I felt, had turned their backs on me. But there was one entity which found grace again and again in my eyes, always new, always alluring, never threatening, never excluding: Paris. The city captivated my imagination and tapped my feelings. If it was exact that one could only live fully when inspired, then it was to Paris I owed my jolt to life. As with the Frankenstein monster who was plummeted with lightning bolts until he briskly stood and walked, so did I too feed upon the city of unending generosity. His generosity, for such was Paris to me, a Renaissance lad with ribboned calves, a full bourse and flowing hair.

I would eventually be accorded all of Paris' favors in equal portion, but at the outset, thanks to Léa, it was the Marais--and Mammy--I came to love best.

Living with Mammy was a moving experience. From the slightly opened door between our rooms I could observe her from my bed while reading. One evening I was watching her as she sat at her dressing table. With her middle finger she applied a small blot of rouge to one cheek and, leaning well forward to see it clearly in her mother-of-pearl mirror, she closed the opposite eye and focused her attention on the spiral movement of her fingertips as they spread the blot over her angular cheekbone. After a few moments she dropped her hand onto the tabletop and squinted at the result. Disapproving, she put her finger into the tiny, delicately carved rouge box and prepared to repeat the process once more.

I had watched Mammy spend hours that way, rubbing in rouge and wiping it out. Suddenly she was shaken by a sneeze. Powder sprang from her hair in little clouds like a footfall on dry earth. She took a handkerchief from her blouse cuff and very daintily blew her nose, giving it a wrenching tug at the end. She studied her hanky with a puzzled stare as though just discovering it. She looked about the room, then back at the hanky. She placed it on the dressing table. Not satisfied, she picked it up by one of its corners. She seized the cane she had recently taken to using and pushed herself to her feet. She gazed right and left until her eyes fell on the chest of drawers. She went to it, pulled out a drawer and shoved the hanky inside. She thought for a moment, mumbled something, and fished the hanky out again. She gave an exasperated sigh. She turned nervously towards the door leading to the kitchen. From inside came noises of crockery being set out on the table. She eyed her room again, this time plainly agitated. From the kitchen came Nène's shrill voice.

"Are you ready?"

"Ready for what?" she murmured to herself. She looked at the hanky. "What does she want me to do with this?"

"Are you coming to dinner or are you going to remain there all night doing nothing?" came the voice.

"I'm coming!" Then to herself: "What should I do with it?" She stumbled towards the door to the kitchen, hesitated, and finally moved towards her bed. It was clear she was going to put the hanky under the pillow. As she went she murmured something I could catch only because I knew Mammy. "I can't stand any more. I can't stand any more."

Nène came to the door of Mammy's room, and I went back to my book. "Are you coming or not," she barked. Mammy thrust her hands behind her back. "Yes, I'm coming, I'm coming," she responded as rebelliously as she dared.

Nène returned to the kitchen. I heard Mammy shuffle around her room a bit more. Then she approached my door. She listened. I coughed so she would know she could come in, but still she hesitated. Only after a few seconds did her meek, cheerful voice filter through. "Are you there?"

"Is that you, Mammy? Come in." She hurriedly pushed the door open. She looked preoccupied. "Can I help you, Mammy?"

"Me? No, I came to see you…. Are you going out tonight?" She stood in the middle of the carpet. She seemed out of place in my room. We were both too eager to please the other, to find a common ground where none existed. Mammy was beyond the circle of life, beyond the touch of the things that concerned me most.

"No, Mammy, Léa's coming this evening and I'm still not ready."

Nène shouted from the kitchen: "Your soup will be cold. Do you want to come?"

Mammy glanced crossly in the direction of the kitchen. "Yes I want to come," she mumbled. Then looking back at me and fluttering her handkerchief impatiently she asked: "Where am I going to put this?"

"You usually carry it up your sleeve, Mammy."

"Oh, thank you. I couldn't ... you know, I'm very fond of you." She made a stilted movement in my direction, her body rigid, her arms slightly raised. I rose and embraced her on the cheeks. "I like you very much," she said, "it's true."

"I like you too, Mammy."

I waited a moment before adding, "Hadn't you better go and eat your soup?"

She nodded and shuttled out, banging her cane on the table and doorjamb. I went into the washroom to shave. From the kitchen I could hear Nène scolding her. "Would you sit up. Up straight! Oh, listen, you just have to look in the mirror to check your posture. Not now! Now you're eating. Oh! Your handkerchief is trailing in the soup!"

Nène entered the washroom to wash out the hanky in the small porcelain basin. I stepped aside for her. "What can I say?" she yelled back to Mammy in a conciliatory tone which I guessed was more for me. "Years before we kept handkerchiefs there, but not today. It's so dirty to have it against the skin. There are pockets. And me," she continued, addressing me more than Mammy, "I'm losing my time following you around. I haven't a free moment for myself. Too bad for my paintings. Too bad for the exposition. But when one has wasted all of one's life anyway, what does it matter now?" She paused. "All one's life running after ideals, believing in others, helping those you love. Then one fine day they don't need you anymore." She paused. "And your friends are dead." She paused. "And then what good are ideals? Léa is right to choose friends younger than she. She takes care of them; the rest of us can wind up in the cemetery for all she cares."

Something was heard breaking in the kitchen and Nène stormed out. I continued shaving. "Oh! One would think you do it on purpose!"

came Nène's voice. "Don't you think I have other things to do than clear up after you? Are you going to use your serviette?"

"I have my serviette..."

"Wipe your hands, I tell you!" A sudden, almost alarming silence descended over the kitchen. Only the sound of dishes being placed in the sink filtered through.

"Is your hair naturally curly?" I glanced into the mirror. Mammy was behind me, leaning against the door. On her face was a smile of enchantment. She entered the tiny cubicle. "It's very nice, all curly. Do you like Paris?"

"Yes, Mammy, very much."

''Especially at this moment," she said. "There are many interesting things to do in Paris: expositions, conferences, the Louvre .... You've visited the Louvre, I suppose?"

"Yes, Mammy, a number of times."

"It's always interesting. There are lovely dresses. Are you going out tonight?" "I'm going to remain here, Mammy. Léa's coming."

"It's always agreeable to receive guests. Do you know her?"

"Yes. You know Mammy, I'm quite busy..." I saw her wince and turn. "Mammy! I have a new record. Would you like to come into my room and listen to it?"

"Very much," she said, putting on her biggest smile. She went into my room and sat gingerly on the edge of the bed. I put on the record and returned to the bathroom. Mammy listened to the music for several seconds. Then she strained her neck to see if there was anyone in her room. Finding it empty, she rose and hurried inside. I went to my bed and turned the record player down. Mammy was sitting at her boudoir, putting on her makeup as before.

I went back to washing up. Soon I heard Nène enter Mammy's room. "Do you want any dessert?"

"Are you taking some?"

"I asked if you wanted any. What difference if I take some?"

"I don't know..."

"What don't you know? Whether to take dessert or not? Is that what you don't know?"

"Well, I'll take a little," signed Mammy.

"Don't forget you have to take tea later with Léa. You mustn't fill yourself."

"Then I won't take any dessert."

"Will you decide!"

"Yes, I won't take any." And to herself, "We have quests."

Back in my room I closed the doors to the washroom and to Mammy's. I put on a shirt and changed into clean trousers. I was combing my hair when Léa's voice came from Mammy's room.

"Where's Nène," Léa asked. Her tone was flat, but out of breath.

"In the kitchen." I could hear the rustling sound of Léa's coat falling on Mammy's bed. "I hope you've come to arrange my affairs. I received money this morning..."

"That was last week."

"Yes, and I don't know what they've done with it."

"Everything's in order." Léa's voice was loud. She was facing the door to my room. "There are papers in my drawer. I don't know how much I've been credited."

"I've taken care of it.... Is he in his room?"

"No, I don't think so. I haven't seen him. You can sit down," she offered.

"Good evening." it was Nène entering Mammy's room.

"Good evening." Léa's tone was as emotionless as it had been with Mammy, but with a harder edge. "I received the papers yesterday and I wasted all morning going from bureau to bureau trying to find out what they mean. Wasted, but I think I'm getting close to settling things."

"What papers?" asked Nène.

"The ... where is he?"

"In his room."

"Oh? Mammy said he wasn't here."

Nène turned on Mammy. "You know he's here; you've been talking to him all evening."

"Of course I know," protested Mammy.

"It doesn't matter," said Léa rapidly. "Perhaps you could prepare the tea, Mammy."

I heard Mammy's cane strike the bedstead. Nène's voice rose up again, "I'll go and help her." The intonation told volumes of what she considered Mammy capable of doing. Nearly immediately there was a light scratching on my door.

"Yes?" he yelled out. Léa came in.

"Oh, I thought it was Mammy," I said.

"I'm not bothering you? Good evening."

"Not at all. Good evening." I stood and took her proffered hand. Of late Léa had taken to pressing my hand in hers for longer and longer periods. A sentiment of embarrassment, not unlike that I had experienced at the New York YMCA, made me lose my footing. "Would you like to sit down?" I asked, to break the hold. My free hand indicated the only chair in the room.

''No, I'll take the bed. It was my room, remember?, and my best years were spent nestled up against the headboard, easel on my knees, drawing." She said this in a curious voice she had also adopted of late. It was a girlish voice, insinuating and flippant. She lay out over the bed cover and gave an unnecessary tuck to her skirt, bringing it down over her knees, a gesture I would see later, in Jamaica, when Linda did the same until, exasperated at my inattention, she raised it a notch each day.

I took the chair. Léa's presence filled the room. I felt very uncomfortable with the door shut, and while I listened to her talk about her childhood I kept an ear trained to Mammy's room, reassured by the clacking of her cane. Léa's attitude towards me could not have been more correct. Yet she had initiated an overly exclusive bond between us, one beginning when I allowed her to surreptitiously thrust money into my hand while we stood in line at the cinema so that I could pay for her, Mammy, Nène, whichever of the children came along, and myself.

Then came long walks at Vincennes, Chantilly or Versailles. At first the children remained by our side, all of them sharing in the conversation. But soon Léa pulled me away to visit sights that did not interest them: the Orangerie, the king's apartments, the chapel. I resented their absence. I had grown to like Vincent more and more. The boy's spontaneity, lack of all artifice and animal instinct pleased me. Often Vincent would put his arm around my neck and hang on to me as we strolled along. To Mireille's taunts *"C'est pas masculin, Vincent!"* He would growl at her like a discontented bear and proceed exactly as he pleased. The long visits through the chateaux and outbuildings were tiring and boring, and Léa's incessant explanations wearied me so mentally I came to despise the places. My legs hurt from the snail pace we kept and I was continually hungry. I wanted to run with the boys out of view of the girls, tug at their necks too and talk about whatever interested them.

Finally Léa came to infringe upon my privacy. She took to dropping by at any time of the day, and each visit began with a handshake and tiny forward movement as if she wished us to embrace French style. During her visits she suggested promenades throughout old Paris that I could not decently decline. Anyway, I preferred going out: anything to escape the intimacy of the apartment.

"I came to talk to you about your trip," she said. "You've been with us for two months now and I'm entrusting Sylvain to your care." Her son and I were leaving Paris the following day by bike and cycling to the Alps where we would join Léa, her daughters and Bertrand at a chalet offered them by the clergy of St. Paul. Vincent was going to a camp for boys, something similar to the American Scouts. It was a secret to no one-- other than to me at the time--that Léa received no child support from her husband, and even though both Mammy and Nène contributed to their own personal upkeep, Léa assumed a certain number of their expenses. There were never fewer than ten to twelve of us at table. Léa gave me at least one meal a day, and never did I pay for anything, snacks, metro tickets, cinema or museum entrances when I accompanied her. "The family, all the family, has come to like you very much," she continued.

Her generosity was confusing. As a boy I was treated by my father as Nène treated Mammy in her advanced age: I could do nothing right. As one failure added itself to another, my sense of confidence all but evaporated. Even worse was the humiliation. One example among many was the day Father met with some friends at a corral. I was seven or eight and had never been near a horse in my life. Without the slightest instruction, he put me on the saddleless, bridleless animal and told me to grip the mane. When he struck the horse's butt to get it moving, I fell to the ground where I was left to pick myself up, shamed by his refusal to make even the slightest gesture of tenderness. He had turned his back on me, preferring the company of his friends, each with a flask, their feet stamping the frozen earth, their eyes watery from the cold and alcohol, studiously looking away from the child who'd disgraced his dad. I always thought that humiliation was the worse punishment possible, worse than failure, and that it was largely because of it that I did what I did later. Humiliation, the penance those scumbags wished me to drunk down to the dregs. No, I never knew a moment of tenderness from that man, except when...

"It's traditional in France," Léa went on, "that when such trust is exchanged, it is marked by a sign. At such times two people use the informal *tu* with each other. I suggest we do the same." I already *tutoyed* the boys, and they me. What Léa was suggesting was quite extraordinary, given the difference in our ages. As though to underline the point, she reddened and was suddenly at a lack for words, a rarity for Léa. Luckily she managed a grin which, when added to my awkward thanks, spanned the tension between us. Mercifully, Mammy's scratching and hesitant entrance saved the moment. *"Madame est servie!"* she announced proudly, her mouth turned up in a delightful smile. Léa and I followed her out.

CHAPTER ELEVEN

Sylvain

The following day Sylvain and I left rue Geoffroy l'Asnier for the Alps. Mammy gave us a kerchief send off from the fifth-floor window. Nène was painting somewhere and Léa had taken an early train with Bertrand, Mireille and Christiane. Sylvain and I rode to the bank of the Seine and followed the cobblestone street that bordered it out of Paris. Dawn had broken an hour before, but the city slept on. Fruit and vegetable vendors were filling their street-side pushcarts with produce and garbage trucks crept at a snail's pace while Africans emptied refuse cans into the revolving teeth at the back. Café *garçons* polished copper counter tops and bakers dumped warm croissants in their display windows.

Sylvain and I made good progress, a hundred kilometers a day, ten hours at a stretch. The weather was marvelous that year. Everyday there was sun. The small routes we took were lined with plane trees, the fields were full of wheat and corn, the serpentine roads empty of cars. We turned brown, our thigh muscles and calves hardened, and we developed raging appetites. We had an endless choice of camping sites that summer, when the average Frenchman could afford hotels. We picked grassy camps, camps situated outside the lofty walls of medieval towns, camps with swimming pools and camps bording lakes.

France was a heartrendingly exquisite country. Our itinerary took us over green plains pierced by the distant steeples of roman and gothic churches, across the ubiquitous fields of wheat, along towering seaside cliffs and through gorges obscured by mists. We followed river valleys between hilly lowlands, sometimes cycling faster than the huge coal-loaded barges plodding upstream. We swam in village cataracts with husky farm boys, handsome and deeply tanned. The roads into the heart of the Alps followed vales scoured out by pre-historic glaciers, leaving them amazingly accessible to bicycles.

The only hitch to the trip was my relationship with Sylvain. The French boy cared nothing for the state of his hair, clothes or body. Although sixteen, he seemed dead below the belt, a sexual indifference which deprived him of initiative and aggressiveness. The result was a person whose head compensated for a lack of sensorial reaction to life. He read nothing that wasn't a school textbook. As far as I could detect, he had but two passions: his bike and English. I took advantage of his passivity, outlawing all English in our conversations. I bullied him into playing linguistic games, the end product of which was my fluency in French at Sylvain's expense. The more Sylvain gave way, the more I demanded. Despite his severe shyness, I got him to do the shopping for us both, and the cooking as well. If something was done incorrectly, I bawled him out, employing the expressions he had taught me.

My mistake was believing that his servitude was unlimited. Sylvain was a moody, despondent child inured to the outer world, uncaring about anything detached from the inner spring he himself fed from. That spring had the tenacity of iron. Somewhere along those days I went too far and Sylvain withdrew the last few feelers which joined us. He refused to speak to me, he slept plastered against his side of the tent, he bought and cooked his own food. I tried to snap him out of his muteness, even profusely apologizing for what I had done to alienate the boy. Sylvain, having grown convinced that I could never be trusted, made no appearance of even having heard me, an attitude which turned out to be justified: I would quite simply have never made any sacrifice on his behalf. Despite all of

Sylvain's former loyalty and kindness, and the fact that it was thanks to him that I had gained entrance into the family, his unpardonable sin was that he failed to elicit even an atom of emotion in my emotion-starved breast.

At the chalet we were greeted as prodigal sons. Sylvain was quartered with Léa, Bertrand and his sisters in a grange-like room full of cots. I was given a room to myself, one scarcely larger than the bed, but my own. A small kitchen into which we all squeezed for our meals separated the two rooms.

Outside the chalet the mountain slope fell away into the far-off valley where the town of St. Sigismond lay under a matinal cover of ascending fog. We wore sweaters all summer round, but the valley was warm enough for swimming in the muddy ponds outside the town. Léa was endlessly patient with her brood on the marches through the woods down to St. Sigismond. During those few times she remained at the chalet, I accompanied the girls and Bertrand to the swimming ponds. I still could not understand Bertrand's clowning, and resented being the brunt of it. For his part, Bertrand did not take well to my knuckling him.

The best times during those days were late at night, when the children lay asleep and Léa and I took tea together. We often discussed the children. Léa was as perplexed as I about Bertrand. A child living within his own world is as cold and unattainable as a mountain summit. What could he be thinking, this pimply lad who was the first in his class, friendless, considered a clown in his family, and exiled alone in the marshy, Siberian complexity of puberty?

Sylvain was another topic. He wandered off during the day, as much a loner as Bertrand, but applying his energies in more recognizable ways. He hiked, he cycled and he swam. He remained aloof of the children, yet contributed to the table conversation. Usually laconic, moments of speech would come over him with the sudden, turbulent vitality of a summer storm. Then he would stutter, his speech unable to keep afoot of the tale wanting release. He was exclusive and fragile. He took only a fleeting part in what interested the rest of us, and never did he make demands for things like money or clothing, seemingly surviving on fresh air and water. Léa stood inalterably at his side. Sylvain, she insisted, was a true individual who made claims on no one but himself. As I got to know her better, and our views on the children focused more frankly, I mentioned some of the problems Sylvain's irascibility had created during our tour. Invariably Léa took her son's side in a way that seemed illogical, yet so implacable as to allow no rebuttal. Only concerning Sylvain would Léa pull rank: I was aghast, but she was in charge, and her boy was taboo. During an average day she addressed Sylvain with fewer than a dozen words; nothing more appeared needed to cement their bond.

Letters began to arrive from Vincent from camp. Despite his age and Léa's liberalism--which allowed the boys and girls to come and go as they wished, never demanding explanations for their behavior, never prying into their personal lives--and despite a room shared with two other brothers, one of whom, Sylvain, was older, Vincent had managed to approach adulthood perplexingly ignorant of certain matters. His first letter contained a detailed description of the Scouts' sexual prowess. He instinctively sensed that he would be opening himself to possible derision should he put questions to the other boys, some of whom were younger than himself. So he asked his mother. Léa spoke to me about the matter late one night. She was furious at the camp's lack of supervision. She was embarrassed to bring up the subject but who else could advise her? Ignorant as she was concerning the sexual bent of the writers she read and the artists she, as an art teacher, was supposed to know by heart, it was not totally surprising that she felt, as I had years before, that her son was exposing himself to practices which would lead to dementia. To agree with her would place me resolutely on the side of normality; to disagree would make me a pervert, and in that case wouldn't Léa be justified in wondering what dirty things went on behind my closed door? Yet for Vincent's sake, I decided to come clean. I said that in America the subject under discussion really wasn't a problem. Of course not, she interrupted, but in France it was. I let her run on for a while. America was too clean and healthy a country for such practices, she said. She wanted to believe I was pure ... and I acquiesced.

In the meantime another letter from Vincent came. There was a change in tone: a new self-awareness, references to fresh sources of energy, absence of comments about boredom and loneliness, comments common in his first letter. Léa hurriedly posted off a list of do's and don'ts. I sent a man-to-man note in the same mail. In fatuous generalities I told the boy that there were mysteries beyond the scope of women. Vincent never answered the letter, but upon his return it was clear from his attitude that it had established a complicity neither of us would forget.

CHAPTER TWELVE

Léa

After lunch one afternoon Léa suggested we attend a *fête foraine* in a village over the mountains. All of us set off, even Sylvain. Distant snow-covered peaks hemmed us in from all sides as we made our way up and over the summit above our chalet. The forest gave way to rocks and wind-flattened grass. Overhead clouds closed in, cutting out the sun and bringing on a sudden chill. I led the way, carefully heeding Léa's indications. She and the girls sang *Our Shepherd, Our Leader*. Bertrand was out of breath and had difficulty keeping up. Sylvain brought up the rear, absorbed in his own reflections. Léa's lips were turned up in a Madonna's smile. She never concealed the pleasure our strolls gave her. Little by little the girls' contentment rubbed off on me. I put an arm around Bertrand and helped him along. The boy nuzzled into my side like a starved calf taking comfort at his mother's udder. I smiled indulgently at Léa. Inside, I felt a pang that tore my heart to shreds. Sylvain continued behind, cut off from the family circle.

At the fair we shuffled aimlessly from stand to stand. The village was made of two-story pointed-roof houses interspersed with shops. We all ate a crêpe, the children instinctively aware of their mother's precarious finances, and none asked to ride the merry-to-round or shoot darts at the balloons. The locals hung around in loose groups waiting for something to happen. Anything was an event: two dogs chasing through the mud, the arrival of a farm boy on a motorbike, even us.

To cover our boredom, we used the threatening sky as the reason for returning home. Halfway back the excuse became reality. The sky went black with enormous clouds. In the distance, sheets of rain and thunder rolled across the valleys. We were in the thick of the forest when the storm caught up. Rain pounded down in torrents. Lightning struck in dense volleys. Between flashes the forest went pitch black and the trail disappeared. In a matter of seconds we were soaked through, cold and at least I owned up within myself to being frightened. Bertrand resembled a drowned rat. Then we came upon more unfortunate than ourselves. A mangy, waterlogged dog lay whimpering in the middle of the road. With each thunderclap he let out an appalling wail. Bertrand broke away from my side and ran up to it. I told him to stay back because the animal was filthy and might be dangerous. Ignoring me, the entire family surrounded the animal. Bertrand bent over to pet him. Rewarded with grateful licks on the hands and face, Bertrand fathered the beast in his arms. We again made off for the chalet, but the mood of the group had totally changed. The girls picked up *Our Shepherd*. Léa took Bertrand's place at my side, her hand wrapped around my own in my parka pocket. I joined in the singing; Sylvain did so as well. Soon we were skipping through the driving rain and sloshy mud oblivious to our misfortune.

Back home, Léa threw out towels for all of us. Bertrand made sure the dog got the biggest and fluffiest. The kitchen stove was stoked and tea put on. We gathered around the tables, the girls looking helpless beneath their ropy strands of hair, the boys resembling gummed-down gangsters from the Roaring Twenties. We were all tired and by nine only Léa and I were left awake. I helped her wash up the day's dishes. I had put on pajamas bottoms and she was wearing a thick woolen housecoat. Her manner was strangely--nearly defiantly--calm. It was a mood I had detected before in patches. She seemed talked out, and was humming. I dried the last fork and asked her if she would excuse me, as I was dropping with sleep. Her answer was "Poor little boy; poor little, little boy." This inexplicable familiarity was followed by another: she wrapped her arms around me and kissed me on the lips. I was breathless, my mind a blank. She was sighing, her breasts pushed into my naked chest. Then she released me, and turned back to the sink. From her profile I saw the same smile à La Gioconda. I mumbled a goodbye and left. She responded only with a nod. First the tea, then the sympathy.

In my room the impossibility of my position terrified, humiliated and angered me. How did she dare do such a thing? Did she think I was so dependant on her as to allow *that*? The more I reflected on the situation, the more furious I became. Plots formed in my mind as to how I would avenge myself. Then I heard a noise outside the door. My anger evaporated and fright took its place. The door was locked but I rushed an armoire up against it. Thinking she might come through the window, I shut that too and covered it with a blanket. That's how I remained throughout the night, the next day, and the next.

Early the following morning Léa came scratching at my door. I remained silent. She returned at breakfast and asked me to please open up. At lunch she came back and pleaded with me in a very low voice. I heard the children approach the door. I heard her tell them I was feeling ill. I didn't open up for food, but later that afternoon I leapt from the window and ran to a nearby farmhouse for cheese and milk. Later I heard the children make their way down the slopes, off to pick strawberries. Léa's voice wasn't among them. I knew I was now alone with her in the chalet. I could not give in, not before I made her pay for the previous night, not before she learned a lesson she would not forget. I cared for her friendship, but I was far more willing to give it up than to sacrifice what I thought of as my scruples. Yet I feared her pleading. As Odysseus' crew, I made balls out of bread and water and stuffed them in my ears, cutting off outside noises. Only the quick, frantic movement of the doorknob told of her presence on the other side.

I slept uneasily that first night. Alone on the soft bed, adrift in the night's blackness, I found I could withdraw into myself as I had never been able to do before. Even the sense of touch seemed helpless without the guidance of my eyes and ears. The threat of Léa beyond the door pushed me into dreams of my mother. I saw her welcoming me home from Europe, her tears, my father's halfhearted reception, the dinner in front of the TV, and the first night back in my own bed with its childhood memories.

The second day the girls came to visit me. They respectively asked entrance. I hated to ignore them. I pretended to be asleep by snoring loudly. Léa was a poor psychologist. She should have sent Bertrand or announced a letter from Vincent. The second night I dreamed again of my mother.

On the third day I came out after lunch. Léa had sent the kids away and was waiting for me outside the door. She took my hand and led me to a grassy knoll near the chalet. There she turned to speak to me. Her eyes were very red. Perhaps I was standing above her, because she appeared small and diminished, not at all the lioness who had raised five children. She began by saying that she was terribly saddened by my misinterpretation of her intentions. Her tone was soft and pleading. I told her I considered her a second mother. That was also the way she considered our relationship, she said. As far as she was concerned, the incident was closed. She leaned heavily against my arm and we returned to the grange where my lunch awaited me in the oven. Afterwards we had tea.

We went back to our Paris formality. We no longer talked about the personal lives of the children. Subjects of a sexual nature were avoided. Yet she would not relinquish my arm when we went out for walks; it was a right she had definitively abrogated to herself during the storm. Never once did it occur to me that had I been like most other boys, I might have welcomed Léa's interest. She could have brought me, sexually, into the world; sexually, she could have undone the harm of my childhood.

At the end of the week I was obliged to leave them. Autumn term would begin soon, the first of another two years of university. Then would follow two years' service to a president, the assassination of whom brought my alienation with the country of my birth a step closer.

CHAPTER THIRTEEN

Just too doggoned bad

We assembled in a large barracks room where we milled around like army enlistees, middle-class, doubtful of the decision that had brought us here, and trying to keep face. The room was drained of light by dark clouds piling up over nearby Jones Beach. We were *pecnos*, a Jamaican word meaning clods and country bumpkins. Our suitcases were new and the boys, like most middle-class Americans, had crew cuts. Some were discussing the fight of the century between Ali and Frazer, while a few of the girls talked about that year's hit, *Love Story*. None knew what he or she was waiting for. This most extreme, deserted point of America was where our traveling instructions ended. Beyond was the sea; we could go no farther.

One boy near me, a stocky hockey-player type, was making a complaint to one of the few girls in the group, in the strangest accent I'd ever heard: ''I just took the shuttle out of Staten Island,'' he grumbled. To which the girl said primly: ''I was provided with an air ticket from Carbondale.'' ''Christ! Where!?'' he asked incredulously. On the other side of her stood a boy with an expression so lost his eyes were glazed. He was husky and crew cut, obviously first-of-the-family-through-the-university like me. He was from Kalamazoo. ''Where!?'' asked the hockey player, bringing the boy into the conversation.

There was a Negro, just one. He was big, strong, handsome, funny, schooled and threatening. His name was Frank. He actually went around introducing himself. Frank was also from New York, and he too was making jokes about his twenty-minute ride down to Jamaica, the N.Y. borough. Unsure of how to approach him, the first Negro--the word favored at the time--I'd ever met. I decided it would be prudent to observe him from a distance, a curious decision from a volunteer whose destination was another Jamaica, this one the Jamaica West Indies, a whole island of blacks.

A boy named Charlie, overweight, his features sagging, drifted unnoticed about the room, as he would skirt every group that formed up during the coming weeks, an expectant look as though hoping someone would whistle him over, which no one ever did. He stopped next to a volunteer named Sophie, a small loud girl from Louisiana. She befriended him in an odd way later during the training period. At the moment he was complimenting her on a pair of huge earrings jingling from her lobes. ''Yeah, they're keen,'' she answered, ''Wanna wear 'em?'' In Jamaica, when she took up with Frank, she came bursting back into a teachers' meeting from the toilet. ''Jesus, Frank, there's a gigantic turd in that bowl,'' she screamed, ''you wouldn't believe it! Really, it's nearly as big as your dick.'' Crude stuff for the era.

Spring came late to New York that year, but for me it made its entry at 3:30 p.m., an hour and a half after the volunteers had all been scheduled to meet together in that large barracks room. The door opened and in sidled Mark Splatz. Tall and around twenty pounds overweight, he wore a white shirt carelessly stuffed into shiny black slacks, and on his feet were huge inch-thick rubber-soled shoes worn for comfort or economy, I couldn't decide. His black hair looked like a haystack pitched by unskilled hands. His face was not unattractive, his eyes were as black as the coal in Carbondale, and in his mouth was a stogy Churchill would have coveted. He trudged in chin up and haughty, bringing to mind the photo of Roosevelt with the holder and cigarette jutting from his lips. *He* wasn't nervous. As with Frank, he went from group to group introducing himself in an accent as thick as the hockey player's. When someone caught his interest, he went straight to him with all the elegance of a bull amidst porcelain. He charged forward, head in advance, cigar and eyes up like a swimmer's. When he came to a stop, his body straightened to the inflexible rigidity of Yogi Bear.

Mark differed as much from me as Laurel from Hardy, but the vibrations were straight on. From that moment I ceased worrying and started enjoying. There was no dog-encircling-dog. The New Yorker came right up and said I'm Mark and who are you? The Tupperware Party approach. My feelings for him were exclusive and restricting; his for me were open and without ambivalence. Mark disseminated largess; I soaked up his crumbs. Never did he wish to be anything other than leader and teacher; never did I want to be more than the bright, attentive student. Mark's curiosity extended to all the Peace Corps candidates; mine centered exclusively on Mark. By nature Mark's impulses were sensual. He experienced a canvas, music and the books he devoured with a part of his body that had little to do with his head. There was nothing of the cat about him. He was a pusher and a go-getter. I saw some of New York's grubbiest and toughest-looking freaks make way for him on the streets as he charged forth, the stogy blazing a trail, a Moses among the Pharisees. Mark took what he wanted, be it a person's loyalty or the essence of a tableau. And since he sufficed unto himself, others measured up to him, or were spurned. There was nothing of the cat about him, except the cat's sensibility. He had to be stroked and made to purr. He reacted to what touched his soul, not his brain.

In contrast, my feelings were all cerebral, and although I had nothing of the intellectual except the intellectual's pretensions, I nonetheless existed through my mind. Mark's interests led to an abominable dispersion. Since everything was of potential interest, Mark had to find time for everything. My mind, on the contrary, led me with near infallible certainty through the shoals of wasted effort. I had long since learned to discriminate between what could or could not be of profit. Indeed, the only time I erred was when I gave my sensuality free rein. Then I courted people like Mark, and left myself open to disaster.

The volunteers' training program took place at St. John's University. A succession of scholars herded by Professor Pinchard, an anemic brooder, put us through variegated courses in Jamaican West Indies history, patois and customs. A string of polite Creoles from the island tried to help us bridge the gap between Jamaica virile-sons-of-Africa and Jamaica former-British-colony, a gap the Creoles themselves were having difficulty bridging. Most had Oxonian accents, smoked pipes and wore tweeds; they sheltered a condescending paternity towards Americans, and harbored a harsh--yet strangely respectful--opinion of their prior British master. The volunteers, America's new ambassadors, were left with the impression that it would be our responsibility to make up for previous colonial excesses.

The classes at St. John's were obligatory. In one way or another Mark by-passed half of them. Since I could have him to myself only at the times he wasn't at the University, I did likewise. The two other New Yorkers, Frank, the Negro, and Rob, the boy built like a hockey player, gave up their freedom on the outside to live on campus in one of the dormitories with the rest of the Peace Corps aspirants. Mark kept his New York residence and commuted back and forth from Queens to the borough of Jamaica. That way he missed breakfast and dinner and all the after-dinner activities the Corps thought indispensable for our conversion into a team: charades, scrabble and monopoly. I avoided the team play, losing myself in Xenophon, Plutarch and Herodotus, increasingly certain that, because of my ''nature'', I would have found fulfillment only in the Age of Pericles (5).

Often Mark didn't come back after having lunch at his house. When Professor Pinchard requested a reason for his absences, Mark pointed out the uselessness of their training, an evaluation, he continued, that anyone with an iota of intelligence would come to. He sympathized with Professor Pinchard for having to follow Peace Corps instructions as to the programming of the curriculum, but only mediocre applicants would accept such inanity. ''If you don't agree,'' he concluded, ''you can deselect me when the time comes. That way, at least, we'll know where you stand.'' I nodded at Mark's side, ever his yes man. If Mark went, I would surely go. Yet if Mark were allowed to remain, I was in danger of being sacrificed in order for Professor Pinchard to assert his authority against the less dangerous of the two.

Afternoons found Mark and me playing handball at a club in Queens or swimming at the Y. Mark was an admirable athlete who carried his stomach hump like a resilient dromedary. Several times Rob tagged along. Even he, a passable model of the discus thrower, could just keep a close second to Mark athletically. Rob fawned over Mark and bullied me. Mark never interfered. It seemed to me that New Yorkers had a blind spot for weakness, and took it as a personal affront to their will to survive. But Mark's shadow allowed me admittance into his and Rob's conversations, a dubious honor because of the vernacular they shared, gibberish I could rarely catch the meaning of. The locker room became the high temple of virility and comradeship. Trained for years to hide myself behind a façade lest my difference be discovered, with the two New Yorkers I tried my hand at loud whistling and locker door slamming. Safely inverted between the muscular brackets that were Mark and Rob, I let myself admire the nudity about us. It was like breaking into the Play Boy Club and catching the bunnies as naked as on the centerfold. Drawn especially to those of Spanish extraction, the first uncircumcised boys I had ever seen, I at times felt the spontaneous urge to turn to Mark and Rob and say, Christ, get a load of that one! (6)

I welcomed the bond that drew men together as evidenced by the closeness of myself, Mark and Rob, but I suffered from the fact that the secret to the ancient Greeks had been lost: that man can be bound to man intellectually and homoerotically, and forge with him that most coalescing of pacts, a covenant based on equality, both mental and physical, and sexual autonomy.

Once their showers taken, Rob went back to St. John's. Mark and I took the subway--that unfathomable riddle which would have daunted even the cleverest Theseus--to various favorite places. One was the Frick collection, easily the most beautiful, the most serene temple of art I would ever discover. Even there Mark charged around like a bull, but a bull with padded hooves and muzzled snout. He took up a stance in front of a picture so totally that one felt he was either the director of the place or a lunatic; in neither case did anyone press to find out. He commented on the art as if it were he the artist, continuing on even when I, too tired to take any more in, took shelter on one of the marble benches around the central pool, gazing at the statuary, palms and galleries of paintings.

Our second hideaway was the Athena, the only movie house at that time to show old foreign films. Nestled into one of the moldy-smelling over-stuffed seats in that overheated theater, I saw some pretty weird-looking creeps dart silently in and out of the exit. Longhair, burly coats, unshaven or bearded and all stag, anyone would have taken the place for a porno house if the flicks on the screen weren't Gabin-*jeune*, Michel Simone and Gérard Philippe. Mark and I took comfort in the thought that back on the ranch Rob and the others were being welded into a team by means of canasta and What's My Line. We never admitted it to each other, but we were gnawed by the incessant thought that our game of hooky was costing us two years in the West Indies.

Unfortunately, as we exited the theater one night Mark said he would be going home to sleep, not back to the University dorm. He had broken a promise to return with me, and I was furious because this wasn't the first time he hadn't kept his word. What David Niven had written about Errol Flynn--that one always knew where one stood with him because Flynn *always* let one down--was alas true of Mark (7). I stalked off to face the subway alone. Of course, I took the wrong direction, and with one thing and another in that miserable hellhole I didn't get back until five that morning.

Home for me was a room with three beds and two cots. It was my first experience at sharing, and I disliked it. The guys made noise until all hours, they monopolized the bathroom and they looked on me with scorn because I wouldn't take part in their pastimes: I refused to shuffle-and-giggle-and-ah-shucks-should-we? on the doorsteps of strip joints; I despised their music, their idiotic jokes and their pigskin heroes. The underlying abyss was, as always, sex. Without that common denominator we were invariably at odds. The boys farted openly, they belched like Turks, one used the can while a second pissed in the sink and a third combed his hair looking over his shoulder. Mark was as manly as any of them, and except for whom he screwed, Mark's interests were mine. We both liked music and our favorite topic was books, and we were both keen on sports: Mark competitive ones, me those made for loners, like swimming and athletics. Yet when the volunteers had their three-day battery of psychological tests, Mark came out an A-1 male while I had to go through an unexpected interview with a bulbous-nosed, toady-skinned shrink.

"Uh, the results show you like paintings, sculpture and arty things like that..." I had marked the No Interest box on any question in the least compromising; the corrector had drawn the right conclusions anyway. "Uh, you're a loner ... you know, the type that'd rather sit in the house all day sewing than toss a ball about. Now, Jamaica's a very masculine society and we're not sure if your skills (?) would go over well there..."

I jumped up and sputtered so violently I showered the shrink with spittle: ''I'm no goddamned queer if that's what you're getting at, and if a guy can't like a picture you might as well shut down the goddamned museums...." The shrink stopped me with a wave of the hand and a supercilious grin and said, "Uh, that's not what I was getting at...." and changed the subject. During the mid-training deselection--based nearly solely on the shrink's report--I was left unscathed. Charlie went though. I cringed at the thought of his limp-wrist rebuttal to the same accusations. When Charlie got the word that he was no longer one of the volunteers, his jowls sagged further still, he went white, and meekly protested, "Well, why *me*?" while giving us all a look of abysmal distress. Sophie came up to help him leave the room before he broke down. He pointed a hip towards the door and followed it out. I wondered if Charlie's sacrifice-- statistically there had to be at least *one* among us--had saved me. But I couldn't help wondering how the tests had shown me up and not Mark. Mark who had at least as much "sensitivity" as I, and more "arty" knowledge in his little finger, I knew, than would probably accumulate in me during my entire life. Coming as it did at the beginning of the '70s, such gay phobia didn't seem particularly unjust or even out of place to me. That I had to go through it was just too bad, *just too doggoned bad* (8).

.

The weeks rolled on and the end of training was in sight. Visitors from the Jamaica West Indies seemed to become more apologetic as the date of the embarkation for their island approached. Professor Pinchard looked increasingly haggard and he had an increasingly insistent way of eyeing Mark and me that made us cringe at the thought of the final deselection. Mark--ever the pragmatist--became more perspicacious in when to, and when not to, cut classes. Our attendance at the Athena accordingly dropped perceptibly. Mark took to sticking around the dorm at night, and while the others poured over Jamaican Industry and Commerce brochures, I sat in a corner slumped over an old pickup listening again and again to the season's hit "Dominica," sung in French. I thought increasingly of Léa. More and more she took the form of angelic succor.

Two months passed and the day of the final deselection came. So far fifty percent of the volunteers had been dumped. Not that it was a bad group. There were perhaps too many individuals for St. John's mediocre tastes, we consoled ourselves in thinking, a way of explaining our own insipient failure. So our last morning at the University found us in the same dark classroom which had welcomed us at our arrival. In an adjoining room sat our jury: Professor Pinchard, the shrink, teachers and the Jamaican guests. Their decision would be forthcoming, the volunteers were told. All morning we waited for a sign from that room, but none came. We returned after lunch, most of us as sick in the stomach as ship passengers. The afternoon went by hour by clogged hour, without a sign of life from behind the little gray door. Mark and I had jokingly accepted our fates; rarities like us didn't stand a chance. During the afternoon the joking ceased; no one was even talking anymore. At about six one of the girls broke down into sobs. Later still, we were herded to the cafeteria for dinner. Back by eight, we expected to find little envelopes with our destinies hastily scribbled inside. But still there was nothing. The psychiatrist came in to tell us the discussions were still going on, and would we please be patient. He looked as haggard as a beachcomber. He made his announcement to the room; none of the volunteers benefited from actual eye contact.

By midnight we felt the farce had gone on too long. We would jointly resign and force the government to give us another training period elsewhere. Our grumbling must have reached the ears of the potentates within, because one of them, a young Catholic priest, came to tell us to go to bed. There would be no decision that night. We all protested the incredulous cruelty of making us sleep with such a sword of Damocles over our heads. Then Professor Pinchard made a sudden appearance behind the back of the young priest. He announced that the waiting was over. He would circulate around the class, he said, and those he pointed to would please go into the room he had come out of. He made the rounds. When he came to me I went so pale I thought I'd faint. Professor Pinchard was himself ashen as a corpse. He looked me straight in the eye-- an avenging angel--but passed by, his hand stilled by the intervention of which god? He went over towards Mark. Poor Mark, for the first time ever his outward strength deserted him. He looked like a child who had lost his pony. I didn't know if it were better to stay where we were or go into the next room. I just prayed that Mark would suffer the same fate as

I. And Mark did. He too was passed over. Professor Pinchard disappeared into the other room with the majority of the volunteers. It therefore couldn't be us who would see the West Indies. ''Yes, yes,'' said the priest left behind, ''you are the chosen!''

CHAPTER FOURTEEN

Buba

Duckenfield a year later. Cycling under trade wind clouds rising like anvils, I made my way past the hillock called Kingston Crag and started the descent into the plain below. Miles of pine-green sugarcane rippled before me like fields of unripe wheat. Duckenfield town and the toy-sized plantation factory lay beyond, and beyond them the sea, as gray as the sky overhead. The dirt road I peddled over led from this, the easternmost tip of the island, to the asphalted Main Road where it turned up north to Montego Bay. The air around me fluctuated from hot to cold as the clouds freed or blotted out the sun. If I hadn't had to go to the intersection I would have been on the beach at Holland Bay, a promontory where all Jamaica was drawn together like the tied-off mouth of a balloon, before disappearing beneath giant breakers. I spent a lot of time at Holland Bay.

At the intersection called the Crossroads I parked my bike at the post office and went into the meat pie shop next door. The East Indian boy Buba sold me a patty of meat and curry resembling a tortilla. When I had first arrived on the island, the meat pies had burned my guts and given me dysentery. Now I considered them, as did the other inhabitants, medicinal. Buba was slim and well built. His eyes glistened like fine black pearls. Above white healthy teeth and delicately penciled lips was a lightly sketched moustache. I had seen him yesterday on the beach near the fishing hamlet of Holland Bay. I'd made out his copper skin and black pubic bush from a long way off. He was running circles about a group of laughing black girls. I'd approached as close as discretion allowed before stripping down to my swimsuit. Buba's rod swung listless and heavy, with the ponderous luxury of the money pouch Renaissance boys wore at their sides. He tried to grab the girls, to get his fingers into their sexes. When he succeeded his rod rose to the enviable proportions of mixed-blood sixteen-year-olds. He and the girl he caught escaped into the palm bushes. When they came out, a few moments later, the game resumed. Sometimes they ran close to me. Once I saw a long rope of sperm ooze free from Buba's glans as he lunged for the girls, two of whom already had peeling splotches of dry cum on their upper thighs. Later Buba came and squatted down beside me. My erection inside the trunks made Buba giggle. He must have felt sorry for me. Volunteers, if they were to be judged by this one, were as continent as priests. He smiled his regret. He took up his flaccid sex in hand and milked it from the base to the tip. He snickered at the resultant accumulation of sperm on his fingers that he flicked away as I had seen him do when he blew his nose into his fingers. Then he strode off.

Now, with those same fingers, he shoved the patty over the counter top. Buba's eyes hardly registered my presence. He didn't say thanks and neither did I when I left. Outside, waiting for the bus from Kingston, I ate the patty. It was Buba's, and Buba was beautiful.

Mrs. Field, the principal's wife, came out of the post office. She shifted her ample weight from haunch to haunch, making the frilly fringe of her dress shimmer. Mrs. Field had a pleasant smile and manner, both guileless, and large flabby arms that wielded a cane in true colonial fashion. A few tiny tots caught between her and me as she approached curtsied away like a school of fish, each with a quick "Orning, Mz Field" on her lips. I didn't get an "Orning". I didn't whip.

"On the town, this bright morn?" She meant was I going to Kingston.

"No, Mrs. Field. I'm waiting for the bus."

"Way ya ah go?" (Where are you going?) a slip into patois she wouldn't have made had she not just come from speaking it with the postmistress.

"A new volunteer's getting off here, Mrs. Field."

"Will 'e be at da school?"

The volunteers were foisted off on them like that. Yet for Mrs. Field it would mean more free time at home.

"I don't know, Mrs. Field. I haven't seen her."

" 'Er! Well you been lonely enough, Mister." She laughed, an implications that white coffee was more to a white man's taste, an idea she would never have accepted had I not gone through a whole year of abstinence to prove it: as with suicide, it was the irrefutable attestation of a belief. I wanted very much to tell this touchingly charming person that I was not the normal volunteer, and that up in the north Mark was screwing his brains out.

"If she does work at the school," I said, "I wonder where Mr. Field will put her?"

Mrs. Field frowned. Her heavy jowls flapped about like a basset's ears. "Wit' da childs. We can' 'ave 'er in da ubber forms."

The upper forms were for end-of-studies pupils whose future was the cane fields; learning was hardly foremost in their minds. In the squat building made of cement floors, cinderblock walls and zinc roof, I taught 9 rows of students, the first 3 of 14-year-olds, the middle 3 of 15-year-olds and the last 3 of 16-year-olds. The girls came and went in green pinafores between pregnancies. The boys wore dark khaki shorts and shirts. All were barefoot. The building smelled of chalk, mold and the vinegar-acidity of the adjoining sugarcane factory. They all studied more or less the same thing, on an increasing scale of difficulty. They were certainly not unaware of the hopelessness of their positions. Outside the windows the cane fields were being burned out patch by patch. Their fathers waded into the still-smoldering underbrush, machetes in hand, cutting down the cane stalks now clear of leaves and debris. Insects swarmed about their scarf-covered heads. Centipedes six inches long and thicker than a finger dropped onto their shoulders. Sweat poured down in black rivulets over their ash-smudged skins. That's where the 16-year-olds would be next year. In the mornings, before leaving Daddy P's house, I often wept at the futility of my coming to Duckenfield. Every morning I played Tchaikovsky's *1812*, with its trumpets and fireworks, to try to buck up my spirits. Had I had the guts, I would have resigned after the first six months.

"Duckenfield no place fa' young girls," signed Mrs. Field theatrically. Did she mean the naked beaches? The boys with their flies left undone? The screwing outside the cinema? The Greenhouse Hotel? To adapt to Jamaica, as the shrink had foreseen, was to adapt to its sexuality.

The Carbondale girl had asked to be transferred back to America the very night she arrived. She had run screaming into her bush-town post office at three in the morning, waking up the mistress and forcing her to send an urgent telegraph to the Peace Corps representative in Kingston. He had had to drive out and pick her up that very morning. The reason she offered him was blackness. The unlit villages disappeared into the inky folds of the jungle at sundown. In the houses shadows shuffled like moths around the sparse glow of oil lamps. At dinner with her host the first evening, she had seen him gradually disappear into the surrounding obscurity as the light outside the cabin was drawn away into the West. Only eyeballs and the flicker of teeth remained suspended Cheshire-catlike in midair. Later in her bed she put her hand up in front of her eyes. She could see nothing; it was totally invisible. Outside, the crackling, gnawing sounds from the jungle approached the pleated walls of her room, sending her into hysterics.

"She could be old," I said to Mrs. Field. "Some volunteers are over sixty." Mrs. Field's eyes opened wide with surprise.

Had I been on less intimate terms with Jamaica I might have feared that I would be spending a part of my time protecting the volunteer from crazed white-flesh hunting rapists. But in the Jamaican countryside, crime was little known, and rape unnecessary. Whites were as protected a species as the koala bear. Once Johnny, a superbly handsome charcoal Jamaican, called in to see me after a visit to the factory doctor, a fiftyish Bristol matron.

"My sex was hurtin' me," Johnny said.

"What did she say?"

"Keep out of Greenhouse Hotel," he snickered.

"How did she examine you?"

"She make it hard."

"Hard!"

"She always make me get it hard when I'm hurtin'."

"What does she do?" I asked.

"She fills to see where it hurt."

"Christ! Has any other white woman ever touched you?"

"The plan'er's daughter. She see me when I bring a package to her mamma. She say coma ah here, Johnny. She say let me see it."

"Did you?"

He shook his head, grinning from ear to ear. His expression reflected the folly of a black messing around with a white girl. The thought was there; but buried in a hundred years of subjugation.

"Well, Mister, I go on home," said Mrs. Field. She clasped my hand in fingers as hard as a knuckle-duster, then waddled off a few yards before a car turned off the Main Road towards Duckenfield. She waved it down and climbed aboard, giving the driver a far less ingratiating smile than she had given me, but one infinitely more personal.

The bus soon came with its usual delay--its Jamaican-time delay. The sun came out to greet the brilliant carriage of red, green, yellow and blue enamel. It pulled into the Duckenfield road, swerved back towards the Main Road and came to a shuddering halt. Packages flew from all the windows. Relatives appeared from nowhere to amass them. The ticket collector sprang from the driver's cockpit onto the roof of the bus where he untied and threw down bundles. The passengers stepped tiredly out, their arms burdened with children or animals, baskets of fruit or bolts of checkered cloth bought in Kingston. I crept close to the exit so the new arrival would not panic at finding herself alone. The waves of people debarking swarmed around me. I looked up into the black, sweating faces as they came into view and descended. The new volunteer was being a lady.

When everyone had stepped out she finally made her appearance with the suddenness of a magician revealing a dove or, in her case, a duck. She stood at the top step and looked around. She looked everywhere but at me. She was a big girl with a large case in one hand while the other tugged her shift down over not insignificant thighs. She descended one of the three steps and resumed her scrutiny. She had big doe eyes and a bigger nose. Her hair was pulled tightly back at the sides and disappeared into a sailor hat with the rim turned down.

Look you bitch, I said to myself, if you don't see me I'll make you carry that case all the way back to Duckenfield. Except for the factory's female doctor, I was the only white within twenty miles; she could at least recognize that.

But no, I had to tap her on one of her knobby knees. "I've been sent to meet you," I said, biting the inside of my lips to keep down my anger. She focused on me at last and gave me a tight smile that took some of the puffiness out of her cheeks. I'm Linda, she said, as soon as she came out of her daze. I was too mad to remember that the six-hour drive from Kingston did that to people. The steep curves driven over at twice the sane speed, the horn blasting away, the heat, the packed conditions--she had probably stood up all the way--were as mind-altering as drugs.

We started up the road back to Duckenfield. I toted her case and she pushed my bike. Even with it to lean upon she waddled like Mrs. Field, although Linda, the ever-practical girl, wore flat shoes, unlike Mrs. Field's high heels. A couple of jeeps passed. I didn't hail them. Linda probably admired my not taking advantage of my color. The reason of course was that I didn't want to test my popularity, and show myself up in her eyes.

She settled in at Mrs. Henry's. Linda was colorblind, and had she not fallen in love with me she would have been one of the few female volunteers to go native. Mrs. Henry was colorblind too. White skin, to her, was a particularity like the shape of one's nose, which seemed to be desirable like the Swiss franc. It was good to be white because that facilitated things, but there was nothing intrinsically better or more beautiful about the color. Mrs. Henry's house was a one-story pink cinderblock affair. A widow, she managed a candy store in Duckenfield. Most nights she spent with men friends at their places. She laughed at Linda and me all the time. We were better than the Keystone Kops as far as she was concerned.

Before leaving to pick up Linda I had resolved that I would bring her back and then drop her like a hot potato. The very last thing I wanted was a girl volunteer. Mark's partner was male and so was Rob's. I began to think the Peace Corps knew what it was doing. But on the way to Duckenfield I found that Linda was a pretty nice human being. So I elected to hang around a bit. After all, I owed her a little presence, her being a New Volunteer. My fury was Olympian, then, when at the door to Mrs. Henry's she dismissed me like a servant who had stolen her watch. She wanted a bath and a rest. I nearly stumbled over myself in my haste to get away from the place. I would never return I decided, so help me God never.

CHAPTER FIFTEEN

Daddy P and Edna

My home was a white cinderblock building next to Mrs. Henry's pink cinderblock. There Edna and Daddy P were waiting for particulars. Both were sitting on an L-shaped couch, listening to the wireless, as Daddy P called it. Edna--tall, super-slim Edna--was slumped sideways in a position between sitting and lying. She was sleepily fanning herself. She was already very black, but around her eyes were circles of a darker shade still, giving her the appearance of a raccoon. Those eyes, nearly always half-closed, now opened excitedly as I entered. "Wa ja know?" she demanded.

Edna was a sexy girl. Any other volunteer would have given his eyeteeth to have her in the same house with him. She liked me very much, and it was a consolation to her that although I had never asked her out, I had never asked anyone else out either. Now she opened her eyes wider still, only falling for half the negative things I was telling her about Linda. Edna, who didn't look upon a white girl as a rival, pointed a finger at me and smiled her smile: You'll wind up in bed with her yet, was what she said in gist. Then she dropped the subject, her interest in Linda going no further. But Daddy P was a woman's man. He wanted details.

For all practical purpose Daddy P was white. The only negroid feature was his crinkled hair, now as white as he. Daddy P and Edna had met me in Kingston when I came out the year before. We had driven back to Duckenfield late at night in Daddy P's old Vauxhall. We went around the coast and up and over the island's knotted feet like cars on a roller coaster. I caught glimpses of the moon on the sea and occasional car headlights coming towards us that appeared and disappeared like a bouncing ball. Daddy P and Edna were very kind, but I was already half-dazed, a victim to the initial stages of culture shock. Kingston had been an anthill of activity, a shantytown capital, hot, dirty and depressing. Duckenfield was considered a hardship post. It was perched on the easterly tip of the island, a macho land of plantation laborers and fishermen. Through what perverse reasoning had the Peace Corps sent me, Mr. Arts, to that citadel of brute force?

We arrived in Duckenfield late in the evening. The place was a black pit. Other than the headlights, there wasn't even the glimmer of a lamp anywhere. Daddy P insisted I meet the schoolmaster, my new boss, Mr. Field. The school was just next-door, Daddy P said. I stumbled alongside him while Daddy P flashed a torch ineffectively over the rutted roadway. He directed it at the school building. It looked awful: gray and dirty, overflowing with desks and stinking from an outdoor urinal on the edge of a schoolyard playground of drought-cracked clay with crevices large enough to break a foot. Mr. Field came out of his house. He held a lamp up in his hand. His first words were Goodnight!, the Jamaican hello. His temples and cheeks appeared swollen and oily in the yellow light. He spoke with an oxford accent, as did Daddy P. The missus was behind Mr. Field. By Jamaican standards he had made a good marriage. He was coal black, while she was only chocolate. We exchanged but few words. Coming out we had stopped at a roadside eatery where we consumed curry patties and bottles of a fizzy orange drink. My guts were on fire and all I wished was to retire to find a place to vomit.

Back at Daddy P's that first night I was shown to my room, a large one that connected to Daddy P's by a bathroom. It had been Edna's before. Edna was relegated to the maid's room, one less than half the size of my own. Every Jamaican house, small-scale colonial copies, had a place for a maid which usually served for doing laundry. Edna was a teacher in the lower forms at the school. She was Daddy P's reputed daughter. Only much later did I learn from Mark that she was Daddy P's mistress. It's true that I had often heard them whispering together late at night. It was true too that I surprised Edna leaving Daddy P's room on the weekends when I got up early to go to Holland Bay with Linda, and Edna had slept in late. On one of those occasions she had come out in a white slip, her hair mussed, her arms raised in a luxurious stretch, and her mouth distorted by a soul-gratifying yawn. When she caught a glimpse of me those raccoon eyes opened as wide as silver dollars. I apologized for scaring her and she said, smiling, that Daddy P was feeling ill and she had come from bringing him a cup of tea. Other times when I had seen her coming out of Daddy P's room she said she had been making up the bed or dusting. Never had I suspected anything. For Mark, it had only taken one visit to discover. With hindsight I now remembered the particular tone Edna used during those mornings. It was the airy tone she used when telling her primers fairy tales.

Early the first Sunday morning after my arrival Daddy P knocked at the door on his side of the bathroom to awaken me. We had agreed to go swimming before the roosters crowed. The roosters had preceded us a bit, but the hour was nevertheless early. Off we went through the cane fields on the dirt road that skirted a bamboo enshrouded river and the fishing village of Holland Bay. The air smelled of very pungent vinegar. The cane stalks swayed on either side of the car door, so close the windows were left closed to protect us from being slapped by the foliage. Soon the cane fields came to an end and Daddy P brought the car to a gingerly crawl as we crossed a marsh of gray clay, inch-deep brackish water and scurrying crabs. Beyond the marsh rose palm-crowded dunes, and beyond the dunes was paradise.

We stopped at a place Daddy P favored and we began to disrobe. I was immediately assailed by clouds of mosquitoes and black sand flies that stung like fire. I ran over the dune and onto the beach. A wind struck me full force, a fabulous wind, warm and caressing, that swept away the insects. I stripped to my swimsuit and waded into the rollers. The water was cold but I continued until I was knocked over with a punch that sent me flying. Over and over I rolled in water that could not have been more than a few feet deep. It was impossible to get my balance. Finally I was literally ejected onto the shore. I stood up. My eyes smarted and my chest glowed red from where the roller had pounded me. The goggles I had brought were missing, as were, I discovered, my trunks. Daddy P came up from behind laughing. I was laughing too. The breeze was now cold. Daddy P took me by the arm and led me back into the rollers. Like a silvery fish Daddy P jumped up and over the first wave, disappeared under a second, and then came back up into a leisurely swim in the placid depths beyond. I did the same. I was laughing when I joined Daddy P, from the joy of this new place, from my nakedness, from the intense cold.

The next day some excuse or other took me up to Linda's, the day after that too, and all the others to follow. We became inseparable. She taught the lower forms in a cinderblock shack with a corrugated-metal roof next to the main building. She occupied one end of the shack with the trustful infants who composed her form 4. On the other side of her blackboard was Edna's form 3. Then came Miss Gerber's form 2 and finally Mrs. Field's form 1. The children chanted their lessons rhythmically, all in a voice, whether they were doing their timetables or reading from the impeccably, painstakingly written sentences on the board. Linda darted about like a mother hen, bravely smiling, occasionally wincing when Edna brought down her cane over the hand of an inattentive dreamer.

"Spare the rod and you's spoils the childs, Mister," Mrs. Field tutored me my first day in class.

Mr. Field and I had the main concrete building to ourselves, Mr. Field on one side of a cement wall, me on the other. Mr. Field taught history and geography with all the seriousness of a nuclear physicist, and his pupils paid better attention than young Pierre Curies. From time to time I heard a sharp firecracker-like explosion, as Mr. Field wielded his cane. As for me, perhaps I didn't believe enough in the future of my protégées to do them physical harm. Everything was against them, even being black in a country of blacks. Only lighter skinned coloreds had a real chance at lower middle-class clerical jobs in companies, banks and the service industries.

During the winter rains classes were sometimes impossible to reach because the children could not cross the flooded fields and waist-deep swamps from their shacks to school. Since Daddy P and Edna were almost always home, Linda and I took to passing the days and parts of the nights at Mrs. Henry's. We talked, we gossiped, we ate marvelous meals Linda's

German-born mother had taught her to prepare. On shopping tours to Kingston, Linda would disappear into all kinds of specialty shops in order to dig up things like real chocolate chips for cookies, peanut butter because I loved it, pastry sugar because I was a nut on sweets. We ate on the veranda under candlelight, picking avocadoes off the trees for entrées and mangoes for dessert.

Later in the evening we read together, propped up side by side on her bed. At first, Linda made a big production of pulling down her skirt below her knees. But as the weeks passed the skirt was hiked steadily upwards. The hiking began with a vengeance after a visit from her mother, Mamma Hoenig.

CHAPTER SIXTEEN

Linda

Mamma came out about six months after her daughter's arrival. She was a stocky woman, a chain-smoker who kept a cigarette in her mouth until the ash attained incredible lengths, flickering it only in extremis into a tiny silver ash box that never left her hand. She and Papa Hoenig still had guttural accents and an old-country propensity to homemade bread and parent-supervised matches. It was clear that I was the game, and what had started as an amusing visit ended in a ten-station crucifixion for all concerned.

The Hoenigs deplaned at Kinston with a gift of a ten-pound ham, the sight of which I found so welcome I quickly decided to place myself at their disposition during the coming two weeks. I expected that Linda would have to introduce me to Mamma and Papa. Instead, they rapidly pecked their daughter's cheeks before setting on me: "We don't know who you are!" they guffawed, Mamma giving me an appraising once-over that would have made a Thanksgiving turkey blush. She obviously didn't place me in her superlative column, but I apparently made the adequate square, the one next to save-for-a-pinch. She had an unsettling way of eyeing my package when I wore my swimming suit, as though pondering the load of *jüngen* I would be capable of engendering. Mamma and Papa hired a car, and off we went to Duckenfield. During the trip they discovered that I was of modest lineage; I, in turn, was informed that they had two houses on Lake Erie, and as Linda was there only child....

We arrived in Duckenfield at midday. I assumed that Linda would like to be left to talk with them, so I said I'm off to Holland Bay, I'll drop by tonight. When I did return for dinner--as I had been invited to do--I found the atmosphere glacial. The Hoenigs had installed themselves in Mrs. Henry's room and now Linda and Mamma were cooking up an extravaganza. Maybe you and Papa should get to know each other, suggested Mamma. He and I went out on the veranda, but since Papa was thinking of ways to bring up Linda and I was determined to avoid the subject, neither of our minds was clear enough to permit much give and take. During the meal Linda and I told the Hoenigs about our classes, Holland Bay, Daddy P, Edna, Mrs. Henry and Duckenfield in general. Mamma sat across from me, staring at me as from a drunken stupor, the ash growing longer and redder as night came on.

The next day we went on a picnic to Holland Bay. I was cross that morning because I felt the Hoenigs were going out of their way to be unfair to me. I had the feeling they held me responsible for gross neglect when I failed to do things as elementary as open the car door for Linda. They failed to understand the down-to-earth relationship their daughter and I enjoyed. I didn't want to be a knight in shining armor and Linda didn't expect it. Later I learned that their real disappointment was that I hadn't taken Linda's hand in mine even once. I had thought of a lot of reproaches they could have harbored, but certainly not that. After the picnic I strolled off alone down the beach for a couple of hours. I liked Linda, but Linda plus her *familie* was too high a price for what we shared. We rode back to Duckenfield in absolute silence.

The Hoenigs cut their vacation in half, leaving at the end of the first week. Three days later, when I came for dinner, I saw Linda all red-eyed. This was really a first. Only after a great deal of pressing would she tell me she had received a letter from Mamma that displeased her. She wouldn't discuss its contents, but long after I had left the island, after Linda had written to say she loved me and I wrote telling her why that could never be, she wrote and told me about the letter from Mamma, who had understood everything down to the last dot on the i's and bar on the t's. Naturally, Linda hadn't believed a word.

We resumed our dolce vita *à deux*. Up the Main Road was Bath, a village of flowers and thermal springs where a volunteer from Linda's group, Mary, was stationed. Mary was proud of and entirely devoted to the Jamaican family with whom she shared her three-room shack. For all purposes a nun, Mary took nourishment--like bacteria-feeding nodules-- from the haven of an ideal.

"I'm a virgin, you know," she announced to me at the Cascades one day, making Linda pull a long, how-does-she-dare-come-out-with-things-like-that face and turn away blushing. I was left gaping, not so much at the confession as at the incredible solemnity of the declaration, as if she'd admitted to having a venereal illness.

Me too, I could have by rights answered, and added that it was little indeed to blow one's horn about.

Mary was kind and generous, very short in stature and still on the decent side of chubby. She had wiry black hair and wore a huge crucifix between two mounds of mesmerizing amplitude.

From the village of Bath we hiked up a trail through luxuriant jungle to the Cascades, a dozen basins of water as clear and ice-cold as the glaciers of the Tetons. We sunbathed on the marble-smooth banks and dove in when our skin became flushed. Occasionally we came upon bathing blacks and mixed-blood East-Indians, like Buba. Their naked virility squelched any thought I ever had of going nude, and I could only pity Linda's future husband whom she would appraise along these outlandish standards. Unlike Sophie, the volunteer from Louisiana who unhesitatingly used the word dick, Linda and Mary neither saw nor spoke evil, but an increase in their lighthearted chatter betrayed a repressed anxiety. Although I admitted to myself that I went to the Cascades in the hope of such encounters, I felt guilty that Linda thought I rode all those kilometers just to be with her.

I had been long in letting Linda accompany me to Holland Bay. It had been my last refuge. For a year I had walked its shores. I knew its every shallow, its every undercurrent. During countless hours I had lain on its sun-gold slopes, becoming one with its sands. It had browned my skin and hair, and given to my eyes the indelible squint lines Linda had been the first to point out. Over the calm sea beyond its breakers I had watched the passing of the faraway sail-shaped thunderclouds, and witnessed the slanted fury of torrential rains that seemed more to rise up from the ocean than descend from the skies. Once I had even cycled to Holland Bay to see the passing of a hurricane. Holland Bay village had been evacuated. Only I was left to witness the skin-stinging winds and icy downpour.

Linda's coming to Holland Bay changed my habits. No longer could I romp without trunks; nor could I let the afternoon's vibrant heat prepare my body for that solitary pleasure which not even sun or sea could rival. No more could I walk for hours on end lost in thought or in nothingness, nor sit hypnotized before the grain of a piece of driftwood, or stare endlessly at the to and fro of a sea plant stirred by an invisible underwater breeze. Linda brought order and games. My diet of coconut meat and tepid curry pies was replaced by crab cocktail, hot buttered pumpkin and fruit delight. Linda put up with my every caprice. Once I made a meal of raw onions like the ancient Greeks. Not only did she have to support my breath afterwards, but she insisted on holding my shaking frame as I heaved my guts out.

We built a hut of bamboo poles and leaves. It was there Linda would have given herself late one afternoon. I recognized the sign on her sad, dusk-gray face, an instant when she had the beauty of a mourner. It was Léa's face that day outside the chalet. I knew the moment and let it shrivel away.

Other than the Cascades and Holland Bay, the third place that was ours was Kingston Crag, a hill overlooking Duckenfield, crowned with the dark, jungle-invaded ruins of a former manor house, called the House that Folly Built because the owner had made cement from ocean sand, the salt content making the mortar crumble almost immediately. We picnicked there on its grassy slopes, and watched the clouds float over the cane fields and disappear into the gray line dividing heaven and sea beyond Holland Bay. I realized I was just killing time the day we unexpectedly came across Buba who was searching for a stray goat. I took him aside to ask his business. Were the boy to give me a simple nod, a year and a half of pent-up need would find its issue. But I had nothing to offer, just as I had nothing of real value for Linda.

One night Linda and I went to the cinema. Located in the middle of the single block-length street that comprised the whole of Duckenfield, it was wedged between the Chinese hardware shop--itself packed as tightly and orderly with merchandise as a clock--and a saloon darker than a coffin where white rum was sold. The expensive places in the cinema were wooden benches with hard backs located at the very back of the room, unofficially reserved for whites. Up in front were rows of the same benches, but backless. The men sat on the right of the room, the women on the left. The film was an Italian adventure triangle. In its heated parts boys jumped up swinging their fists at the flickering images of the villain making off with the damsel. The adults contented themselves with flinging beer bottles at the stained screen. Cigarette butts were flipped through the air when smoked down to the fingers, making for a continuous flight of fireflies throughout the projection. I tried to get Linda out rapidly when the *Fine* flashed on in the dark, but duty obliged her to wait and ask Mrs. Henry, whose huge figure and yellow gown had deflected a disproportionate amount of light during the screening, her opinion of the movie. It was Linda's way of snubbing the plantation whites for not taking more of an interest in the thoughts of the blacks. At the exit I pointed up to the starry heavens, but Linda chanced to glance down the narrow alley between the cinema and the saloon. "What are they..." formed on her lips, but the visible rhythmic movement of the couples lined up along the cinema, the women against the wall, the men humping them, informed her. Only a brief "Oh" slipped by. She then looked up with me, and, indeed, she said rapidly, it was an amazing night.

We lapsed into silence, a silence broken by the Howdy's and Goodnights that came from invisible passers-by whom we tried to identify by the sound of the voice. One voice I knew, and one face I could make out from the night, that of Buba smiling. He was passing in front of one of the shacks that had a faint yellow lantern in the window. I pulled him into the pale light. The boy's teeth gleamed under the black strokes of his nascent mustache. His eyes were glazed over and askance. Automatically I looked down at his knees. They were covered with dark-brown and slightly wet patches of dirt. Buba had been to the Greenhouse Hotel. I wondered which of the high-buttocked girls walking past carried his white essence. Buba laughed drunkenly and reminded me for the nth time of his brother's marriage. I let him go and returned to Linda, left waiting in the middle of the rutted road.

.

The next day, a Saturday, I was walking down to the Crossroads Church for the wedding when Balla, Buba's brother, pulled up to give me a lift. I slipped into the back between Johnny and an equally handsome black friend of his, Kupa Tula. Balla and Buba rode up front. I leaned forward, resting my elbows gently on the brothers' shoulders. Everyone was dressed in his best suit. I let my hand drop onto the fabric of Buba's white sports coat. Beneath I thought of the bronzed muscle and the wiry tendons I had so often seen at the beach.

Balla was going to wed a Negress, not one of those they had all shared at Holland Bay, but a girl from his hometown in the central highlands, a girl virgin to these parts. Buba was kidding Kupa Tula and me about when we planned to get married. I stiffened until the obvious dawned on him. I said I would marry after Johnny. Buba said I should marry after Kupa Tula. I suggested we marry together in a triple ceremony. Buba agreed and broke into a wondrous smile. I pictured myself standing next to him at his wedding. When the time came it was his hand I would take and his lips I would kiss. Yet I knew the closest I would ever come to those lips would be their imprint on the bride's own, that I would share after him.

That night Mrs. Henry threw a party for Balla at her candy shop for a fee. The displays had been moved to a back room where some women were stirring up a huge pot of goat curry. Up front one wall was stacked two meters high with beer cases; one of Mrs. Henry's nieces sat behind a small table selling the stuff. In a corner was a hi-fi with enormous speakers that Mrs. Henry had hired from Kupa Tula. Rhythmic skaï music blared out at full volume. Overhead, a single light bulb hung naked. Everyone who entered the shop immediately started dancing singly over the cement floor. They danced, drank and ate to the beat. I was alone; I hadn't insisted enough for Linda to feel wanted there. Edna came over to me. She planted herself squarely in front, her hands on her hips, and laughed mockingly Why ya no dance? I said I would later but she grabbed my hands and pulled me onto the floor. I tried to copy the others but I was a sack of sticks in comparison. Edna pretended to be disgusted by my awkwardness. She stopped, smiled with her large eyes and said, Come wis me. She dragged me to the table. Mrs. Henry's niece reached for a beer but Edna fingered a bottle in the corner of a lower shelf. She made the girl pour me out half a glass of auburn rum. I hated the taste of the stuff. Edna again shook her head in mock contempt. She went into the back room and came back with a plate full of curry goat, seasoned as hot as purgatory. Once my mouth was suitably on fire I cooled it off with the rum. I went back to the dance floor with Edna. This time I did much better.

Again and again during the night I went back to the beer table. My money was refused, my patronage valued. I drank and danced, danced and drank. I must have done the equivalent of ten miles of jogging to that hypnotizing beat. A perfect euphoria descended over me, that silenced my brain and freed my legs. Sometimes girls took up the place before me, sometimes it was men. I saw smiling faces and foreheads dripping with sweat. My clothes were drenched. Black faces, Chinese faces, Edna's raccoon eyes, even perhaps Linda's concerned frown, I was totally beyond knowing. My body turned and swirled, yet no matter how free it became, I could only just keep up with the total abandon of the others.

Then into the light came Buba, still dressed in white. His movements were slow motion compared to the others. Elegantly he swayed his hips and nodded his head. The girl he was with timed her rhythm to his, sliding into his hollows. I slowed too, the three of us forming but one being. I closed my eyes, and when I opened them again Buba was directly in front, his eyes nearly shut. I could make out each stroke of his brows, each curl of his lashes. His black hair was oiled and the curls glistened. On his forehead were transparent drops of sweat, and around his flared nostrils was the moisture of a blushed sleeper. His lips were closed and at rest. He bobbed back and forth, his head down, his hands joined together at his fly.

A feeling of overwhelming despair descended on me. I felt as if I were going to weep, and within me a voice that belonged to the god of my youth bellowed Cry! And I did cry: like a shrill whistling wind through a labyrinthine skull, like the oozing ears of the strangled goat, like the sucking gasps at a milkless tit, my tears slid dry from the angelic canvas, white from the bullet-bored brain, translucent through the skin shade. I blacked out.

Daddy P found me early the next morning in the rubbish barrel at the bottom of the terrace steps. I had fallen in while trying to make my way home. Only my head and legs were sticking up. The can rim had scraped away the skin on my back. I was forever to carry the scar.

CHAPTER SEVENTEEN

Mark

From up north word filtered down that Mark had gotten a girl in trouble. At the same time, I received an invitation from him to come for a visit. Even though there were only three months left to my contract, I rather cavalierly insisted that the school let me off for a week. I left Linda and Duckenfield and set out for Kingston on one of the hated buses.

The Kingston bus depot, where we pulled in after six hours of mind-joggling starts and stops, was as alive with hawkers as an Arab souk. Food and drink venders, shouting in patois, shoved their way through the rainbow-painted buses, serving departing passengers who had taken over their seats with all the finality and ostentatious possessiveness of desert sheiks. I waded through sidewalk stands selling food, combs, mirrors and toys. Out-country whites received a dispensation from the hordes of peddlers: British austerity, coupled with the vertiginous decline of the pound that year, placed them beyond temptation for cashew nuts, mangoes and soda water.

In the predominant white section of the town was a drugstore, the meeting place of volunteers coming in-town. That was where Mark and I met later the same afternoon. Mark had a way of announcing things last minute. His invitation to Kingston left me only three days to give the school notice, and now I had barely slid into the vinyl booth before he informed me that we would have to go back on the bus Mark had come down on.

"Couldn't you even get a night off from school?" I asked.

"It's not the school. I forgot to ask the Peace Corps for permission."

"You forgot?"

"There's been some trouble up home and I didn't want them to know I was coming down."

"Like what?"

"A false alarm. One of the girls was puffing up. Her father made the school principal telephone through to Peace Corps Headquarters here."

"You must have been scared shitless."

"I hadn't been careless."

"One could break, I guess."

"None ever has."

"So you're here without permission."

"Yup, the corpsman's favorite game," grinned Mark.

The Peace Corps gave consent for one social visit to Kingston a month. Mark was in every weekend. This was only my second trip in as many years.

"Okay, order up. How's Rob?" I asked, and Frank and so on. Mark knew it all.

We stuffed ourselves with a malt and a banana split and exchanged information. We had nearly finished when Mark suddenly stiffened. A bullet had finally come into the chamber. In through the door walked the Assistant Peace Corps Director, a blond stud in a smart khaki suit, a dead-ringer for Redford.

The stud would inevitably make his big bi-yearly inspection at Duckenfield while I was on the beach, and had never once found Mark at his school. Only real volunteers like Linda and Mary and the Kalamazoo guy were where they were supposed to be. But he was fair play, and as proof he sat down with us without asking why we were there. He reddened though: he hated being taken for a ride.

Mark was uncommonly nervous. He dreaded being kicked out of the Corps only a few months before the end. His peccadilloes boiled down to drunkenness, absenteeism and fornication, all chronic. Compared to him I was a saint. But compared to him I must have seemed pretty milquetoast in the Assistant Director's eyes.

It was time for us to leave but Mark refused to give the Assistant the idea we were being chased back to work. So we stayed on, Mark and the Director arguing over twenty-one months of accumulated grievances until, to get rid of us both, the Assistant offered to drop us off at the bus depot in his immaculate jeep.

Once the bus left the city limits the sap ran out of Mark and he abandoned me for sleep. The drive into the interior of Jamaica was totally different from that along the coast. We passed through desiccated flatlands of red dust where single whitewashed mud houses stuck up like lonely tombstones. Gnarled, leafless witch trees were the only sign of vegetation. With the demise of the setting sun, the cauldron-hot afternoon faded into a thickening haze of blue.

We arrived in the dead of night. Lanterns came out of the black mountain jungle to snatch away the discharging passengers, and then disappear like swarms of firebugs. I could see nothing. Mark made me latch on to the back of his belt. We stumbled up a steep incline. Then Mark's voice came through the night calm and authoritative:

"Can we hold on to your donkey, Joseph?"

"Grab a tuft, Master Mark."

Mark guided my hand to the raspy back of a shivering beast as invisible as the disjointed voices.

At the door to Mark's house we were met by the servant carrying a very dim lamp. Mark kissed her and introduced me. We were offered food but were too tired to accept. We were shown into Mark's room, a box just big enough for a modern imitation-wood bed, a shelf of books over the headboard and his record player. The girl hesitated before leaving us. She was very young. Her hair was braided into dozens of tight knots and she wore a checkered blue pinafore, open wide at the breasts, of the same material tablecloths and headscarves were made of. I had the distinct impression she expected me to take her room during my stay, as her body crowded me backwards toward the door. Mark told me to throw my gear in a corner and left with the girl for a moment. When he came back we wordlessly undressed and slipped under the sheets. I thought that perhaps I should have offered to take her room. But gallantry wasn't my forte when I was this close to whatever it was that drew me to Mark. I soon fell asleep.

The next morning we had a breakfast of coffee, toast, breadfruit and mangoes. The house, on stilts, was perched high on the slope of a valley. The dining room window opened on to a stupendous view, a green dell of tall grass and orange orchards. Holstein cows with enormous udders grazed at the base of the orange trees. Had the house fallen from its stilts, we would have tobogganed down into the bucolic scene as pristine as a Swiss postcard.

After breakfast we went back to Mark's room where we listened to music and talked about books, both of us sprawled over the patchwork coverlet. At noon we had a meal of sardines, rice, cassava, breadfruit and oranges. I met the mistress of the house, a timid woman who kept out of our way. At teatime she had the servant girl bring us her specialty, a drink of sweet condensed milk and water that she colored with a pink syrup and cooled with chunks of ice she bought from a passing iceman on a donkey. Mark drank his but mine went to the pigs living under the house.

In the late afternoon we went for a walk to Mark's school, the same cement buildings as at Duckenfield. The teachers greeted Mark with rather awesome deference. A few children came running up for a pat on the head, but the majority kept their distance. We went to a nearby shack that served as the town bar. The proprietor seemed to know Mr. Mark well. We had half-glasses of rum. A few men came in. Rum was sold to them in all amounts, some minuscule and only coasting a pence. Cigarettes were also sold, separately from an opened pack. The shack was dark and airless. The men's sweaty, deeply etched faces reflected the light from the cracks in the wall planks. Their gray oil-strained khaki shirts and trousers hung from them in formless folds as though held up more by strings than bone and sinew.

Back at Mark's, we did more talking and listening to music. It was the time of *Welcome to the Monkey House* and *Rembrandt's Hat*, the *Concierto de Aranjuez* and *Concerto pour la main gauche.* I was very marked by Mark's tastes. My own library at Duckenfield read like an advanced course in Jewish lit. The rum brought out tensions I had hardly been aware of. Problems with Linda, my future after Jamaica, Buba, my lack of commitment at Duckenfield, and now Mark at my side: all combined to bring on a numbing fatigue. I felt I could have slept for years. At the same time, I because overly maudlin. My back to Mark while he read, I listened to Bernstein's *Kaddish* and silently wept.

That evening we went to the plantation director's house. All along the black roads voices--women's voices--hailed Mark from somewhere beyond the folds of night. His replies were stern, brief orders for them to be patient until later on. How could he go with so many? And how could the women accept his promiscuity? I imagined open thighs hovering amidst a terrifying oblivion, all waiting like restless mares for Mark to cover them.

We arrived at the house unannounced. Mark was received royally by the planter and his wife. We were seated in overstuffed armchairs in a room of teak woodwork and huge overhead beams. We were brought whiskies and cigars. Mark animated the conversation as if it were he the host. The planter was tall and thin, a bookkeeper upon whom England had imposed the adventure of a foreign post. His wife was a tight-skinned, gray-haired stringy woman with world-weary eyes. Neither she nor I said much; our position as consorts seemed enough. The few times I did intervene my voice was shaky and rapid, leagues away from Mark's assertiveness. Even Mark's most trivial statements were coached in irrevocable finality.

Whisky followed whisky, each glass interspersed with a liqueur the director insisted Mark judge. Mark invariably tasted loudly, paused to let the *goûter* take hold, pronounced the product every good, then frowned as some obscure aftertaste made him qualify his judgment with an addendum that, he quickly admitted, did nothing to reduce the excellent quality. As time wore on, Mark slumped more and more into the cushions. I half expected him to call the servants in to show the bookkeeper and his wife out. In truth, the place was indeed suited to him alone.

Around nine, an ungodly hour for the sticks, Mark abruptly rose and excused us. I thought we were going home. Instead, Mark led me to a simple cinderblock house not unlike Daddy P's. We were greeted by a very suave Jamaican dressed in a baggy corduroy suit. His curly hair was rust in color, about the shade of his skin. The Jamaican was the Minster of Something or Other, back among his constituency to do some hand pumping. He knew right away what Mark wanted. We were led into a room the size of my bedroom in Duckenfield. Against one wall were two wooden chairs that the gentleman quickly added a third to. Opposite the chairs was a stereo at least eight feet long, with enormous built-in speakers. The Jamaican, politely addressing me but clearly talking to Mark, described how he had had it brought piecemeal to the island and assembled. Mark remained mute, absently pulling at the rum he had been offered. Other than the stereo and chairs, the room was entirely bare. The Minister asked Mark what it would be that night. Mark said the *Sixth*. The Minister hurried through a stack of records shelved away in the center of the monster. Occasionally he briefly pulled out a jacket and told us the history of its finding and its circumventing passage past Customs into the island. At last he put on a record. First came scratches in a room now quiet and waiting. Then came the most glorious sounds my ears had ever known. We listened with rapt attention, Mark more than all. Record after record was put on until the symphony finally came to its magnificent end.

It was Mahler, and the symphony told a story: three blows on an anvil, the first weakening the mythical figure the symphony described, the second announcing his death, the third annihilating him.

I left the house enraptured. I couldn't thank the Minister enough. Mark seemed cast in a mood, but as he walked in his purposeful stride back home he beat the air with an invisible baton, humming the music he was conducting. I asked him why he hadn't made conversation with the Jamaican. Mark replied that our *presence* had been enough. Only years later did I find out what Mark meant. But at the time I had been incapable of identifying those of my bent, and naturally assumed that Mark had too.

At the house Mark collapsed on the bed in a drunken stupor. The next day we would go to Montego Bay where Mark's parents were coming in to see their boy and vacation. I was expected, Mark promised. A room had been booked for us both. Again I fell into a troubled sleep. Mark, Linda and me; if only it could have been Mark and she, at least then something would have turned out right.

We took the bus to Montego Bay early the next morning. Since we caught it en route, we were forced to stand at least until Ocho Rios, a four-hour ride through a jungle of cascades and dripping leaves larger than platters. Mark was in no mood to talk. Gripping the overhead bar, he let himself be jogged into a nightmarish torpor. I had only taken a few sips of alcohol throughout the long evening, but my head was as sodden as Mark's. I dreamed of the two of us, just Mark and me, returning to New York to continue our studies; I thought of the adversities we would surmount, just the two of us; I dreamed of our successful careers; our New York apartment; our friends, intellectuals and artists; the book-strewn walls which would nurture our minds. I thought of loving Mark--not a sexual love as with Buba, for I wasn't in that way attracted to Mark--but a shared complicity which would give substance to the whirlwind of emotion that welled up within me. The fatigue of the past several days, the pressure of the things left continually unsaid between Linda and me, an unknown future but three months away, and the presence of Mark who drew from me feelings deeply buried, all combined to produce near-disabling lassitude.

On we rode, hour after hour. At Ocho Rios no one disembarked, only more people got on. Dead tired, we slunk down like tramps on the filthy back steps of the bus. It was noon. From Ocho Rios we hugged the coast, a hundred meters above the shimmering ocean below. The beauty was mind boggling, but the rattling bus and our imprisoning thoughts sent us into lethargic oblivion. Jamaica was truly Eden inhabited by Cain.

For another three hours we woke and dozed. When we did get to Montego Bay, Mark came alive with new energy. He ordered a cab to his parents' hotel. From then on things moved terribly fast. At the lobby we found out that only a single room with a single bed had been reserved. Mark seemed embarrassed but muttered something about things being taken care of. For the moment all he wished for were his mother and father. We went through the lobby to the outside swimming pool where winding steps climbed up to the terraced rooms. *Christ, again I'm not wanted*, a voice throbbed within my head. *Neither by my parents, nor by him.* On the top step I took hold of Mark's arm and spun him around. My distraught face silenced Mark's irritation.

"I've got to tell you Mark. I'm homosexual and I love you. And I won't be staying."

"Oh, Christ, what a time to come out with something like that!"

Mark looked as if he'd been kicked by a mule. His parents chose that precise moment to step out above us. As they came forward to kiss and sputter, I heard Mark say, "He won't be remaining with us...." I spun around and ran from the hotel.

I cried all the way to Duckenfield. For the day and night the trip along the coast took, I wept. One life had come to an end. I would turn my back on Linda who had loved me, and on Mark who had seared my heart with the white-hot brand of humiliation. I promised myself that never again would I face my parents or the hearth of my youthful memories. I would turn my back on the nation that had made me. I feared the future, but loathed the past incalculably more. I would seek elsewhere to be made whole.

BOOK II

CHAPTER EIGHTEEN

Philippe

From Jamaica I flew to Paris where my life, in part thanks to the sums banked for two years, was once again my own. It was there I found first love: the love of a city, and that of a boy. All before had been compost from which a plant had taken root--crooked perhaps--but willful and sunward.

I returned at the end of autumn, *la saison triste*, days of haze, brittle leaves and wet cobblestones. I took up a life supremely suited to me, the monastic celibacy of a monk. For months I contented myself with remaining in my room at rue Geoffroy l'Asnier, reading and listening to Mammy shuffle through the corridor beyond my door. All else was silence, the silence of a street abandoned in the white heat of summer by even the pigeons, a street so serene the powdery snows of winter lay trackless at day's end. A silence so deep I could discern Mammy's sighs as she sat at her window, waiting.

At night I ate at Léa's and afterwards we walked along the lamp-lit quays of l'Ile Saint Louis. I discovered Hesse, which so impressed me that I began the study of German. Within myself I too felt the struggle of Goldmund against the abbot Narcisse, Narcisse who burned for things fine and obscure, lamp-lit and *triste*, Narcisse whose vocation it was to be a martyr, to sacrifice himself so that another could experience life. Beyond his readings, beyond the abbey, Narcisse knew no bodily passion. I was indeed made to tread his steps. But my body, so long somnolent, was increasingly inhabited by a restlessness for things my mind was ever less successful to still. The ways of Narcisse came to seem piteous beside those of Goldmund. The great *élans* and terrible deceptions known to Narcisse seemed inadequate because they were wholly of the spirit. Goldmund's acts, because initiated by the body, appeared direct, honest, more tangible. He knew love, something that seemed to me wondrously beautiful by the emotions it inspired. But Goldmund's love could survive only as long as his body remained worthy of worship; it was a love destined for a suicide's fate. Through conviction and nature I belonged to the descendants of Narcisse, but the sure hands of hazard directed me into the path of Goldmund.

And so the day came when I put my books aside and left Mammy's in search of the adventure which would inalterably deviate the flow of my life. My loneliness had become too unbearable; an insistent force in the pit of my stomach, leaden and aching, pushed me towards my kind. I had the chronological age of an adult, but an inner clock had ground to a halt in adolescence, saving me from the concerns of my contemporaries. Like a stele, I was frozen in eternal youth, oblivious to the passing of time.

It was again autumn, and in autumn the Louvre was devoid of tourists. There were rooms no one entered, not even the shuffling, inhospitable guardians. On that particular day I felt wholly alone. The accumulation of years and deceptions, the constant failures with those I loved, like Mark, and those who loved him, like Léa and Linda, had pushed me into the deepest of myself, a weighty, heartsick desert devoid of life. The misery of my condition made my throat choke. I felt the pressure of tears wanting release, but could hardly understand the provenance. Didn't I have Paris and my books?

I entered the Salles des Vases grecs. There were four connecting rooms, all perpetually empty of visitors, even in summer, with one guardian asleep on his wooden chair, nose, jowls and chins piled like building blocks upon the crest of his faded blue uniform and shopworn gray shirt. The light from the grilled windows was as leaden as the dark clouds outside; in some parts of the rooms the vases could scarcely be made out in their glass cases. The rooms were cold and damp, the floors squeaked.

I was studying a vase depicting a bearded man looking over his shoulder at a comely youth, when the immense doors behind me opened. From the reflection in the showcase I saw a boy enter quietly. The boy cast a long gaze at my turned back before going to one of the display cases opposite. It became rapidly clear to me that what took up the boy's attention was not the row of vases lost in the shadows, but the image of myself on the mirrorlike surface of the glass. As we circled the room the boy saw too that the young man with the bent head never let him out of the reflected field of his vision. My heart was beating so fast I feared it would block the use of my tongue. I recognized with an astonishing clarity that the moment was now: either I assumed my destiny, or that destiny would forsake me forever.

I turned towards the boy. He was small and impeccably dressed in a navy-blue velvet suit and tie. His hair was as blond as summer wheat and wildly curly, toppling over his forehead and onto his shoulders. His eyes were blue, smiling and unsure. On his lips played a grin that came and went like the ebbing of the tide, there when I looked his way, away when I glanced back to the case.

My reaction to his presence surprised me by its explicitness. While I had envisaged sex with Mark, the thought had been devoid of desire. Even Buba had filled me with wonder and longing, not lust. But as the boy neared, I felt a warmth and hardness that distended my baggy trousers. I felt grateful for this force that awoke my senses, quickened my blood and gave existence to a day otherwise shallow and, were it not for this boy, lost to memory. Instinctively I knew that as the older it was for me to make the first move. I was little accustomed to initiatives. It was Léa who had taken the decisive steps, as had Mark and Linda. I felt proud that I could act with purpose and courage at the time of my own choosing, and at the welling of my own heart. I put all the savoir-faire of my twenty-two years of substanceless experience into one moment in the Salles des Vases grecs.

"Wouldn't it be better if we went through the museum together?" I asked in French so accented the boy laughed. "If you want," was the answer. Those were our first words, Philippe's and mine. Whatever came afterwards originated from that request and its acceptance.

"It's a beautiful vase," smiled Philippe, indicating the man and the boy.

"It's Ganymede being led to Olympus by Zeus," I said and quoted: "Now to the son of Cronos came the Trojan lad, with the seriousness that comes with adolescence, and the god rejoiced."

We did not stay long in the Salles des Vases grecs. We left the Louvre. I took Philippe home to Mammy.

"How do you like Paris, *mon beau monsieur*?"

Mammy was regal in her gold-leaf Directoire chair, her blue cotton house robe closed to her lace-encircled neck. She had served us tea and nothing was missing. With Nène away painting St. Auxerrois, Mammy was mistress of herself. "And how long do you count on staying?" She needn't have applied any rouge for our visit. The presence of Philippe awakened the color in her sallow cheeks.

Philippe was my first and only visitor to Mammy's. He couldn't have been better chosen had I the pick of all Paris. Irreproachably turned out, his locks the exact effigy of Mammy's favorite poet, Byron, Philippe's candor and laughter were those of the Little Prince come to earth. He had the gift of love for old things, a love encompassing ancient coins, antiques and elderly ladies. He answered Mammy in a most particular voice. It was musical, gaily rising and falling, meridional in its singsong, full of sun and children. It was preceded by a laugh of embarrassment, an engaging laugh, a laugh that made you want to sweep him up in your arms. But then it could become resonant and gravelly, a voice that took its source from deep in the throat. And finally, it was a hesitant voice, a voice that expected to be interrupted, and the laugh was there to take the edge off if it was.

On the way to Philippe's train at the Gare d'Austerlitz I stopped off at a shop on the rue de Rivoli to buy him a book of reproductions. He was very moved. As we walked down the quays of the Seine into the Jardin des Plantes, Philippe talked about himself, his studies in archeology, life in the cloistered home of his parents and the even more cloistered sea port of Brest. His seemed a strange universe. I tried to picture his house, its upright piano, the clear walls awash with light, the doily-protected cushions and the canary in its white cage. Philippe's father would be easy-going and sloppy in comparison to his son; his mother would be a small tightly wound woman, the bringer of order in their closed world. Brest I could imagine too. Carless boulevards and disciplined pedestrians who waited at the traffic lights, dances for chaperoned young ladies and the neighborhood *boulangère* who had an eye open for unseemly behavior. It hurt me to think of the boy locked away, but I was far from imaging that such a place could interfere between us. At that stage, love for me was a question between two beings only. It never occurred to me that we would both come with a load of past baggage, and have to make do.

I saw Philippe's train pull away from the platform. Our goodbyes had fit the occasion, grave and bordering on tears. There was now someone that I was responsible for; my acts would have to measure up to what I imagined to be Philippe's expectations. I would go back to my room. I would read. I would make myself better still.

Philippe's train pulled out and all I held of him was his address, *poste restante*, carefully printed on a scrap of paper. Philippe left and I went back to my room, joyous for the boy's existence, torn already by his absence.

We had not kissed, nor exchanged a single vow of love. It was later--when the doubt set in--that I would turn to undying promises and eternal sermons, the glue of building blocks of sand. Later still would come the exchanges of blood oaths, and then blood itself.

But at the time I took Philippe's faithfulness for granted, as I assumed Philippe did mine. I had taken the boy home to meet Mammy, not to go to bed. Again, only later would I learn that with my clan encounters originated in the bedroom; they did not evolve to there.

Back home Nène came into my room to tell me that Mammy had been seeing visions. Should Léa find out, Nène feared, she would have Mammy put in a home. And after Mammy, eventually Nène herself. She stood before me, shaking and nodding her head, searching my face.

"I'll talk with Léa," was all I could find to say.

She left satisfied.

Three days after Philippe's departure I received the first of many letters full of love and hope for the future. I wrote back in the same vein: we had come together in order to accomplish the Platonic reunification of their separate halves into a single whole. If we were pure in thought and intention our couple would survive; together we would have the strength to confront a hostile world, apart we would slip into the void. Both of us were terribly anxious to see the other, and when I suggested that I come to Brest--even if I had to stay in a hotel--Philippe readily accepted.

The trip took a stultifying six hours. I hated trains. I hated the rocking that lulled me into a druglike half-sleep, I hated the people and their foreign smells, the restricted movement, the communal toilets and the lack of privacy. Yet I rode six hours to Brest and six hours back, and that every weekend until Christmas of that year. To supplement the Peace Corps money I had squirreled away, Léa helped me to find employment as an English teacher. At Mammy's my steady diet was crêpes, literally milk and flour. The major part of my expenses went to pay my passage and hotel.

That first morning the train pulled into a city vaulted by clouds and built around a cold harbor of gray battleships, a provincial, isolated city of colorless people and little ambition. I checked into a hotel and went off to a *pâtisserie* to await 11 o'clock, the time I had agreed to phone Philippe. The boy's voice was hesitant and nervous. I could imagine a woman's ear round a hallway door. I told Philippe where I was and he promised to come at once. I hung up, my stomach knotted at the thought of this, our first full meeting. I was no longer a university graduate or a Peace Corpsman who had been the friend of a sophisticated New Yorker. I was neither a world traveler nor great reader. I was only a teenager out on his first real date, an adolescent who had put all his eggs in this one all-consuming basket.

Then Philippe came, and the angels deigned to descend. It was really he of that first encounter. The same smile, abashed and earnest, the same impeccable velours, bow tie, and cheeks as ruddy and flushed as the incipient winter could have bitten them. We sat for tea and *éclairs* and conversation so taintless and credulous a priest would have praised it, had he not known of the passion that united these two lads.

Philippe suggested going to the north coast where he had reserved a table for us at a Cliffside restaurant frequented by the best of the Finistère. We took a bus there, the only passengers. We rode through a denuded landscape of rock and wind-flattened yellow grass, the ascetic, mist-haunted land of the Druids. We held hands. Each had only eyes for the other.

I knew I would have not passed through this world in vain if I could find a friend--a brother and lover--immutable and just, loyal and deserving. I carried within my breast the mystic quest for the missing half of myself. With this other being I would swear eternal love, as the Ancients had over the tombs of Hylas and Iolaos. And in reality my nascent love for Philippe would have to prove strong. We were two unprotected sprouts in a gathering hurricane. There was no civilization anywhere to acknowledge our attachment, no literature to praise the beauty of our union, no rites to give holy and everlasting assent to our passion. We lived amidst disgust for our particularity. Moreover, the boy was dependent on his family. It was not I who could assure his support. One day Philippe would be inevitably torn between parents and lover. When they discovered the unique nature of their son's liaison, a liaison that in their eyes made their pure, beautiful boy a walker of the shadows of perverse acts and unnatural sighs, the habitué of an underworld of putrid and damning wants, how would Philippe react then? Would he leave them for me, or me to please them? What could Philippe demand of himself, he who was still an adolescent? What could I demand of him, I a flour-eater who survived by the grace of others?

Problems to come, yet on the bus we both felt that the universe was manipulating things in our behalf, that somehow we would pass through the loops of a net which had entrapped all others. The fledgling sun seemed to make an appearance for our sake; even the burly bus driver, we thought, would have nodded acceptance for a passion so devoid of evil.

The restaurant was four stars, the only one outside Paris and Lyons. We walked up a gravel drive hedged by Rollses and were ushered in by tuxedoed waiters and seated at a table with a dazzling array of glass and floral arrangements. The disdainful glances at my *caban*, the knowing eyebrows raised at the obvious intimacy of our relationship, and the display of opulence made me shrink behind the bewildering expanse of cloth and silverware. Only after our first glasses of Muscadet was my courage piqued to rise to the occasion. Philippe ordered for us both, and it was he who led the way through the labyrinthine conventions of eating snail, crayfish, crab and lobster.

Silver platter followed one after the other, glass after glass was drained. Philippe was very aware of the couple we formed. In his hesitant way, part laughing, part blushing, he assumed the dominant role. He would save his American from barbarity; together we would go from good things to the best.

At times Philippe would punctuate his utterances with statements of the most dire sincerity. "We'll have to stay together, no matter what"; "We can't allow anything to come between us"; "There must be loyalty and fatefulness." I understood his love, but not his urgency. I had assumed Philippe was as virgin as I and, like me, took faithfulness for granted. It never occurred to me that he could have had other lovers.

To my stupefaction, Philippe paid the bill. Over my protests he placed a note on the waiter's salver, giving the *garçon* an embarrassed smile for my lack of polished assent. I had come with a hundred francs, thinking it twice as much as necessary, although now I knew it was far less than even half the sum. Philippe joked that it was his father's contribution. It was a grand gesture from one whose youth would normally have led him to expect the opposite.

The cliffs descending from the restaurant were empty of life. Not even a sea gull ventured out into the sluggish afternoon. The sky was again overcast but the morning chill had lifted with the dew and mist. We took a trail down the steep slope to a landing of boulders a few feet above the restless waves. We chose a flat rock with room enough for both of us to lie out on, Philippe on his back, I on my side facing him. Words quickly gave way to kisses, and kisses to the urgency of the moment I had awaited my entire life. With trembling hand I unfastened Philippe's tie and undid the top button of his snow-white shirt. My lips went to the boy's neck and the hollow of his throat with its delicate chain and crucifix. The heat and perfume from his body drew me on to unleash another button and still another. I folded back the white oxford cloth and embraced the upper, lightly-bronzed chest. Philippe pulled away. From his lips came the first No's, low and guttural. Please, Philippe, I begged, uncovering the tiny nipples. My lips nursed at the twin medallions, deeply aroused by their erecting hardness. I felt Philippe give in to the caresses and pushed on. My teeth skirted over the interlocking muscles of his stomach and my forehead pushed into the delicate navel, feeling the rush of blood and breath as throbbing as the sea.

Before my eyes were shirt and buckle. I grasped handful after handful of the cloth from out the recesses of the boy's waist. There seemed no end to the linen, crisp and white. It came out unending from the trousers and swept over the rock, providing a bed as soft and scented as a field of hyacinth. My fingers followed the line of soft blond tufts from the navel to the belt. My nostrils inhaled the leather, my teeth bit into the clasp. I pulled the tongue loose from its buckle. Philippe rose up on his elbows. "Not here!" I unhooked the clasp and the zipper opened of its own. No!, Philippe called, grabbing the open folds of his trousers. Please, Philippe, please, I begged. I seized the corduroy at the pockets and pulled down. The shirt bellowed free from the narrow waist and floated out over the boy's brown shoulders like a sail cut from its moorings. From the taut arc pushing up into the white briefs I knew he was as ready as I. This was the moment, nothing in the world would make me let it go. Please, Philippe, please, please, please, please. The boy lost his balance and tumbled back onto the rock, his trousers crumbling down to his knees. I brought my lips to meet his. My body pressed him flat. My fingers slipped under the band of the shorts and only seconds were needed before the blond curls dropped onto the field of white and his blue eyes looked up glazed into mine. I felt Philippe's small hand jerk at my own belt. In the space of a breath I stripped first him and then myself. I was in awe of his body, ecstatic at his nakedness. Philippe brought his hands up to my chest and pulled me down over him. *Mon amour*, he whispered in a voice no longer hesitant, *mon chéri*. And we slipped onto a wave long and mounting, rising to a distant shore and the breakers there that would split it asunder.

We were both very quiet on the way to the village square where we would await the return of our bus. Since we still had time on our hands, we slipped into a Roman church of black weather-pocked and lichen-embedded granite. Philippe caught hold of my fingers as we crossed the portal into the cold, dark stillness. He approached the font and dipped his finger enwrapped in mine into the pool of blessed water. He made the sign of the cross over me and over himself. We moved silently to the low wicker prayer stools and kneeled before the altar, our fingers still locked. After a few moments Philippe looked up at the wood image of the crucified Christ. With his right hand he took off a ring from the second finger of the left. He placed in on the first finger of my right. Tears flowed from his eyes and from mine. Still without exchanging a word, we rose and left the church. All the way back on the little bus our hands were joined. We felt that never would either of us be alone again. I knew that Philippe was as moved as it was possible to move a body and a spirit. As for me, it was the most beautiful day of my life.

Back in Paris we communicated by phone. Philippe would notify me that at a certain hour he would call from the post office in Brest and I was to answer from a café near Léa's.

The café phone booth was located in the basement, in a corner across from a piss trough and two toilets. At the foot of the narrow, winding staircase was the supervisor, a stout shawled woman who sat behind a dialing apparatus and box of change and *jetons*, knitting. A former prostitute, she had confided to me that she had met her late husband when he had come down for a piss the night Pétain had signed over France to Hitler. Suspicious and disdainful, she surveyed her clientele as they stepped up to the trough, heads stooped and shoulders hunched, her eyes alert for mischief. She was hardest on old ladies who used the toilets and took their time, leaving the minimum tip on their way out. Her head cocked to one side, she followed them with a beady stare all the way to their destination and all the way back, searching out an indication that they had made work for her, ready to pounce on the first sign of hesitation or an ill-advised attempt to climb the steps without depositing their ten *sous* piece. When a real gentleman left her a proper coin, her puffy jowls lit up and there came from her bloated throat a hiss of gratitude which, in its eagerness to come out, ended in a burp, putting her enormous body at rest. She was a good woman who asked no more of her patrons than that they leave behind conditions as benign as the relieved expressions they wore as they left. Should one flinch and portray guilt, she would track him with such a stabbing stare that invariably he stumbled on his way up.

With me she was at first cold, but her black eyes warmed with the assurance that I would leave her twenty *centimes*. Night after night I took a seat near the *cabine téléphonique* waiting for Philippe's call to come through. Night after night she swabbed the tile floors, checked out the damage to her bowls, and said the comforting words, "A little late tonight, but he'll call," and he always did.

Our conversations blended with the severity of the surroundings: Keep courage. We'll be together this weekend. I love you. They'll never separate us. We'll come through together. It is destined. We're special. We're the exceptions. God meant it to be so.

We made dates to go to church, Philippe in Brest, I at St. Geneviève. On the same day, at exactly the same minute, we would light candles, Philippe for me, me for Philippe, both for God. We would pray for the strength to remain pure and united no matter what.

On the weekends I took the accursed train to Brest. Over coffee at the same *pâtisserie* I hatched plans with Philippe on how to get him past the concierge of the shabby hotels in which I stayed. Once inside the airless room, we jumped at the slightest crack, and in general lived in fear like thieves. On an average weekend, Philippe could get away from his parents no more than two hours in the morning and two in the afternoon. The rest of the time I had to walk that ugly town, sleep in those seedy sunless hotels.

There was nonetheless a silver lining on our horizon. Philippe promised to come to Paris to spend Christmas Day with me. It had been arranged somehow with his parents, and as a gage, he sent me his gold chain and crucifix. Through all of October and November and December it was the gas upon which I ran. We would buy real matching rings at that occasion; at St. Geneviève we would take our vows before God.

At home relations with Léa degraded. One night she had a terrible fight with Nène.

"I'm dying of thirst," she said to Mammy as she entered the apartment. "Can you make me a cup of coffee?"

"Of course my dearest. Where's the coffee?" I heard her shuffle to the kitchen door. "Do you know where the coffee is?" She asked Nène. "Léa's thirsty."

"It's here in the kitchen! Where else do you want it to be?" Came Nène's high-pitched answer.

"Oh, all right," pouted Mammy.

I could make out the creak of the chair where Léa placed her coat. I heard Nène come into the hall.

"I've spoken with the members of the family," said Léa to her. "We've decided to put Mammy in a home where someone can take care of her."

"And me?" asked Nène shocked. Confronted with Léa's silence, she changed tactics. "Mammy would be bored in a home. After all, it's *her* place here. She has a home and a pension, and I'll remain with her as long as she needs me. There's no reason..."

"But Mammy needs surveillance. You know if she falls you wouldn't be able to lift her. You need your own freedom ... a chance to voyage ... to paint." Léa pleaded in the patient, altruistic tone parents take on to sway their children.

"Everyone's agreed?"

"Mammy needs help, and the older she gets the more she'll need. God forbid, but if something happens to her here she'll be without anyone."

"And if I fall, you'll do the same thing to me."

"Really, that's not the question...."

"You'd do it to your mother, you'd do it with your aunt!"

In the end, Nène got her way and Mammy stayed. But a few nights later Sylvain came to tell me that Mammy had been hit by a car while crossing the rue de Sévigné. The accident had occurred at six but a swimming class had kept Sylvain from notifying me until two hours later. Actually, when I opened the door I found him standing there mute, a piece of paper in his hand. I took it and read down to the part about the car. I looked to Sylvain for details. He was stifling a yawn and would say nothing. At first I thought he had written the note so as not to break into sobs. But I saw that he was angry, angry I hadn't finished reading the note through because it was in English and he wanted me to correct it. It was full of faults and he wanted it corrected.

I asked to go to the hospital right away but Sylvain didn't know where it was. He was in a hurry to get home and eat so we returned to Léa's together. There I learned that Mammy had fractured her hip. Everyone was playing cards and laughing; for some reason Sylvain's off-the-cuff comment that it might all end in the cemetery made the boys giggle. Nène left the room in a huff, her eyes red and running. Léa conducted herself with the proper gravity at table, but after a little wine they were all laughing and thinking of other things. Even Nène felt better. She remarked how easily Mammy healed. Besides, Mammy had never been sick a day in her life, said Nène.

I knew of the cost of hospitalization in America and in a respectful way I asked how they were going to meet it. I was told that everything was paid by the Social Security, and that it was cheaper having Mammy in the hospital than feeding her at home.

Later that evening, after the children had gone to bed and Nène had turned in, Léa and I took a cup of tea in the kitchen. The scene was to come back to me often. She was bent over the oven basting a chicken she was going to put up in cold lunches for the next day. The girls had noticed the ring on my finger, she said, and were curious as to its provenance. Of course she knew of Philippe and my trips to Brest. If anything, she was content I had a friend, a male friend who had been able to draw me out of myself.

"It was a gift from Philippe," I said.

"That's strange," Léa answered vaguely, still basting the chicken, "a boy giving another boy a ring."

"Not if he loves me," I said.

She stood up and turned to me.

"And I love him, Léa. I love him with all my heart."

Tears rushed to her eyes.

"I'll never accept that," she said, staring, "never."

"And yet...." I made for the door, crying as hard as she.

Never again did she come by the apartment; never again did I see her; she never did accept it; and Mammy never again came home.

.

A week later I walked through the dark slushy streets to the ultimate telephone call before Philippe's arrival in Paris. Philippe's letter had hinted of problems with his parents. I had written to tell him that he must come anyway. Nothing could take a place above the promise he had made. He had to prove his love by coming. An hour before, I had lit a candle in St. Geneviève. I had begged God to bring Philippe to me.

The old woman was at her place, her body mummified in cloaks and scarves. He hasn't called yet, she smiled. It was Christmas and the blond boy was our Christ child. With him coming, a world of belief would open up. Belief in God, belief in Philippe, belief in myself, belief in our two halves. We would build a fortress, and from the rafters we would look down on others like wise owls, content, needing none but ourselves, living for none but ourselves.

I sat in that stinky corridor, huddled despondently in the heavy *caban*, my ears trained on the phone cabin, my heart heaving against the shadows that closed about me. We would have to scrimp and save. God knew how much effort it would take just to provide Philip with what his parents could already offer. Nothing must be allowed to interfere with the beauty of our couple. He is of my body, I thought, and I of his. Nothing impure can touch me so long as we remain unsoiled. Philippe would inspire me to limitless heights. For Philippe, I would remake the world in our image.

The phone rang, sending a feeling of pain and revulsion through my stomach. It's for you, Monsieur Boyd, cabin 1. Philippe? *Mon cheri... Oui, mon amour*, I got it. *Oui, mon cheri*, I love you. *Oui, mon coeur*, I believe in you... But Philippe, you must come. Philippe, it's been promised for months. You must do this thing. Philippe, our lives depend on your coming. Philippe, even if you must take a train and remain ten minutes before returning, you must do it! The same voice, hesitant and troubled, carrier of more pain than I could bear.

I came out, reeling from the blow. The woman gave me the look of a mother who suffered for the son she knew too unarmed to adjust to life's shifting fortunes. Was she mirroring my own grief, or had she listened in and become an accomplice of the love Philippe and I had fought to build? I left the booth, never to return.

CHAPTER NINETEEN

Reiner

The entrance to the restaurant was a colossal beer keg. The curved doors opened on a cloak vestibule followed by a wall of heavy red-velvet curtains that, once folded back, gave onto a dining area of dark oak-paneled walls. The room was long and lighted by a single candle on each table. The only clients present, four boys, sat at a bench to the left of the room, presided over by an elderly heavy-set woman with ample blond hair and eyes narrowed to slits. The place looked expensive. I made a movement of retreat when the *Kellner*, a remarkably good-looking boy my age, came into view through the back kitchen and made his way towards me. I was directed to a small table on the right of the room across from the bench. The *Kellner* gave the woman a nod and backed off a few paces while she got up. All warmth and bearing the cherubic smile of an angel fallen to drink, she offered me a flabby hand and arm crenellated with bracelets up to the elbow, welcoming me to the Volla Poulla.

She repeated my order to the *Kellner* whom she patted on the cheek, then returned to her table from which stories and laughter and one *prost* succeeded another throughout the long night.

I was surprised at finding myself there, simply because I'd been inspired by Goldmund and Narcisse, and because I'd lost Philippe and Léa. But I was young and my future lay before me, or so I thought. I had loved and lost: Wasn't life made of such experiences? Thanks to the variegated past, I was now, I believed, better armed to confront the future. I'd read enough to know, as Nietzsche had written, that what didn't destroy me, made me stronger. Wasn't that the end purpose of sufferance? Yet the truth was that, without knowing it, the future I so ardently desired was behind me. I had had the possibility of having a real family, thanks to Léa, and I'd messed it up. But how could it have been otherwise? She wouldn't accept me for what I was, and I certainly was unable to change my nature to suit her demands. My failure with Philippe was far more serious. How could I have asked him to choose between me and his family, those who had cherished and pampered him for long years? How could I have acted like a lout in ordering him to toe the line? It was a make-or-break kind of ultimatum that I'd also lost. And, moreover, how could I have known that the beginning of the end would start this very night, in this very place? Abandoned by a father who beat me, and a mother who welcomed me into her bed, I saw the origins of my desires but was unclear as to the roots of my hatred. Had I bottled up too much in a heart that finished by imploding? The bad weed had been sown and I was the result, although it could all have been prevented if, only if, always if, Léa hadn't turned her back on me, and if I hadn't turned mine on Philippe. The tragedies, the vengeance: all due to real or imagined humiliations, all useless, all of which could have been avoided. Had I not been mistreated from my earliest youth, my crimes might have remained mere fantasies, like my killing Reiner. But no. Here I was at the Volla Poulla where the end, as I said, was just beginning.

While waiting, I studied the boys. One had short-cropped blond hair that appeared too yellow to be real. He wore a levis jacket over an unbuttoned shirt. On his feet were fishermen's knee-length galoshes. He had sharp inquisitive blue eyes that he occasionally focused on me. Across from him I could see the back of a man obviously in his late fifties. He had a thick head of white hair carefully brushed, an impeccable white silk shirt and dark trousers tailor-cut to minimize the waist spread. My attention was interrupted by the *Kellner* who entered from the kitchen with a beer. I leaned back to receive it but he went by to a corner table next to the velvet curtains, half-hidden by a screen. There sat a man in his fifties, lost to the shadows. Even the candle on his table was out. At the same moment, the velvet curtains suddenly parted and a tall blond boy came bursting in. The young *Kellner* greeted him with a handshake. He took the boy's sheepskin coat deferentially and started to lead him to the bench. The blond boy gave a brief shake of his head, as much to say, Not tonight, tonight I need peace, and he looked about for a secluded spot. His eyes fell on me. They were inexpressive eyes, nearly sagging in weariness. His face was very pale. His regard was diverted by the woman who rose. She bathed him in kisses. They sat for a moment at a corner table nearby, she talking animatedly. Then she got up again and insisted that the boy follow. He seemed reluctant but allowed himself to be directed to the long bench. The woman exchanged a glance over the boy's back with the man behind the screen. It seemed to say, What a tiresome performance.

I dawdled over my food and a few beers until midnight. I imagined Philippe seated in front of me. I could hear his deep, naïve laugh as we maneuvered our heads through the candlelight, Philippe trying to bring out the clarity of his eyes and blond hair, me bringing attention to my best profile. I didn't want to return to the hotel. Alone in the dark night I would unconsciously reach out for the naked shoulders and the slope of Philippe's back. It had been three months and he still refused to leave me untroubled.

I raised my hand for the *Kellner* and made the signature sign. To my surprise, the woman immediately got up, as if awaiting my summons.

She leaned over my table, her skin hanging from her neck and chest in crisscrossed webbing, and shouted in German into my ear. At candle level I could see every capillary in a face gorged with blood. She was terribly drunk. Would I come to the long table, she asked. Taken unawares, my reflex was to nod. She righted herself and put a hand to her chest that ineffectively ironed out the folds. With the other hand she made a shoving movement to the approaching *Kellner* who instantly stepped away.

No one other than the white-haired man acknowledged my presence as I sat beside the woman who placed a strong, firm hand on my leg, and continued the conversation. I could not understand a word they exchanged, but felt heartened to be squeezed in among them. If Philippe came in now, he'd see that I was no longer alone. Then I could magnanimously leave my new friends and take the boy to a corner table where we would begin the task of reconciliation.

The white-haired man facing me paid attention to the woman but pushed things in easy reach of me, a tumbler, vodka, some crackers. His head had indeed an impressive mane. At the open neck of the impeccably clean shirt a dozen gold chains lay in a woods of crinkly gray hairs. After nearly an hour, the man took advantage of something which had sent the woman into howls of laughter by saying, Really, Anna, the boy understands nothing, let me at least translate for him. She gazed at me with eyes red and swollen, and pinched my leg so hard I jumped. *Ja*, she said, in a tone of surprise that I considered myself neglected. I wanted to protest, but already she had turned away and the man, leaning forward, whispered, "It's no use, she can't hear you," he said in English.

"You've never head of Michael Rolf, Dear Boy," he continued in the exaggerated intonation too characteristic of his clan, "but in Berlin I'm a king at my trade. I'm a designer and my layouts are published in every major magazine in the world. Today I received a card from Fonteyn who's coming through Berlin, and next week I'll be in New York as a guest of Capote. I wish I could take my darling *kätzchen* along with me but he must stay and work at the job I found for him."

The darling cat in question was the boy in fisherman's boots sitting next to the woman. His name, Ulf, and the boy himself, made me think of a young wolf, a shorthaired beast with clever eyes and hungry grin. Ulf said little, slumped over his vodka, absentmindedly fingering a gold chain with a silver fish. A few days later I would see the chain around Anna's neck.

"He only works at the Hilton, you know," Michael went on, "but one day my Ulfi will be head receptionist there. He just has to learn English and French and know the right people. I can help him. That's what we're for, people in my position, that's our responsibility. My parents were very poor. I'm forty-eight and I've worked years to get to the top." Although hopelessly lost when it came to estimating age, I nonetheless felt I could safely add ten years to the man's version. "But I'm also humble and can remember what I went through."

Michael looked at Anna. The table conversation was on cars. Anna took her paw off my leg, a movement which noticeably loosened Ulf and disturbed Michael. He leaned towards her to whisper what sounded like placating words. Her only response was to send the waiter, Denton, for a bottle of Bavarian white wine. Michael pressed her with more whispers. She laughed and dismissed him with a *Meine Katze, virklich*, and turned her attention to the bottle she opened herself. Michael fell back into his seat. He gave Ulf a long, reflective glance.

"Dear Boy," he said, "when I met Ulf he was nothing. He made sandwiches in a small stand on the Ku-Damm. He was young and I thought he had potential. I introduced him to all my friends, taught him manners, tried to get him to read, took pains with his dress, but as you can see…." he shrugged. "But you know, Dear Boy, most of these people began where Ulf was. And then one day, they too met someone like me who took an interest in them and lifted them up. They made many friends and those who were smart have worked to the top. You know, nowhere outside our clique could a boy like the one sitting next to Anna," he went on, lowering his voice, "become an actor after just being a salesman--and all because people helped him and gave him a chance. But you have to have some brains. Looks will do for the first part of the road but later, when you're older, you must be prepared."

I looked over at the actor. His face was indeed handsome although expressionless, his eyes dull to the point of milky blindness. He spoke in clipped statements, in a voice resonant and beautiful, ending each intervention with a self-satisfied snigger that left no room for dissent.

"Denton's a good example of what I mean," said Michael, nodding at the *Kellner*. "He's a lovely boy, everyone wants him. But he's not ... a part of our clique. He came three years ago from Berlinzer and met Anna in the Grünewald. He stayed with her for a while and she got him a job here as a waiter. Everybody gives him good tips. Now he's married and has a son and a beautiful house near the Ronensee. He's smart. Everyone told him he should be a movie star. He went to acting school and since has done some advertising on TV and film dubbing. But he hasn't quit his job here and he won't until the big break comes. He doesn't sleep around. If a producer wants him for a part, he waits until the contract's signed. Ashton, the gentleman in the corner, comes here every night. He's the conductor at the Opera. He loves Denton and they go everywhere together. Last year Ashton invited him and his wife to his place on the Riviera and then to London. Ashton's introduced him to a lot of people. No one knows if they've ever slept together, that's how discreet Denton is, and that's another reason we all like him. He doesn't use anyone and he doesn't ask for anything. If people want to help him because they like him, that's fine. Otherwise, he's everybody's friend."

At the moment, Denton was seated with Ashton, in conversation. I could have gotten acquainted with myself by knowing Ashton because we shared many of the same tastes, and although I was inexperienced, I wondered, even then, if the solitary Ashton was what the future held in store for me too: a Denton, slim and dark complexioned, serious, intelligent and respectful--seemingly the opposite of any of those at the long bench--the sole consolation in my own old age.

Michael asked me about my family. I had received a letter from my mother that morning. I had skipped from paragraph to paragraph, past the Your mother went shopping... Dad went trout fishing... scanning the lines for the words dead, has just died, terrible accident, the ways I had learned about Al and my Uncle Bob, killed from exposure during a hiking trek in the Uintahs, and would soon hear about Bud, a victim to age, and Bill, dead from gluttony or drink or both. Clark had inherited the place, immediately leaving it in the hands of Bill's son-in-law, an ambitious hotwire, while Clark spent what remained of his life island-hopping around the Pacific.

"Dear Boy, I like silk and finery," said Michael, reminding me of Mammy when he took out a lace handkerchief from his cuff. "At my home I have leopard-skin rugs and zebra canapés. Ulfi wears jeans jackets and those horrible boots that he thinks make him look *männlich*, but in his wardrobe is a wig, Dear Boy, and if you look closely you'll see his eyes are shadowed. I know what he does while I'm away, don't think I don't. He is only twenty-three and if regular workouts in bed are responsible for the aging process, his face registers retirement. But he has such an exquisite body, My Boy, if you only knew...."

Later, when I gave Ulf English lessons, Ulf made that body abundantly available. I could not arrive at his apartment without finding him in the shower. At first Ulf donned levis and sat legs wide apart; then a bathrobe, legs crossed; bathrobe, legs open; towel; towel up with testicles in repose on the armchair seat; then towel accidentally open, exposing a phallus that was more than ample reason for Michael's investment; finally briefs, the pouch of which he perpetually kneaded like Rudy at Bud's. But the view of the wig slumped over a lampshade, and a way he had of posing, turned me off. Ulf did come in handy later, though, when life with Reiner was turbulent and Ulf, the hotel pusher, provided me with drugs.

"Like Denton," Michael went on, "we all began here ... yes, in this very restaurant ... all of us waiters, *garderobe* boys, dishwashers, cooks ... yes, even I. We all had our start with Anna, all except the actor, Reiner. He was too proud. He came when he was young and Anna fed him. He desperately needed to be around people who had more than he, more money, more experience or a more important job. He was the poorest of us all, was Reiner. He said that one day he would succeed and the rest of us would come hat in hand to him. Well, for the moment he has succeeded. *Vierzig Karat* has played a full year and is still going strong. All his life he took. He took how to dress, how to eat at table, how to know the value of objects. He's used us all, Anna first, me and my connections, even poor Ulfi. Like all of us at the beginning, Reiner had ambition. He got through actor's school with the money given him by a married industrialist. Then he waited. He waited for a job. Week after week, month after month. The other students were taken on one by one, but not Reiner. Every day he made the rounds of film agents and the theaters. Always nothing. He grew thin and motley. His industrialist went to Switzerland where his wife was giving birth to twins. Soon Reiner was down, literally, to his last egg, and that fell from his trembling hands onto the kitchen floor."

He took time out to pour himself and me some vodka. Anna, Reiner and Ulf were busy enjoying a story the actor was telling them.

"Anna and I took him under our wings," he resumed, "until his industrialist came back to set him up in a men's clothing shop. Never did he give either Anna or me thanks, worse, he took one of Anna's lovers right from her bed one morning while she was out buying cigarettes, and he fixed Ulf up with a rendezvous with Leisa, the drugged slut who plays the lead with him in *Vierzig Karat*. Even the industrialist he eventually cast off as punishment for going to Switzerland without providing for him. Over the years we've seen things at this table concerning Reiner, you can bet on that. But never could we rid ourselves of him. Perhaps it's a feeling of culpability. He said he would succeed and to a point he has. The others said then that they would too, and look at them now, all hardly better off than Ulf. Still, I believe firmly that every dog has its day, and it's on that cheerful thought that I must excuse myself." He ceremoniously handed me his card, letting me know that he was doing me a great favor.

As Anna escorted Michael out, Reiner and I fell into conversation. The tone was light and Reiner charming. I had no difficulty accepting his invitation to his apartment. After all, I was alone in a foreign city, and the boy was really very handsome. For Reiner, the moment contained an amusing turn. Anna had singled me out for her own attentions. Here was an opportunity to pay her back for a number of slights, as well as pretending to do Ulf, who feared losing Anna, a favor reimbursable later on in hash.

Reiner made an announcement to the table in German. Anna, entering through the curtains, shouted for champagne. Denton came with a quarter bottle that Anna seized and uncorked. Her small, bloodshot eyes were very moist. Everyone was jabbering merrily except for Ulf who appeared tired and sorrowful. Reiner guided me out of the Volla Poulla, holding me firmly by the arm. The others followed. It was bitter cold.

Unmarked snow covered the streets. Reiner had retrieved my *caban* and his own sheepskin coat. We got into his sports car. Anna loomed above the windscreen with the champagne bottle she shook before letting the fluid spurt out over the roof. The people outside were yelling things at Reiner who was laughing back. It finally occurred to me that they were baptizing the car. "She's very nice," I said. "Yes, she is very nice," Reiner answered in the restrained and somber voice he was always to use with me. I was reminded of the line from Cyrano de Bergerac when the musician asked what music to play. "For a woman an air gay," Cyrano answered, "for a man, *triste*." That was Reiner that night and thereafter, *triste*.

CHAPTER TWENTY

We drove through the streets of Berlin, deserted streets lit by yellow lamplight that caught the steady, slanting fall of snow. Reiner spoke in low, rich English, correct in its syntax and Shakespearean in its melodiousness. He spoke of the particularities of each district we passed through. He spoke as only Berliners speak of their city, with feeling as total and nostalgic as a boy fallen calf-eyed in love with his girl, married her, fathered their children and reaped the bounty of the faithfulness written on her face, one line at a time. Reiner's seriousness worked its way with the icy cold into the marrow of my soul. I fell under the spell of that voice, and admiring of the beauty it described. For me too, Berlin would become unique.

We parked down the street from his apartment on Trabener Strasse. Side by side we tramped through the snow. Reiner ushered me into his apartment, a single large room. Two walls were of wood paneling, one with a niche and bed, the other with a white sofa that matched the wall-to-wall carpeting. A third wall was taken up by a bay window with lowered slats. The last was covered with light brown fabric. It had two doors, one leading into the kitchen, the other to the black-tiled bathroom. Reiner showed me around. The bed had a fox coverlet he had brought back from Russia. Above the sofa hung a modernistic painting of a pistol, aimed at the viewer, going off. On either side of the sofa were end tables, each supporting a vase filled with fresh red roses. In front of the sofa was a coffee table flanked by two armchairs. Between the two doors stood an antique secretary with a tiny stool. Above the secretary rose a gold-columned lamp with a black lacquered shade. The room was meticulous. Each object picked up--a jade figurine, a quartz egg--was replaced precisely where it had been. There was no dust. When I congratulated him on his cleaning lady, he looked at me as though I were mad. No one would be entrusted with his objects. Nothing in the apartment had been placed there without a meaning for this boy who was just my age.

The best is outside, Reiner said. He had an ill-definable laugh that was almost a snigger. He seemed to be saying, It's truly great, if you're intelligent enough to see it, but he could as easily have meant, It's nothing, but you'll like it. He lowered all the lights with a dimmer, then snapped them off. He went to a corner of the bay window and turned a handle that raised the jalousie.

The clouds outside had cleared away and a full moon shone on a small dark lake over which a breeze tossed up ripples. Reiner flicked a switch that brought trees from the shadows and lit up a patch of lawn that sloped to the lake's edge where there was a small bark. He flipped the spots off again.

I could not move from where I stood. I felt him come to my side and look with me into the garden at the moonlight playing the same invariable tune on the flickering water. We stayed like that a long time. Seen by anyone from across the lake, we were no more than two wintry shadows that formed one when Reiner bridged the space between us. He kissed me lightly on the lips. I started to tremble so hard he had to take me tightly in his arms to steady me. Oh God, I heard him whisper.

After a few moments, Reiner mentioned a nearby woods. Perhaps we could take a walk there.

We drove to a forest surrounding a large lake. Reiner parked the car and we rounded the lake on foot, he with his arm around my neck, and I wondering what I had done to elicit such a reaction, praying that it would not wear off, and frightened to death of bed and my measuring up to the boy's anticipations. The lake was white and partially frozen over, the shore boot-deep in snow. We stopped near a fallen tree trunk and Reiner turned to kiss me. The shaking recommenced.

"The champagne was for *us*," Reiner laughed, the image of Anna in his mind's eye. "I told them all I was taking you home with me. Never had I done that before. You wait, the telephone won't stop ringing tomorrow." My stomach filled with butterflies.

He drew me to him and again we continued our walk. As we came full way around the lake we approached a tiny bridge. Reiner hugged me tightly as we went over it. In the middle we stopped and looked over the side. *Ich gehe mit Dir über die Brüche*, he said in Schillerian tones. Then in English, "With you I will cross the bridge. There will not be another."

We went to Reiner's car and drove back to Trabener Strasse. Inside his room he lowered the slats, sealing us off as in a sarcophagus. He opened the bed, placed his own clothes neatly on the couch, and undressed me. We entered the white sheets. Reiner supported my head against his chest with one arm while with the other he lit and slowly finished a last cigarette while we listened to *Suzanne* by Leonard Cohen. Then he turned to me, and the most beautiful night of my life spun on and on in that artificial darkness which kept out even the first flicker of the mounting dawn. Reiner's infinite tenderness ignited my passion, and my passion ignited his. Again and again we found the wellsprings of feeling and shared pleasure until he finally fell into sleep, curved into the slope of my back. For one hour, two hours, three hours I thought of the ways I would make this boy proud of me and earn his faith. Then I felt Reiner's fingers encircle my lower stomach and stroke my sex into readiness, and again we spun out the night.

.

The following afternoon we were awoken at two by Ulf on the phone. Reiner took the call nestled in a sea of soft pillows and linen, one hand on the receiver, the other playing over my bed-warm body. I had slept very poorly. I had never slept with anyone before, as Philippe had always been obliged to return home by dinnertime. During the endless night I had not moved a muscle for fear of waking him. My head would not stop going over the events of the evening before, the encounter, the walk through the woods, and the future that would now be mine. Reiner had slept dead to the world, his arms enfolding my chest, his forehead implanted in the nook of my neck. I was nonetheless alert and responsive. I listened to the slow, deliberate voice, even more deeply resonant in drowsiness. I couldn't understand much of what he was saying, but he was obviously content.

When Reiner hung up we began one of his days, upon which all the rest were immutably cloned. He opened the jalousie. He was naked and beautiful, yet like me he spurned complete nudity, quickly slipping on a pair of immaculate white briefs. While he poured his bath he gave me instructions for breakfast. Coffee beans to be ground like this, with this many spoonfuls in the filter; the boiled eggs clocked at four minutes, here's the hourglass; the toast done this brown, the butter this soft; this much cream; this much sugar.... The litany continued but I was a capable acolyte.

Reiner's baths were wonders. He was wetted, soaped and scrubbed down to the most remote pore within the most inaccessible crevice. Toes were trimmed, quicks flattened, hangnails clipped. His ears were operating theaters of propriety, his nose a hecatomb for loose hairs, the underarms the proving ground of odor-conquering scents. In bed he smelled of sandalwood, a perfume that went well with the vase of roses, the thick carpets and the down-filled quilt. Above the bathroom lavabo was a 60-watt light. You see, it hides nothing, he said to me, grim faced. He worried about his hair thinning, but still washed it daily; he worried about the shadows under his eyes, yet continued to smoke and spend the night at the Volla Poulla; he worried about his muscles losing tone, although his only form of physical activity were the daily walks in the Grünewald. He seemed to get a perverse satisfaction from evoking the day when he would have to give up his niche as *jeune premier*.

After bath and breakfast we trotted off to the Grünewald where we repeated the round of the previous night, this time in the company of heavily coated, distinguished burgers walking their hounds. The movement was clockwise, a river of humanity encircling the lake. Reiner's strides were purposeful. His sheepskin coat flapped about an exquisitely tailored French shirt and razor-creased beige trousers. He smoked a Lord cigarette thoughtfully, studying me, my *caban* and corduroys, like some of the other passers-by were observing their animals, hopeful they wouldn't be disgraced by a canine fight or an untactfully placed dog mess.

We left the woods and drove for lunch to a tastelessly furnished chandelier and bay window restaurant in the Ku-Damm. As Reiner opened the car door on the street side, he knocked over a girl riding by on a bicycle, a load of books in one arm. She got to her feet and while brushing the snow off and scanning her coat for rips, she had the temerity to mutter something about his being more careful. Reiner flew into a horrifying rage. He literally swooped down on her like a hawk, giving her a brutal tongue-lashing. His face was livid with choler as he spit out the word *scheisse* and others I recognized as insulting by the girl's flinching. He left her speechless and barreled his way into the restaurant, sputtering in English, "Doesn't that bitch know who I am!"

A waitress came and took our orders. Reiner's mood was now indescribably foul. I tried to joke him out of it but when he gave me one of the looks he'd given the girl, I clammed up. I ate a salad but Reiner repeated *scheisse* as he turned over his, evidently dissatisfied with something in its seasoning. I had ordered a hamburger and he a steak. Reiner gave my plate--naked but for the parsimoniously filled little buns, a frugal choice because I was there at Reiner's invitation--a disdainful regard, and made a comment under his breath about American tastes. When he cut into his own meat he howled for the waitress. She came and a dispute irrupted that ended with Reiner overturning the plate on the restaurant floor, reminding me of my father. The waitress shrilled her indignation and Reiner rose up menacingly in front of her, shouting in English, And when you serve, you can at the least wash your fingernails, you dirty… and then a German word with the resonance of sow. "We're leaving", he called over his shoulder, but I was already up and behind him.

Back at his apartment he gave me some odd jobs to do like fetching cigarettes from a nearby *Tabakwaren* while he did his voice training. From a pay phone I gave a ring to Michael and told him I was going to the theater that night to see Reiner's play. Because Reiner liked to be there an hour early, he said he would drop me off at an adjoining café. I told Michael I would like to wear something smart for the evening, but had not come from Paris with a suit. Michael said Ulf would lend him one of his. Some were at Anna's that Ulf hadn't bothered to move when he got his own apartment. I was to go there. Michael would phone ahead to say I was coming. As Anna's was on the other side of the small lake, I had only to walk around it to get there.

Her flat was in a post-war block of brick housing, up two flights of stairs poorly lighted by occasional cubes of translucent glass. She came to the door, her cheeks ruddy and puffy, dressed in a pink housecoat open at the breasts. Behind her was the partly closed door to her bedroom. I saw a hand reach out and snatch up a pair of white shorts from the floor. Before the door to the bedroom closed I caught the rapid movement of a naked figure.

Anna led me into a living room filled with old sofas, a bookcase of hand-me-down paperbacks and walls of amateurish, impressionistic paintings. She spoke no English so she just sang out cheerfully, *Koffee? Koffee?* while nodding her head affirmatively. As she occupied herself in the kitchen I heard some scampering in the hallway, then knocking at the front door, Anna's *Wer ist da?* and a surprised, *Mein Ulfi! Komm' herein!* Ulf entered the living room like a servant overstepping his mandate, his head low and his shoulders stooped, his hair mussed up, and although I did not find his face attractive, I could pleasantly picture those white shorts moving up thighs of corded muscle.

Ulf spoke in an ingratiating, resonant voice certainly patterned on Reiner's. He was a good mimic. He sat beside me and while we waited for Anna he asked about the possibility of having English lessons. I agreed on a first rendezvous. Just as Anna returned, Ulf went out to get me a suit. As he crossed Anna he noticed she had put on a piece of jewelry. He gave her an exasperated look and said something about a provocation. She came in all smiles. She had no more than put down the coffee and cakes when she drew my attention to the silver fish and necklace she wore, those I had seen around Ulf's neck the night before. *Von meiner Katze Ulfi*, she beamed. And when he returned, *Nicht wahr, mein kätzchen*?

Ulf shrugged disarmingly, an engaging you-know-how-it-is grin playing across his face. The telephone rang. Anna returned from the hallway and announced, pointing to the receiver, "Herr Reiner Rolf." It was hard for me to interpret her smile. It seemed to say, You've been caught with your hand in the cookie jar. Reiner was courteous, impatient and questioning over the phone. Whatever gave me the idea of going there? What surprise? Was Anna alone? Well, he finished, come back where you belong and don't say a word to Michael about Ulf's being there when you see him tonight. I gulped down the rest of my coffee and left a bemused Anna and a slightly anxious Ulf. On the way home I wondered how Reiner knew about my meeting with Michael.

Reiner was still doing his voice exercises when I walked in. I came to discover that he was as proud of continuing them as was a former athlete who still worked out in the neighborhood gym. Reiner put on the

Magnificat which I failed to recognize, a confession he duly scorned. While waiting for him to finish in the bathroom, I smoked one of the Lords he had left lighted. It was my first cigarette.

CHAPTER TWENTY-ONE

Reiner dropped me off in front of the café. Since Michael had not arrived, I went into the men's room and put on Ulf's suit. It was a good size too big but an improvement over my *caban* and corduroys.

Outside, Michael was seated at a table waiting for me. Over one of the chairs was his cashmere overcoat. He was wearing a very expensive looking sweater and a scarf knotted under his Adam's apple. His mane was as full and shaggy as his Cossack hat perched on the overcoat. He asked me how I had spent my first day with the star. His eyes were so friendly, his manner so disarming that I found myself going into the details of Reiner's behavior, his punctiliousness, his inexplicable hot and cold attitude towards Anna and Ulf, his furies, the moments when he would show me great tenderness, others when I felt little more than a domestic, the dichotomy of his love for the theater on one hand and, on the other, his hatred for those who comprised it. What I did not tell Michael--what I was too ashamed to confide--but what Michael seemed to sense anyway, was the disdain Reiner harbored for both Michael and me. I had only been with him one day, yet already he made me feel that my life was empty compared to his. I was a sloppily dressed, hamburger-eating American who wouldn't know Bach from the Beatles. As for Michael, Reiner never said anything outright, yet his way of not saying things, or a certain condescension in his voice, hinted that Michael was at the zenith of his profession and could only go down. He sneered that Michael was mocked by his friends because of Ulf sleeping with Anna. "Can you imagine, losing your lover to an old fag hag?" And, finally, that Michael had always tried--how did he put it?--to fart higher than his ass, and that, at any rate, he was old, so what good was he?

"You know, Dear Boy, the war has produced a veritable nation of orphans, each deprived of the father who would introduce his son into the ways of manhood as surely--if less spectacularly--as a shaman leading initiates through the rites of puberty. Remember that the Greeks sent their newborn to the women's apartments to be raised, and as women prefer men, the boys, by mimicry, did the same. The result was the perpetuation of the homoerotic bond that would forge boys and men into a link stronger than iron. The link had a name: Passion, both intellectual and physical. The Greeks would often fight, wars and petty feuds would sometimes divide them, but forever there lingered the nostalgia of that Passion which gave purpose to their acts of courage, inspired their art, and laid the foundation of a democracy based on the shared experiences and loyalties of their youth.

"From the women's apartments," he continued, "Greek boys were put steadfastly on the path to manhood, first by their fathers, men who were responsible before society for the correct upbringing of their sons, then by the boys' masters whose conduct and teachings were supervised by the entire populace--let us not forget that Socrates was put to death when he was thought to have had a corrupting influence on the young-- and finally by a boy's lover, an older boy held responsible not only before his belovèd's father, and not only before his peers, but especially before the god himself. Zeus would judge the sincerity of the lover's influence because Zeus, through the ascension of Ganymede, was the guardian of boys and their paramours." (10)

"I have a friend in Paris who rid herself of her husband the moment she had had three sons, sons she raised alone. Yet none of them shares our passion."

"A boy can survive without a father if his mother is strong enough to take the father's place. The flaw, if we can again go to the Greeks for inspiration, lies in modern-day Andromaches who overly protect their boys as Andromache fought to save her son, little Scamandrius, from the ways of his father, which were the ways of the warrior, and implied devastation, rape and battle to the death."

I remembered my own mother's protective ways, making place for me in her bed the moment my father left for work.

"Look at Reiner," continued Michael. "Brought up alone by his mother who had suffered the cataclysm of Berlin in war, he was shielded by a woman decided to undergo all abnegation to make of him the vindication of her wasted life. She barred anything external that could aggravate her insecurity or trouble their idyll for two. Thusly locked into his own world, separated from others, her son came to count on the only object which proved invariably true: himself. The outer world with its competition and vulgarity held no interest for him. He came to worship an inner sun every bit as mystically and unquestioningly as Ikhnaton did the outer one. Whatever could magnify his personal worth was placed before his altar. Lost in the depths of his own thoughts and sensations, he related to the outside world on the terms of his egocentric self. People were the means to his goals, he the end. Even as a child he was perpetually on stage. He could never forget himself, he could never lose himself in anything but his own person. Always mindful of his dress and his behavior, his interest in others never went farther than his own reflection in their eyes.

"As he grew he became aware of his difference, a difference which further alienated him from others. His acquaintances despised the clique to which it was his lot to belong, calling it depraved and worse. To survive, therefore, he had to hide his nature. He tried to conform to society's demands. Already turned passively inward, this passivity was magnified as he allowed himself to be carried along the current of life which offered the least resistance, such as a log carried downstream by a torrent. He could not compete with others because the direction of his interests was so infinitely divergent from theirs. Had he not been provided with his talent, he would have found a safe job someplace, in a travel bureau or as part of a hotel staff, like my Ulfi, where the flux of visitors would have given him the illusion of variety and action. Had he wished to capitalize on his esthetic sense, he would have found work as a hairdresser or florist. But as it was, he chose one of the better openings offered his kind, a refuge where his difference was well tolerated, and a place of high esteem. After all, our inclination can't hurt as actor, although it would destroy the career of someone like a judge, say."

"Still," I said, "it's obvious Reiner's above the others. Look at the way he speaks and dresses, and his love of good music."

"If we are pushed into ourselves, what remains other than preoccupations such as reverie, going to museums, appreciating the classics? But we mustn't confuse intellectual concerns with snobbism. The first is an attribute open to anyone and is meritorious. The second, snobbism, is our revenge over those who have forced us into conformity; even the most ungifted of our clan considers himself superior to society in general. We dress better than the others, it's certain; we speak better than they do, that's certain too. We make more money. Our romanticism is more developed, our literature more emotional, our music the loftiest. It was not for nothing that Reiner chose the *Magnificat* this afternoon. We have a marked penchant for inspirational compositions, although what really move us are syrupy symphonies, masses, requiems and other dirges. Of course, there are those who would say our obsession with what is esthetic is only to give us a film-thin smattering of cultural pretension, and that underneath we are all sottishly mediocre, which, for most of us, is perhaps the most certain still."

"Where do you place Reiner is all of this?"

"That, Dear Boy, is for you to discern. But one thing is for sure, he will never change. To change is to deny his difference, his inherent superiority over others, his very originality. It is to become part of the mindless hordes: football on TV, Sundays at the German equivalent of Coney Island, a suburban family with children spoiled on surfeit or junked into oblivion on fads, cults, drugs.

"His difference became his fetish. He lived by it and for it. He associated himself with others of the shadows, constructing a social fabric from the night they frequented. He learned of the places of rendezvous, from the lowest--the street--to a closed cell of friends, of whom I am one. But the price he paid for his new life was dear indeed. There is no fidelity in the land of Sodom. Even at the outset a couple formed of two boys is condemned by a society that refuses any form of deviant behavior. Our boys have neither the understanding of their families, nor the essentials of civilization: recognition of their union, protection under the law, compassion. In addition, in a union of two boys each boy is financially independent; there is no restraint to his walking out. The resultant insecurity sensitizes them to any sign that their friendship might be weakening. The first of those signs is inevitably infidelity."

"You almost say that as if infidelity must occur."

"My Boy, nothing is stronger in nature than sexual curiosity. Today we fight for sexual monogamy as tenaciously as we do for a monotheistic religion. Believe me, it's the greatest *malentendu* of our time. It is as stupid for us to act as sluts as it is for us all to take the veil; somewhere in between lies sexual fulfillment, not the dogma of fidelity which we take as much on faith as we do the existence of the one god."

"I won't be unfaithful to Reiner. And if he were unfaithful to me, I would leave on the first plane out of Berlin." Michael shrugged and gazed disinterestedly outside the restaurant window. Small groups of people had formed in front of the theater.

"When they move in," he said, "it will be time for you to go across."

"If being as we are were only bad, we'd all be going to a psychiatrist in hopes of changing."

"But you would lose your *uniqueness*, and besides, there are auxiliary compensations. You belong to a group that takes care of its own. It is not exclusively thanks to Reiner's acting ability that he has come this far. Ours is an exclusive club, and the most workable Freemasonry in the history of the world."

"Based on beauty."

"Based on contribution. One gives what one has, but one must give. I have not survived for beauty's sake," he said laughing, ''At least, not *recently*. Yet I have position, and friends, and, let us not forget, *a* friend-- wayward gipsy though he may be."

"And if he becomes exaggeratedly wayward, there are ten to take his place?"

"No longer for me. Ulf is the last. With him, as we say in German, I shall buckle the belt. With Ulf I have come full circle. There will not be another Ulf, nor a surrogate Ulf. I have had my fill, Dear Boy. One must really know when the time comes to leave the table."

A time that would come sooner than I could possibly have guessed.

"I've led a *fabulous* life. I've known boys. Oh God, you wouldn't believe the boys I've known. Especially following the war, they were just everywhere and so *accessible*!" At the memory of the boys who unclothed before his eyes, who permitted caresses and penetration in order to stave off starvation, his lips trembled like a glutton's on the verge of devouring a leg of lamb. "I have memories that until death will keep me on a permanent high. I have been free, really free. My money has been mine, and with it I have offered myself a standard of living beyond the dreams of the masses. There is nowhere on the face of this earth worth visiting, Dear Boy, that I have not trod. There is no nectar worth the tasting that I have not tried. I have known the pleasures of true love, and those of promiscuity; there are none higher. I have sought the Ideal Love and have found it four times. I have orchestrated my life to play on the endless variation of romance found and lost. I shall go out on a crescendo."

"With Ulf?"

Michael shrugged me off.

"I just hope you'll be as lucky. As your youth vanishes and you find less and less success among the generations coming up, a horrible abyss will open before you. Believe me, the loss of youth is the first death, the second and real one is a salvation in comparison."

"Well, when I'm old," I said, "I won't pay attention to the mirrors. I'll break them." Nène was like that, I remembered. There were certain mirrors she refused to look into.

"It is true that Narcissus cannot age without his mirrors," Michael laughed, "but the true mirrors are not those hanging on the walls. They are too willing to be dupe to rationalization. No, the true ones are the eyes of those around us; the eyes of those we desire: they will not lie."

"So eat, drink and be merry."

"And make love, my Dear Boy. You've lived in Paris, you said. Remember Molière's words: *Tout le plaisir de l'amour est dans le changement.* That's what I tell Ulf. Let lust be his ruin, since all else is fake and mockery."

"Were Ulf's beginnings like those of Reiner?"

"Like Reiner's, like yours, like mine. After all, throughout the past hour I have only been speaking about you."

"I had a father. He survived the war."

"Death is not the only cause of the absence of those meant to push us in the right direction. There's indifference. Alcoholism. There are many reasons why sons turn away from their fathers, or fathers their sons."

I couldn't deny that.

"And here is the greatest misconception of them all. For us the conflict is no longer that of being like our fathers in order to seduce our mothers, it is the opposite: Help will come only when we renounce our mothers to follow in the steps of our fathers. It is the only way out."

He rose after offering that recondite piece of information and pointed outside. The theatergoers were hustling there way inside. It was obvious the play was about to begin.

CHAPTER TWENTY-TWO

The play began on a beach in Myconos when Young Boy, Reiner, met Mature Woman, Leisa. His entry was stunning. A barefoot blond-haired blue-eyed Adonis in t-shirt and levis, his voice was light and sonorous, his sexuality blatant. His displacements were perhaps a bit stilted and perhaps he lacked in spontaneity, but the audience was entranced by him, and it was a heady thought that of them all it was I alone who knew the source of that sexuality, hidden beneath folds of denim and soft white cotton.

The second act found Reiner in Paris to be with Leisa and her daughter Mimi. Very Old Grandmother suggested to Leisa that Reiner's interest in her was only a classic maneuver to get at the person he really loved, the daughter. Leisa believed all and returned to the arms of her former lover, a well-preserved gentleman as middle-aged as she. Would Mature Woman lose Young Boy? Did Young Boy love Young Girl? Would Middle-Aged Man always be faithfully there to welcome back Mature Woman? And Why was Young Girl so admiringly amiable to Middle-Aged Man? In the end, Very Old Grandmother recognized the error of her facile analysis and reunited Reiner and Leisa. Mimi, of course, got Middle-Aged Man who enjoyed a sexual renaissance. On the way out older men eyed young girls and the young girls were perhaps thinking Why not? But only I was headed towards reality.

In his dressing room I found Reiner by himself. When I showed surprise at the absence of admirers, he told me about the night of the Première. Years of work and worry had gone into his preparation, and then at last a starring role. Months of rehearsals at the end of which would assuredly come fame. But the night of his great success, after the final curtain call when he had stepped into the back alley, his face still slightly made up, he had found himself completely alone. Nothing had changed. From then on returning to the theater was like going to a factory.

Seated in front of his mirror, those drained eyes staring back at themselves, his face pale and lifeless, my spirits were crushed by the web of despair Reiner relentlessly spun over those around him. Through the alley I felt his bitterness, in his sports car it was so overwhelming that it chocked off conversation.

At one the next afternoon the phone woke us. Reiner's voice was low and somber as usual, refined, grave and elegant, but there was an inflection of disbelief and a note of anger. He spoke for quite a long while before hanging up, giving me time to put out coffee and toast on the coffee table.

"It was Anna," Reiner said. "Michael's suicided," he continued, his disarray passing into his grammar.

Poor Michael. He had prided himself too much on that leonine head of his to put a bullet there. He had aimed at his heart and missed, taking, the doctors guessed, an hour to bleed to death. Blood was all over the apartment, claw marks where he had pulled himself. Decided on death, the only thing untouched by blood was the telephone itself. The neighbors had not heard the shot. Nothing had filtered through the lacquered Chinese screens, rugs, low couches and deep folds of the leather-tapestried walls.

Michael had left a note with the names of those he wanted to attend his services. He had requested Verdi's *Requiem* to be played in the background, one of the dirges he said gays so favored. The list of names was a Who's Who of Berlin. Reiner insisted on being part of the funeral even though he hadn't been listed. Anna and Ulf were also excluded, but they too would ultimately turn up. Michael had no family to survive him.

The death of Michael changed nothing in Ulf's plans to learn English. To the contrary, he needed company, and as I was running short of money, we saw each other daily for lessons. Reiner did not seem disconcerted by my absences. To the contrary, what he took for my lack of ambition began to mine our relationship. More and more he asked himself where I fit in in a world in which only people of importance could help him advance socially and professionally.

A week later, Reiner received a midnight telephone call. There were pauses, a number of sighs and an ugly, cold blue regard aimed at me. When he hung up his manner was instantly remote. I asked for an explanation but when none was forthcoming, I told him it was better we quit friends now than let our relationship become bitter. It sickened me to see how easily I had let myself be manipulated by this boy, and how I had come to do his bidding like the obedient German hounds paraded around Grünewald. I was sick too at the thought of leaving him. I told him I would return to Paris. When he saw that I was serious, he consented to divulge the contents of the call. A friend had warned him that I was sleeping with Ulf. I was too taken aback to speak. For me faithfulness was not a thing to win, it was something taken for granted. I told Reiner I would definitely leave now. If Reiner could believe such a thing, we did not deserve to remain even friends. I was not yet so attached that I could not walk out. I would suffer, but to go through more humiliation was surely worse.

It was then that he did the totally unexpected. He asked me to sit in the armchair, and kneeling before me he opened a tiny drawer in the coffee table from which he drew out a small box. Inside was a necklace of gold and a gold heart. He put it around my head, in place of the one

Philippe had offered me. "Don't you know I love you," he said, "and that you must stay?" The actor's eyes were filled with tears, as were mine.

But there was a "but", Reiner said. I would have to prove myself. As of tomorrow I would have to look for new lodgings and get a job. I would also stop giving Ulf lessons--not because Reiner believed the telephone caller, but to stop the gossip. He would help me. He would do everything to get me on my feet. Once I had my own place and was financially well-off, our relationship would be reestablished on a basis of equality. I understood the reasoning and could only go along. It was a test, not unlike the test I had put Philippe through.

To celebrate the necklace, Reiner did what he preferred most. After bathing, he came out of the bathroom, his cock long and heavy with knowing what was coming. He put on *Suzanne* and lay out over the fox coverlet, making himself harder still by rubbing his organ into the soft fur. The sight of the broad back and hairless ass, rising and falling, thrusting and retreating, the first sighs, just audible, the way the ass formed deep dimples with each thrust, made me mad with lust. Watching him was in a way like watching myself, as we both were mirror images of the other, the same height, both well-built, hairless and handsome. Only in our coloration did we differ: Reiner blond and blue-eyed, me raven-black in hair and eyes. I shucked my corduroys and manipulated myself through the taught white briefs because that's what excited him. The more my organ distended the cotton, the more the tissue stretched forward and the first emission of what the French call dew seeped through, the more he wanted me to take him. While his eyes were fixed on me, I went to the dresser drawer where I took the lubricant I used to stroke myself to even a greater length. Then dropping my briefs, I took two fingers charged with the substance to the bed where I kneeled beside the cheeks and inserted the oil, my excitation redoubling with his moans as I penetrated him with my fingers. The only hair on Reiner's body was the fine line of dark down between the twin mounds that I parted, while my right hand guided my cock into the opening. I pressed my whole body into the boy who raised his head just enough so I could lean over and plunge my tongue into the waiting mouth. At the maximum of my dimensions, I pushed into him with my knees and with my feet anchored in the coverlet. I fucked while waiting for him to come first, which he at times did by forming a sheath with his hand, or, as he did now, by just rubbing himself against the fur. I awaited his cries before releasing my own seed in jet after jet of an orgasm so long I could visualize my boyhood friend Doug dropping his jeans and freeing himself from the briefs he pulled down just under his balls, his cock so taut it flapped against his stomach, already moist but too young to come, quivering over the nascent pubic bush, meager yet black and dense despite his age. The image of Doug, fisting himself, doubled my climax. When I finally withdrew Reiner turned his head to again drive his tongue into my mouth. I drank his breath, thinking that at present I was far, far from the caresses, so innocent in comparison, to my lovemaking with Philippe.

.

The next day I moved in with Anna, and that night I took over as *garderobe* boy at the Voila Poulla. The arrangements were hideous. During the day when Reiner was away filming commercials or rehearsing for an upcoming play, I paced my room with nothing to do. I could not concentrate to read, I lit one Lord off another, and always my ear was pitched for Reiner's call, which would mean a walk in the woods, or lunch, or perhaps an hour behind the closed jalousie. At night I sat in my cage accepting coats at precisely the hour that Reiner came in to take his place at the long table. I awaited my friend's arrival with spit and shine correction. Reiner stayed never more than a few minutes with me, either because the situation did not lend itself to conversation, or because he did not want to be seen by too many people taking with his lover, the cloakroom boy. After Reiner's passage into the main room I paced the aisle of coats. I paced so doggedly that Anna had to come out and ask me to make less noise. The worst was at 1:00 when Reiner went. He was usually too tired to wait until 2:00 when I would be free to spend the night with him. As 1:00 approached, I shed tears of rage at the remaining coats that kept us apart.

I became dependent on Ulf. He gave me pills that reduced the tension, helping me to act more normally. Then I took to drinking. Denton brought me tiny glasses of vodka throughout the evening. Everybody drank, none more than Anna, but I couldn't hold mine. On one occasion I had to be literally carried home. I let my appearance go to pot, and kept my room in such a mess that Reiner vowed to never step foot in Anna's again. I even began stealing. I gave out the same cloakroom ticket several times and pocketed the difference. It was a Volla Poulla custom, and Denton had shown me how to do it. But the director, as on to the ways of boys as Clark, came one night for a coat count and threatened to sack me if the theft continued, adding that I had only been hired to please Reiner.

The end finally came one evening when Reiner deigned to take me home with him. Anna had agreed to check out the last coats and so we took off at midnight. The following day Reiner had a TV series to record in Cologne. He would have to get up early for the plane. In his usual way he calculated every second, how much time to reach his apartment, how much time to get prepared for bed, how much to fuck, how much sleep, and the exact second he'd have to rise the next morning.

He put on *Suzanne* and in bed he removed the chain from around my neck, both signals that we would make love. But this time I could not react. Minutes and hours were flickering through my mind. Hurry, hurry. I felt Reiner's lips descend to my cock which refused to respond. In disgust he turned over. I tried to caress him to arousal, but he shrugged me off with a Save-it-for-Ulf retort.

At three in the morning I slipped out of bed and went back to Anna's. I had decided to earn my fare back to Paris. Yet even there, who would be waiting for me? I thought of Michael and his vision of the future. It was the most miserable, the lowest ebb my life had ever reached.

.

Yet through some miracle I pulled up my socks, as the Brits say. I found a job at a language school that paid twice what I had been earning in Paris. I got an apartment of my own. I bought some decent clothes. I took up going to the opera, to ballets and recitals. And more, I gave up Reiner. After explaining to Anna the reasons for my leaving, I packed up and moved out without leaving a forwarding address. In the space of two months I had given up every bad habit I had acquired. There were no more pills, no drugs; I was eating regularly and sleeping better; I didn't drink. Only smoking continued, although on a far lesser scale. Yet I could not forget the German boy who had been a moment of real life in a sea of mediocrity.

And so two months later when we ran into each other at a bus stop, my heart throbbed with the stampeding of a thousand horses. Our accidental meeting in the city of many millions was scarcely believable. The fact that Reiner's car had broken down, thus obliging him to use the city transit system, only reinforced the feeling of destiny inherent in the reunion. Reiner was immediately charming and conciliatory. He told me how he had scoured Berlin for a trace of me. He begged me to return. I refused. I was doing too well to go back to the nightmare of insecurity built on those humiliating phone calls beckoning me to his side like a court page. Reiner told me what he'd been doing. I told him about myself. He confessed that he had gone to a sauna looking for me and wound up seducing another boy. The information at first enraged me, but soon I found it reassuring. He was telling the whole truth, surely the proof of his having turned over a new leaf. We talked for two hours like that, in the middle of the sidewalk. Finally he begged again that we go to his apartment. He was young and handsome, and I wanted him, so once more we took up together.

CHAPTER TWENTY-THREE

The relationship continued from where we had left it, with hardly the loss of a stitch. I became as nervous as ever, Reiner as withdrawn, but this time I had work, money and my own place, conditions affording a semblance of stability. I suffered through the actor's black moods and fits of temper and, worse still, his absences. But there were moments of deep physical exchange, and it was then we called up the best in each other. It was the moments of intimacy which saved our union. Afterwards came the spells of brooding and unhappiness. I knew the first would never compensate for the rest. The only question was when it would all end. Two weeks later I found out.

Michael had told me about the industrialist who had sponsored Reiner while he was out of work, even opening a men's clothing store for him to run in Berlin. Suddenly Reiner got it into his head to visit the gentleman. The industrialist lived in Bokenheim, outside Cologne. Reiner would take me along; we would travel by car. Because the theater closed on Wednesday, we would leave Wednesday morning for Bokenheim and return to Berlin Thursday during the afternoon. Reiner had to get permission to leave the city from the theater authorities. Should he fail to get back for the Thursday evening performance, the theater would lose a great deal of money. His departure was okayed but he had to take out an airline ticket from Cologne to Berlin in case something happened to his car.

We left very early Wednesday morning and got to Bokenheim late in the afternoon. Reiner was a terribly irritable driver, cursing every motorist who overtook his sports car. We arrived worn out, my head splitting from the death-march pace and the ridiculous lengths I had gone to to humor him.

The industrialist welcomed us half-heartedly. He was a middle-aged corpulent man with gray hair and a frank and firm manner. I was introduced to his wife and Jean-Luc, his boyfriend. Jean-Luc was ill at ease, not for himself it seemed but for the older man who had to put up with the visit for old times' sake. The industrialist had evidently filled in Jean-Luc on the former relationship, as well as the pitfalls of life with the actor. Reiner conducted himself as on conquered territory. He treated Jean-Luc as the industrialist treated me: a momentary amusement to be momentarily endured. The industrialist's wife was self-effacing and totally dependent on her husband for her subsistence. She had presented him with two sons, both at boarding schools in Switzerland (11). The house was a huge modernistic affair of plants, piled carpets, stainless steel fixtures and bay windows. She showed us through it, the industrialist trailing miserably behind. We got to see the boys' rooms, and even Jean-Luc's. With such a dismal welcome, I could not fathom why Reiner had chosen to drive all that way to spend just one night, especially as the actor's attitude towards the industrialist had been atrocious since our arrival: See what you've lost?, he seemed to be saying. I'm now a star and you're stuck with a car salesman. The industrialist had indeed met Jean-Luc at a car showroom where he worked on the Champs-Elysées.

We were served drinks in the salon. Reiner sat in an armchair across the room from me. The industrialist sat with Jean-Luc. His wife emptied the ashtrays. The conversation centered around Reiner who was in perfect command of himself. He spoke about his work with fulsome, self-mocking verve, laughing at the ways of fate, unaware that no one but he himself was amused. I could only catch patches of what was being said, but a lot of the actor's monologue seemed to deal with do-you-remember-when reminiscences to which the industrialist grunted nervously.

At around six the conversation turned to what Jean-Luc was now doing in Bokenheim. Reiner commented that he had heard the industrialist had opened up another men's store just for the boy. Yes, the industrialist concurred, and he has his own car and his own apartment in town, a convenience, it was left unsaid, for when his sons were at home. Reiner suggested that they visit the store. Over the French boy's objections that it closed at 6, Reiner answered with a smirk in his voice that as Jean-Luc was the director, he certainly had the keys. We climbed into two cars and off we went. The shop was located in a giant mall. It was very chic, very French. Jean-Luc showed us around. Reiner liked this and that, he picked out jackets and trousers from the racks, laying them in piles over armchairs provided for the customers. We were there a long time while he tried on one item after another. I sat in a corner, exhausted. Sometime during the evening Reiner came to me and gave me a lapis lazuli fish to fasten to my necklace. It was an exquisite object that I greatly appreciated, even though Reiner threw it to me like a pirate flipping a doubloon to the ship's cabin boy from a chest already running over with treasure. Reiner turned to Jean-Luc and pointed out all the things he was taking. Jean-Luc huddled with the industrialist as Reiner waited for the bill.

When we left the shop Reiner was deathly white, but my spirits had risen, thanks to the gift. Jean-Luc returned to his own apartment.

At the house the climate was macabre. The industrialist went off somewhere leaving Reiner and his wife in conversation in the hallway, in hearing distance of me, left to myself in the salon. Like two traumatized Andromaches, consoling themselves over the excesses of the Hector they shared, Reiner and the woman jointly lamented the insecurities and abuse that united them.

Finally we all came back into the salon and sat facing each other, nearly wordless. Reiner stared across at me with absolute loathing in his eyes. Drinks were offered but there was no food, and no talk about where we would be put up. At eleven, Reiner suddenly rose and said he was leaving. The industrialist and his wife rose too to see him out. I got up, at a loss at what was in store for me. Reiner came over and said he was taking me back to Berlin because he didn't leave garbage in front of other people's doors, and because he needed someone to keep him awake on the autobahn.

When Reiner seemed more calmed, I asked him Why? Why was he angry? Why was he taking everything out on me? I asked him how he could offer a gift one moment and treat me as garbage the next. Reiner paid no attention to me but began to rant about the industrialist and his lover. Half was in German, half in English, but the import became evident. Reiner was beside himself because he had been made to pay for the clothes he had chosen. They had given him 10%. He had gone to Bokenheim for clothes he had expected to get for free. I counted for nothing in his anger. I had been a convenient target because Reiner had not dared confront the industrialist with his own hypocrisy. I kept repeating, You came all this way to sponge off your friend, and you turned on me because he didn't come through?

In my heart the feeling of bewilderment changed to one of hate. I hated this boy whom I felt did not deserve to live.

.

It was 8:00 p.m. in the dark apartment on Trabener Strasse. The telephone was ringing. It rang insistently for thirty seconds, then stopped, then rang again, and again stopped, the repetition continuing into the lengthening night. Moonlight entered the room through the slats of the jalousie lowered over the bay window. The light filtered through curtains stolid like sentinels, and was caught in the uneven folds of the thick rug that extended to the dimly lit bed in the opposite niche, its sheets rising over an inert mass. The phone rang on, but so intense was the room's silence that its cry was muffled by the grained walls, voluminous sofa, pillows and deaf ears of the entwined bodies under the cold, crinkled sheets and dense, cold air that accumulated above them.

At the door at the end of the entranceway the theater owner began knocking. He was impatient, yet there were brief silences of control. The telephone continued to ring. The knocking gained. Someone had gone around to the jalousie and was scratching to find a grasp. Their fear of the silence within drove them to a frenzy of tugging and kicking. But the silence remained unbroken and its persistence muted those who would force it. They stopped.

A key scratched at the iron lock. A stark yellow streak of light moved across the floor and up the curtain. The room gasped a breath. In comic slowness men entered, their heads bent in apology for their presence. The room was intact. The intruders marveled at the geometry and balance and fine taste of the young king it housed. They were perhaps surprised that the young king himself was still there, realizing the rarity of unopened tombs, but their surprise was less, for the moment, that he was lying not alone.

They hurried to him, but they knew by the too cold air and beautiful stillness that the young king as no more.

.

"*Hey*!" Reiner punched me in the arm. "I took you along to keep me awake."

The German's eyes were nearly swollen shut with sleep. He looked out at the road through tiny slits. His face was very pale, very set. Sometimes his eyes closed completely and I would shake him. They opened slowly, the car never straying from its onward course, and I wondered if even now I was being tested. Outside, the night was black, the headlights picking up occasional patches of fog, some of which startled me by their sudden appearance. There was no conversation. We were dead even to thought. Glimpses of film played through my brain: The small plane that would take me from the oasis that was Berlin; the flight across tiny pastures, lakes and pine-covered mountains. I saw Reiner in the sauna where the inevitable fetishism had drawn him. I saw him slamming his cock into the lips of a kneeling boy he held violently by the hair. This is for Mother, he cried, pummeling the crystalline mouth, this is for poor Reiner, for lonely Reiner, for lost Reiner. This is for those who wanted to bridle me, for the kids who had more than me, the teacher who caught me stealing, the coach who said I couldn't act, the industrialist, the producer, the whole fucking theater; those who didn't trust me, believe in me, listen to me; those awaiting the telltale smudges under the eyes, the first wrinkles, the thinning of the hair; those who have never used more than my face and my ass; those who want me to fail, to be one of them ....

I too had joined them, the others Reiner had tricked and loved and cast aside. Only, I would be the last; it was I who would deliver the annihilating blow. I saw Reiner returning to the apartment, silent, closed off, lowering the jalousie that entombed us. I saw him lay out his clothes over the armchair, daring me with his eyes to touch him, to kneel at his crotch and encompass the cock with my mouth through the white briefs. I saw him set the clock and roll over to the wall, leaving the place he deigned to be mine. I too undressed. From the kitchen I took the sharp-edged steak knife. I turned out the light and placed myself under the sheets along Reiner's back. One final kiss, I whispered in the actor's ear, please, Reiner, please, don't leave me like this, please my dearest, one last kiss, please Reiner, please ... please. Enraged, the actor turned to me. I placed the knife against the sternum and plunged it up and under and up. Reiner rolled to the wall and then back to me. Under the sternum and then up. He rolled back to the wall, and then back to me. Under and up. The blood coursed out wondrously warm. We rolled together again and again. The heat was marvelous.

.

I awoke to the constant turning. There was no panic. Not for an instant did I realize what had happened. I was on the ground, outside, draped over something, perhaps a stone, which pierced me in the back. The car blazed nearby. I thought I was in the mountains with the Scouts. The boys had gone for twigs to feed the blaze. But why was I lying there? Why wasn't I helping? I blacked out.

Reiner was bent over me. His hand was toying with the fine gold necklace and crucifix Philippe had sent from Brest. The feeling of it during sex irritated him. He jerked it away and tossed it into the folds of the carpet.

When I came to again moments later, still alone, I knew where I was, and from the hissing and monotonous moan of the flames, I knew too that Reiner Rolf was indeed no more.

.

I was hospitalized for three months before flying out of the city-island for a new life in Paris. Letters to Léa had gone unanswered; requests for money from home were met with equal silence. Father had definitively abandoned Son but, as I admitted, only after the realization that his boy had turned his back on him years before. There was no doubt in my mind of my mother's love, yet she could do nothing more for me that would jeopardize the truce the passing of time had brought between her and her husband.

Fortunately, my gift for putting money aside bought me the time to get a teaching job, during a period in France known as the Glorious Thirties, thirty years of full post-war employment. I took an apartment that faced the park surrounding the Sacré Coeur, and enjoyed trips to Greece during the many months of paid vacation afforded to teachers.

I tried to banish my past with Philippe and Reiner to an obscure region of my brain, where I had relegated the equally obscure events of my youth, an obscurity befitting of Laurent.

CHAPTER TWENTY-FOUR

Laurent

The convent-like rez-de-chaussée on Avenue Clichy he shared with his mother was a meander of lightless corridors with dark heavily curtained rooms, worn sofas, display cases of bric-à-brac from desultory voyages, the whole patrolled by a naked cat who had lost her fur through illness.

I had seen his mother only once, blocking the traffic at Clichy while dislodging long mantis legs from the back seat of the taxis in front of her porte-cochère. A casque of long well-called-for blond hair enveloped the fine nose and strong chin of a face sun and disappointment had melted into the flaccid, sagging remains of a used candle. Yet Laurent's resemblance to her was nonetheless remarkable. He had the same high forehead, the same strong chin and nose. His great height and ramrod posture had a stateliness that in her had soured. Only in their hair, his black and curly, did they differ.

Laurent and I had scurried into the Hollywood Café. Laurent had said we needn't run from her, but both of us wished to avoid a meeting. I knew she had a habit of giving her blessing to those of Laurent's friends Laurent came to ultimately dislike the most. Between Mother and Son a morbid symbiosis had evolved over the years that permitted any unfaithfulness short of outright rupture, that admitted even sexual deviation. I was to learn much about Laurent's mother, and the battlefield they maneuvered across at Avenue Clichy.

Laurent's father had fled that battlefield at Laurent's birth. His mother farmed Laurent out to country relatives, hayseeds who shared their silent, abject meals with an unwanted mouth, alternatively ignoring him, mistreating him, prodding him, with less attention they paid the family dog, which at least earned its keep. The baby found he could gain grudging notice by pushing his food bowl to the floor or causing his highchair to waver back and forth until he and it went hurling over; even acts of self-inflicted punishment drew attention: biting his hands, wrists and arms, ranting, holding his breath until he turned plum purple.

I had seen a result of Laurent's immolation at Clichy. In the Spartan room she had ceded him, the armoire, desk and narrow bed frame were covered with knife slashes, varnished over and invisible now to all but touch, or when viewed from the side in the gold light of his desk lamp. Then they appeared as a kind of cuneiform, recondite and indecipherable.

The first time I noticed them I was sitting at the desk while Laurent lay on his bed stroking Smoky. "*Oui ma fille*," he said, tickling her naked thighs, *"Oui ma puce, t'es une belle fille."* In all the world only they were oblivious of her monstrous ugliness. She danced the dance of the seven veils under his raised fingers, writhing to the grave masculine monologue like a cobra to a flute. Time and again she lured Laurent down the black corridor past the room where Mother and Son dined while listening to the 8 o'clock news, before moving on to Mother's bed to spend the remainder of the evening in front of the flickering blue TV. If his mother entertained while Laurent was out, she fastened the main door with the burglar chain. He had to keep coming back until the door was unlocked, sometimes not until dawn. In the kitchen Smoky begged for food Laurent spooned into a dish already full, and from which I never saw her eat.

.

In Myconos Laurent explained the knife cuts. It was a late afternoon on Jacomi's porch, pale blue with a tint of dusk that would thicken until drawn across the horizon like a curtain of navy velvet, sweeping away the sea and the distant island of Naxos. We sat about the table on which our plates were piled with small fish Laurent had cleaned and I had fried, and French fries mixed with onions and tomatoes.

Laurent opened up when satiated with sun, fishing and food; abundance made him generous. Talking prolonged the evening, as did draughts of restina, tinkering with the oil and vinegar, a Gauloise. Fresh and warm from the shower, dressed in identical navy-blue turtlenecks and jeans, tired, content, thinking of bed, it was a part of the day neither of us wished to end.

Laurent knew the story would please me. He never took my side against her, but he exploited the enmity. "We had moved into Clichy," he began, breaking off the filter of the Gauloise provided by the army. "All day long Mother had been hysterical about her crystal glassware and lacquered tortoise, and the figurines she keeps in her show cases. After making the movers sweat their pourboire she freed them. I asked for a reprieve too to go for a beer. But Madame had a visitor, a woman colleague she wished…" Laurent searched for the words I provided: "…she wanted to show her balls to." "Permission was declined," he picked up, "and I was sent to my room to put it in order. The balance tipped. I went more or less nuts. Mother said moments later she heard things being broken and me moaning. When she opened the door she found me on the bed, my knees drawn up to my chin, my teeth sunk into the palm of my hand, the letter opener I'd used on the furniture on the floor."

During the days on the farm, Laurent took care of the farmer's animals, especially the baby calves, rabbits, chicks and puppies. He passed hours fishing from riverbanks into dark pools of stagnant green scum. On Myconos he would stand from morning till night on a polished stone a few yards from the seashore, and there in the hot sun, his fishing pole resting in his right hand against his thigh, he would stare into the swirling eddies as if hypnotized.

Bit by bit the bare threads of a fragile kind of stability began to form themselves into a safety net. By force of habit and routine he adjusted to the farm surroundings, and the people in them adjusted to him. His shy beauty won over the girls, and although the boys taunted him his reluctance to join in their more violent games, they were kept in abeyance by farm chores and their own pastimes. Besides, the encompassing plains and hills were immense, ideal for escape. Had he been lucky it was there he would have remained, one of the minority of youths in France to stay on the farm and, because rural life was considered especially hard for women, he would even have been dispensed of the social obligation of taking a wife.

But like the witch of the fairy tale, his mother, the aging mantis, sprouted wings and swooped down to uproot him from the semblance of balance he had been able to eke out.

In Paris he was moved from school to school as she worked their way up the social ladder. Laurent was quiet, secretive and alone. At home his occupations centered around his room and the cages of pets his mother was forced to put up with. On winter vacations they shared the same ski instructor, he on the slope, she when he had dropped off to sleep. "Once," he told me, "she was coming in from off the mountain with the monitor. I was waiting outside our hotel, just a few yards away." I could see him bundled up like a penguin, stiff and erect. "I took a step or two towards her, just when the cornice from the hotel broke off and fell exactly where I'd been standing." There was a kind of awe in his voice, as though he had the presentment about his luck, that it would see him through anything, even her, and, in due course, even me.

At puberty Laurent's personal isolation became more heightened still with the full awareness of the bent of his sexuality. Fearing to speak of it at home, and knowing only too well his peer's opinion on the subject, he found himself increasingly cut off. He became more introspective, acquiring an inner knowledge so keen that it deprived him of spontaneity; his egotism developed; he stole from the world the crumbs the world held back. He became infinitely more partial, self-centered and unforgiving than the bullies who occasionally preyed on him.

He led two lives, one inner and exclusively his own, the other outward and artificial, built upon the values his mother and others thrust on him. But of the two beings, the internal truth and the outer lie, it was the secret child within his breast who ruled. If no one else could be counted on, if family, friends and parent were all found lacking, at least he had himself.

Later, when I was accused of initiating the events leading to the tragedy, I knew that it was not I who had wished Laurent dead. Laurent was awaiting the death that only he himself could bestow. He wished for the sleep of uninterrupted dreams, for the pool of waters so black that none but his image showed through. Like an only star, he wished to be alone in a lonely universe. He wished the implosion that would turn that star into itself, the cataclysm that would sweep the water from out the pool like a film in reverse, leavings in its place nothing.

Laurent was often despondent, often indifferent, because he knew the truth: never would he find another whose beauty would ignite in him the spark of life he himself fired in others. And later, were he to have lived and lost his beauty, what consolation would he have found living with a mother whose only occupation was the quest for the Fountain of Youth, a hag rummaging through life like a scavenger through a refuse dump in search of the scraps that would prolong the little attractiveness she had left. What consolation would he have found when youths no longer said, as he passed by, that phrase from Musset: *Voici une belle nuit qui passe*?

Just weeks before the end I had lain with him on the rug in my bedroom, my head resting on his naked chest, listening to his heart. Laurent's father had died at thirty from cardiac arrest. "I know I haven't long," Laurent said, speaking perhaps of the genetic defect or perhaps of the few years he believed his beauty would last. He smiled, then laughed as he felt my tears. I knew, in effect, that he hadn't long.

We had met in May, a precociously sunny May not unlike summer except for the summer's starker light which turned Paris into an Aegean resort. Along the quay St. Michel bare-chested boys lay against the cut-stone embankment, their faces turned upwards to the sun, a slight smile playing on their lips, the heads of their girls cradled in their laps. Laurent was finishing military service then and wore the dark-blue blouson, beret and wool trousers of an airman. I had come up to the Hollywood Café to get him and we had strolled down to the Trinité. We sat on the iron chairs in the park in front of the church, our feet propped up on a bench. The park was fresh and already jade-green leaves--so sun-soaked and so translucent that their emerald veins stood out like the blood-engorged hands of the old--burst over the ancient oaks in the midst of the unseasonable warmth. Laurent drew out the moment by extracting a Gauloise, then slowly lighting it while turning it in his fingers like a cigar.

"I've got one piece of good news," he said, "and one piece of bad." With Laurent there could never be uncut good; every act was sundered by a prism, unvarnished, disparate, accepted in its entity or deflected away, with the loss of Laurent himself.

"Let's go for the good first." It I could read on his face, but an interval was handy to shore up the dike before receiving the bad.

"The good first. Well, I've got the two-week perm for Myconos, at the end of August."

Laurent in the jet, in the little white plaster house; Laurent with Jacomi, Franchesca and Maria; Laurent in the rocks at Super Paradise; fourteen nights in the same bed with Laurent.

"*Mon cheri*..." I stammered. Words of desire and a longing as mournful as the last wave on the last shore of a world gone dead. "You'll need a speargun, *mon Amour*, and a knapsack and a rubber boat..." and, I knew, all the luck extractable from a luck-impoverished universe. "And the bad?"

"I told you I had a rendezvous with the doctor...." The gay one, who always insisted, to Laurent's amusement, that he strip naked. "He says I've got a heart murmur, confirming what I told you about my dad."

That, I knew with relief, would be God's worry. For the moment we switched to departure dates. Laurent proud of his permission. Proud of our plans. I watching Laurent; making mental notes; thinking that the boy had to go home to Clichy soon, and wanting to send him back happy.

''And Mother?"

''She's going to Indonesia with a girlfriend." He seemed proud of her, too, that cave-dwelling Circe who bartered my mortal lover for a cruise with blue-haired matrons. "She'll be away lots making plans, so I'll be able to come by more often," meaning afternoons of sex with Laurent, sex that was the weathervane of our relationship. At the end of long days spent at one of the suburban swimming pools we would go into the changing room, both of us in the same obscurely lit cabin, and undress. The building's coolness after the sun's heat, the unique smell of the lockers, the nudity of the boys content with their virility, all served as an excitant. I would invariably strip off my trunks first, then Laurent, his back to me. At that moment the air was so thick with the accumulation of the day's want that my head literally swirled. I would stretch out my hand and gently touch Laurent's white buttocks. Laurent would turn towards me, his member already rising, an expression of hesitation on his face-- almost of duty--and the fleeting, guarded avowal of the pleasure he did nothing to initiate.

In French the act of love is called the "little death." It was like that for Laurent. He became quiet, more locked up in his own thoughts afterwards. The interests we had shared just minutes before came to an end. Laurent retreated from the world we had ruled in common, to the other Laurent knew so well--his own solitude. For me it was the opposite. Like a man starved, I could not free my mind until my body was freed first. Then I became more open, less dependent on Laurent's moods, far happier, far nearer my real self. For me it was *la petite vie*, the flame that ignited life.

From the Trinité we walked to Paris Plage, a quay of the Seine near the Tuileries. There, sporting g-strings, golden bracelets and necklaces, skeletal bodies stretched out in the sun, so different from the heteros at St. Michel. Despite the horror of Paris Plage, there was always the premonition that the couple we formed would not last, that someday we too would be searching partners there among the nearly dead. We walked through the alleys of Montmartre, Laurent in the cut-offs he favored, down to Place Pigalle. "*Eh, t'as de belles cannes!*"--you got swell legs--the whores shouted to Laurent who grinned. "*N'est-ce pas?*" he answered. Past the tourist coaches, the Live Shows, the acrid smell of bars--not unlike the smell of those I had known when my mother had gone looking for my father--to Avenue Clichy and home.

Greece had followed, and the first morning at Jacomi's. I was up at five to prepare Laurent's breakfast. At six I went into our room where I set a bowl of coffee on the edge of the bed. I blew the fumes towards Laurent's bushy head lost in the folds of the pillows. The boy's brow and nose were humid, each curl of hair fell over his forehead as if fingers had placed it there, and each eyelash stood out from the others, separate, long, thick and black. His cheeks had a ruddy hue, soft and sheet-lined. I waited for his nostrils to flare open like a young stallion's. Then I left him alone. I returned to the kitchen with the coffee I put on a back burner. Five minutes later Laurent came out.

Naked, his sex slightly distended from the warm bed, Laurent seated himself on the straw chair in front of the table and dropped his chin to his chest. His brow was knitted and his nose pinched, giving him the likeness of a Cocteau ephebe.

I placed the coffee in front of him and pushed the biscuits, jam and butter in reach. Laurent made a clumsy *tartine*, thrust it into the scalding coffee and chewed, his chin still on his chest, a total economy of movement.

Half an hour later, on the trail that descended to the beach of Super Paradise, both of us were singing. Nothing could have warned us of the turning that day would take, a day which had its origin a year after the death of Reiner, and began on an evening when I left my Paris flat in search of a newspaper.

CHAPTER TWENTY-FIVE

Literally at the door to my apartment building I had stumbled on Ivan, a Chilean model and neighbor out walking his basset hound Gigolo. We struck up a conversation. Ivan was three days unshaven and feverish from a bout with the flue. He went up to bed after inviting me for coffee the following day. Thus began a friendship in which Ivan sought company through his illness, and I the words which would eventually seduce him.

I learned that Ivan was in love with a certain Floyd, an American my age, a rent boy who summered in Nice. Floyd's main hangout was a grange-like bar, La Villette. It became mine too. My plan was to discover what influence Floyd had over Ivan, and then use the knowledge to win him over, a scenario of such naivety that it was proof to what extent love can blind he who's smitten by Eros' arrows. Night after night I took the same table, ordered the same beer, and soon became a habitué. From my usual corner in the black rotund sale I stared across the vast empty dance floor to the dimly lit *East of Eden* poster of James Dean. Floyd usually came on Thursdays and Saturdays or Sundays. His body, ramrod straight, moved easily through the groups on the floor's periphery. The darkness of his clothes made him hard to follow as he wove his way from acquaintance to acquaintance, halting briefly to exchange a word or a nod. Occasionally he played the pinball machine, but it was evident he did not care for the momentary notoriety of its dim blinking lights. He was a creature of the shadows, I supposed, who let his game come to him. Floyd's routine was as immutable as my own: a quick turn around the room, a beer, a few short exchanges of conversation, a quick trip upstairs, and then he was gone. I guessed at the curly hair and broad shoulders, I felt more than heard his heavy boots, and at times I caught the glint and faint tinkle of a ring of keys he wore at his side (12).

"How can one live with a prostitute?" I would ask Ivan, meaning how could Ivan prefer a gigolo to me. Ivan just smiled. To know Floyd, Ivan's silence suggested, was to know Ivan. Covering the walls of Ivan's room were pictures of the models Ivan posed with, handsome guys Ivan had had, boys, said Ivan, a poor second to Floyd. The boys in the pictures were youths with but a hint of down descending the navel, hairless nipples on squared-off chests, firm skin, faded jeans, a lazy, proud, amused, knowing glint in their eyes--the kind of fresh-meat that queers would kill mother and father to possess, Laurent had once said, referring to the old men looking for male trade at Place Blanche.

It was when Ivan took up with a Marine who had been lent by the Ministry to form an honor guard at one of Ivan's fashion shows that I decided to meet Floyd. I could understand Ivan's sexual interest in the Marine, a straight kid with a big wang who fucked him in the men's room minutes after Ivan had nodded his willingness, and a second time during the cocktail party after the show, to the amused grins of the Marine buddies he had confided in. The gain for the Marine was twofold: on the one hand he entered the world of showbiz, a promotion for a guy from Tarbes in the Hautes Pyrénées, and on the other hand Ivan promised him girl models by the basketful, as the French say. No, there was nothing mysterious about the Marine, but Floyd's attraction needed elucidation.

At the end of the month I followed Floyd upstairs for the first time. There were a number of corridors, dark, and a number of rooms, nearly black. One of them, the largest, had a faint red light overhead that made the occupants of the room visible only to eyes grown accustomed. The room was narrow and long. Floyd stepped just inside the door and leaned against the wall. I entered and took up a position against the wall facing him. Floyd was wearing his usual apparel, a blue shirt and levis with a wide leather belt. I had what the French call a *débardeur*--a sleeveless undershirt, navy blue--and beltless jeans.

At the end of the room a blond boy was half-sitting, half-standing against a table, his buttocks pressed into its edge. In euphoric abandon he was kissing a dark-haired kid bent over him while two others were busy unbuttoning the two boys' shirts and lowering their trousers.

Someone standing next to Floyd let his hand skirt his thigh. When he met no resistance, he turned to embrace Floyd who jerked his head away. The guy didn't insist. He dropped to his knees, opened Floyd's fly and covered him. To give one's prick was nothing; to give one's lips was a form of involvement. Floyd showed no expression. He stared straight ahead, at me. I hoped for someone to sink to his knees in front of me too, and, sure enough, a boy came in--a better-looking boy by far than the one between Floyd's legs--and planted a hand over my crotch. I gave Floyd a long theatrical look and walked out of the room.

The next night I returned to La Villette. Floyd came at his usual time. I followed him upstairs again, and again we faced each other across a space hardly more than a stride in width. Floyd shunned the groping hands around him. I did the same. After a few minutes I left the room but halted at the top of the stairway. Floyd came out nearly immediately. He came towards me with unseeing eyes, turned to descend, but then stopped and, on the spur-of-the-moment, faced me and smiled.

Without realizing it, this was the third blow to the anvil in Mahler's *Sixth*, as foreseen years before in a Minister's home of concrete blocks. The first, Philippe, weakened the hero, the second, Reiner, announced his ruin, and the third, Laurent, annihilated him.

I made a sign with my head for us to go down for a beer. In a corner of the dark room we stood talking. My month-old mistake became clear after a half-dozen words. This boy was French, not American, and despite a maturity in excess of his years, he was hardly even twenty. There had been no succession of summers in Nice for him.

In the street we walked together towards Avenue Clichy for the first time. The air was warm and fresh, the lampposts blazed as through polished glass. I caught a look at his profile. I couldn't believe my eyes. I felt the hair at the nap of my neck bristle, then a feeling of immense relief. This boy was too handsome. Never would he allow me into his bed. The relief came with the realization that we could spend an evening in talk before I took my leave with dignity. I thought of the Greeks; if he could not be lover he would at least serve as companion. It was the role I had desired with Uncle Bob and Mark, it was the role... Suddenly, as we made our way down Clichy, another memory, buried until that very moment, opened before my eyes like a long-lost tomb.

.

During my last year in high school I had met up with a loner called Eric, a boy I had seen stalking the campus all winter dressed in a heavy faded-green overcoat which had impressed me because it was European and had been worn in the German Wehrmacht. Eric slumped in chairs and never had his head out of a paperback; he was dark of complexion, handsome, distant and saturnine. I could not remember what turn of fate brought us together, but that first spring after graduation we decided to go to the Grand Canyon in Eric's car.

We set off via Vegas, at the time a dusty oasis begging for tourists. As with Mark, Eric's intelligence was so sharp it seemed as tangible as an object. Years of a steady diet on science fiction books had set him free from earth, and his smugness about being born a bastard made respect for convention irrelevant.

We drove up to the curb of one of the flamboyant casino fronts with bulb-lit marquee, nothing like the fountains and nude statues that would be there a few years hence. Still underage, I stopped respectfully at the entrance. Eric, as young, sailed past the guard's nose and went into the bar. A few moments later he sauntered back, another guard at his side. How old are you Sonny? the guard asked me. So hypnotized was I by Eric's smug grin that I didn't hear the question. ''Did you really do it?'' I asked. ''Sure,'' came Eric's answer. ''I don't believe you,'' I said. ''Smell,'' shrugged Eric, leaning forward, opening his mouth wide and drowning me in exhaust. His breath wasn't laced with vomit like my father's, but there was definitely something on it. ''Christ,'' I blurted out.

The next day found us at the bottom of the Grand Canyon. It had taken hours to hike down, and now we were at the edge of the Colorado, a swift river of beige mud. The shore had beach-fine sand, white, and for all we knew we were the only inhabitants left on earth. The Canyon walls rose in red and yellow layers so far above us that only a narrow strip of sky was visible, but the sun had risen to the axis of the strip, showering us in golden light and warmth.

"This isn't a place to be dressed," shouted Eric, and he stripped. I sat on the beach and watched. There was something in the way he had said that, something in the purposeful, deliberate way he dropped his clothes that hinted at a sad, fatal kind of courtship. The overwhelming beauty of the boy's nudity produced in me a feeling of abject lethargy, a reaction that was to occur again and again throughout all my life when confronted by a situation that I was incapable of controlling. I simply didn't have the experience and the maturity to cope with Eric like that. My desire was too strong, it robbed me of all will. I wished only to lay my head on the sand, to sleep and never again awaken.

My lethargy loosened Eric's inhibitions. He went waist deep into the water, but finding it too cold, he romped around the rocks beyond the beach in search of firewood. I joined in half-heartedly. At one point he threw me a stick and insisted we were two sword-wielding musketeers. Only when the sun was dead, and the cold air from the river forced us to dress in sweaters and parkas, did I return to normal. Around the fire Eric talked about a girlfriend. "I'll be your best man if you marry," I said. "That's how I imagine you," answered Eric, "always second best, always doing something for others; you're the rays of the sun, but you'll never be a sun."

That hurt.

But a second later when Eric apologized, the hurt formed a scar. Yet it was true: I would always be the rays to someone else's sun.

.

That was how I accepted things that night as Laurent and I walked to Laurent's apartment with its heavy scent of femme and poor naked Smoky. Laurent opened a bottle of whisky, his mother's, and we drank it together. Just before dawn Laurent asked if we hadn't better turn in.

I knew it. I swear before God that I knew it: Laurent would be the last. Seated on the chair at Laurent's desk I knew it. Watching him undress, I knew it. There would not be another. He would be the last. And that's the way it turned out to be.

Neither of us was laughing now. Could some momentary premonition have told Laurent that this rite would be his last too? He reached up and pulled me to him. There was the heat of our young bodies that would never know old age. We came willingly into one another's arms, drawn only by the maleness that was ours to share. Each of Laurent's movements, even the most imperceptible, told me of his needs. I could do for him that which he could not do for himself. I brought him to heights that only other hands, only another mouth, could help him attain. We were one in the most complete sense, because we were the same. In an hour I would leave, and Laurent would let me go. We would surely be wise enough never to attempt to recreate this. And yet, even before the end, I was thinking: if only there could be once more, just once more.

At dawn I slipped away and made for home. Garbage trucks groaned up the steep streets to Place Clichy. Blacks and Arabs headed for their slots at Renault or the abattoirs. The air in Pigalle was cool and clean. Behind closed shutters the city's whores lay entwined with young tourists who the evening before had bought smelly leather Stetsons from sidewalk Congolese. Few of the soldiers I crossed walked as proudly and cockily as I. Their faces were deathly pale, their acne abnormally red in the morning blue. They raced back to their barracks blurry-eyed, focusing on one slab of pavement at a time. After being one with Laurent, I was one with the world. I even felt a pang of affection for the middle-aged fruit waddling in front of him, the backs of her high heels cut out to make way for the feet, her hairpiece askew, a morning shadow on the chin and upper lip.

I didn't feel like going back to bed when I returned home. At eleven I was at the sink washing a stack of dishes and listening to Mahler. On one of those impulses that defy reason I put down the sponge and stared through the kitchen window. Grass and trees covered the slopes that rose to the Sacré Coeur. In the center of a patch of green, where a bit of the zigzagging trail could be seen, I glimpsed a splattering of blue. I opened the door-window and stepped onto the balcony. The blue came languorously into the sunlight. My heart tore at my chest. I opened out my arms. Laurent made his way down the slope, a child's playful smile on his face.

I had time to give my hair and teeth a brushing before I heard him at the door, a light I'm-expected scratching. He came in wearing the same smile, a satyr with reason to be pleased with himself. I moved into arms built for the protective role that would nevertheless be mine.

I prepared a late breakfast, then Laurent moved on to the balcony chaise longue while I finished the dishes. From the kitchen window he could see the back of his curly hair. He drew out a pack of army-issue Gauloise from his shirt pocket. Carefully he surveyed both ends of the cigarette before ripping off the filter the Health Minister ordered be furnished with the cigarettes--the parade grounds of Les Invalides were strewn with them. He leaned back his head and settled in to his smoking.

Later I moved into the cool shadows of the drapes. Laurent wore his satyr smile as he rose and came to me. Our second.

In the afternoon we went to Deligny, a swimming pool afloat in the Seine across from Paris Plage. The pool was surrounded by cabins available only to those who offered big tips. Inexplicably Laurent and I were shown to one. When he was naked I touched him tentatively from behind. The reaction was instantaneous. I sank to my knees. Our third.

At five we left Deligny and crossed over the Solforino bridge to the Tuileries. It was shirtsleeve weather, a miracle for so early in spring. In the Tuileries we sat at a table over beers. After-work crowds raced along the tree-shaded paths. The air was cool and our skin pleasantly warm. The beer went directly to our heads, making us laugh. Laurent was trying to shake off the thought of his mother whose plane had returned from an African holiday. I was very tired and very happy. My only thought was when we would meet again.

I walked him back to Clichy. In front of the street entrance he leaned over and kissed me. "Now they all know," he smiled, and disappeared through the porte-cochère. I returned home through those crisp, breezy streets, streets the coming summer would fill with harsh white light, heat, dust and the racket of the 8 o'clock news. I cried tears of joy. I knew it was too good to be true. I knew too I would not survive the future which precluded the continuation of our two lives as one.

CHAPTER TWENTY-SIX

The next day I went to Les Invalides--the army and air force H.Q. situated in the building housing Napoleon's tomb--to meet Laurent when he came off duty. I sat on the low wall bordering the moat, smoking the mopping my forehead. I had passed by the Grands Magazins and had rushed to escape the worst of fates: missing him, making him wait, putting his devotion to a test. Laurent came through a side entrance down the street at precisely six with a large group of people who surged forward like racers released by the shot from a starting gun. I would have recognized him at any distance, even had his bronzed face and curly black hair been obscured. His gate was both languorous and airy, like a yearling fighting back the vestiges of adolescent élan in deference to decorum. He smiled when he saw me, a sheepish, cocky grin, full of himself, yet timid, a smile that tore my heart with the wonder of its beauty. Laurent was in civilian dress. I met him every day and every day he wore the same brown trousers, brown-checked suit jacket and brown tie. I seemed the only person who saw through his drab clothes into the extraordinary and handsome lover I had discovered.

We went to a nearby café. I placed a beautifully wrapped package in the center of the table that we both studiously ignored. A surly waiter came and I gave a surly Reiner-like command. Over coffee Laurent told me about the people he worked for, the woman who tried to out-balls him, a guardian who made him wear his jacket in the corridors, a new recruit-- so pretty Laurent blushed recounting him--who spent the day staring at Laurent from across their abutting desks. "He's a daydreamer," Laurent said, "but it's troubling." "Would you ... if..." I halted. "Why not? I mean, what would that change...?" Laurent's essays at truth cost him dearly in the countenance he lost when trying not to hurt me. His forehead buckled, his chin fell and he became tongue-tied. But he would not lie. In all the months we were together he never once implied he loved me. Here, on the third day of our meeting, I was already asking for accounts, making him justify himself.

We got up to go. Only outside did Laurent break down. "You left a package behind, didn't you?" "No, it's not mine... So it must be yours." Laurent went back to retrieve it. Again we crossed the Seine and the Tuileries, the Grands Boulevards, the Trinité and Avenue Clichy. We kissed and once more Laurent sauntered into his apartment building. On my way back to Montmartre I pictured him opening his package and finding the superb portable shaver, black, sleek and masculine. Already I dreamed of Myconos, of Jacomy's little white house on the plateau overlooking the island-strewn sea. The phone was ringing when I got to my door. It was Laurent. He had been touched by the gift, the beauty of the object, and puzzled by something of such importance so early in our relationship.

I hung up, incredulous in my love for the boy, swelling with pride at the emotion I had invoked from my handsome lover. For it was this the highest goal: to awaken Passion, from which all that is good and inspirational draws its source.

Day after day when Laurent was off duty we went swimming. Night after night when Laurent worked late I would meet him at Les Invalides. We wandered home through the warm streets of Paris, hands touching, briefly entwining; we used apartment entrances as lovers' coves; the pent-up sexuality of the day drove us to a fury of touch, lips and ardor quivering on the edge of release. I drank from Laurent's mouth the very breath of his life--like Bacchus I could not drink my fill of the essence of Laurent's beauty.

Often--after mornings in the alcove beyond my balcony, or afternoons when the heat of the canicular spring found vent in the cool shadows of locker rooms, or evenings when Laurent's mother was out and I gained access to his boyhood bed--I would return home satiated, my mind at long-last clear, my eyes weighted with fulfillment. Then I would think myself finally free of the boy.

Yet in my bed night-stalking Eros would awaken images of the day: Lying side by side in the grass of a newly discovered pool, my hand lost in the hollow of Laurent's swimming suit, my thumb gently plying over the viscous tip of the obscenely protruding shaft, the look of bliss on the boy's face as he rode the incredible waves which would fill my palm with the source of his virility, while about us a dozen people dozed under Helios. The locker room when he dropped his swimsuit; the fleeting caress that sent a shivering-ripple up the small of his back; the instant lengthening, thickening and uplifting; our locked naked bodies, my nipples hardening, taking their pleasure against his chest. The moment of Laurent's cry, muted into the grass, smothered beneath my hand from the ears of other boys in the locker room, free and sharp in the sealed confines of Laurent's room. Then again, alone in my own bed, I would have to yet again bring myself release, while gleeful Eros sat smiling.

Mornings Laurent came for breakfast. Over toast and coffee we spread out maps and planned a trip to Yport on the west coast of France where we had decided to spend Pentecost. Neither said it, but we knew that on the outcome of this first adventure would depend the future of our journey to Myconos. Laurent borrowed guides from his mother describing the most scenic locations. He got a laissez-passer out of Paris from the military. To give us a head start on Parisians who would also take advantage of the long weekend holiday, I arranged for a friend to call me in ill at the school where I taught. Since Laurent lived near the *gare* St. Lazare his job was to put together train times and bus schedules; I was to arrange food parcels, games and music.

Laurent's enthusiasm showed through his usual placidity. In the back of his mind he awaited the falling tile--the French equivalent of the roof caving in--but he put up a good front. He sighed resignedly as he accepted his duties, yet he accepted then with burgeoning alacrity. I plied him with dreams: the sea, the early-spring sun, the mussels and promenades. If it rained at Yport, as it usually did at that time of year, I knew there would be Myconos to compensate later on; if it turned out as I hoped it would, I imagined our lives as a pyramid rising one block at a time, lifting us above two broken childhoods.

The morning of our departure we met at the Hollywood and walked to St. Lazare. From the window of our compartment Laurent saw an army friend from Les Invalides waiting on the opposite platform. He went off to say hello, lighting a cigarette as he made his way down the aisle. I saw him jump from the wagon and walk over to his buddy. Laurent was smiling for the first time that morning. Men looked at him in that slightly awed, slightly embarrassed way they did girls of great beauty. Their conversation lasted hardly a minute. Laurent came striding back, content. "It was exactly a year today I left from this very quay for boot camp," he said, "exactly a year to this very day. You can't tell me things don't happen for a reason." My mind struggled to decipher the associations he was making between that first departure and our own. The comparison seemed in our favor for the encounter had put Laurent in a good mood, but who could fathom why? I rode the crest of the boy's contentment. Soon the train jerked into movement. We both lit up a Gauloise. Laurent eyed the buildings enclosing us in cliffs of brick and mortar. I watched Laurent. "That's where I went to school," Laurent said. "Over near there was where a gang of us used to play cards. There's the municipal swimming pool where..." His voice was drowned as we left the rest of Paris through a tunnel.

Our voyage had begun.

.

The train pulled into Fécamp at noon, a town of winding streets and gray buildings with shutters closed against the sun. Laurent bought some croissants at a *pâtisserie* and we went to an old café in a back street. The interior was wood paneled, dark and smelled of coal. Ricard ashtrays lay on metal-legged tables. The proprietress came from the backroom to our table by the lace-curtained window, angry perhaps at having been disturbed during her meal. The café was totally empty. Laurent drank his café-au-lait and ate his croissants slowly, his forehead creased. I kept a close watch on the white enameled clock on the wall. It was my responsibility to keep us on time. The café was cold. Laurent fetched a white turtleneck sweater from his baggage and pulled it on over his blue levis shirt. He was very quiet. I studied the large hand of the clock as it climbed up the black roman numerals. I was anxious to get us going: only movement gave meaning to our displacement.

As the crow flies Yport could not have been more than five miles away, but the road wound up and beyond great chalk promontories and through forests of stunted and twisted evergreens before descending to the tiny harbor stitched tightly between two limestone cliffs. Our task was to find lodging. I dreamed of a room giving on to the bay. It was in that direction we first tried. Narrow streets flowed one into the other like rivulets, all leading to a windy little esplanade with a casino and modern hotels overlooking the vista of a muddy plain at low tide and the withdrawing sea. Behind the harbor old gabled houses climbed up into the hills. Of a common accord we decided to try there. On the way up we stopped at two café-restaurants with rooms. Everything was reserved for the next day by Parisians. We were nonetheless given the name of an old lady who lived in a Victorian mansion near the top of the hill.

Once in Greece I had met a fellow who had taken a fancy to a young boy on the beach. Spurned by the kid in his attempts at seduction, the fellow led me to an old church built on the foundations of an ancient Greek temple. There he prayed to Hermes Trismegistus to sway the boy's heart or wreak revenge. The following day there was a great commotion on the beach. I discovered that the kid the fellow desired had been hit by a water-skiing boat and shredded in the propellers.

Since Laurent was a Gemini--and therefore Hermes his protector-- I taught him the Trismegistus prayer that would bring us luck. An elderly woman came to the door of the mansion, dressed in white and lace. Both Laurent and I stood smiling like village idiots while she informed us that her rooms were taken. But there was a hesitancy. Would a single bed in her kitchen possible do? I frowned at Laurent and asked if he was against our sharing the same sheets. Laurent shrugged. I accepted. We paid in advance and were shown to a room the size of my Paris apartment, with fridge, stove and sink. When the woman closed the door we jumped in muted joy and ran to the giant windows overlooking the bay, the gulls and the cliffs below. We dropped down on the bed into each other's arms, children who had pulled off the biggest stunt of their lives.

We unpacked our swim gear, a chessboard and cassette payer. Clouds were coming in over the sea and the temperature was dropping. We put on windbreakers and went to explore the town. There was hardly a soul anywhere. We found a Prisunic and did our shopping. Back at the room I prepared ham, eggs and cheese for dinner. We were both praying for sun the next day, but hesitant to ask Hermes for a second miracle. We played a game of chess and turned in early.

The next morning Dawn, the Sun's sister, preceded her brother in his rising, blushing at the sight of young lovers entwined. Beside me Laurent's naked body lay warm and flushed, his legs lightly apart. I encompassed his warmth in my own and gently rode that inert body to a bliss the Sun himself surely envied. Laurent admitted pleasure, but he rarely sought it. I knew I could content him sexually, but never did Laurent rise to the erotic heights he inspired in me. Could it have been my perhaps excessive devotion for Laurent, I wondered, which stunted Laurent's desire?

The sun shown through the window. Romping naked at the tail end of winter seemed simply too incredible. Our bags were packed with swim gear and lunches. We had but to hoist them and move out.

Half a mile down the beach we discovered a natural wonder. A gigantic chunk of the upper cliff had broken off and slid down to the shore. Now it stood surrounded by water, waiting to be scaled. We made our way up its side to the top. There we came upon a second miracle, a plateau as flat as a table, covered in verdure. We chose a spot not far from the seaward edge where we could keep an eye out for intruders. The sun soaked the meadow grass, drawing the blades upwards. Above us the cliffs hovered as though suspended in a sky of faultless blue. Hawks jumped out from the upper tiers, screeching and cawing. Laurent threw his shorts, shirt and swimsuit on a half-buried log and lay out naked on a large towel. Like the grass, his face sought out the sun's rippling rays. I put our lunches and drinks in the shade of some rocks and undressed to my trunks. I found a place nearby, opened a book, and it was thus we passed the next two hours, Laurent asleep and I watching him over the top of the pages.

I must have dozed off a few minutes. When I raised my eyes I saw Laurent looking at me. His body had already taken on a reddish flush. As I watched, he languorously brought up his knees a little and parted his legs. His cock lay long and heavy and flask across his thigh. The pubic triangle stood out sharply from the soft white skin. Laurent's matted chest swelled to the heat, and his breathing seemed labored. He closed his eyes and turned his face once again upwards to the blue sky. I put my book aside and stood up noiselessly. I undid the string to my trunks that fell to the grass. Laurent guessed the movement. He opened an eye hardly a millimeter, the space to survey me through the lashes. My nakedness and arousal brought a thin smile to his lips. He closed his eye and from his throat escaped an involuntary groan. I knelt down between his legs. There would be no preliminaries. Laurent was still flask, but it only took a touch, even the minutest touch, anywhere, to bring him to life. I ran a finger over the hairs below his testicles. This time the groan came from the very center of his being, and his cock stretched up and over his navel. Bringing my head down to Laurent's waist, my mouth added a second source of warmth to the sun's rhythmic beating. Laurent moved his chin upwards, lost in the waves of pleasure, each sooner and more intense than the one before. I let him come over his stomach, rope after rope after rope. I caught one pearly thread with my hand and brought myself off in seconds, adding my essence to Laurent's on the still-throbbing chest. I slumped to the boy's side and we slept until noon. We were young and we were beautiful; if there was shame, it was that our love seemed to stumble behind the uncomplicated generosity of our bodies. Veritably, this act was the proof that in this life there was at least this one untainted permanence.

.

We packed and left Yport the next morning. At the train station in Fécamp we were appalled by the number of vacationers waiting on the Paris quay. The ticket man said that if we waited fifteen minutes longer there would be a second train, a special one put into service to pick up the overflow. The first train came and the mob shoved its way aboard. There were people even standing up in the toilets. When it departed Laurent and

I found ourselves alone on the platform. The second train entered the tiny *gare* ten minutes later. It was made up of converted cattle cars to which wooden benches had been added. The lack of comfort was amply compensated for by the luxuriousness of space. We had the whole wagon--perhaps the whole train--to ourselves. The morning had passed in packing and taking the bus, the early afternoon had been spent waiting in Fécamp. Now the sun was dropping into the west, its rays already a ripe gold. We sat across from one another. The sun warmed our reddish-brown faces. Laurent's black hair was a lighter, softer shade. His eyes were heavy with weariness and his face drawn. But never was he more handsome. As the train shuddered along, his eyes closed in sleep, a boy with the shadow of a man's beard. I knew that only my strength and the promise of a decent future would keep him with me. Yet I was gnawed by the feeling that one day I would be deprived of Laurent's love, that he would leave me shipwrecked before our voyage came to its natural end. What does one do then, when the tide goes out? If one is smart, he goes out with the tide. And the train went on, into the golden dust of the declining sun.

CHAPTER TWENTY-SEVEN

Monday was Laurent's turn to be on late duty at Les Invalides. He was to call me at six to tell me when he would be free for me to come for him. By eight the telephone had still not rung. That Laurent had been held back was obvious, but was it so impossible to reach a phone? I walked aimlessly the length and width of the salon, crushing cigarettes on the slate surface of the dining table already strewn with butts, a half-empty bottle of gin and a bowl of tiny lumps of melted ice. La Rochefoucauld had written that there was more self-love than love in jealousy. Without doubt the pain I felt was for myself. I was aware that the boy had been forcibly cooped up in Les Invalides all day, and if that were not enough, he would perhaps be obliged to spend the evening there too. But why? A late replacement? Someone had fallen ill? One of the teleprinters he had to survey had gone on the blink? A surprise inspection? Or was he at that moment sharing his cot with the boy across the table? I felt splintered like a mirror and totally incapable of gathering together the pieces. Again and again my brain told me that feelings of jealousy, as feelings of revenge, were only wasted self-pity. I would have to rise above the limitations I inflicted upon myself. Yet it was one thing for a cripple to tell his legs to walk, another for them to obey the command.

At 8:40 Laurent called. He was home for a short bite, then he had to return to Les Invalides for the night. He spoke in a low, nervous voice. Was his mother prowling the corridors demanding--like Smoky, like me--her stroke before the boy could withdraw to the calm of Napoleon's tomb?

I smoked another cigarette, drank a final glass of gin and took a valium which gave a night of dreamless oblivion.

Tuesday Laurent taught me poker. We sat on the thick white rug in front of the fireplace. The lethargic heat rolled over us, and furtively I watched the clock on the mantel pass the fifth hour. All day we had stayed hemmed in. All day I had awaited the late afternoon twilight. The routine had become immutably the same, but I was panicked lest there be a change. I was jealous of whatever deprived me of Laurent's presence, yet when Laurent was with me I languished before the multitude of hours we had to somehow inter. It would soon be 5:30 and Laurent, as always, would have to be home for dinner with his mother by 7.

Finally he laid down a bet and then his hand. He yawned as he gathered up his winnings and the cards. God, I thought, another round. But Laurent put the deck aside and rose. It's time for my bath, he said, his face expressionless, blushed from the heat and dulled from having remained motionless so long. He took off his shirt, trousers and socks and placed them over the chair facing my desk. Right back, he murmured. I heard water running through the pipes. I closed the curtains and turned on the lamp on the chimney. I put a final log on the coals, a cassette in the deck, and stripped down to my shorts. Laurent returned wrapped in his bathrobe. He sat down on the rug before the fire while I went into the bathroom.

When I came back I saw his briefs in a little pile on top of his levis. He was spread out over the bathrobe. I dropped the towel from my waist and gently knelt beside him. Laurent opened to me, to my hands and tongue, he opened to the warmth from the fireplace, to the beautiful waves building between his legs. His head lay back into the folds of the robe, his face at rest, his chin rising to meet the mounting swell. His cheeks reddened, his lips parted, his breath carried the crest of a tide now irresistible.

Later, he curled up on his side, his knees drawn to his stomach, his head tucked forward into his chest. I wrapped him in the trailing folds of the robe and lay beside him, fitting my body around his, burying my nose in the damp curls at the nap of his neck. The fire burned low. Only the sound of shifting coals and the snapping log broke the room's silence.

Laurent napped by my side for half an hour. Even as the boy rose to dress he knew something was wrong. He surveyed me from his great height, but it was a trait of his not to ask questions; he would not provoke; he let ripen. Yet exceptionally, on the way down the mountain, he quietly asked what was the matter. I said I was just tired, and I did feel tired, tired and carved in stone.

He felt there was something else, and repeated his question. I wanted him to come to my aid, but what weighed on my heart could only be explained in words impossible to share; in words I myself dreaded to face. Yet below Pigalle, in front of the Arkansas Saloon, in an attempt to laugh off Laurent's insistence, my eyes nonetheless filled with tears and it all came burbling out, my uncertainties, my fears and my love. Laurent listened with a pained expression that made me love him still more.

Sex was the barometer in the relationship between two men. All that was sublime and grand had its roots in sexuality because it was love the inspirer of enthusiasm and generosity. It was through love that one surpassed the limits of good and bad. The trial by sex united two beings in a bond in which nothing was hidden, in which all was open. One could not cheat at the decisive moment that demanded the peak of physical and mental will. A man cannot feign the conclusion of intimacy in the way a woman can.

Back in my room, at the time Laurent had had his pleasure, I was himself pitched as high as a violin that one tremolo would have sufficed to set off. I needed Laurent as a fetishist needed his totem. It was Laurent the object of my love, not only the final harvest of the seed that would bring me rest. But once satiated Laurent had turned over, the glutted male, leaving me to my own devices. This was not an unknown boy at the Villette where even there, in the dark corners, there existed the unspoken code of reciprocity. This was my lover, with whom I had shared Yport, whom I would introduce to Greek friends in Myconos.

All this I tried to explain to Laurent, there on the street amidst cabaret pimps and the street-wise residents, my eyes filled with tears that would not stop.

Laurent paused to put together his thoughts. Then came his rebuttal. It was the stress of work, the pressure of putting up with his mother, fatigue from the trip to Yport. I was in no way to blame.

I let pass the reasoning and latched on to the last phrase. Laurent's look of innocent bemusement somehow saved face for us both, and in front of the door to his Clichy apartment I merited a pat on the ass and a long kiss which sent me back up to Montmartre thinking what a fool I was.

The doubts nonetheless festered, later, during the long hours in search of sleep. The doubt that Laurent was turning away from me physically because he had never really been strongly drawn to me, the doubt that the boy had never planned for our relationship to go this far in the first place. Again I was forced to exchange a valium for dreamless sleep.

.

The days passed, each with its lot of crises, but each crisis, I told myself, had served to cement the relationship. The first fire of our encounter had banked, a bit, for Laurent, but a fuller, better understanding offset the first rage.

We shopped together, canvassing the stores for an inflatable dinghy, a speargun, fins and snorkels. After work I would meet Laurent, or if Laurent got out early he would come to the Institute where I taught. From the forth-story window that looked out on the rue de la Sorbonne, I would see him make his way up the sidewalk and sit on the low wall opposite. On one of those days he brought along some line that he painstakingly attached to leader, hooks and weights. He was oblivious to the students passing in the street, to me at the window, oblivious to all but the confines of his task.

In the overheated room where I was giving summer classes in order to augment the stack of bills I'd need for Myconos, the students were sleepily taking notes. One was a Polish girl, a divorcée and model. Another was a young tennis player of exquisite looks who had seduced each of the girls in the class. For nine months I had had to compete with him for the young ladies' attention, put up with the girls' bickering, stand by while one of the girls broke down in tears, another stormed out of the room, and all, sooner or later, dropped out. Just the Polish model remained, the only one who had laughed off her own three-day affair with the boy. Meanwhile the kid looked impassibly forward, blond and crew cut, never disturbing a soul, his sleepy blue eyes seemingly blind to the havoc he caused.

There was an Iranian student, a woman of unknown age, dressed in black skin-tight velvet jeans, a black silk blouse under a black shawl, black hair masking most of her face, and silver knee-high boots. Behind her, in the back row, was a woman in her late forties dressed in a pinstriped suit with matching raincoat, scarf, umbrella and shoes. She had invited me to a bar by means of a mysterious telegram signed only with illegible initials. As it was during the period of my infatuation for Ivan, I hoped it was from him. There she asked for private lessons while putting me up at a Biarritz hotel across the street from her and her husband's hotel. When I declined, she left me to stand the bill.

Four remaining students: it as really time for the summer courses to come to an end.

·

Early on the morning of our departure we met at the Hollywood. Laurent's eyes were half shut, his smile dimply, his humor excellent. A strong bluish down gave a manly cast to his cheeks still hot from sleep. We gathered up our stuff and splurged on a taxi to the Air France depot where we took the bus to Le Bourget. Our plane was already outside on the asphalt. I hated charters. Even in the best of times the French were undisciplined, now they were nearly clawing over each other to be first at the boarding gate. Ordinarily I remained seated until the last passenger had exited the waiting area. But this time I was with Laurent. For nothing in the world would I be seated away from the boy during the coming three hours. It was also Laurent's first flight. I wanted him to have a window, and not just any window.

I approached the outskirts of the crowd. There was a possibility of recognizing a steward. On more than one flight I had come across an old disco buddy who put me in first class and kept me furnished in champagne between bouts of love making in the john. No such luck this time. On the other hand, I saw that the aircraft personnel were strewing out the baggage at the tail of the machine, a measure that existed at the time because of the delicate political situation in Greece. The passengers would have to pick out their own before boarding; those not claimed would be left behind in case someone had inserted a bomb.

I went back to Laurent. "You take care of the luggage. Leave the seating to me." I left him with a fresh cigarette and made my way through the masses calling out loudly and clearly *Pardon*! *Pardon*! *Pardon*!, stepping around those who would not displace themselves. The majority took me for someone from the charter agency. I halted near the boarding rope, unable to go further, obliged to halt behind the fanatics who had been standing for hours and would have killed their children rather than let an interloper through.

Finally the flight was announced, the rope dropped and we spewed ahead. I made for the ladder, dismissing the stewardess who tried to point me in the direction of the luggage with a big smile and a very polite "I haven't any." I was the first up, the first in and the first seated. I piled Laurent's window seat with his sweater, a newspaper, the charter menu and a vomit bag for good measure. So fixed was my stare, so ill-bred my countenance, that no one dared even ask if the place was free.

Laurent came on, one of the last, as fresh as a daisy. I had seen him below pointing his stubbed-out cigarette at what was ours, although, as usual, he began with his. He settled back in his seat. On his face played a Cheshire-cat smile. He was content. The first day had started as I had planned it. Myconos would go the same way. And then the rest of their lives the same way still.

Laurent looked out the window and I studied his profile, the bronzed neck, the black locks, the light down above his lips, and the nose with its ever-present dew at the ridges. Laurent did not turn to see my tears. The engines roared and the plane shook. We moved forward and advanced down the runway. Laurent leaned his head back into the headrest. He looked straight ahead, his lashes long and thick. It was as if he felt my emotion and had the discretion to leave me to my thoughts. I leaned back too and let the pressure of acceleration hold me immovable. This is it, I thought, we are OFF!

CHAPTER TWENTY-EIGHT

The first day of our life together was Laurent all over again.

He was as thrilled as I, he was tender, loving and marveled, yet always with an ultimate hesitancy, a final denial to give completely of himself, to be truly tender, veritably loving. He was himself, Apollonian in the moderation of the sentiments, aerial in the emotions he chose to demonstrate.

The agency bus dropped us off at our hotel. Laurent grinned like a little kid. He had to try out the carpet with his bare feet; the terrace with a view of the Aegean; the shower, behind the closed translucent door of which he worked himself into an erection, deliberately exciting me by pushing it up against the glass, humping it while his hands kneaded his nipples, waiting for me to join him.

We took a bus into Athens, to an outdoor taverna I had discovered the year before. Laurent was amazed at the salads, piles of tomatoes, cucumbers, olives, onions and goat cheese, and the giant bottles of Hellas beer. From our awning-sheltered table we looked out on a blue sky and the white sun-stark streets empty of Athenians taking their afternoon naps. Satiated and feeling slightly heady, we made our way to the acropolis.

Each man has a place in life to which he is predestined, and it was the wind-swept plain of marble that rose like a vessel above the undulating city that belonged to Laurent. As a black opal is embellished in a setting of gold, so was Laurent adorned on this site to which he returned after a diaspora of two millenniums. He was of those who had been the beloved of Solon, Themistocles and Alcibiades. Above all, he was the Antinous of Hadrian. He was of the languorous ephebes who spurned the athletic field for the talk outside the oil and perfume shops, those who spent the afternoons posing for statues as Dionysos and Apollo, those, finally, who possessed the gift of turning night into day and day into night for the ones they loved. He was of none of the dominant classes of that ancient city, yet it was upon the likes of him that the literary and artistic inspiration of the Age of Pericles was founded. How could one admire the glory of that far-off era, I felt, without understanding the mores which fashioned it (10).

Now it was I who walked beside him, wondering why it was to me that this boy, this handsome, living boy, had been confided. It was a sacred trust by a prankster-god like Hermes, avid to see just where beauty and adversity and blind luck would conduct these two mortals.

Nestled in the flank of a hill below the Pnyx was a terraced café with a superb view of the acropolis. We arrived in time to see Helios sink like an amber in a shroud of violet mist. We ordered ouzo, anisette drinks that sweetened the breath and freed the inhibited mind. We were both very happy, very content with the smooth march of events. We reached out to one another, each trying in his own way to pinpoint the other, to discern with whom it was he had thrown in his lot. Over our heads hovered the threat of failure, a sword of Damocles poised to wield the disjointing blow that would send us back into the desolation of our separate abysm. Even then, with sun, air and freedom at our feet, we only half believed in a common future. Somewhere laid in wait the fissure we would mask until it ineluctably yawned open beneath us. Why? Because life quite simply could not be so beautiful.

I told him the story of a Greek boy whose statue we had seen several times throughout the day, and whose head resembled Laurent's to an uncanny degree.

"Antinous was a goatherd adopted by the Roman Emperor Hadrian who bestowed up him gifts of every kind, from the best clothing to the finest villa. Once on a voyage to Egypt Antinous went to the oracle at Siwa. 'The Emperor has done everything for me but I have nothing to give him in return,' said the boy to the sage. 'There is one offering left to you,' replied the oracle, 'and it is the most precious. If you go to the Nile and drown yourself, every year you would have lived will be added to those remaining to Hadrian.' The following day the boy's body, lifeless, was fished from the river."

"I see what remains for me to do," smiled Laurent.

"Hadrian had a thousand statues erected in the memory of his belovèd,'' I continued, "and a thousand cities named for him. But he lived for only four more years." (13)

"If Hadrian died so soon, what then was the precious gift of which the oracle spoke?" asked Laurent.

To this conundrum I could only add another: "There were two Argive boys who, when their oxen could not be found, harnessed themselves to their mother's chariot and pulled her to the temple of Hera where she could worship. To thank her sons for their filial love, their mother asked the goddess to bestow on them her greatest reward. Hera responded that the boys should eat, drink and make love, and when satiated come to her temple to pass the night. The boys did so and the next morning it was there their mother found them, dead before the goddess's altar, proof that the greater blessing is death, not life, for it spares us from disillusionment and the wreckage of time."

I looked at Laurent and my heart welled up. It seemed to me that the boy was more completely a part of me that night than at any time before. I was certain Laurent felt safe in my hands, unafraid of my ever letting him down. He must have known that the light in my eyes was there uniquely thanks to him. Yet something else told me that this boy, whose body was so alive and warm and welcoming, had never chosen to be of this earth. He would have abhorred his own death in the way the Greeks shunned immoderation, yet having known too many worldly things too young, he was tired of living, and silently condoned the goddess's gift which freed one from incertitude, fear, sickness, degrading age, the inacceptable lose of beauty and the palling of memory.

Laurent held his ouzo and smiled wanly. The sun had set; his face took on the bluish tint of the crepuscule. His eyes and hair were blacker still, his features set. I knew Laurent's smile of greeting and the smile when he was proud of himself or abashed or indulgent; I knew the smile when I set a present before him, and the recondite smile when I came to him in the late afternoon; the smile to mask impatience, to signal complicity, and the one which came at the end of a quarrel. I even knew the smile of deep contentment, although never in the midst of love--that was a tensing, tinged with wonder and disbelief. But this smile I would never see again. It was the smile of serenity. As with the frenetic humming bird at day's end, Laurent had come to rest. All the Houses of the Universe had coincided in bringing forward this one moment of respite, and it was I who had provoked it. It was I who had brought him to a place of peace.

We wandered home through the deserted half-lit streets, our hands entwined. For me too it was the ultimate peace.

.

The next morning we were up at six for breakfast. A lone Greek served us in the large dining room where the tables had been laid out the night before. The Greek was young, dark, his eyes swollen with lack of sleep; his kinky hair wanted another pass of the brush. Beneath the fairly recently pressed white trousers a colorful striped swimsuit, serving as briefs, could just be made out. His legs certainly held the marks of mosquitoes from the Spartan, unscreened bedroom he rented in a small cinderblock house not unlike Daddy P's, or sand fly bites from an adventure on the beach with a tourist, most likely female. Modern Greeks championed the grandeur of their ancestors without adhering to the passionate friendships which had made that grandeur so unique.

The unknown aspects of the Greek boy's life brought me to wonder about what had made Laurent. I who had waited years for my first experience with Philippe tried to imagine how and with whom the boy, still so young, had made the discovery. Laurent told me that the first time had been with *un monsieur* he had met while descending the Champs-Elysées. He had told the story of that encounter several times with differing details, but each version ended by saying, "*et c'était très bien.*" Laurent related another version while we were strolling along the rue du Four near the Bon Marché. We came to a sign indicating a huge underground parking lot. Laurent told me that a swimming pool used to be in that spot and that while taking a shower *un monsieur* demonstrated the art of onanism, and then returned to his flat with Laurent for further instruction which turned out to be *"très bien."*

At seven we took a cab to the airport. At eight we boarded the little fourteenseater to Myconos, an ungainly dumbo-like box, more bus than aircraft. Laurent was thrilled. Again I was first on, and again Laurent had the window seat. "It's beginning to be a habit," he smiled.

At nine we landed and were walking down the rutted road to Super Paradise. I was happy I was in a position to make the discovery of the island easy for Laurent, especially since my own arrival the year before had been a continual hassle, the language then unfamiliar, lodging, avoiding the tourist traps. Now I led him through fields bursting with ripe tomatoes, onions, peaches and wheat, the air smelling of the sea just over the next set of hills, the sun rising in a sky of faultless blue.

''Why Super Paradise?" Laurent asked.

"What the Greeks call the Big Boat leaves Myconos town around 9:00 and takes the tourists first to Platyalos, more a family beach. The guys that discovered the second beach saw that the girls there were topless and so decreed it to be Paradise, the name which caught on. It's favored mostly by young heteros. Those who continued on to the next beach after Paradise saw that the girls there were bottomless, and cried out that this must be Super Paradise. In reality it's an alcove where the water's deeper, bluer and more transparent, far more beautiful than the other two beaches and pretty much reserved for guys like us.''

As we neared Jacomi's house I hoped I would be recognized by the women in the fields, and that was exactly what happened. One of them saw me and pointed me out to the others who dropped their tools and came to offer their hospitality. I was showered even beyond my own expectations with warmth and kindness. Laurent, I'd like you to meet Zakaro, and this is Franchesca and her best friend Anna, and this is Athonia. We were received and blessed. Laurent was very moved, and I knew that these, my friends, were the greatest witnesses in my favor so far. Away from Paris and its bars, life seemed so infinitely simpler, and the direction of our future immeasurably clearer.

Jacomi had adopted me because not only would I sit at his restaurant hour on end studying Greek, I also treated Jacomi and his wife Maria and their little kid Nikola as if they were the most important people in my life, which wasn't far from the truth. So Jacomi lent me his house the previous year, in thanks for which I left a wad of 1000-drachma notes on the kitchen table when I left. The act so incensed Jacomi that he had a friend write to say that I wouldn't be welcome back if I ever did anything so stupid again.

So now, at Jacomi's, I found the key in its place under a ten-gallon can of earth and flowers. Laurent and I entered the narrow kitchen that led to the bedroom. Two tiny rooms, far from a palace, but they were ours. From the terrace Laurent gazed to where the plateau broke off into the sea, as calm as a giant lake, its pale azure surface fusing imperceptibly with the sky on the horizon. Tiny fishing boats could be made out, trailing silver ribbons at their sterns.

Anxious to get to the beach, we blew up the boat and carried it down the twisting, often nearly vertical path to Jacomi's restaurant. The cane-roofed terrace was filled with tables and guests taking late breakfast. I went into the whitewashed building and was greeted with screams of welcome. I pulled Jacomi and Maria out to meet Laurent who stood like a country bumpkin at the doorstep. Jacomi's friends, Alakos and Stomati, followed on our heels, as did little Nikola. The introductions were very boisterous. Laurent blushed from head to feet. Never was he more boyish, never had he seemed so completely disarmed as before the manifestation of warmth. He also appeared embarrassed to be singled out from his peers, those at the tables looking at us. But I was used to such treatment and felt at home.

We took a table and had an early lunch, squid, country salad, fruit and orange juice. Stomati came to sit with us. He openly admired Laurent and asked me all sorts of questions about him. Stomati despised the gays who were just beginning to frequent the island, and never gave the slightest indication that he--or any of my Greek friends for that matter-- suspected that I was a part of what he called--in an effort to be polite-- "anomalies", the squawking, preening, emasculated queens draped over the chairs around us, their sordid snobbishness--rings, amulets, bracelets, necklaces, gold watches, an occasional earring--gleaming in the rising sun.

After lunch we hurriedly cast off in our dinghy and paddled to the Big Rock, a refuge I had discovered at the point of the promontory between the bay of Super and the beach that followed, Hellos, a long ugly strand of squat gray hotels. It was a cove protected by claws of talus. Overhanging the cove was a boulder of gigantic proportions, a break away from the mountain above, the top of which was a smooth slab of granite. We moored the dinghy and climbed the boulder to admire the view. The sea in the cove was green and calm. Beyond, the water was choppy and royal blue. In the far distance the island of Icarus rose up like a huge dorsal fin, temping and terrible in the unnaturalness of its form and the red sheen of its totally vertical surface. To the west was Naxos, a gray stegosaurus hump.

Laurent shucked his clothes but I wore a bathing suit until it was worn away by the rock surfaces three days later. From then on I too went naked. Laurent hunted up a branch to which he affixed the tackle he had arranged weeks before, line, floater, sinker and hook. He gave me a rapid peck on the cheek like a husband off for work, and climbed down to the rubber boat from which he fished in the cove all of the remainder of the day. I stayed above reading, brushing up on my Greek, and watching him.

The sea was too noisy for us to talk, but occasionally I heard a grunt and looked down to see him display a multicolored fish about a finger long.

At six we made our way back to Super. We were tanned, weary and hungry. At the restaurant we wolfed down two plates of squid and smoked a cigarette while Maria served honey cake and coffee. The boats to Myconos town had long since taken the queens back to their hotels where for them the evening was just beginning. The beach at that time of the evening had been forbidden by Jacomi to his family. At both extremities boys who had awaited the calm and growing dusk grouped together in little orgies. When finished they went romping into the warm sea which lapped sleepily on the sand, their hard-ons, still thick and pointed, preceding the way. They then dressed and, as there was no road to Super Paradise, made their way by foot back to Myconos town, a full three hours away. From inside the restaurant Laurent and I could hear the Greeks washing plates and pans.

The trek back home served to finish us off. We had showers, more coffee and went to bed. It was only eight-thirty but dark. Laurent lay on his stomach over the white sheets. Thanks to Yport he was already as brown as mahogany except for the reddish strip around his buttocks. I climbed above him and covered his back with lotion, massaging him as I myself had been taught by an expert the year before. By the time I lowered my lips to take up the place of my hands, Laurent was breathless with desire, his body an even ruddier hue still. This was the thirty-fourth day since our meeting, our fifth night together, and one of a nearly perfect series of physical communions. Spent, Laurent curled up against the whitewashed wall and immediately found sleep. I doused the oil lamp and lay out beside him, planning the morrow.

CHAPTER TWENTY-NINE

The next morning we were up and on our way to Myconos town at seven. The sun had long-since risen over the jagged hills and meandering wall-enclosed road, but the air was still crisp and fresh. After an hour's walk we reached the heights above the town, an oasis of white encased in the blue setting of sea.

By eight we entered the first streets of the labyrinth which ultimately led to the port. Everything was painted white: the two-story houses, the chapels, even the pavement. Only the abundant flowers and plants over-flowing windowsills and spilling from every balcony broke the uniform incandescence. Myconoans went quietly about their business. Behind closed shutters the tourist population would sleep for at least another few hours. I took Laurent to the shopping street where we filled up on what we needed back at Super Paradise, coffee, canned milk, tomato paste, spaghetti, lemons and cookies. All other fruit and vegetables would come as gifts from Zakaro.

At nine we went to Franchesca's. She and her husband Apostoli, like nearly everyone in the hills, had a second house in Myconos. The living room had a marble floor lustrous from polishing, a modern couch, coffee table, armchair and a plastic construction for bric-à-brac. I had come with a pink vase from Paris that she placed there. The kitchen was of marble. Its stove, fridge and sink were far more up-to-date than mine in Montmartre. She had an upstairs bedroom with bath. Everything was spic and span. I could imagine poor Apostoli having to literally undress at the front door before being admitted entrance. I felt contrite in the presence of Apostoli. During my previous visit Franchesca had taken an immediate liking to me. One day Apostoli came to see her at the home of her parents in the hills near Jacomi's, while she and I were having tea. With admirable daring and honesty, she made clear to me that she was free by standing up in front of Apostoli and literally shouting, "There's nothing between Apostoli and me. Nothing!" To illustrate that she and he were mere friends, she cast her arms apart in a dramatic movement showing separation. Apostoli tried bravely to smile, but it was clear he preferred to be dead. Now, months later, they were a married couple. Apostoli was a big, nice-looking guy, strong as an ox, whose first love had plainly always been Franchesca. He had clearly replaced me in her heart.

Franchesca cast aside our request for coffee and prepared an entire breakfast of eggs and bacon, the first bacon I had had since leaving America. But Laurent and I were eager for the beach, so when conversation--terribly curbed by my lack of vocabulary--petered out, we rose and took our leave. At eleven we were back at our house, and a half hour later at Jacomi's for squid.

The afternoon was spent at the Big Rock. Laurent took along his underwater gun. To my surprise, he came up with a fish on his first dive. Then came another, and another. As the afternoon went by, the Big Rock began to look like a hecatomb of sliverthin perch.

On our way back home Laurent suggested we cook the fish. While I took a shower, he cleaned them, and while Laurent took his, I fried them up. We had plenty of lemons and a five-gallon drum of olive oil Jacomi put aside for the restaurant. When Laurent came out of the bath I had him peel potatoes. While they too were frying Laurent moved our table onto the terrace and in the coming dusk there we sat, both in navy-blue turtleneck sweaters and jeans, in front of the finest table we'd ever feasted our eyes on. The fish were crusty and brown, the fries crisp and golden. We regaled ourselves like two survivors. The French say that hunger comes through eating. For us it was true. The food was so incredible that I had to put on another batch of fries that I laced with sliced tomatoes, onions and vinegar. Later Laurent cleared the table and prepared himself a whisky and coke, I a cup of coffee. Life was never so wonderful. At nightfall I got out the lantern and we went to pay a visit on Zakaro, Franchesca's mother.

"Much wind!" she explained in Greek, throwing her hands around like a windmill and motioning to the leaves curled in the corners of her adobe terrace. She threw her arms about Laurent and yelled Welcome, Welcome as she ushered us in. At the little table inside, her husband Yorgos sat reading. He smiled and pointed at the paper. "Karamanlis in Paris," he said, "with Giscard d'Estaign." Their daughter Athonia sat on the bed in the shadows of the lamplight, knitting. She was very shy in the presence of Laurent. She never yelled out her usual greeting to me when Laurent came.

"Cold!" Zakaro shouted and hugged herself. She gave us a liqueur to drink, more appreciated by Laurent than me. We talked about fishing, about jellyfish and snakes seen on the trail. Snakes never failed to move Yorgos. He could entertain all evening with anecdotes about how Athonia had nearly been bitten by snakes, as well as Franchesca, Zakaro and himself. Zakaro shook her head and sucked at her gums while reliving the stories. When she caught my eye we both broke into big smiles of complaisance, reminding me of Mammy. Don't men exaggerate!, Zakaro seemed to be saying.

At nine we went back home, made love, and slept.

.

The next morning found us once again on the Big Rock. The sea was too rough to risk the dinghy. Laurent had me fishing now. We both could think of nothing but the dinner the fish would provide. At lunchtime we climbed back on the Big Rock and I broke out tomatoes, cheese, bread, hard-boiled eggs and cans of fruit juice. We ate ravenously while the sun dried off and browned our naked bodies. After cleaning the things away I went to Laurent and sat beside him. I ran my hand over his broad shoulders. The skin was coated with a velvet layer of fine sea salt. I played my fingers through it, tracing a path down to the small of his back. Laurent turned to me. He brought his hands to my waist and turned me so we were sitting face to face. We kissed. Our hands went down to the other's sex, and so sensitive had we become through the touch of sea and sun, that only the briefest friction brought us to ejaculation. After we jumped down to the pool and washed off.

Hardly an hour later I was reading when I felt his mouth covering my sex, taking it in completely, sucking until it became to big for his mouth. He jerked off the length he couldn't cover, massaging my testicles until I came, nearly as rapidly as the first time. His cock was very hard. I took it in my mouth, it and his seed.

The act gave me sudden hope for the future. The only time Laurent had initiated sex was the first night in his room. After that he would allowed me to do whatever I wished with his body, but never would he do more than touch me with his hands. The normal pattern of sex between us had been first Laurent's orgasm provoked by me, then mine which I brought on himself while Laurent caressed my nipples. I knew in my bones that such one-sided sexuality would eventual end the relationship.

My joy at that moment gave me a brainstorm. Why not go into Myconos that night on the Big Boat, I suggested to Laurent. Franchesca would certainly put us up. Laurent jumped at the idea, as happy as a puppy. So at five we climbed up the gangplank onto the Big Boat. Little Nikola, Stomati and Alakos came down the beach from the restaurant to see us off. We were welcomed by the captain's mate who knew that I was a friend of Jacomi. We took place on the bow, our feet dangling over the bluish green depths a yard below. Laurent was so tickled he could hardly sit still. I got out my camera and shot a role of film, talking to him as I pressed them off, trying to make him smile, trying to shoot the angle where the sun added a red tint to his bronzed face. "There's something I want to tell you Laurent," I said, snapping picture after picture, my heart beating furiously. My happiness had infected me with the hope that I would meet a favorable response to my words. Not necessarily other words, just a sign that would not close off the future. All felicity hung on the reaction to come. "*Mon cheri, je t'aime...*" the breeze blew through Laurent's curls and spread wide the collar of his blue shirt. He was a god reincarnate. Fearing he had not heard, I repeated, "*Je t'aime* Laurent." The pictures taken at that moment reflected a cloud crossing his eyes, bringing on a dark, brooding cast. I flicked away the tears the moment of emotion had drawn forth. He was not pleased. God, why couldn't things be right just once!, I thought, swallowing hard. I finished the role and sat at his side. The wind dried my cheeks and the blazing sun enfolded me in a sheath of warmth, but within I trembled from a cold marrow-deep. I could only take what I could, while I could, I knew. There was no other way.

At Francesca's we met up with a whole houseful of visitors down from Athens for a religious festival that I had known nothing about. We were well accepted, but our cut-off levis and open shirts did not fit in with the men and women dressed in their Sunday best. We stayed just for sweets and liqueur. Franchesca was upset at not being able to put us up, but even the couch would be taken by her guests. From there we went to another Maria, a friend I had kept from my first visit to the island. She let rooms but hers too were all occupied. Her whole family was living in their kitchen so that she could rent out even the living room and their bedroom. We stayed for Greek coffee and then headed back to our plateau on foot.

Laurent's gaiety had evaporated. I told him how I regretted his disappointment. I promised that I would arrange things with Franchesca or Maria so that the next time we would be sure to have a bed. Laurent said nothing. We walked up the road from behind Myconos into the hills in the last blue of the spent evening. From the airport onwards we made our way through a night lighted by the generous Milky Way. Laurent paid no attention to me while I tried to get through to him, my efforts spanning the gamut from shameless pleading to my own attempts at silence. Still the boy said not a word. Only at the gate to Jacomi's did he reach over and take his hand. "What was it, *mon cheri*?" I asked with relief. "I was angry, and you just happened to be there."

In bed Laurent rolled over to the wall. I lay beside him knowing I could do nothing more to pierce his armor. I couldn't offer him more than my love and my complete attention. I was reduced to impotence. An hour later he turned to me and said he was sorry. "I know, *mon cheri*," I answered, but my heart knew too that Laurent's words were meant more as a salve for the coming days than a really felt understanding of how deeply he was hurting me, of how irrevocably he was hammering in the wedge which would split us asunder.

Before dawn the following morning I left him in the warm sheets and went back to Myconos to do some shopping. The sun was well up by the time I returned to Jacomi's. I had decided that if Laurent wasn't there I would not go down to the beach to find him. I understood the boy's cholers; I guessed at the motivations of his actions. Many times before the shoe had been on the other foot; I had been pursued by others whose love I could not reciprocate. I knew that if I stuck it out long enough he would be mine in the end--a kind of consolation prize after Laurent had gone through a life of continuous disasters. But I was too proud to admit such an insipid outcome.

Yet Laurent was waiting, seated on the low wall in front of the house. We went to the Big Rock fishing. It was the only time I felt no desire to make love to him. For Laurent it was the opposite. The moment he stepped out of his clothes he was hard. He strode up to where I was putting our lunches in the shade of some boulders, his cock level with my head, coming seconds after I took it in my mouth. After lunch he kneeled behind me. He felt the cock against my back and the encircling hands on my nipples. Again I turned to him, unable to refuse his beauty, his need, and the groaning that made me mad with lust. Later still, while I sat leaning against the cliff wall reading, Laurent sat between my spread legs, his back against my chest. I put the book aside and ran my hand over the massive pectorals trickling with sweat and heaving with desire. Leaning over Laurent's shoulder I watched him as he slowly pulled the prepuce up and over the precum-soaked crown of his glans, again and again and again until he erupted for the third time in the space of two hours, his youth and vitality sending a first jet onto the rocks above my head. Back home we cooked the fish. There were cherries from Myconos, Laurent's favorite fruit.

CHAPTER THIRTY

The following day Laurent's brooding began again. On the Big Rock everything went wrong for him. He hit his head twice on the cliff walls as he swam up from plunging. He scraped his back sliding off the Big Rock into the pool below. He stumbled and bruised his feet, and finally he lost his snorkel. That day I decided to leave him under his black cloud. At the house we took our showers and then strolled to see Anna, Francheska's neighbor and friend, who lived in a small adobe house in sight of Jacomi's. Laurent was introduced to Anna's hundred-year-old father, his blue eyes sightless behind milky veils, and Anna's mother, also a hundred, cheerful and crippled. Both parents sat on their respective beds, the old man eternally counting his rosary beads, his wife asking us a stream of questions, her sparsely toothed jaws breaking into laughter at whatever I answered. We were shown things neither of us had seen before: a rack for weaving, a stone trough for pressing grapes, hanging wicker pots for draining cheese, brick ovens for baking bread. The house was as spotless as a newly minted penny. What a dream it would have been if Laurent and I could have lived there, I thought, cut off from all but ourselves.

Saturday we had breakfast at the restaurant. The beach was empty and would remain so for many hours more. For a change we went to what I baptized the Lagoon, a bay beyond the Big Rock, a far larger cove and shallower, surrounded by low hills accessible to the tourists who wanted to get away from the beach for more privacy.

All day I watched Laurent as he stood on a large rock a few yards from the shore, hardly moving except for an occasional flicker as he tried to hook a chary nibbler. During the afternoon the upper hills began to fill with other boys, all naked, all seeking each other out. From the shaded hollow where I read and where Laurent came to drink we could survey them, unobserved. Boys who had just arrived at the beach, their skin sickly white, were nearly always paired up with darker boys who knew the lay of the land, choosing them because they were virgin to the island.

Later Laurent donned trunks and wandered off into those same hills. I could not forbid his curiosity and every fiber in me said I must have trust, but I was heartsick each minute he was away. When he did return, twenty minutes later, he seemed very content, as though he had come across a particularly instructive display that had advanced his knowledge a notch. He went back to fishing.

At home that night I went into the serious dressing of Laurent's wounds. He had cut and bruised himself all over since our arrival. Most of the sores sun and air had healed, but others the seawater had festered. I took alcohol to them. When I had finished, Laurent's feet were more bandage than skin. Laurent fingered the long scar across my brow where I had fallen against my father's digging machine and which, later, had been reopened by the pitchfork when, in front of my uncle Bob, I had tried to spear the carp. He asked about the scar along my spinal column, when I had been ejected from Reiner's car. But the story of that scar I kept to myself.

.

Sunday was the worse day either of us had ever had together.

Laurent insisted we go to the Lagoon where we fished throughout the morning. After lunch he wandered off into the surrounding hills, completely naked but for sandals. Playing nursemaid to Laurent's fishing pole, I watched him slowly disappear from view. As the minutes passed, each with the speed and gravity of a glacier, my jealousy knew no bounds. I sucked in air in angry half-sobs, my body trembling with humiliation. Hadn't he seen enough in the bars, clubs, saunas and backrooms he haunted? Was our friendship so inconsequential that he would repeatedly put it in question, knowing the suffering he caused to the person who was his host and his lover?

I stood on the rock and shook with despair. Only after waiting two hours did I kick the pole into the lagoon and wade ashore. It was then Laurent appeared. My rage blocked my voice in my throat. Laurent took a measured look at me, got the drift of what I'd been thinking, and went out to the rock to recover his pole and stand over it throughout the rest of the afternoon, wordless. I went skin diving. The cold water and Laurents presence--for it was that suffering, the absence of the person one loved-- brought me around. I went out to talk to him. This time it was Laurent's turn to be outraged. He wouldn't utter a syllable to anyone who had thought him unworthy of trust.

The day was supposed to have been a happy one. That night we were going into Myconos. At five we walked back over the ridges to Jacomi's restaurant. Laurent deigned to speak to me, but the tone was spiteful, accusing me of having misunderstood him as he had always been misunderstood by those who expected the worst of him. We again fell into silence, but the difference was that I was as determined as he to not give in.

At the restaurant I went into the communal showers while Laurent sat with a Paris acquaintance of his on the terrace, a dark-complexioned boy outstandingly handsome. It seemed clear the two had been intimate, clear too that Laurent hadn't gone into the hills totally naked just to take in the scenery. If anything, my distrust was heightened because I knew the pull of temptation, like that I felt for the kid in the shower beside me, his buttocks muscular and lightly haired, his heavy dick swinging like a pendulum, and my crazy desire to reach out and touch the thousands of droplets that shimmered on his brown skin, each reflecting a thousand suns. My thoughts were broken by Laurent who came back to tell me that the friend in the restaurant was only the owner of a club where Laurent had once worked and so, he added jeeringly, I wasn't to be jealous.

I replied that I no longer cared. Perhaps Laurent deserved someone better than me, but I didn't merit his behavior. I told him he would have access to Yacomi's house as long as he wished, a hint that the relationship between us had otherwise come to an end.

Laurent's chin began to tremble uncontrollably, a movement that his whole body picked up. His forehead wrinkled up and tears shot from his eyes as he sobbed his heart out. I couldn't believe my eyes, nor could the boy showering who immediately left. "My God, what have I done?" I whispered. "Oh God, what have I done?" I took him in my arms and his body collapses around me. "Good God, Laurent! Oh my God, my God!" I tried every form of comfort. I promised I would never leave him, that I would do anything to make him happy.

Laurent brought his tears under control. There and then I swore to myself that I would never push things so far again. It was my role to protect the boy, and in the name of God, protect him I would. I felt Laurent's back stiffen. Already he was moving away from me. It didn't matter. I would prove I could be counted on. Laurent asked me to return to the restaurant while he made himself presentable. I left him looking like a soul lost to the world.

Laurent's friend was sitting at Laurent's and my table. I sent him packing, an act that infuriated Laurent when he returned. I explained that we needed to talk alone. I assumed the entire blame for what had happened. Never, I told Laurent, had I realized the tight rope upon which he walked. My job was to at least bring us back to point zero and then maintain the status quo until things could look up. We talked for a long time; rather I talked. Never had we been so glum.

The rest of the afternoon, following a pattern increasingly familiar, was exquisite. We took the Big Boat to Myconos. We went directly to Maria's where a large room with a double bed awaited. The air, sea and excitement of the town completely transformed Laurent's humor. For the first time that day he permitted himself to be embraced. We went to Franchesca's for coffee and then to the street of shops where she helped Laurent pick out a sweater for himself. His spirits were totally restored. He became as shy and blushing as a baby. Franchesca and I were all over him: the sweater and arm sleeves would have to be lengthened, a pocket would be put in on the inside for his cigarettes, all to be finished by the next evening when Franchesca would pick it up. Laurent let himself be pried over. Standing amidst Franchesca and the women shop assistants he made one think of a bride at the first fitting of her bridal dress, so guileless and awkward was he.

From the stores we left Franchesca and headed for the port cafés for ouzo. We drank too much. Alakos came by and offered us a round. Maria's husband insisted that we have another with him. Over the harbor the sky irrupted in a completely unexpected display of fireworks. We had come into town on some Greek festival, perhaps Independence Day. Laurent raised his glass and touched mine. He and the night were so beautiful my eyes clouded over. Laurent's eyes too were full of an emotion the drink guaranteed veritable. Once more I promised myself that I would never abandon him, that I would bring our boat to safe anchorage.

We went to the restaurant of another of my friends, Marco Polo, for a fish dinner under plane trees. Then to Maria's for love and bed. The lesson of that day could not have been clearer. Through thick and thin I would stick by Laurent's side. With Laurent even the most minor things would take on meaning, without him I had taste for nothing.

The next night, back at Jocomi's, I took Laurent through his anointing, massaging him as he lay on his back, the lamplight casting gold darts over the brown, deeply relaxed body spread open to me, his head resting on an arm, his eyes closed. The glistening, curly hair of his underarms and pubis, so black and virile, awaited the appeasing eruption of his hard cock, and ensuing sleep.

This time I stretched out beside him and waited too. After a few moments Laurent said, "Well, that started off well," and turned to the wall and fell asleep. I could only ask myself if I had created this devil through my pandering, or had he always been like this and I was just becoming aware of it.

.

Tuesday, my birthday, seared me for life. I insisted we go to the Big Rock over Laurent's preference for the Lagoon. It was the first day on the island that the weather was partly overcast and the sea choppy. Despite the mounting wind, I ceded to Laurent's request that we take the dinghy. We caught no fish that day and late in the afternoon we boarded the dinghy for the trip back to the beach. But the moment we left the sheltered cove we were surprised by the wind that picked us up like a balloon and threw us into the sea, the dinghy covering our heads. We held on to its sides and managed to right it, but all our belongings were lost, the fishing gear, the clothes, the remains of our lunches. Over my objections Laurent dove to retrieve some of the objects. He surfaced once with the palms, a second time with our sweaters, and as the wait for the third immersion drew itself out I descended undeerwater a few meters but saw nothing, absolutely nothing. Back at the surface I was seized by a panic that made me hurl his name. Terror gripped me in the stomach, shriveling my body into a withering leaf. Still I cried out Laurent's name, on and on. A fishing boat picked me up minutes later.

.

In adolescence I had left the world of my parents because I had harbored the conviction that although I did not know what fate lay before me, it would assuredly be better than the past which trailed ignominiously behind. I had known Paris and Philippe the Day, Reiner and Laurent the Night.

I never saw Laurent again. His body was retrieved by a police patrol boat and claimed by his mother. There was an autopsy, revealing not a drop of water in his lungs. Laurent had died of massive heart failure.

I had vowed to protect the boy, I had promised to be there when I was needed: I had done neither. When undressing that first time in Laurent's home I had known that there would never be another, that Laurent would be the last; in this I had been right. What had begun in the obscurity of the convent-like rez-de-chaussée on Avenue Clichy, home of a naked cat and the mantis who appropriated my lover's body, would find its closure in the obscurantism of Port Beausoleil.

Laurent had been young and perfect. Like a Greek stele his beauty would never age. He had been saved from life, from disappointment and demeaning death. It had been the unspoken pledge from the beginning. I could only wonder if, perhaps, as with Antinous, this was Laurent's parting gift. If so, the wait for my own salvation would not be long.

BOOK III

CHAPTER THIRTY-ONE

Frédéric

The year following Laurent's death Boyd was invited by one of his students, Marie, to the Riviera, a land famous for its princely villas, cinema festival, sex and drugs, where the regional Golden Youth exploited life to the hilt, without rules, beyond limits (14).

As he pulled up in front of the Gaillard property on his motorcycle, Marie's brother Frédéric came through the French doors of their one-story Mediterranean-style red-tiled house, and crossed the lawn to the picket fence to greet him, as if he'd been sitting at the window awaiting his arrival all morning. Frédéric locked the gate behind Boyd, careful to keep in a languorous-looking black-and-white Great Dane the size of a pony. Seated on his motorcycle, Boyd dominated the boy who came at him with a rye smile, an outstretched hand, and a quick and warm ''Welcome!'' One eye was noticeably larger than the other, giving him a guileless Popeye cast. He was shorter and younger than Boyd, his waist padded in baby fat. Boyd was immediately aware of the absence of rivalry in the proffered hand, and the uncomplicated friendliness in the quizzical gaze. The boy appeared to appraise Boyd with that big Cyclopean eye, and find him, like Mamma Hoenig, acceptable breeding stock.

Behind Frédéric both French doors flew wide to admit the passage of Madame Gaillard, a huge woman whose tent-sized gray shift was slightly pinned-in at the midsection to suggest a waist. She wobbled forward on flat shoes, her face the portrait of a Spanish dowager whose sad Pekingese eyes were rimmed by tears of sacrifice and inbreeding. She could not bring discomfort to even the servants she had had in Madrid, and for her children's sakes she would overturn heaven and earth to spare them from suffering.

Dropping Frédéric's hand, Boyd took up hers, offering words of thanks for her invitation, to which she mumbled I'm so happy, I'm so happy, as though it were he the host. Then Marie came through the doors in a staged arrival, a petite damsel in modest white shorts and white Lacoste sports shirt. Her hair was as back as her brother and mother's, shoulder length; an amiable smile crossed her face as she leaned upward to be embraced on the cheeks. Caught up in the emotion of the moment, Frédéric yelled a full-throated Spanish exhortation into the silent, bluish late-evening air, a Fascist salute meant to inspire one onwards to glorious feats. Boyd knew that the family had lived many years in Spain, and now measured the consequences.

That night in bed he listened to the Great Dane patrolling outside his window with heavy paws, while Frédéric's bed creaked up a storm on the other side of the shared bath separating their rooms, as it had his and Daddy P's. Boyd, lost in the folds of the bedding Marie had made up for him, felt an unfamiliar serenity. He had made an ally of Frédéric by letting him take his motorcycle onto the beach at dusk, where the boy literally flew over sand and dunes, the water lapping at the bike's wheels, Boyd's head planted into his shoulder blades, paralyzed by his daring, yet exhilarated in the company of the boy who seemed to know no fear. Marie told him that there were metal pins holding parts of Frédéric's arms and legs together, all results of motorcycle spills. He wondered if the pins inhibited Frédéric's bedroom performance. By accident Boyd had observed the girl--Sylvie, he learned later--enter through the bedroom window. Were women able to fathom the behavior of men, Boyd asked himself, behavior which even for Boyd was often enigmatic? Could Sylvie understand that Frédéric, the salt of the earth, an overstuffed teddy bear, generous and affable, could at other times become violent as he seemed to be now, driving between the girl's spread legs, thrusting as if his life depended on the expulsion of the pent-up forces at the confluent of his thighs? Boyd remained obsessed by the act, by the imagery of one's inserting one's self into the body of someone nearly totally unknown, provoking and receiving a pleasure nearly unbearable in its intensity (9). He admired the fearless boy for the traits they did not share. Scarred by the obscure dangers of his early childhood, the battle that occupied Boyd's every moment was defending, tooth and nail, the remnants of his equilibrium. It was a battle to the death against anyone who would try to humiliate him.

And he had unexpectedly made an ally of Madame Gaillard. Watching a *corrida* on the TV whose parabolic antenna could bring in Spain, at a moment when the matador, stupefying in his grace and bravura, just escaped being gored, Madame had grabbed his arm which had been in languid repose near her own, causing her a moment of extreme embarrassment, and the boy one of the biggest frights of his life. He withdrew his arm from the sheets and studied the nail marks, still visible. He had assured her that it was a pleasure for his arm to be at her disposition should she again need it. Hypnotized by the bullfights, by the blood and daring, it took such physical intervention to take his eyes away--*scotchés* was the French term--from the screen. Now the only unknowns were Mr. Gaillard who would not return from a business trip to Madrid for at least another week, and Marie, who for the moment bent over backwards to ensure his comfort. For how long would he be able to use what he imagined to be a savant mixture of seduction and charm until she withdrew, as near to the end of summer as possible he hoped, the welcome mat? From one of his students he had rented an apartment in Rome for September, but he much preferred staying right where he was, and allow himself to be pampered.

Marie accompanied him to the beach the next morning. Matinal in his habits, she had volunteered to rise early so he could breakfast at dawn on coffee and the croissants she had driven into Cap Martin to buy warm. Stretched out over the sand, the sun not yet up over the palms, he had to admire the charm and discretion of the young girl, the feminine blue-flowered bikini on what was otherwise a boy's body of supple muscle and firm buttocks. She was a feline creature, handsome in a permanent way that would see her into graceful middle age. She carefully left a strip of sand between her towel and his, and never did she embarrass him with a more than sisterly regard. The conversation came easily. There was nightlife to discover, outings of which he would do well to avail himself, and descriptions of friends, hers and Frédéric's, and anecdotes about local personalities. At eleven she returned to the house to help her mother with lunch. Clearly, thought the boy, his body numbed by the sun, the threat to his balance--threat ever lurking in the shadows--would not come from her. Despite the life-long feeling of anxiety, at that moment his conscience, at least, was as pure as his body. Denis existed in a far-off future, and Yves Brun and the bastard on the *Kitty* were even more distant still. Nothing on that serene beach could portend the sorrow triggered by two dogs, which would culminate in the death of Frédéric.

That afternoon, while Frédéric again made the springs creak and Mary and her mother napped, Boyd returned to the beach with Sultan and Sultan's companion Scot. Scot had shown up for lunch after a night of roaming. The retriever had been bought as a pup by the Gaillards for the autumn hunting season, but as Frédéric never got around to teaching him the proper comportment of a bird dog, Scot grew up to obey his own inner urges. It was Scot who had imposed Sultan on the family, bringing the mastodon for dinner and making a fuss until Mr. Gaillard filled a plastic wash basin with a mélange of bread, rice and milk that Sultan contentedly swallowed, so happy was the orphan in the proximity of Scot, while the retriever was treated to his usual meat. Scot proved a good provider. He would go to one of the tourist restaurants and howl to beat the band, flittering between the outdoor tables and chairs to escape the proprietor, a dog smile and grateful lick to an outstretched hand, until the owner finally brought a bowl of food to get rid of him, a bowl Scot would nudge along with his snout to the curb where Sultan was peacefully stretched out in the shade of a plane tree. They would share the repast in turns, under the astonished eyes of the diners who even, on occasion, applauded Scot's intelligence and devotion to his friend. As Scot was never satisfied with a single bowl, the propriator was obliged to phone

Frédéric who eventually drew up in his car to whip Scot into the back seat with his belt. After a few words of regret to the restaurant owner and an offer to pay dismissed out of hand because the Gaillards were well-known winter clients, Frédéric took Scot back home, Sultan following at a steady thirty-five kilometers an hour. Then would ensue a couple of hours of peace for the Gaillard family before Scot wandered off again.

Boyd was pleased to be in the company of his two protectors. At the boy's usual place on the beach, Sultan slumped down on a corner of his towel like a snorting rhinoceros, panting into Boyd's ear while Scot ran along the edge of the thundering breakers, scattering the tourists like swarms of sparrows when he shook the water from his pelt, earning furious epitaphs in German and Dutch as he toppled umbrellas and sprayed sand on oiled bodies. The stretch of beach in front of the Gaillard house had been allocated to the nudists, to the chagrin of all the Gaillards, but especially to Frédéric who with his friends had, at night, twice burned down the drinks stand that catered to the foreigners. They also slashed tires of cars bearing the nudist emblem. To inhibit voyeurism, the municipality put up signs specifying that suited bathers could pass through the nudist region only along the waterfront, leaving the nudists undisturbed on the upper beaches like lolling walruses, shifting their flesh from underdone to done, depending on the number of hours or days since their arrival. The disturbing presence of the dogs permitted the Gaillard family to sunbathe where they pleased. Not satisfied with that, Frédéric and his companions--local boys his age known by the police as the vandals who spray-painted the nudists' cars--plunged into the center of knockers and bullocks, emptying the area around them like the sudden appearance of a school of sharks among a herd of seals, commenting loudly on the human wrecks the tide had washed up, debris without the sense to mask their imperfections with the clothes God had provided for the purpose. Frédéric himself never appeared in less than knee-length trunks and a sport shirt pulled down to his navel.

Scot tirelessly dropped a small branch in front of tourist after tourist until one would fling it for the dog to fetch. Most often it was Boyd that Scot recruited, pushing the piece of wood onto the boy's towel with his muzzle, then stepping back and barking until Boyd complied. At first the boy enjoyed the sport and basked in the dog's attention. But eventually he grew tired, while Scot remained undaunted, willing to chase the object into the worst breakers, or dig it up when the boy buried it under one of the giant logs the winter storms washed up on the shore. The insistent barking was grating. It was ridiculous to feel picked on by an animal, but Boyd came to feel that Scot was taunting him, deliberately preventing him from getting a few moments of peace. The barking drew the attention of the other bathers to the boy's discomfort. Once Boyd went in swimming, only to be followed by Scot, a chunk of driftwood locked in his jaws. The boy seized the animal from behind and tried to mount it, his weight pushing the dog underwater. But Scot kicked free, his nails inadvertently digging into the boy's chest and thigh, leaving long gashes and drawing blood. Furious, Boyd drew Scot into the upper dunes out of sight of the tourists. There, after each bark, Scot received a snout-full of sand hurled at him with all Boyd's might. The dog only retreated a few feet, shook the sand from his muzzle and eyes, and then pounced forward again, yelping as insistently as ever, accepting fistful after fistful of sand in the face, but careful to not venture close enough for Boyd to gain a hold on his collar.

On the beach Sultan had taken over the Boyd's towel and was looking out to sea, his battle-torn ears trained on his friend's cries.

That evening a storm blew up over the Gulf of Genoa, loud and torrential, pelting the roof and sucking at the shutters, glutting the gutters that fed the overflow into the sand at the house's foundations. Boyd went through his belongings, those in the wardrobe and the chest of drawers, those in the joint bathroom, arranging them meticulously. Every few minutes a separate source of splashing was added to the night's cacophony of water and thunder, the sound of Sultan's heavy pays making their relentless rounds.

The next morning no one was surprised at the absence of Scot. Boyd went off to the beach with Marie in the morning and again, alone, in the afternoon. Sultan preferred the comfort of a patch of porch-shaded grass while he awaited Scot's return. The scenario repeated itself for a week, until the return of Mr. Gaillard from Madrid. That morning Sultan refused to let Boyd out of the house.

.

Mr. Gaillard was an amiable businessman, content to peddle his pharmaceutical wares in Spain, from hospital to doctor's office, from Madrid to the remotest Spanish village, building up a clientele for the stress-reducing capsules he had invented and which kept his family fed and clothed, maintained two households, one in Spain, the other in Cap Martin, and permitted his daughter to take English classes, classes that gave the girl an excuse to winter in Paris, classes that both father and daughter knew--owing to the family aversion to studies--would come to nothing. Mr. Gaillard's staff in Madrid took care of the administrative details and the actual production of the medicine. When he was not traveling, he spent much of his day stretched across his bed in shorts and undershirt, on the phone, conducting his affairs. His hobby was fishing from his Zodiac which he did as he had done everything, with unruffled patience and thoroughness, as uncomplaining of life's vicissitudes as Job.

It was in the company of the senior Gaillard that Boyd passed through the front door the morning Sultan attacked. Both were heading off for a day of fishing. The old man had just the time to interpose himself between the dog and the boy, his command over the animal imperious and decisive, shouting Sultan down with complaints of his behavior to a guest, just the right pitch in his voice when he put out his hands to take Sultan's head under his arm and pat his back. Sultan snorted and shook as though freezing, dribbling strands of saliva that stretched to the earth. Mr. Gaillard kept the head in the vise of his bicep and chest, ignoring the muffled growls and drooling, and pulled the animal from side to side while taunting him playfully with a tone not exempt of tenderness, "So what is it, Sultan? Scot's absence got your dander up? Huh boy? Is it Scot that's got you all tangled up? Com' on, less fine Scot. Com' on, Sultan, les go ge' Scot."

Mr. Gaillard forced the dog in the direction of the trailer on which rode the Zodiac, stroking the animal's flanks and talking to it. But as Boyd took one step off the porch, Sultan wheeled around and began a rabid barking. "Get his collar and leash," Mr. Gaillard yelled to Marie. All the family had come out when Sultan had first started acting up, Marie freshly combed and dressed in her white shorts, Frédéric in a long-legged swimming costume and--proof of the urgency of the moment--bare-chested, his stomach extending over the upper button strained to the limit. Madame turned away shaking her head, "If he keeps this up it won't be safe with the children around," meaning Marie and Frédéric, as well as Boyd.

The dog was collared, leashed and patted by Mr. Gaillard and Marie. Once he had calmed down, Mr. Gaillard asked Boyd to approach the car and get in. Sultan kept an eye trained on him, an eye that became crazed and bloodshot when Boyd entered its field of vision. Immediately he began a low growl but let the boy enter the car without making a move in his direction. "We'll have to keep a close lookout on him," said Mr. Gaillard, shaking his head. Nothing in the gentleman's comportment suggested that Boyd was responsible for Sultan's inexplicable conduct.

When they returned that evening after, for Boyd, a stultifying six hours trawling for fish, both man and boy had forgotten about the dog. Boyd opened his side of the car and exchanged a few words about the catch with Frédéric, his head sticking out of his bedroom window, when with sudden fury Sultan came barreling around the corner of the house, sending up clouds of dust and nearly tripping over himself in his haste to get at the boy. Frédéric shouted for the animal to halt. Boyd decided to stand firm in the face of the snarling beast and again Mr. Gaillard had to hurry to deviate the animal's course. Mr. Gaillard led Sultan to the back of the house where he prepared his basin of food. Boyd continued in, his gait stilted and his hands trembling.

At night Marie usually walked the dog. That night it was Boyd who went to the cedar chest where the collar and leash were kept. He went straight to Sultan who was crouching in the position of the sphinx alongside Mr. Gaillard's chair while the old man watched television, absently stroking the animal's back. Visibly taken by surprise, Sultan let himself be collared, and although he did not groan, his eyes thickened with approaching madness. Under his black and white pelt spasms shook the muscles along his spine and over his ribs. He refused to move. "Let me take him," said Marie. "You can come along."

The moment the leash was placed in her hands the dog rose and preceded them out of the house and down the road to the beach. After a few yards Marie relinquished the leash to Boyd. The instant she did so the dog's step began to falter, to slow down, and come to a halt. Boyd passed ahead of the animal whose head was turned studying Marie a yard farther back. When the leash was taught, Boyd faced the dog. To his chagrin he saw, over the animal's back, all of the Gaillard family out on the porch, surveying the scene. Boyd lightly pulled at the leash and encouraged Sultan on with gentle words, reddening in the bluish dusk when the animal completely ignored him. Madame Gaillard went back inside, frowning, followed by her husband. Frédéric came up and asked to try. With the leash in his hand the dog trotted forward, shaking his head like a pony, but with the same demented expression in his eyes. "Take hold of the cord with me," suggested Frédéric as the two boys and Marie continued to the beach. The new development did not escape Sultan who missed a few steps before deciding to keep up the gate. "Now I'll let it go," said Frédéric, which caused the animal to sit down the moment he did. "Beats me," he shrugged, leaving Marie and Boyd to the problem. Marie took the leash and the rest of the promenade was effected without words.

From then on the boy had to be escorted to the front gate by a member of the family. Sultan, his front feet dug into the ground, his chest muscles trembling with rage, barked and drooled, his eyes blood-red, while the neighbors standing out on their porches watched. Each day back from the beach Boyd bent his head in insouciant casualness and studied the glass from bottles along the roadside, pulverized into splinters by the passing cars, as shiny as diamonds in the blinding sun, and waited patiently at the gate while the dog hurled and someone came out to bring him safely in.

It was Mr. Gaillard who suggested that the boy take over the preparation of the dog's dinner. "An animal never bites the hand that feeds it," he assured the boy, inferring, from the tone of his voice, that there was a moral there for humans too. The dog would not approach Boyd while he mixed the concoction, but his hatred was not enough to impede his appetite once Boyd had gone back into the house.

·

The boy found Mr. Gaillard's work habits Bohemian. The old man woke at five to walk Sultan and "scarch the beach for evidence of Scot," as he said to comfort the animal. He then prepared his wife's breakfast that she took in bed, manipulating her massive balk into a sitting position by giggling her stomach ballast from side to side while propelling herself with her small feet. Mr. Gaillard sipped his coffee at her side, taking the quarter of the bed his small body required, his shorts drawn over hips narrow as a clothes hanger, his armless undershirt in folds at his sparrow chest before stretching out to envelop a paunch resembling a six months' pregnancy. After Madame rose he slipped off into a half sleep until it was time to take to the telephone. After lunch he went out on the Zodiac with Boyd.

For the boy, an afternoon of endless hours on the rubber boat, deadened by a swell as repetitious as a metronome, was the price he felt he had to pay to work himself into the old man's favor. Mr. Gaillard sat perched on the fore-air-chamber like a ravaged seagull, the few remaining strands of his white hair sticking out askance around his ears, the ubiquitous sleeveless undershirt drawn over his breast, while the baggy shorts he was partial to were immodestly agape at the thighs, obliging the boy to avert his eyes.

In contrast Boyd was all muscle, his chest brown and squared, his waist trim and girded, the pectorals well defined. Fine droplets of sweat beaded their way from the silky black tufts of his underarms to his hips and black trunks. The boy smiled meaninglessly at the man when he caught his eye, a smile of dimples and bright eyes that came in compensation for the conversation neither required, the old man using the outings to straighten out his business in his head, the boy because he had only his presence to offer.

As for Frédéric, he and Boyd were together far less than Boyd would have wished. Frédéric stuck out on the beach in his knee-length shorts and flamboyant shirts. He tried to avoid eye contact with the reclining bodies spread out over the sand in front of *his house*. Inadvertently he might catch sight of a breast resembling a stranded gelatinous jellyfish, the brown nipples the shriveled texture of wilting mushrooms. Or a hairy anus displaying a single testicle entrapped between scissored legs, making one think of ''hemorrhoid cancer'', as Frédéric put it. At night Frédéric went disco-hopping with a group of friends, excursions Boyd had forcefully declined in order to please Madame Gaillard by keeping her company, only to find out later that she encouraged her son's sorties as a way of meeting girls. Sylvie, Boyd learned, was Madame's nemeses, and although she treated the girl with perfect correction, on one occasion she inadvertently confessed to Boyd, her head indicating her son's door, that Boyd mustn't think she approved of the situation. Boys from Madame's social class could sow their oats where they would, with the sole exception of their parent's house, in audible distance from their mother and sister's bedroom. Madame

Gaillard immediately regretted her outburst, an outburst which nonetheless brought tears to her eyes, so hurt was she by her boy's conduct. Sylvie was her son's guest and entitled to the same politeness as was Boyd. In reality, Madame Gaillard considered herself her children's guest for as long as they wished to have her. Outside the family, she knew from experience, there was only chaos. Even her belief in God was predicated on a ruthless bargain: He would exist for her so long as He cared for her children. God had tried her patience a first time when Marie lost her maidenhead to a neighbor boy both mother and daughter adored. Then came Frédéric's motorcycle crash, and the rods of steel which now kept his body in one piece.

She insisted that her boy clarify his intentions before he compromised Sylvie's future. Unknown only to her and her son who had been away in Madrid at the time, that particular girl's future had already been compromised when at the age of sixteen, after a night of heavy drinking at the Monaco Bronx, she gave herself to all comers, still a respectable number at that predawn hour, in the parking lot behind the disco reserved for card-carrying members, the local sons of rich landowners, none of whom had the gallantry to offer the comfort of his Porsche or Ferrari. This was but the climax of sorts to an itch began earlier still with her idiot brother. On the family private beach she and a group of her girlfriends would gasp at the dimensions of the weapon God seemed to have bestowed in compensation for the boy's mental derangement. There was no difficulty enticing him into the basement from which they would leave one at a time, basically in the state they had entered, since where was the sin when the boy couldn't measure the consequences of what he was doing--or, more pointedly, tattle to others? The story got out, eventually, when one of the girls criticized her lover for lacking, in centimeters, those supplementing Sylvie's brother. The wantonness excited other boys who began whispering in Sylvie's ear about bigger and better, the culmination of which took place at the Bronx disco, when the members banded together in a Bacchanalia worthy of Messalina.

Her son had imposed the girl's presence on the family. At the age of eighteen it was either that or he would find lodgings elsewhere. Madame hadn't known a night's untroubled sleep since. Sylvie was of a good family, her father a doctor, her mother a nouveau-rich socialite-- everything Madame Gaillard, who had real money and from way back, detested. There was a vulgarity in Sylvie that the girl did her best to mask by patronizing the old woman. Sylvie lacked interest in anything outside of clothes and partying, and she suffered from intermittent illnesses brought on by excessive drinking on the one hand and, feared Madame, female troubles on the other.

Boyd's mistake during his sojourn with Madame Gaillard was his unshakable assurance that the path to her heart was by way of filial concern for her person, an approach not unlike Sylvie's. He unabashedly smiled at her with the adoration of a stage-door Johnny; he went out of his way to accompany her into Cap Martin or Monte Carlo to be of use carrying groceries and chauffeuring the car; he bought the family pastries nightly, but only the ones that had her preference; he cleaned the house windows and carried out garbage; and he was careful not to soil his sheets, protesting when she came to change them every few days that it was quite unnecessary because he was clean, an observation which displeased Frédéric who had his removed every other day. He even let her take over the washing of his briefs, although he himself insisted on placing them in the machine. He refused alcohol, he didn't smoke or stay out late; he emphasized reading as his greatest pleasure, and sat between Monsieur and Madame for the nightly film, placing his arm in reach of hers should the screen show something frightening. It was unclear to Boyd why he cavorted in such a manner, but one thing was limpid: his need to please and be accepted was limitless, and his desire for affection as deep as a well to China.

But Madame had a son, and had she wanted another she would have engendered him. She married very late for girls raised in the Maritime Alps, at thirty, having spent the entirety of her precocious youth on a motorcycle, carousing. She had been the opposite of the woman she was to become, a young girl game for anything, refusing the concepts of reasonableness or righteousness. As the only daughter of a rich landowner in the provincial graveyard of Sospel, a town twenty kilometers inland from Menton, she knew she would have no trouble finding a suitor when the time came to settle down. Her dowry was solid and she hadn't the least qualm in spelling it out in a prenuptial wedding agreement. Mr. Gaillard had been the least handsome of the pretenders to her throne, but the only one of any real imagination. Evenings with him were spent in dreams of honey, real honey from real bees that he had turned into a hard, suckable health food his customers could carry with them like candy, obtaining the nectar and energy of what he conceived as being the nutritive basis of nature. Honey could prolong one's lifespan, he contended, cure diseases thanks to its anti-bacterial composition and, with constant use, it could ward off cancer. He had figured out the process by which he could harden the liquid treasure without harming its benefits, a first step in making him an eventual captain of industry. ''We'll have a town house in Paris next year,'' he promised the children, ''and a yacht soon afterwards.'' In reality, he cared nothing for money. Nor did Madame, the proof being the hundreds of thousands of francs in checks she wrote out year after year to bring the product to industrialization, checks for which there was as yet nothing more substantial than a tiny one-room factory in the industrial section on the outskirts of Menton, built by Mr. Gaillard while Frédéric went through school, now run by Frédéric while Mr. Gaillard sought out distributors for his honey candy as he was doing for his blood-pressure medicine. A few outlets existed already, but as yet not enough to pay for the factory's electricity bill. In the meantime, Madame continued writing the checks.

She had had fifteen years of pre-marriage memories, followed by two beautiful children. All she wanted now was grandchildren, a houseful to compensate for her unwillingness to go through childbirth more than twice, births which had left her as she was, bloated as a bullfrog, and gave Boyd, unscathed by time, the misconception that what she was now, she had always been. With that degree of ugliness what could life have been for her in the past, he thought to himself, other than kitchen and church? Her passionate dislike of Sylvie centered about Madame's deep-seated certainty that the girl, frail of health, was too concerned for her own person and personal desires to be able or willing to give Madame the children she and her son desired.

When Marie suggested that her teacher visit them for a week or so that summer, Madame Gaillard jumped at the opportunity as a way of extracting her son from himself, and weaning him away from Sylvie's influence. During the previous Christmas holiday Marie had talked endlessly about the teacher the girls were gaga about. He was certainly a playboy, the girl assumed, but one who seemed to have some preconceived notion that a teacher should not date a student. An invitation to Cap Martin could not be misconstrued as a ''date'', she managed to convince herself. Madame deduced that such a boy would be able to convince her son, through his example, that there were greener pastures beyond Sylvie, and that a boy should play the field before settling down. On the other hand, if Boyd were the playboy Marie felt him to be, perhaps he was now ready to recognize the unique opportunity to set his sights on someone like Marie, her fresh young beauty, her sizable dowry. At any rate, Madame needed a young son-in-law willing and capable of begetting the numbers of grandchildren she had in mind, the whole horde of children her fortune would finance, and although she could not explain why, it was in acres and acres of laughing progeny that she would finally find self-completion, and even a kind of salvation. All else was futility and wasted time.

What promise, then, when Boyd pulled up on his white motorcycle. What hope in a lad of his youth and personal beauty. She questioned Marie about their rapport after the first day at the beach, content that the boy was showing respect. Even as day turned into week, and week into month, Madame Gaillard refused to take Boyd at face value. He could not satisfy himself with sea, books and television, she reasoned. She would have been pleased had he palled around with Frédéric, but her son refused to leave Sylvie's side. Madame would have gritted her teeth had

Boyd taken his motorcycle into Monte Carlo for a night of slumming, but she would have understood the motivation and anyway, it would be better for him to run wild now, she knew, than later when he had a wife. But night after night he stuck to *her* in the darkness of the parlor, breathing as heavily as a seal, wasting his time on the ersatz way of living that had become her own. Not even Mr. Gaillard could stand more than a few minutes of the television soaps Madame favored, before getting up to walk Sultan.

When she regretfully came to envision the possibility that Boyd was no more than the recluse he seemed to be, she hoped that he was at least a sincerely hard working, pleasure-shunning boy, a byproduct of the Protestant genes she knew to be his, and not a Catholic Tartuffe, which would mean the damnation of them all.

.

Back on the beach that afternoon, free from the supervision of the Gaillard family, Boyd took off his trunks and stretched out naked over a large sea-blue towel belonging to Frédéric. He loved to let the sun play across his muscles, to catch the light and shadows in the ruts of the corded knots of his abdomen. He flexed his biceps while closing his eyes to the sun, raising his chin and knees, opening his thighs to the scalding heat. Near him a boy in black swimsuit put out his own towel. It was a boy from down the road to the Gaillards', from the house Marie sped past in horror, the one in front of which Frédéric slowed down to see if the occupants were up to any reportable violation of the commune's laws on morality.

That night Frédéric had agreed to let Boyd treat him, Sylvie and Marie to the cinema. Boyd looked forward to the outing. He was fond of Frédéric, and had the boy not been totally taken up by his girlfriend, Boyd was certain they could have found adventurous things to do over the summer. Frédéric was indeed a breakneck, a boy whose father had taught him absolute disdain for any form of fear. That, Boyd could admire, he who had been a mamma's boy living his life in fear that his father would break something more than his nose. And he loved Frédéric's family. He loved the stout woman who would grab onto his arm and then turn a violent red; he loved the old man who put up with his company, who could be silent for hours with the boy, proof that he accepted him as part of the family. He stood in awe when Frédéric did crazy things like driving his unlicensed Ossa motorbike over the dunes and onto the beach, helmetless, rearing up on the back wheel, making the nudists snatch up their children as he shot by, kicking up sand over their belongings. Frédéric considered himself a through-and-through Spaniard. Boyd liked to hear him shout his military slogans, which he did some mornings outside Boyd's door to let him know that lunch as ready. Boyd imagined the slogans to be something about mothers and children rising up to protect the country from the invader who Shall Not Pass! In reality, they were fascist exhortations, inviting the populace to rise up and slit the throats of the Republicans.

Boyd, his organ stirring due to the pulsating warmth of the sun, turned over onto his stomach, taking his time with the placing of his sex up into the soft tissues along the underbelly. The boy next to him had turned on his side, facing him, his knees drawn up to make a protective hollow from the eyes of the rare strollers who still remained for the last of the day's warmth. Within the hollow his thumb absently played over the distended tissue, like a guitarist whose thoughts were elsewhere.

Boyd traded Frédéric story for story concerning their numerous sexual adventures, each more coarse and phony than the other. That in reality Boyd was still a virgin made him smile, especially as his astrological sign was Virgo. ''Virgin'', he now said to himself, ''Virgo and virgin.'' The thought caused him a moment of joy, the ecstasy of being young and footloose, free from those who would collar him and shackle his independence by dictating his wants and by challenging his conception of himself. He was free to come and go as he wished, to mount his motorcycle and be off, to make himself as welcome as a pasha by those who wanted him, to spread out on a distant beach in the warmth of the sun, and listen to nothing but the endless repletion of the surf and the beating of his heart. The moment of joy caused him to shove his hips into the folds of the towel, bringing his sex up hard between the firm sand and the interlocked bands of his stomach. He opened his eyes to slits and was surprised to see a jet of gray mucous leap with uncanny force through the boy's black swimsuit, followed by a succession of spurts of decreasing momentum, the last of which made the boy, whose eyes had been riveted to the small of Boyd's back and his firm naked buttocks, cave onto his towel, his breath as racing as Boyd's heart.

That night the four of them left the house for the cinema, Frédéric and the two girls forming a protective hedge around Boyd. Sultan came around the corner stumbling like a drunkard, long streams of bloody saliva dripping from his snout.

CHAPTER THIRTY-TWO

Boyd had come to meet some of Frédéric's friends. One of them, Eric Navarre, sometimes spent the night rooming with Frédéric. Boyd agreed with Marie when she said he was considered the most handsome boy in Cap Martin. Tall, dark complexioned, black hair, Boyd kidded Marie about why she seemed immunized to his charms. She shook her head, smiled knowingly and remarked on his ''reputation''. Boyd had once ridden around Monte Carlo in Eric's car on some errant for Madame. Eric had commented that if Frédéric was crazy about Sylvie, it was because she was the first to put out for him. But Boyd came to learn that there were other reasons that accounted for Frédéric's ardor. Her father was a doctor practicing in Nice where they had an apartment, as well as a house at Cape d'Ail and a ''cabin'' in the woods outside Sospel. As the medical profession was highly respected in France, marriage to her would be a step up for Frédéric and his inventor father. As for Sylvie herself, she was at that moment with a French boy she had noticed at the beach. He was tall and slim, nicely turned out in the French way: lacking the noticeable muscularity of a surfer, but with taut, unexaggerated pectorals and hard, though not excessively knotted abdominals. He was now humping her in the dunes, treating her as the bitch she was, ramming her with full thrusts, rotating his sex so she would know she was being fucked, finishing in her mouth, the ultimate degradation and the French preference for birth control, compared to what Mario, another of Frédéric's friends, had told Boyd was the Italian way: up the ass. It was the story of her life, and in marrying Frédéric she was taking what was left to her, a step down. Boyd's closest encounter with Sylvie had taken place the week before at the Beaulieu disco La Mandigotte. Seated at the same tiny table with Frédéric and Marie, she had kneaded the calf of his leg with her foot until he finally stood up and brushed off her shoe marks from his levi's. Both brother and sister were too tipsy to catch on to what had been going on. One didn't need to be a genius to imagine the future Sylvie reserved for the boy he desired as a friend.

.

During the afternoon following the outing to the cinema Frédéric and Boyd were joined at the beach by Eric and his brother Phil. They preferred to meet at the beach rather than the Gaillard house because the presence of Madame obliged them to endless courtesies and meek demeanor, while at the disco their speech was rendered inaudible by the sound system. As Eris threw down his towel next to Frédéric, who raised himself on an arm to face him, Boyd joshed him about a girl Eric had fancied at the disco several nights back, who had slipped through his fingers.

''I'm not going to be one of a dozen flies buzzing around some new bitch,'' Eric answered. Upon arriving, the Navarres had shaken hands with the boys, a custom that never ceased to amaze the American. The rite would have been respected even had there been twenty of them, and even if they had all seen each other but a few hours before, boys shaking hands and kissing the girls on the cheeks. Boyd got Phil, a boy with a hair-lip that cut through his skin like a meandering gorge. The flesh-colored, hairless walls of the scar seemed to want to split apart each time the boy's perpetual snarl tore at the sides of his face, sides like the asymmetrical plates of continents trying to break away to form elsewhere a pleasanter landmass. Tiny pinpoints lined the gorge on both rims, remnants of the sutures that hadn't succeeded in repairing the damage. So choleric had Phil been as a child that no amount of care had prevented him from scratching the stitches that tugged at the surface. He too wore a shirt to the beach, doctor's orders to keep the sun away from a second scar, this one from his throat to his navel, where he had undergone open-heart surgery to repair an auricular deformity. He cared nothing about his scar reddening in the Cap Martin sun, but during his recuperation the forced inactivity had transformed his food into fat, and until he lost it he preferred to keep covered, especially in comparison with Eric and Boyd. Their muscles and firm skin did more to attract girls than his flabby gut.

''Why a fly?'' asked Frédéric. Only eighteen, his shirt-covered stomach seemed to tower about the taut strings of his knee-length swim shorts like a snow-white Fujiyama towering above a plain.

''Flies buzz around shit,'' Phil scowled, answering for his brother

Boyd could not join in the conversation. His repugnance for Phil sealed his mind to thought. Even the muscles of his back rippled in spasmodic repulsion to the physical proximity of the boy whom he tried to please in deference to Madame.

''He's right. She was shit,'' said Eric. He kept on his shirt, perhaps in sympathy for Phil. Their father was a lawyer who worked in Nice. He had a house a few hundred yards from the beach at Cap Martin, overlooking a storage shed where he kept a boat for water-skiing. While their father stayed over for days at a time in Nice, he had someone, usually one of his sisters, supervise the Cap Martin house and his sons during summer vacations. This year no one had been willing to do the job, and Phil and Eric found themselves on their own. They immediately installed a girl hitchhiker in one of the rooms, hoping she would put out for them in exchange for the lodgings. The girl would have come through for Eric but not Phil, and as Eric was the kind who shared with his brother or went without, the summer had so far bestowed little pleasure. The girl was finally ejected with such screaming and insults that the neighbors alerted the boys' father. He took an early vacation to put some order in the Cap Martin household. Phil, as the youngest, now had a nightly curfew, the result of which was more freedom for Eric.

''Ever been sucked off by a black?'' asked Eric. ''Phil and I were last night, right Phil?'' Phil, his eyes shut, grinned deeply. ''In the back of the car. The bitch did us both, right Phil?'' Phil grinned deeper still, his mind on his BMW 1000 motorcycle that he much preferred between his legs, and whose obedience was total. The silence of wind and surf when he cut the motor was far more preferable to the cries and curses of the girl hitchhikers Eric was always imposing on him. For all his vulgarity, Phil had the ear of Madame Gaillard who admired his intelligence, and what others took for his irascibility was, to her, his way of surmounting life's blows. Phil's mother had been a bed case since an automobile accident when the boy was an infant. His father had more or less abandoned him for his work, and Eric treated him like a punching bag during his younger years. He had been sent off to boarding school where he had been beaten up because of his lip, and following the heart surgery, which had nearly cost him his life, he had shown near heroism in the face of the debilitating pain.

As Navarres, old French stock, owners of entire segments of the highlands in the south-east, the boys felt there should be no bounds to how they lived or expressed themselves. Boyd shouldn't have been surprised when Phil asked him, shortly after his arrival at the Gaillards', how it felt to marry into one of the great fortunes of the region. Before Boyd could answer, Phil went into the details of what the Gaillards, incorrectly as it turned out, possessed. Forest lands, stocks, various titles and bonds, the house at Cap Martin and an apartment in Madrid, a townhouse in Nice and pied-à-terre in Paris in the 16th district. Boyd had informed Phil he was there on vacation, and that the Gaillard money was their own business. He had then gone off for a swim, firmly decided to avoid the boy whose intuition was just a bit too prescient.

After bullshitting about blowjobs, Frédéric and Boyd went to the house for dinner before driving to Lynx for a stag party offered by one of Frédéric's best friends, Michel Canton. Madame had prepared a treat for them, confie de canard. They ate silently while Monsieur watched the news on television. Later, around the chocolate cake Boyd had bought, Monsieur brought up the subject of Sultan's death. ''The veterinarian got the bleeding under control, the heart was back to normal, the respiration was less shallow…'' He paused.

''In brief,'' cut in Boyd, remembering a witticism he had read, ''he died cured.''

No one caught the joke except Monsieur who gave a chuckle despite himself.

.

The Canton house at Lynx was surrounded by several hundred acres of pine forest. The fortune had come through the mother who managed the land herself, selling off tracts to provide her two sons with a Porsche each, as well as their own apartment in Nice, where they could retire with the pick-ups they knew would be undesirable at their mother's home, a columned mansion she had had built along the lines of Tara in *Gone with the Wind,* and which had cost her half her land. It was only the land that had value now that pinewood could be imported from Scandinavia cheaper than it could be processed in the Alps, and each year a certain amount of land was sold to pay for the boys' education and cover the family bills. When her first husband died, Madame married Mr. Canton, the local postman. Such were the Cantons, Frédéric explained to Boyd on their drive to Lynx. At the time of their mother's passing, the fortune would disappear completely between the boys and their sister, Marie-Ange, along with death taxes which would take nearly half of the inheritance. Boyd was quick to catch the disdain in Frédéric's voice at the mention of a *postman* being the boys' father. Although he had succeeded in putting Lynx on a paying bases before he too died, to Cap Martians he was never more than a letter carrier, and the boys' mother a sentimental fool who had married for love, thusly fouling her sons' bloodline. Now she never left the mansion. Entertaining was done in the "cottage" built for the boys' pleasure, a luxurious two-story tower of glass and imported wood beams that dwarfed the Gaillards' house.

For the evening Frédéric had put on a blue suit and Boyd wore his best corduroy trousers and a sports coat lent by Frédéric, in which he swam. The car was met by Mario, a friend that Boyd had as yet not met. Mario had come from a few weeks with his family on Lake Lagano where he had bought the clothes he was now sporting, considered the height of fashion by Italians his age: silver trousers flared out at the waist and taken in at the ankles, black piping down the legs, a matching jacket resembling the double-breasted, gold-buttoned waistcoats worn by the sea captain in the year's television hit, *La Croisière s'amuse*, opened on a pink shirt and slim leather tie. Only Mario, square shouldered and ram-rod straight, exuded the charm and assurance to carry it off, winning grudging acceptance from Niçois boys who despised the Italian fashion-plate faggots who worked in their restaurants and made off with their girls. The Cantons and their friends were decidedly conservative in comparison to the Italian: short hair, white shirts, dress slacks and polished shoes. Their fathers would have easily recognized themselves in their sons' dress, in the football and car conversions, in the tendency to drink too much, the use of outmoded lexis, even the same election slogan they had invented was still used, years later, by the boys present: P.S.=P.D., the first initials standing for the Socialist Party, the second used to describe queers, *pédés*. The fathers had been less open and crude, perhaps less promiscuous, but just as breakneck, *pressés*, the arbiters of the regional conception of virility, a conception Boyd was soon to discover. Drugs were occasionally tried at Lynx, but took second place to cigarettes and alcohol. Dealers were in as much danger of being tarred and feathered as the owner of the concession on the nudist beach. Lynx was a protected plot of France where Family held the reins and Elders sat in judgment, where tradition was rooted in land, intermarriage and exclusion, a fascist mentality Mario found as conductive as that in his own Alpine homeland.

Michel Canton came up behind Mario. He knew the social amenities, intimately cordial to Frédéric and accepting Boyd enough to throw a hand over his shoulder and dig his fingers into the padding of Frédéric's sports jacket. He saw them to the bar and made sure they had drinks. He then drifted away and from a distance turned with the intention of giving Boyd a once over, but by then it was too late as Michel Canton suffered from myopia of near-clinical blindness. Too vain to wear glasses, and unable to support contacts, his friends had long since decided of a common accord on ways to shield him. They would clear furniture away as he approached, and did not hesitate to enter a car when he drove, despite a series of accidents ''occasioned by others'', they inevitably said when testifying in his favor. Michel Canton's brother Alain was more reserved, and only slightly less near-sighted. His attention span was limited to seconds, and this, combined with the vague glaze of his eyes as he tried to focus on an object or person, lent him the aura of an intellectual, an impression somewhat justified as he was considered the brain of the family, and only his dissolute youth, said his friends, kept him from making the most of the academic career his mother dreamed for him.

Jean-Charles, a friend of Frédéric's who often came over to the Gaillards' to watch tennis on television, sat with Boyd. ''Swell place they've got,'' Jean-Charles said, nodding to the immense wall-length fireplace where a number of boys stood with drinks, talking. Others, in time to a rock beat, swerved and writhed on the dance floor in front of the fireplace. A massive spiral staircase of intertwined teakwood beams led upwards to, Boyd supposed, the brothers' bedrooms. Bay windows gave onto the garden of lawn, cypress and conifers. ''And just wait for the entertainment,'' Jean-Charles added, winking lasciviously and drinking in the same motion.

Jean-Charles was the only boy who stood out from the others significantly. His hair looked self-cut while the other boys went weekly to Monte Carlo to the Rivera's best salon, ''manned'', they laughed, by the only queers any of them had ever allowed to approach within fist-swinging distance. His suit coat was not well cut, and his trousers showed too much sock. His shirts had nothing of the 100-franc quality of those around him, nor were his nails as trim and clean.

Boyd watched as Jean-Charles joined the others, going from group to group, playing the shuffling servant when a boy wanted a drink, complementing them and getting them to laugh. He had invented a name for Frédéric's intimate friends, the Coyotes. It was he who had initiated the burning of the drinks stand on the nudists' beach, and the slashing of the tires of cars bearing the nudist emblem. It was his suggestion, so off-the-cuff that each boy took it as his own, that decided how they would spend their evenings. Jean-Charles had added a new drink to the menu of the best nightclub in Cap Martin. The drink was called the Chicass, and was to be served to the vacationers who invaded the beaches in their Cardin swimsuits and the disco in their YSL jumpsuits, financing their outings with what they had squirreled away during eleven months of labor as postal workers or bank clerks. To the puzzled look of his friends, Jean-Charles had explained, ''It's French and English for chic assholes.'' He had a real American jeep from the last World War and he was known for being a kamikaze rugby first-liner, an awesome talent to this group of boys who rarely roughed themselves up, except during the hunting season, when their fathers let loose the caged pheasants they had raised during the summer. Only Jean-Charles was favored to drive Michel and Alain Canton home when they were blind drunk, a role he was allowed because they considered him as threatening to their caste as a teddy bear. One of the few boys present forced to work, Jean-Charles sold insurance. All of the boys' fathers had bought some, and all of the boys eventually would.

Boyd supposed the entertainment to which Jean-Charles had referred was the young girl coming down the central stairway, dressed in the gauze caftan of an Egyptian belly dancer. To a drum solo the boy responsible for the records put on, she performed a kind of dance of the seven veils in front of Michel Canton who sat in an armchair, straining myopically in her direction.

''Jean-Charles said she's the evening's amusement,'' remarked Boyd to Frédéric who came up to refill his glass.

''She's Michel Canton's latest,'' said Frédéric. ''And before him she belonged to Eric Navarre.''

''Not bad,'' commented Boyd evenly, never forgetting that Frédéric was the brother of the young lady he had been invited to Cap Martin to squire.

The girl vanished during a lapse in Boyd's attention span, although he did notice a growing number of boys stepping outside, to take a leak he assumed. ''It's to vomit,'' said Frédéric, ''so they can keep on hitting the liquor and caviar.'' Such decadence seemed inconceivable to the boy, an offense to his Calvinist legacy. At first Boyd had only taken polite sips of his drinks, when he couldn't do otherwise. In the recesses of his brain he harbored the fear of having inherited his father's alcoholism. But now he hit the bottle freely, overcoming even his disgust at why the boys were retching in the garden. Unfettered from inhibition, he stood and danced, awaiting the dawn and the sea and beach over which he would lay out for the thousand years it would take to return to normal.

It was Frédéric, so drunk he would later claim he remembered nothing of that night, who came for him at what must have been three in the morning. Prepared for his ride back to Cap Martin, Boyd followed him into the woods behind the cottage. There, in the dark, a small group of boys circled the girl who had been dancing for the head of John the Baptist. Now naked, she was giving head to Michel Canton while Alain sodomized her through his open fly, his back inches from a tree. A couple of the boys watching were stroking their organs to keep them up, ready to take their places. Boyd felt his own sex surge in his pants. He cupped it and felt a bodily need for release the likes of which he had rarely known. He put his hand in his pocket, content to bring himself off while watching the other boys, each of whom seemed removed from the scene, nearly disinterested, as if waiting their turn at a school urinal. When Michel finished in the groan of a wounded beast, Frédéric pressed forward and insisted that Boyd hadn't had any yet. ''You haven't done any screwing in all the time you've been my guest,'' he whispered in the American's ear, his hand cupping his ass, urging him onward. The boys made room. ''Thanks, but I pass,'' he said, remembering the first words in French he had learned playing cards, that first night at Lea's. Mario leaned against the oak trunk Alain had left, and let the girl take over the unbuttoning of his fly and free an erection that was dribbling enough to lead one of the boys to suggest he had already come. She blew him while he held his head tilted back. Eric Navarre took Alain's place behind her. Mario came to orgasm in seconds. Someone took his place while Mario shook his cock free of sperm, and went behind the oak to piss.

When they finally got home, Madame was up waiting for them. With her boy safely in his room, she returned to hers.

.

Boyd had been invited to Cap Martin by Marie for a month. As the time was now up, he prepared to leave. On what was to be the last fishing trip with Mr. Gaillard, Frédéric decided to come along, an unheard of event since the boy hated fishing as much as Boyd, the endless hours on the boat with Mr. Gaillard rocking silently back and forth with the waves, the old man's thoughts on business, what the French called the family jewels poking through the leg hole of his shorts. Boyd's arrival had freed Frédéric of the obligation to go out at least a couple of times a month. But today Frédéric and his father had something in mind that they wished to talk over with Boyd privately.

Driving towards the wharf, Frédéric leaned forward and placed his arm and chin on Boyd's shoulder. The physical gesture was more a symbol for Frédéric than a spontaneous movement, but for Boyd, who had grown very fond of the boy, it was a kind of reward for his loyalty. ''Marie invited you last month, and for the coming month Dad and I would like you to remain here as our guest.'' Should Boyd have put together the accumulation of feelings he had for the Gaillard family, if he had been able to be honest with himself about the wells of emotion they invoked in him, he would have burst out in tears of joy. Yet sadly, as a result of years of repressing hurts and injustices, each segment of his brain, like terrorists' groups divided into impermeable cells for their own protection, remained detached from the others, sparing him insights into what he was to himself and to what others were to him. He never saw the whole because he worried incessantly over the components. No segment of his life, no matter how minute, was beyond the level of worry. There was nothing unimportant enough for his concern. Through fear of losing track of the infinitely small, he was blind to what life could offer in grandeur and munificence.

Yet his happiness was evident to both father and son. Boyd smiled and thanked them, and he who was rarely loquacious, spent the trip jabbering like a magpie, making sure Frédéric got the life-jacket that was in best repair, as well as sway over the outboard motor, the domain over which Boyd had taken command for himself weeks before. The loveless, malevolent world niched within the boy's brain, hovering on the verge of convulsion like incipient epilepsy, had just been touched by a moment of grace.

This was the peak of his life with the Gaillards. From here on, his hopes and aspirations collapsed like a house of cards.

.

For the Gaillards a guest was a sacred responsibility, someone to be pampered, and it made no difference if that someone was a close member of the family whom they saw every day, one who was the very personification of vulgarity, someone like Phil Navarre: feet on the sofas, cigarette ash on the floor, and comments about this or that bitch he was screwing when Madame (or so he thought) was out of earshot. The next day Mr. Gaillard spent the early afternoon in his lawn chair untangling a deep-sea crab net while Phil, Eric Navarre and Frédéric watched the U.S. Open inside on television. Boyd waited for Mr. Gaillard at the side of the house. He made a dozen rounds of the Zodiac, ensuring himself they had all the equipment they needed, nervous that a late departure would leave him little time to chew the rag with Frédéric when the young man, rising from his usual nap, would lean out of his bedroom window to inspect the catch. He began to eat at the interior of his lower lip, a sure sign he was losing restraint. He knew that Mr. Gaillard was *thinking* and *planning* as he unraveled the line, and that he could spend *hours* doing so.

Finally the old man said they could shove off. Phil chose that moment to leave the house and meander over to the boat. Mr. Gaillard asked him if he'd like to come along, fairly certain, Boyd believed, that, as the boy became easily seasick, he would decline. Phil asked if Boyd would be coming, as though the boy's presence at the door of the car, naked except for his black trunks, his hand nervously kneading the car doorhandle in his anxiety to get underway, could have any other meaning. ''What the hell,'' Phil said, ''if I'm sick it won't be the first time I'll have thrown up my guts,'' and he climbed in the back of the car because Boyd was blocking the front door with his body, a lack of Gaillard courtesy Mr. Gaillard could not help but register.

On the way to the wharf at Cape d'Ail panic began to seize Boyd. It was as if Phil was using up the very air meant for *his* breath. He pictured the boy on the boat, taking the place that was *his* at the motor, *his* seat across from Mr. Gaillard, suggesting they fish at a place where there would be no fish, but where the old man would go just to be polite. He saw Phil monopolizing the conversation, destroying the *silence* which belonged to Mr. Gaillard and him. He fancied the boy giving Mr. Gaillard orders that Boyd knew the old man would obey because it was *Phil* the guest on the boat, and orders to Boyd that he would refuse to even consider, but whose very refusal would hurt the old man. Boyd was struck by his increasing inability to draw in air. He knew that if he did not leave the car he would suffocate. He had no time to consider how illogical his fear was. When the car slowed before a red light, he opened the door and bolted, yelling he had to get home, that he was ill. He ran down the road, barefoot in his swimsuit, while the Gaillard car and boat were stuck in traffic and Mr. Gaillard, his head out the window, his face entirely perplexed, yelled for him to come back.

Two hours later he was home, his feet blistered, too proud to have hitchhiked, but having at last caught his breath. As Boyd knew he wouldn't, Mr. Gaillard did not raise the subject when he returned for dinner. He just informed the family that Phil had been very seasick and vomited the whole time, a satisfying piece of news which seemed to put them all--with the exception of Madame--in good humor. He and Frédéric went off to the Menton Casino where Boyd put a hundred francs on red and won. He insisted that for once Frédéric let him buy the drinks, and that they not go home until they had consumed every cent. Madame greeted them, drunk as sailors, at four in the morning.

The next day accelerated his downfall.

.

At seven Marie tapped on the door to awaken him. Boyd had invited her to lunch at the restaurant of her choosing in the Alps. He downed four bowls of coffee in hopes of steadying his hands and hangover. At around 9:00 they stopped outside of Sospel for gas and for him to urinate. He invited Marie to stretch her legs, but she waited in the car for his return. At the approach of the Alps he had a second urge, and pulled over into a clump of pines. Again he offered Marie the occasion to ''stretch her legs'', and again she remained quietly waiting in the car. In the Alps, at St. Martin-Vésubie, he used the men's room after filling the car's reservoir. This time Marie refused to let him pay, saying her father would be furious. He paid anyway, and suggested she too might want to use the ladies'. She said no, and they went off towards the Cîme du Diable.

Boyd found himself again struggling for air, and not because of the height of the gorges they climbed through. He had felt obliged to invite Marie on an outing of some kind, his way of repaying her for the morning breakfasts, the cold cokes she would bring out to him on the beach in mid-morning, her kindness when making sure he got the best and biggest pieces of cake during tea on the Gaillard veranda. He could hardly do less, he had told himself. Yet a conviction was boring itself into his head, one that told him she was purposely trying to demonstrate her independence of him by not accepting his repeated suggestions that she use the washroom. Even as he drove along he felt the pressure of the four bowls of coffee again building at his groin. It was inhuman, he believed, and impossible, that Marie was not afflicted by the same need. For some obscure reason she wished to spite him by not acquiescing to his superior judgment. The thought that she was trying to make him out as some kind of weakling made him smolder.

Marie was as incapable of guessing the reason for Boyd's change of humor as was Boyd of bringing himself away from the abyss his mind sped towards like a car out of control. She would gladly have used the ladies' had she known it had become a question of saving his sanity. Finally Boyd pulled into a restaurant. Wishing to please him, Marie agreed to accompany him for a bite of lunch. She knew from experience with her brother the utility of a good meal in calming the beast in boys.

They took a table that gave onto the Cirque, a basin bordered by mountains, still snow covered. Boyd went to the toilets, as white as a sheet when she refused to do the same. She's laughing at my weakness, he said to himself in front of the urinal and, at the thought of her scoffing behind his back, he let go a final spurt that stained his jeans.

Slightly nauseous, but far too reserved to reveal a problem she sometimes had at certain monthly periods, she declined to order.

''But that's why I *invited* you here,'' he said, incredulous.

''You take what you want and I'll keep you company.''

''But I invited you here to...'' and broke off, his mouth askew. While he stared at her, the waiter came up and asked if they'd like to order. Lost in his thoughts, as unconscious of his environment as a diver encased in a bathysphere, he heard nothing. The waiter placed a hand on his shoulder and repeated the request. As with Phil the previous day, his mind snapped. ''You touched me,'' he said in a low, menacing growl, turning to the boy. ''Don't you *ever* do that again.'' He got up wordless, threw a fifty-franc bill on the table, and walked out. Marie had to run to keep up. He opened the car door for her as was his custom, but he would *not* give her the comfort of a single word. She could *stew*. They took the road back to Cap Martin, both walled in their meditations.

.

As a boy he had found solace in the haven of his heart where he endured, alone, the hated years of his youth. At the university he had discovered another refuge, the walls of which were lined with books. At the first opportunity he had fled his country, the witness to his failings, to Paris where he accepted the post of professor in a British college, the only American. In the staff room, smelling of cigarettes and musty from windows sealed against drafts, he had found another sanctuary among stuffed armchairs and tables blemished from ancient tea stains, where the conversation among his peers--thick Oxford accents, bifocals and rumpled suits--was serine, and the students served as the butts of their stellar derision. He had no penchant for the things of this world, and his indifference extended to his person: baggy trousers, unironed shirts, a tie he never unknotted, shoes with thick soles, not unlike those worn by Mark, ever in need of a brushing. Had fate not interfered with his chosen asceticism, he would have preserved his mental balance and, as the majority of his colleagues, taken his retirement in a remote village in Province.

But for reasons more pragmatic than esthetic, he allowed himself a personal touch. He needed exercise and decided that weightlifting would be as good a way of getting it as any other. The more his body took form, the more he desired to show it off. He swapped his badly cut suit for jeans that molded to his forms, particularly the curve of his thighs, the focal point of the gazes of his girl students.

Still, he continued to withdraw into the corner of his heart where his true and loyal friend remained himself, censoring even the images which enflamed his solitary pleasures. Had he been satisfied with the outward improvements, and remained a cute prof blessed with an amiable ass, contenting himself with nothing more than titillating young, inexperienced girls, and that until old age deprived him of his new beauty and nascent virility--diluting, simultaneously, the memory of the cruelties of his youth, like water thinning wine--if he had contented himself with just *that*, he would have known--compared to others in the world who endured wars, famine and disease--a moderately happy existence.

But there had been Philippe, Reiner and Laurent, and his immergence from the depths inhabited by the likes of Narcisse, to the real world of Goldmund. A period of calm came with the death of Laurent, but here he was now in Cap Martin, exposed to people and situations that were again threatening his stability: Frédéric in bed with Sylvie who had given herself to her own brother and to most of Frédéric's friends at the Bronx disco, Eric coming in the mouth of the girl at the Cantons' while Alan sodomized her. Frédéric who had insisted, ''You haven't done any screwing in all the time you've been my guest.'' What would they all think if they were to discover his decadent tendencies? He remembered the story of the Greek boy who had been abandoned by Zeus because he felt no charnel attractions towards the youths who were his companions, the ideal of the time. The Greek had resolved his dilemma by committing suicide, a step that intrigued Boyd, since the act had put such a rapid, such a definitive, such a *painless end* to his suffering. The new demands, the new changes, the new *emotions*, were causing him to lose his footing, like a child who couldn't swim, yet was being dragged into the deep end of a swimming pool. And like the child, there was no one to throw him a buoy, because in his heart of hearts there was place for no one but himself.

.

Back home Madame Gaillard waddled out to meet the car. Through the windshield she could make out Boyd, the black-circled eyes, the chalk-white face looking straight ahead as though hypnotized. Marie was staring ahead too, her eyes furious, a lock of hair hanging stranded down the middle of her forehead. Madame shook her head and waited for one of the children to make a first move. Poor woman, how could she have known that the viper she had all but taken to her breast sat coiled on the front seat of that car, and that unless it was cast out now, within a week she would contemplate, like Hecabe, the crumbling remnants of her world.

CHAPTER THIRTY-THREE

A special night for the Coyotes at the Menton Casino had been arranged by Jean-Charles, and Boyd was invited. He asked Marie to accompany him to Nice to buy a suitable outfit. As she knew the men's shops there, he was certain of leaving no stone unturned in his search for something just right. ''He's worse than a girl,'' she said laughing when they returned. ''We went to every store and then back again. There was always a detail that was wrong, the cut of the pocket, legs too narrow or a zipper where buttons would have been smarter, according to him.'' But when he came out of his room, the family was in commensurate awe. He had settled on a pair of white ducks, narrow at the waist and flared at the pockets, a midnight-blue pocketless shirt--unheard of at Cap Martin where a shirt's prime purpose was carrying cigarettes---white socks--a youthful error, regretted Madame--in black loafers. In one of those flared trouser pockets was the hundred-franc bill with which he needed to win at the roulette table if he was going to spend another month at the Gaillards'. ''After all,'' he thought to himself with some justification, ''I can't *always* arrange to be elsewhere when in cafés or restaurants the bills are handed out.''

And win he did, placing the hundred francs on red three times in a row. Besides the Gaillards, there were Eric Navarre and Michel and Alain Canton, Jean-Charles the organizer, as well as Phil Navarre who had somehow freed himself from his father's vigilance. At the moment of Boyd's winning streak Phil was drunkenly making his was through the parking lot, Alain in tow. Between two cars Phil saw a boy pissing. ''Mighty small pecker you got there, son,'' he said and laughed with Alain, leaving the boy, up from Sospel, so angry he wet himself.

In the Casino the others took a table on the terrace of the disco, a superb view overlooking a garden of lawn, cypress and palms, and a swimming pool lighted with four small corner spots, off limits at night, but where a group of boys was skinny-dipping anyway. The air was warm and the sky clear and starry. The beer put Boyd at ease, and for a moment he envisaged taking up Marie's hand and saying something sweet to it.

In the patois of the Southeast, big rugby men were known as wardrobes because they were bulky and built to last centuries, and the mirrored doors might shatter like a chin or nose, but nothing could damage the man within. Six wardrobes made their way onto the terrace, uplifting tables and chairs, and causing the karate black-belt bouncer to absent himself to the toilets to relieve an urgent need. In their midst was the boy Phil had insulted out in the parking lot. Phil rose to make a hasty retreat but was too late. The boy whose pride he had injured gave him a blow to the plexus, gravely indenting Phil's ribcage which was wired to his sternum, shaking up the heart his father knew hadn't long even under the most cajoling of conditions. Phil whitened and collapsed, catching his chin on the jagged edge of a metal patio chair as he went down, ripping it upward until it joined his harelip, impaling his canines into the gums. Alain stooped to help his friend and received a kick to his buttocks that fractured his coccyx. Whelping, he rolled over on his side, knees drawn to his chest. Only Frédéric had time to get in a punch before receiving a blow that glanced off his chin and broke his left clavicle, making him a defenseless target to the rugby men's drunken savagery.

It was then the bouncer chose to return. He convinced the rugby men they had caused enough havoc, and informed them that the police were on their way. Three boys were taken to the hospital where Phil was given a bed, Frédéric a sling and Alain painkiller. Back home Marie and Sylvie gave the Gaillards the details. No one knew what had happened to Boyd who had been right next to Marie until the violence broke out. Everyone overlooked Jean-Charles who, like Boyd, had had the same presence of mind to get out while the getting was good.

When Boyd finally returned, everyone fell on him for an explanation of where he had been. He mumbled something about being separated from the group by a wall he had been pushed behind. He had fallen, and by the time he got to his feet again the battle was over. As he retired to bed, Sylvie could not help noticing how impeccable his white trousers were for someone who had been stretched out on the terrace floor among cigarette butts and tracked-in dirt.

During the following days the fight became the ''*cause célèbre*'' of Cap Martin, retold a dozen times in front of televisions, as the U.S. Open tennis season came to an end. What a sad destiny that anyone should be born in Sospel, lamented the Coyotes, that inland hellhole, freezing in winter, stifling from heat in summer, where most of the hillbillies born there had never even ventured out to see the nearby sea. Sospel had been frequented before the War by socialites and actresses thanks to its mud baths, but today the cures were reserved for the fat and aged as a kind of holiday doctors prescribed for their best patients, paid for by the Social Security. That Cap Martin boys would stand up for an invalid like Phil was proof enough of their valiance and loyalty, especially in comparison to the outsider who had disappeared. Frédéric's friends stopped dropping by as often to see him because, he was told when he met them by accident in the streets of Monte Carlo, they didn't care to run into Boyd. When they couldn't help crossing both boys, the handshake they gave the foreigner was decidedly limp-wristed.

Boyd pretended to be unaware of the ostracism, but the toll it took was devastating. He vitally needed to keep up pretences, to mask the inner void, that wasteland where a shadowy train shunted from empty station to empty station, its load of loneliness stretching, he sometimes felt, to the core of the earth. The world was made up of the mediocre and the incapable, that he knew from experience. If they had turned against him because he had been unwilling to risk a broken jaw or blindness or worse, they would receive the disdain they deserved. Sometimes from his room he would hear the Coyotes visiting the Gaillards. He wouldn't go out to confront the hypocrisy of their smiles in front of Madame, and the sly looks of commiseration they turned on Frédéric. For Boyd they were no more than a pack of animals.

He wanted to stay on in Cap Martin, but was pragmatic enough to realize it was now impossible. In that case, why not take Cap Martin to Rome, to the apartment he had rented for September? Frédéric would come, of course, as would Marie, that was obligatory, and Sylvie if Frédéric was coming, that he could do nothing about. He would invite Mario as their translator, and Eric Navarre. Why not Jean-Charles? He too had disappeared at the beginning of the fighting though no one seemed to hold it against him. He could be counted on to take up the slack should the conversation lag.

But at the last minute Frédéric decided he couldn't leave his father to do all the work alone at the tiny honey factory. Frédéric did nothing to suppress his anger that Sylvie would be going anyway. She had never been out of the Riviera except to visit an aunt in Paris, and for her the trip was an offer of escape from the same faces and the same places that had hemmed her in since birth. Her younger sister had once been invited to Chicago by an American boy she had met at the Menton Casino, and she had been treated like a queen. She had had to return home after her American summer, but her mind had been liberated. Now she was preparing herself for the baccalaureate and then entrance to a university, after which she planned to return to her ''adopted'' American family and her boyfriend there, to start a new life. Sylvie secretly wished for a similar adventure: the son of an Italian magnate was perhaps waiting for her on his yacht off Capri, where fate and chance would have them cross trails. Eric Navarre agreed to go at Marie's insistence. He too harbored dreams of Tyrrhenian sunsets, each evening at the side of a different olive-complexioned *ragazza*. Marie welcomed the excursion in the company of Eric Navarre whom she had known since they were both children. Each summer she had found him more handsome, growing worldly and ever outward with each experience his budding manhood, parents' money and boarding-school liberty in Nice offered him. Marie had been brought up a tomboy from her contact with her brother and his friends, and she took to night life more brazenly than better chaperoned Cap Martin girls, but she had nonetheless decided to be the good-girl wayward lads eventually married, and although she had had a coup-de-coeur for Boyd, her inner heart had belonged to Eric from the time she had taught him to tie his shoe laces.

Boyd had promised to guide the group through Rome. He knew the city well from having passed two weeks there at Christmas, visiting museums. His only request had been that Phil not be included. Then had come the disaster caused by his refusal to participate in the fight at the Casino, the result of which was the refusal of Michel and Alain Canton, whom Frédéric had invited, as well as Jean-Charles' bowing out in consequence. *His* cowardliness even over-shadowed Boyd's own, the boy thought with no particular justification. These withdrawals, Boyd was certain, had inspired Frédéric's last-minute concern that his father was being overworked at the family factory.

.

The humor of the voyagers, when the day of departure arrived, was execrable. Frédéric had told Sylvie that Boyd was against their marrying and Phil had told Sylvie that Boyd had called her a slut, which was the case after Phil had informed him about her incest with her brother. Boyd had also said to Phil, ''I'm not the marrying type,'' which Phil had immediately reported to Marie, along with Boyd's additional comment, ''Never could the dowry of a Cap Martin girl tempt me.'' And Boyd had had mixed feelings towards Eric since the morning two days before when Boyd had entered Frédéric's room, through their mutual bathroom, with an offer of coffee and croissants served in bed to him and Sylvie. There he found Frédéric enrolled in a sheet, fast asleep. Eric Navarre lay against him, naked, also asleep, his white buttocks in contrast to the tanned body, a sight that caused Boyd a moment of throat-parched discomfort, but was only something Eric did when too drunk to drive home. Rumors, gossip, duplicity, lies, incest, innuendo, homo-eroticism: All the ups and downs of these young people were scarcely less perfidious than the dissipated mores of the youths in that session's successful television series, *Santa Barbara.*

Driving down the alley leading away from the Gaillards', Boyd had seen for the last time, in the rearview mirror, Madame's sad face and sagging jowls, the immense, hesitant body, the final tearful look she cast on her only daughter. He loved that woman, for whom nothing more was left than the hopes she set on her children.

Now Eric sat next to him in the front seat, Marie and Sylvie behind, as the car sped along he coast, past Port Beausoleil--the port that would receive Boyd in just two short years--in the dead of night, on its way to Rome.

The moment they left Cap Martin, the private domain of the Cantons, the Navarres and the Gaillards, Boyd took command. The calm, gracious houseguest became a tyrant, as aggressive as if he'd downed a potion prepared by Doctor Hyde. Everything served to unnerve him. He told the girls to stop their "cackling" when their gaiety at entering the Italian Riviera became too vociferous. He ordered Eric to exhale his cancer out of the window when the boy lit up. Eric reminded him that cigarettes hadn't kept him from spending hours in a smoky disco. Boyd informed him that he was now a passenger in the car confided to Boyd by Monsieur, and that he could either knuckle under or take a bus back home.

Eric decided to humor him. Jean-Charles had given him the name of a girl in Rome "who will enable you to fulfill," he had exulted in a flight of lyricism, "even the most unmentionable of your dreams." And with uncanny foresight he had given him the address of a friend who would put them up "if ever the Yankee does something stupid." When they eventually got back to Cap Martin, Eric would let Marie explain to the Gaillards why he had broken Boyd's jaw in front of the Coliseum, which was precisely what he planned on doing.

When Boyd was forced to stop for gas he made everyone fork over his or her fourth of the bill, even though Marie said he had only to charge it to her father. "There's no reason for that," he said, holding out his hand until they all divvyed up. Then he gave them five minutes for toilet and drinks before starting off down the ramp without Sylvie because of her la-dee-da slowness in regaining her seat. Jumping over a flowerbed, she caught up red faced, certain he would have left her behind.

In the car he put on classical music, treating their preference for pop as the mindless idiocy of uneducated yokels. He sped along at 130 kilometers an hour, fast for the old Peugeot, at the limit of what was needed to maintain control of the shaky steering wheel over which he hovered, his head strained forwards inches from the windshield, his eyes hypnotized by the lane markers flipping past like a broken film in black and white, black and white, black and white, the impossibility of the situation poisoning his mind.

He had left everything he loved back at Cap Martin, the breakneck son of the family, the pristine beach, the morning coffee in the peaceful alcove, the sea and breeze, his naked body in the twisted dunes, television with Madame, an afternoon with Monsieur on the goddamned Zodiac, the night listening to Sylvie's moans, and even the glimpse of Frédéric's body encased in that of the handsome boy brooding at his side.

Only the return to routine could have saved him at that point. He needed his bed and sleep, and all the countless other little things he did throughout a day, invariable and unchanging, immutably stable and stabilizing, his body's defense mechanism against the chaos which threatened to plunge body and soul into the black night of his inner self. Had he stopped the car then, the worst may have been avoided, and at the best the vacation would have been a succession of ugly little incidents as Boyd strove to impose his will on the others. But Sylvie chose that moment to demand he stop at a hotel. Slumped in her seat in the back, her skin slack and pale, she threatened to tell the Gaillards if Boyd didn't pull over. "Do something, Eric. He's going to kill us if he's not forced to stop." Her voice had the squeaky pouting of a baby. Her feet kicked the back of Boyd's seat, bringing on the threat that he'd slug her if she didn't stop. Eric stared straight ahead, determined to wrest the wheel at the first sign of danger. Marie tried to convince Boyd that a hotel was a good idea, that the Italian Riviera would be far more beautiful if they drove it by day, that she had her father's credit card, and how nice it would be in the morning to have coffee and croissants on the terrace overlooking the sea.

Boyd wasn't listening. When he became convinced that Eric, deprived of the support of his friends and native environment, would not interfere, he turned his attention on Sylvie. He tried to remember the filth Phil had said about her, and the confidences Marie had made during their first days together. He could probably make her mad enough so he'd indeed be forced to stop the car: to let her out. Eric and Marie would leave at the same time, of course, but not before hearing Sylvie treated as the *putain* she was, which would make the marriage impossible, Boyd thought. He would gain the Gaillards' outer anger--certainly they would never speak to him again--but he would save Frédéric in spite of himself, and win Madame's eternal--albeit silent--gratitude. In his imagination he saw Frédéric come to him through the car headlights, having now realized how right Boyd had been all along, and together they would go off carousing at the Casino, the buddies Boyd had always wished them to be.

Even as a child the boy's innate paranoia had convinced him he detained the inner truth of things. It was his possession of that truth that was the key to his stability. If Marie came to believe in him, she would wake up and recognize Sylvie for what she was. The truth would bring him Frédéric's love and make Eric admire his tenacity and stronger will. The truth would reveal to him the day when his body lost its beauty, he thought bitterly but with courage, his mind wandering from hill to dell, the day when he could no longer perform the acts of his youth, when his intelligence began to erode and his brain metamorphose into pulp. He would then end things with his own hand. But before that day, he promised himself, his eyes filling with the tears of years of acrimony and treason, a good number of others would be forced to pay for harming a boy who dreamed of nothing more outrageous than books and music, sea and sun, and the tranquility of the tomb. The remaining enigma was how to attain that tranquility without pain ... without suffering.

In the backseat Sylvie pouted on and on about the death march. ''He can't even speak French good,'' he heard her saying at one moment, and at another, in a whisper to Marie, something about Phil's saying he couldn't fit in with the other boys, that his affection for Frédéric was *unnatural*, and then, in the silence between two movements of Mahler's *Titan*, he caught the worst of Cap Martin words, ''*pédé*.'' Blood engorged his neck. His throat tightened around the word slut he was preparing to hurl at her. His oxygen cut itself off. Like a vein bursting in his head, there was a red flash behind his eyes. He would stop the car and chock the life out of the bitch. *That* would be a way of saving Frédéric. She would pay for all the innuendoes of a life of innuendoes. She was only right about his not being able to fit in. He had never been like the other boys. He couldn't piss at the urinal with them, but he didn't know why. He had never been accepted, even after years of seeking out the secret to their strength and insouciant self-confidence. Why could he never be at ease in their presence, why did he have to be different? He would have given *anything* to not be different. Oh God in Heaven, he cried out in his mind, Why did you make me *different*!

At that moment they arrived at the toll station of the Genoa section of the freeway. When Boyd skidded to a stop before the barrier, the others needed no invitation to scramble out. Unknown to him, he had been swerving across the road, yelling out his inner thoughts, of not being accepted, of being different, of problems at the urinal, bitches and innuendoes. And also about Frédéric. Yelling that he needed to get back to Marie's brother. The side doors still open, he put the vehicle in reverse, and with the wheels screeching, he turned around and went back down the road, back towards Cap Martin. Crying, Marie went to a pay phone to call her parents. Too distraught to make herself understood, she handed the phone to Eric who, fired up by the adrenaline that enflamed his cheeks, giving to his voice the gravity of a baritone, told Mr. Gaillard that they had been abandoned literally in the middle of the road by the Gaillard houseguest.

''I'm leaving right away to pick you up,'' said Mr. Gaillard, always in control, ''but why was Marie crying something about Frédéric?''

''Nothing, really. Your guest just went bananas. *He* was yelling about Frédéric, and Marie got caught up in the … the … boy's crazy thoughts, I guess.'' Eric went into some detail about how Boyd had been acting since leaving the house.

''*Bueno*. I'm getting in touch with the Gendarmerie at the Menton section of the highway,'' he told Eric. ''For Boyd's own safety I'm going to have to see he's stopped before he does some bodily harm to himself or others. Now you just wait where you are. I'm leaving now and will probably be there early in the morning.''

''*Holy shit*!'' laughed Eric hanging up, grateful to the old man, and not unhappy the crazy *enculé* who'd upset Marie and her family would get what was coming to him.

At the Menton toll station the gendarmes were alerted to halt the Gaillard car and its sole occupant. At the Gaillard house Madame insisted on accompanying her husband. While he waited for her to push into her housedress, he called the Casino for Frédéric. The owner himself promised he would go to the gaming room personally and see to it that the boy returned home to guard the house during their absence. Madame at last made it into the car at the moment her son, hampered by the clavicle broken by the Sospel rugby men, left the Casino on the white motorcycle Boyd had entrusted to his care.

Halfway between the Casino and the Gaillard house was what the locals called ''the ambush'', a spot favored by the cops to give out tickets for speeding or non-compliance to the lights. The real name of the crossroads, and the nearby bus stop, was Massolin. At that time of the night the lights had changed over to a blinking yellow in consequence of the near total absence of traffic. Frédéric arrived there before his parents, but at the same time as a tourist coach. When the Gaillards arrived, and Mr. Gaillard carefully slowed and signaled a right turn in the direction of Italy, there was already an ambulance and a mass of police, and a bus pulled over to the side of the road. In the center of the crossroads was a large dark patch Mr. Gaillard took for oil, and in the gutter at each corner foamy fragments that reflected the blue light of the ambulance and the pulsating yellow of the traffic lights. Frédéric's head, helmeted, had literally exploded on contact with the bus that projected the bike into an empty lot and carried along the body pinned to the front axle like refuse swept up by a street cleaner. Neither of the Gaillards gave a second's thought for the boy they assumed still at the Casino.

At Menton, Boyd's car succeeded in breaking through the wood barrier set up in front of the toll station, but the car's four tires were flattened by the nail-rack the gendarmes had laid out across the road. The car crashed into a tollbooth. Disregarding severe facial injuries, Boyd, pinned to his seat, fought to free himself, to continue his course. He was yelling Frédéric's name when the gendarmes got to him, and even after being extracted through the car window he had to be held fast to the asphalt despite fractured ribs and his jaw broken in three places.

In Genoa the Gaillards found the two girls in the company of *carabinieri*, having coffee. Eric had to be pulled away from a Sospel boy just arrested by the cops, who had been entertaining Eric with stories of drugs and sex orgies along the Italian Riviera. Boys from the Southeast, even mortal enemies like Cap Martians and Sospelois, knew their own, and the colorful life led by the Navarres and the Cantons was well regarded by the boy in custody. Mr. Gaillard was told that Boyd was in the Princess Grace Hospital in Monaco, under surveillance. He decided to drop off the girls and Eric in Cap Martin before seeing in what way he could be of aid to his guest.

By late afternoon Frédéric's identification back in Cap Martin had still not been finalized. When the Gaillard car entered the Massolin crossroads the patch in the middle of the road was still there, russet and peeling, as well as the foamy white substances along the curb. As the bus and ambulance had long since been removed, Mr. Gaillard noticed none of these details. It was at home, later, on the other end of the telephone, that their world would come crashing down on them all.

Frédéric's friends gathered at the Gaillard house. Maître Navarre sent his son Eric to Monte Carlo to gather news about Boyd. Jean-Charles volunteered to go to the ''ambush'' with water and a long-handled brush to clean away the remains that were in evidence. The girls returned soon after with flowers.

Eric went to Monaco accompanied by Phil. As he looked for a parking place, Phil entered the hospital where he found Boyd's jaw wired and the boy in a daze from painkillers. ''Listen careful, Yankee scumbag. When you ordered Marie out of the car last night she called papa Gaillard to come and get her. Papa called Frédéric at the Casino to return home and protect the family silverware. On the way there, on *your* bike, he was splattered along the countryside by a big tourist bus. His brains are still in the road and his guts pushed into the gutter. Because of you he's dead,'' he continued, his voice distorted by sobs. ''Because of a Yankee piece of shit the remains of the best buddy Eric and I ever had are now in garbage bags in the morgue.''

When Eric caught up with Phil outside Boyd's room, he was bewildered by the screams coming from inside, and the scratches on Phil's face that a nurse was cleaning with disinfectant.

''For Christ's sake, what happened?'' he shouted.

''I don't know,'' Phil answered, ''but the doctors had to give him a shot to calm the bastard down.''

Boyd returned to class after a three-month medical leave, weak and gaunt, his skin hanging from his bones like rags on a mummy, and a spark like a low fire in the recesses of his black eyes.

CHAPTER THIRTY-FOUR

Denis

The summer following the death of Frédéric, Boyd signed on as a crewmember on a boat to Rhodes. It was the first time he had ever set foot on a sailing boat and as far as he was concerned he didn't care if he drowned, as Laurent had drowned two years before. He had come to a dead-end in his life. The psychiatric help at the Princess Grace Hospital had offered a reprieve, enabling him to relegate thoughts of self-destruction resulting from Frédéric's death to the obscure convolutions of his brain. Yet he remained mentally unstable, quarreling even with his students, going so far as to invite one of them to settle things by stepping across the street to the park. At the end of the class the student slipped out at the head of the others, never to return. The incident gave him the idea of taking up karate where he soon won a reputation as a kamikaze, indifferent to receiving punches. The *maître* was a colossal black, a Guadeloupian, who had made himself invulnerable thanks to his technique. For hours, weeks and months he would make the boys sit before him, practicing various movements in slow motion, over and over and over, the ankles upon which they sat becoming so painful some cried out and were immediately dismissed, others couldn't rise at the end of the class and had to be lifted up by their companions, their legs still crossed beneath their buttocks.

It was the only dressing room Boyd had ever known where there was no whistling or singing or horsing around. He himself was impassive, dressing, like the others, in troubled silence. He was the only white belt the *maître* would call out to demonstrate on, sometimes hitting or kicking him so violently he would pass the weekend in bed, unable to move. Once he caught sight of the *maître* in the Samaritaine Department Store, seemingly encircled by a protective shield. The girth of a bear, he slipped through crowds like a panther. As the months went by Boyd took on other nighttime karate classes, and then added the weekends. Occasionally brown or black belts would attend the Guadeloupian's beginners' class. Boyd always took them on, and after the first few minutes of light sparing, the time for the advanced belts to see that the boy was dead serious, they would get down to serious fighting. More and more the Guadeloupian would leave the other boys to referee and give advice to the boy and the advanced belts he was sparing with.

The truth was that he mourned for the Gaillard son, and needed to be beaten in retribution for the blood splotch and broken skull at the Massolin intersection. At times he saw Phil's face in the place of his adversaries. Then he hit so hard the Guadeloupian was obliged to remind him he was practicing a *sport*. The wish to see Phil Navarre dead went a long way in his determination to never throw in the sponge, neither on the tatami nor in life. His feelings for Laurent were different, Laurent had been called back by God.

One day in the teachers' staffroom a colleague read out an *annonce* about a boat sailing from the South of France to Turkey. Boyd picked up the paper when the teachers had gone to their classes, and copied down the phone number he called the next day. The decision to board a boat was further proof of his despondency, as he feared water since the day at the lake when his father, drunk, had nearly killed him.

Didier came by in person, between thirty and forty thought the boy, tall, slender, blond, pleasant-looking, a sincere manner and self-ingratiating smile that inspired confidence. ''There'll be a plethora of islands to visit,'' he promised. Boyd signed on for two months, about six weeks longer than anyone Didier had ever had before, and made out the check. The boat would leave from Marseille around the middle of July with just one other boy who had also signed on for an exceptionally long period. It would sail directly to Bonifacio, on the south coast of Corsica, and then non-stop to Brindisi where they would pick up their first passenger, a girl. After that they would sail during the day and anchor at night, occasionally going into ports to pick up other passengers or drop them off.

The boat was in dry dock at Martigues, outside Marseille. That particular model was called a Swan, but on land resembled an ugly ducking. Boyd, freshly arrived, his single baggage at his feet, was being shown the hull by Didier when Denis, the other passenger, returned from an errand. The boy's heart missed a beat. He hoped his embarrassment wasn't evident to Didier, and his unsteady handshake felt by Denis. Denis had been a French champion tennis player, ranking at one time third nationally. Tall, dark skinned, pitch-black hair and eyes, he rounded off his year financially and girl-wise by giving summer tennis lessons at the Club Med. ''Where there's a plethora of pussy, Denis here tells me,'' interjected Didier. ''But this summer I plan on resting,'' Denis inserted , giving a genial smile to Didier, while Boyd looked at anything, rudder, propeller, sounder, water intake, rather than at him, able only to ask Didier why the boat's name wasn't on the transom. ''Didn't get around to it, did I?'' the captain answered sharply.

In the water the Swan's line made the boy's heart sing, although since meeting Denis everything took on new splendor. They set off the next morning, straight for Bonifacio, several days away. As they made their way out of Martigues, clouds rose in the form of anvils, dark and ominous, so beautiful the boy gasped. The wind became strong when they were in the open, smelling of coming rain. Sitting in the cockpit wedged between the man and the tennis player, the boat tilted to such an angle that he found himself staring down at water racing under his feet. He instinctively grasped behind him where his fingers seized a life cable that he clung to, certain that should he let go he'd fall into the white-crested stream surging past the gunnels. Didier and Denis were talking together across his chest, seemingly oblivious to the boy's distress. The memory of his father in the small boat in the middle of the lake resurfaced, making his blood run cold.

The days and nights were broken into watches. In all his life Boyd had never been disturbed during his sleep. Now he was awoken in the dead of night to take the helm, an eye on the stars and an occasional verification of the compass by illuminating it with a flashlight for a second or two. The boat sailed without life jackets, without a safety raft, with absolutely no lights on, all of which was of no concern to the boy who knew nothing of either sea legislation or what was normal equipment for a boat. Because he couldn't sleep undisturbed through the night, he became more and more tired during the day. Soon he found himself rushing off to sleep the moment he was relieved, rousing himself only for food. The weather was terrible and the boat continually battered by waves. He had admiration for the resilience of Denis and Didier who spent all their time outside, while he remained in the cabin sleeping and reading.

Bonifacio was the most spectacular sight the boy had seen outside of the Grand Canyon. From afar the entrance presented itself as a solid cliff wall that, as Didier approached, both boys wondered what suicidal urge was egging him on to crash the Swan onto its sheer face. Only when they were several meters away did they see the slit in the wall's surface, giving way to a channel of overhanging cliffs so narrow that only a fine line of blue sky, sun faded, could be seen at the summit, reminding Boyd of the gorges of the Colorado and Brian. The boat meandered through the bottleneck for a mile, to the port at its end. They docked and headed for the showers. Boyd nearly fell when enclosed in the four walls, fighting for his balance as the floor rose and fell, obliging him to steady himself against one wall while he soaped up and rinsed off. He gained enough of a toehold, though, to ejaculate a week of abstinence with a violence and urgency that emptied his body and left him crouching on the floor, wrung out. When he joined the two others Denis made a comment about how he too had ''emptied every pore.'' Didier's laughter informed the boys that even he, at his age, hadn't been less prolific.

From there they set sail for the Straits of Messina. Most days they were well in sight of the rolling barren hills of Italy, the coast at night laced in a magical string of lights that perfectly outlined every beach, bay and creek. The winds that had accompanied them since leaving Martigues fell once they'd pass through the Straits of Bonifacio. Some nights Boyd had the feeling they weren't even moving. The sails fell slack, but the watches were respected, and as Didier refused to use the motor, its existence was soon forgotten. Little by little he regained his lust for life, aided by Didier who taught him how to set the sails, decipher a map, chart a course and take readings.

Boyd was keen on performing the physical exercises he had picked up in his karate classes. They kept his muscles in tone and his joints loose. Denis was an even greater enthusiast. He had been raised in a special school for athletes, one that gave a general scholastic education while training the participants in the sports with which they would one day win medals in competitions. He added a few basic movements to what Boyd normally did, and both would work out together for a couple of hours daily on the prow of Didier's ship. Didier made fun of Boyd at first, but when he saw Denis follow Boyd's lead, he said nothing more. He rarely interfered with the boys, partly due to his age, partly because he sensed that their respect for his knowledge would be undercut through untoward familiarity. The boys spread out a large towel just behind the jib, and while the boat plunged ahead, they took turns encouraging each other to exploits in pushups and sit-ups. Boyd wore his bathing suit but Denis soon abandoned wearing clothes altogether when they came into the hot weather along the coast of Sardinia. As Boyd held his ankles, the French boy slowly rose and slowly let himself down during the series of sit-ups, his mind on his abdominals. Boyd marveled at the pouch of testicles reaching down to the deck, and the cock shriveled into a mass three times the thickness of his own. The ancient Greeks, he had read, tied up the end of the boys' prepuce with a piece of string to discourage erections during physical exercises, resulting in an extension of the skin, similar to Denis's own, as ample as the stem of a funnel. Didier's equipment was more voluminous still. ''There's a plethora of girls who'll appreciate a workout with this on the voyage,'' he said one day, shaking it after pissing overboard.

In Brendisi they picked up their first passenger, an extremely proper woman in all-new gym gear straight from the box. She talked literature with Didier while being politely avoided by the other two who found her uptight. During the afternoon of her first day aboard, a few hours after they had set sail for Corfu, Denis, fresh from of his sleeping bag following a short nap, was making his way up the ladder from the cabin to the cockpit where Miss Prim and Proper was trying to maneuver the tiller as Didier had shown her. Boyd was lying on the roof in the shade of the mainsail, happy someone else was doing the steering for a change. He heard a gasp and looked down as Denis came into view, his sex nearly perpendicular. After that both boys spent the day naked, making jokes about how lucky she was to be among three handsome virile studs.

They anchored off Corfu and Denis, unexpectedly, insisted that Boyd accompany him to the beach for a meal on their own. In the dinghy, when Boyd asked why Didier and the woman weren't coming, Denis rounded the thumb and forefinger of one hand which he pierced with the forefinger of the other. "She cracked," he laughed. "Seeing us naked was too much for her. Didier told me we'd hastened the inevitable by three days. Especially thanks to me," added Denis with a grin. In taking on passengers during the summer, not only did Didier earn money for himself and for the upkeep of the Swan, he also benefited from the romantic nights at anchor off the coasts of island paradises such as Corfu. "And you?" asked Boyd. "There's a Club Med in Corfu, and others all along our itinerary. I emptied the neighborhood drugstore of rubbers. I'll be invited to tour the Clubs, perhaps even spend the night. Don't worry, I know what to do."

And he did indeed. Each time the Swan anchored off a new coast, Didier, Denis, Boyd and whoever were guests at the time, used the dinghy to get to shore to a Greek taverna. Afterwards they would all return to the boat except for Denis who would either disappear into a Club Med, or go off like a lone wolf. Boyd chose to sleep on the deck of the Swan, from which he could gaze at the stars, night after night, from the warmth of his bedroll. The world had never been so wonderful as during those moments before sleep, in the peace of an anchorage, a soft breeze on his face, and the tranquil lulling of the boat over the perpetual movement of the sea. It was from the prow that he would see Denis swimming back in the early morning, his clothes in a plastic bag. He would greet the French boy as the prodigal son, his admiration increasing in leaps and bounds with each exploit. Denis couldn't take him along to the Club Med, that he understood, but he wasn't avaricious with his tales of what had gone on there, or if there was no Club, how he had rounded up and squired the night's prey.

One thing had really fired Boyd's imagination was when Denis told him he had had a drink with a girl at a street-side café who confided that she was a virgin. Denis leaned towards her for a kiss while, at the same time, he slipped two fingers inside the panties she was wearing under her skirt, into her pussy, the act sheltered from passersby only by the small table.

"*Jesus*! I hope she slapped you!" exclaimed Boyd, certain she hadn't as he knew how evenings with Denis invariably ended.

"She jumped, but crying out was difficult as I had my lips stuck to hers."

"And then … you fucked her?"

"A virgin? Never. They're a source of infinite hassles. Anyway, there are other fish in the sea. And then, when I lost my virginity, I lost everything," he added cryptically.

Boyd was on the verge of asking him to clarify the statement when he thought he saw tears in Denis's eyes. Before he could be certain, Denis had plunged into the sea.

It irked Boyd that Didier confided only in Denis. Denis always knew exactly where they were going and by which route they would get there and whom they would be picking up, since Didier had met them all before, as he had met Boyd. The boy tried to get on the man's good side, to initiate communication, to flatter his ego, to "collaborate" with him-- the word favored by the French--but to little avail. Boyd would spend hours upon hours at the tiller steering, a chore he hated, and he would scrub the boat, a labor of love because he loved the Swan, but there would be no thanks, ever, from the captain.

Boyd wondered if he had overdone his zeal in Italy and Corfu, earning the disdain of the older man. The boy liked languages and had picked up a little Italian during a summer in Rome. He had spent the summer before meeting Laurent in Greece where he had little to do other than swim, eat and study a Greek grammar he picked up there. He had appointed himself translator when the Italian customs visited their boat in Brindisi. Didier had chuckled, giving the boy his head in the negotiations. But he had paled in Corfu town when Boyd greeted the authorities in Greek. He laughed then too, but "yellow" as the French say for something forced, and quipped that while the boy was at it, he could just as well tell them the boat was his. The officials, grateful for his attempts to speak their language, saw them all quickly through Greek red tape.

.

In Athens Boyd again distinguished himself to Didier's discomfort. Because he had been there before, he knew the best restaurant for the price they were willing to pay, he knew where to change money, how to take the subway, the museums they *had* to visit on their short stopover, and even the emplacement of the nearest toilet when they needed to take a leak. This time they picked up a girl who was the opposite of the prude they met in Brendisi, short, fat, loud, her arms over their shoulders, her hands down Didier's shirt. In fact this was her second tour, and when Denis pulled Boyd away from the Swan once she was installed, the boy wasn't surprised but had to ask Denis, "Why do it with someone so *homely*?" "Those aren't your onions," was the French expression used by his friend.

The girl was everything Boyd wasn't, and he couldn't stand her for it. She was fun loving, open, outgoing and unabashedly sensual. She went *naked* on the boat, a right, in Boyd's world, reserved for those who were *well made*, for Christ's sake. She charmed the two Frenchmen, always walking between them while he trailed behind. She had offered to make room for him, of course, but he patiently waited to recuperate *his* place between the two boys once she had left.

And also, she was perpetually sea sick, demanding, without overtly demanding, that Didier and Denis be at her beck and call night and day. She had gastric troubles too, which called for a diet of rice, rice and more rice. She never prepared the food, she never lifted a finger, in fact, to steer or wash the dishes or do the shopping. But she ate more than the other three together, and then proceeded to throw it up, lowering herself over the stern ladder while Boyd made his way to the farthest limit of the prow, in front of the jib even, where he wouldn't have to see or hear anything. She just loved to lie out in the bottom of the cockpit, on her back, obliging Boyd to steer over her head, while her tits fell like giant formless medusas to each side of her thorax. When it was hot Didier and Denis were requisitioned to douse her with buckets of seawater, like a seal stranded on land, and when they were not available she would beg Boyd to do the same, until he inadvertently threw a bucketful into her face, just as she was drawing in air. Although he said he was sorry during her choking spasms, he was abundantly insulted by Didier and Denis while she kept sputtering, ''It's not his fault he doesn't like me, it's mine for not finding the way to the tenderness that's in *everyone*.'' And then in voce sotto, ''Or *nearly* everyone.''

The night before leaving she said to him, ''You know, when I look at you you're always smiling. But when I catch you unaware there's an expression of the most terrible loss, the most fathomless unhappiness on your face....'' ''Bullshit,'' he'd said, smiling--yellow. Chary of her sure aim, she couldn't be off the boat fast enough to suit him. Very early the next morning she halted at his sleeping bag to say goodbye. Boyd pretended to be asleep but she knelt next to his head and kissed him on the cheek. ''*Au revoir, mon chéri*,'' and, ''I'm leaving you a little gift,'' which she place next to his head. It was Greek candy, as hard as steel, which he later flung into the sea. ''How could you have been so cavalier with her,'' Didier said when he returned from accompanying her to the airport, the first time he had ever made a *personal* comment to Boyd, provoking a moment of exhilaration in the boy.

But the moment was brief, and when things continued as before, Boyd decided to give up trying to understand the man. After all, he asked himself, wasn't he at least *useful* enough to not be given the cold shoulder? He did the translations. He left the guys at their table to sip a cold, leisurely beers while he went into the hot kitchens to do the ordering, a Greek custom that, in reality, he adored. He did the paper work in the ports, freeing them to spend their time as they chose. And who did more for the Swan than he? Sure, he couldn't stand their music and crude sense of humor. Their politics were based on the a priori that their elected representatives were all dishonest, in contrast to credulous Americans, as Didier saw it, so willing to swallow anything coming from their own. Tired of Didier's pretensions, he took to mocking the man: ''There was a plethora of ships in the harbor'', he stated in front of Didier and a new guest. ''You know, *plethora*, the big word Didier's always using.'' This didn't win Didier over--it wouldn't, he knew--but he came to feel that the only choice the man left him was to either lie down and take it up the ass, or revolt.

Didier never felt he had anything major against Boyd. He just didn't *feel* the boy. He needed relationships in which he was at ease with men. Boyd's eyes were on him too much. He sometimes felt he was being studied as he studied girls. He liked being around men because men were disinterested. Men enjoyed exchanging information and could be counted on for help; they shared the same interests like sports and cars and, for Didier, boats and motors. Try to talk about *those* with girls. Girls represented a whole other world from the daily one Didier knew with men. He could be special with them; he took pleasure in dressing for them or even shaving when he was going to join one of them. He liked the way they looked at him, and the more their look was provoking, the more he liked it. He liked the way they were pretty and vulnerable and readily took an intellectual backseat, offering no resistance to his judgment. And the way they worked was so *natural,* and pussy felt so fucking good. One of the grudges Didier held against Boyd was that the boy was always in competition with him, even though Didier knew so much *more* than he did. Before they'd left Marseille Boyd had asked Didier if he had remembered to buy spark plugs for the boat's diesel engine. What real kid, Didier wondered, shaking his head, doesn't know that a diesel doesn't *take* spark plugs, for God's sake.

And then it always came back to the way the boy looked at him and didn't look at the female guests on the boat, and how he hung around Denis, flattering him, taking his part, working to turn him against Didier, never in *agreement* with Didier, always an obstacle. Not that the kid was an ''anomaly,'' the Greek word, Boyd had told them, for queer. But Didier knew that sexual maturation wasn't always easy for boys. He had a boy of his own, and he had been a boy. Yet a truly normal boy would follow his lead, since he was so goddamn much more experienced; a normal boy would be grateful that Didier spent a good part of his time imparting his knowledge. Boyd knew nothing about winds or sails, yet was always saying let's do this or let's do that, sometimes, Didier thought, just to provoke him or to prove to Denis that Didier was only capable of saying no. Of course, there *were* a couple of things in the boy's favor. He was *paying* his way on a summer tour where there were fewer guests than usual, he *did* do more than his share of the steering, and he *was* enthusiastic about anything having to do with the Swan.

Didier always kept Denis informed about his plans, despite the fact that Boyd saw them rarely together, as though through a kind of osmosis. The complicity provoked a jealousy in Boyd that Denis tried to lessen by sharing his own projects with the boy. At anchor, he would let Boyd help him fill a plastic bag with the clothes he'd use during his nocturnal wanderings, and as he slipped into the water he'd always turn back towards him and say, ''Don't do any entertainin' while I'm away,'' to which Boyd would hurl back, ''Fuck you!'' with a kind of pleading in his voice, as if he hoped that at the last minute Denis might just turn back and invite him along. Boyd would watch his friend swim away, his eyes riveted to the water long after he'd disappeared from view.

Denis seemed to sense when Boyd's emotional stability was slipping. At those times he would loosen up the boy by telling him stories about the school of athletes he had gone to, about the jokes they played on each other, the unexpected mores and idiosyncrasies of some, and stupidity of others. ''He's lucky he knows how to play tennis,'' he said about one French tournament winner who otherwise ''didn't know his ass from a hole in the ground.'' Denis also told about the musical beds he'd played in the Club Med, how he'd make love to one gal in the w.c. of the Club's disco, then go home with another just after making a rendezvous with a third in her room for breakfast and bed the following morning, and then starting all over again the next day. The gays were the worse, laughed Denis, '' 'cause you have to string 'em on for the tips which are *huge*, while getting off with no more than a hand fleetingly caressing your shorts-covered ass or groping maladroitly at your fly, but even that was pretty rare.'' There was always "traffic" at shower time, when the Gentle Organizers, as the Club athletes were called, displayed their wares.

One night, with Denis ashore and Didier in the cockpit, Boyd decided to sleep in the cabin because rain had been predicted for the early morning. It was perhaps the stuffy enclosed quarters that brought on the same dream. It always began with an old man's visit to de Roquette, the head of the English Department where Boyd taught. But now de Roquette was a real estate agent who sold the man a cabin near a lake. Then Boyd, as a child, found himself on the lake with his father. There was a blazing sun, replaced by storm clouds amassing over the high-peaked summits encircling the lake, and a wind, cold and violent. The surface of the lake became rough, and the boy begged his father to gain the nearest shore. The glazed, disdainful eyes, leaden and unsteady, mocked the boy's cowardliness. Then it was night in a hunting cabin warmed by a huge black iron stove, an isolated cabin on a plain of wind-flattened salt grass. The boy was in bed on the top bunk, his father's dirty playing cards of naked men and women he had found that morning scattered on the bedding before him, his hand cupping his small, child's turgid erection. The rest of the dream was more confused still. His father was getting out of the lower bunk, his back to his son. While watching the back disappear into the yellow light of the stove, the boy promised himself when old enough he would seize his freedom like a slave, never again to return to his shackles. Then it was day. The form on the upper bunk was inert. The anxiety Boyd felt at seeing that dead silhouette, covered with blankets, made him wake up with a start, howling. He was caught by Denis who had returned early and had been asleep in his own sack opposite the boy. Denis took him in his arms while Boyd sobbed into his shoulder. Then hearing Didier descend the stairs, he stifled the sobs and stiffened.

''What the *hell's* going on!'' Didier cried out, angry at being awoken.

''I had a bad dream,'' said Denis, separating himself from the boy.

''It looks to me...'' began Didier, an evil eye turned on Boyd whose face was masked by the shadows.

''I told you I had a bad dream,'' Denis insisted.

Didier turned and went back up the stairway, speechless.

Boyd again clung to the boy. ''Oh god, I need help,'' he sobbed again. ''I love you Denis and I need help. If you only knew how much I need your help.''

CHAPTER THIRTY-FIVE

A few hours after awaking from the nightmare, Boyd exchanged his sleeping bag for the solitude of the prow, leaving Denis asleep in his sack and Didier muttering incoherently in his dreams in the cockpit, entwined in blankets. He didn't sense Denis until he crouched beside him and put an arm over his shoulder. Boyd dropped his head. Denis, perhaps fearing more tears, said to him softly, ''Last night I had a bad dream, it's true. But everything's better today, so you can't hold that against me, can you?'' he asked smiling. Boyd's throat hurt from the emotion he felt for the boy who at eighteen was so much younger than himself, yet nearly a father figure thanks to the obstacles he had overcome since leaving home at age fourteen to become a professional athlete. Denis was the first of a new breed of French, in ways more American than the Americans who prided themselves on experience and independence. ''We don't want Didier to know that anything's happened, do we?'' continued Denis. ''So we'll go on as before, good friends and no more tears.'' Finally, felt Boyd, there was something new in his heart, something other than himself. Again tears filled his eyes. He eagerly nodded his consent, so thankful for this moment of joy.

''Who put the water on the stove to boil away?'' shouted Didier angrily from the cabin. ''Gas doesn't grow on trees!''

''Oh God!,'' muttered Denis, rising to see to the coffee he'd forgotten.

Alone again on the prow, Boyd thought back to other moments that had buoyed him with a feeling of hope and promise. One had been the first real book he read, *The Grapes of Wrath*, in which he discovered that he was not alone in his suffering. He had known the joy of seeing the Grand Canyon and he had taken the train to New York. He knew the excitement of crossing the Atlantic on a ship, and the elation of the incomparable view of Cherbourg in the morning mist. He remembered the trust of the college that offered him his first teaching job, and touring France on a bike. He thought of Frédéric slaloming between the dunes, his ribcage crushed under Boyd's grip, and the eyes of Philippe looking up at him from the shelter of his arms. And here was yet another chance offered by life, a last unhoped-for opportunity ... that he immediately set about screwing up.

They had anchored in the harbor of Paxos, gaining the shore in the dinghy. With a few hours to kill before the opening of the tavernas for dinner, they went for a walk into the heights enclosing the tiny port and its bobbing fishing boats. Coming back down Boyd trailed behind the other two in search of a place to piss. Passing in front of a closed chapel of some sort, he decided to go behind and, with due disdain for the religious symbol it represented, relieve himself against the wall. Buttoning his fly as he came back around the building, he fell nose to nose with a peasant. The peasant summed up the situation immediately and began yelling at Boyd who lagged so far behind his two friends they were unaware of the ruckus. While the peasant went behind the chapel to verify his assumption, the boy speedily ran up to join them.

After dinner Boyd hoped that, in light of what Denis had said that morning, he would perhaps be invited to accompany him on his rounds of the bars, instead of returning with Didier as usual. To his surprise, it was Didier Denis invited to go bar hopping. Didier had been asked before but had refused, laughing that at his great age what he needed most was his sleep, an affirmation that seemed plausible to the boys. This time he said yes. As Didier hadn't prepared a sack for his clothing, Boyd asked how he would get back to the boat, assuming he would have to give up the dinghy to the others. ''Go with the tender,'' said Denis. ''When we finish I'll swim out for it and bring it back for the old man here.'' ''Oh!,'' laughed Didier, ''if I'm that old I'll go back with Boyd now.''

Not feeling tired, Boyd decided to explore the village on his own. By 10:30 his bedtime had come and gone, and as he started to yawn he decided to return to the Swan. The tender was tired up on an empty beach a few yards past the last taverna. He noticed three men sitting nearby who got up as he approached. One was the peasant of that afternoon. Boyd immediately turned on his heels but not fast enough. He was caught up by the others, two of whom cut him off while the peasant began hurtling what were, Boyd supposed, more insults. He couldn't speak Greek well enough to explain himself, and then, what was there to explain? He searched for the expression *I'm sorry*, but all of the sudden his mind had gone blank. In fact, no form of thought remained except for the fleeting interrogation on how karate could help when surrounded by three men. The peasant worked himself into a fury, drawing nearer and nearer to the boy who didn't have sense enough to keep him at a distance. In reality, he'd never seen or heard of a *"coup de tête"* until he received it, coming with lightning speed, the man's forehead slamming into his upper nose. The spurting blood had a satisfying effect on the men who muttered among themselves as Boyd sought to stem the flow with the sleeve of his shirt.

"What's going on here," said a voice coming from the direction of the taverna. Seeing the size of Denis, the men backed away. The peasant began shouting in Denis's direction, and through descriptive gestures he enacted pissing and then pointed to one of the many island churches. Denis caught Boyd by the clean sleeve, murmuring "Come on Cerdan, Piaf'll bandage you up on the boat," and hauled him off towards the tender, covering their progression by shouting out *Thank you, Thank you* in Greek to the men, some of the few words he'd retained. Back on the Swan he let Boyd clean himself while telling the truth of what had happened. "How can one be so *dumb*?" Denis wondered out loud. "You're lucky your nose's already broken. What's one hump more or less...." Boyd began laughing. "This time it was a pleasure," he said, talking through his mouth, "compared to the first." As Denis lacked a curious nature--or possessed a discretion foreign to Boyd--he let the remark drop. Again Boyd was grateful to him, this time because he wouldn't have to drag up what was best forgotten.

.

Denis turned out to be what Boyd called "a real education." He knew an incredible number of things, and didn't mind sharing a portion of them with this boy he found in some ways strange, a strangeness most likely due to cultural differences, rather than any real anomaly. He told Boyd a bit about the incessant romping that had gone on in the dormitories of the Sports Academy. "Some of the teachers were hardly older than us, and filled us in on what things were just 'sexuality' when boys were thrown in together." The kinds of "experimentation" which meant nothing to normal development. "One teacher made it clear that you can't change a tendency. 'If you're born stupid and heterosexual,' he said, 'you stay stupid and heterosexual', or whatever else you're born to be." Then, sitting in the cockpit, at the helm for once, he recounted to Boyd the story of his brother, Gabriel.

Gabriel was much older than Denis. "In fact," said the boy, "it was because mother was convinced that Gaby would soon leave the house that she decided to have me. I was brought up by Gaby, and despite the differences in our ages it's not possible to imagine two closer brothers. He told me everything, included me in everything, and because I knew nothing, I took it all in, the good with the bad, without judgment because I didn't know what good *was*, or bad for that matter.''

An only child before Denis came along, Gabriel's boyhood on the highland slopes of the Pyrenees was solitary and isolated. Peaks as ominous as sharks' fins hovered in the infinite blue sky, while underfoot torrent-hewed and glacier-scoured valleys lay in a mist impervious to the sun and its bone-comforting warmth, where lichens and marble salamanders proliferated, and the night freeze cracked the sheer granite mountains, leveling the land in a twinkling of the historical eye. So when a club-footed black and white kid was abandoned by its mother, Gaby lightened his loneliness by nursing the animal with warm goat's milk from the baby's bottle that had been his when he was nursing, ''and perhaps,'' said Denis to Boyd, ''mine, later.'' He prayed to God that the kid would take to the ruse, laughing to tears as the tiny creature sucked desperately at the imitation nipple, sometimes catching the boy's fingers in its impressment, sending a wondrous chill up his spine. The kid, unable to right itself on its remaining sturdy legs, fouled the corner bed of hay Gabriel laid out for it in the grange, obliging the boy to climb into the underground shelter with broom and dustpan, and air it when the stench became too dense.

Outside the stone and thatched-roof structure the April rains raised up knee-high grass, green and glistening, through which the other kids bounded, their nostrils flared to catch the crisp spring air, snorting tiny geysers of vapor in the heavy dawn haze. Gabriel's mother tolerated the boy's whim and his father, away in the hills from morning till night, waited for the moment when Gabriel was safely out of hearing to slip into the grange and snap the animal's neck. Later, Father reproached Son with having spun out the kid's misery, sermonizing the boy on Nature's vocation to destroy its miscreants. ''Our father was a stern man, and it was his sternness that made him absent to us even in his presence,'' said Denis. Yet the words his father felt obliged to speak that day to still his son's tears were exceptional in their tenderness. ''Instinct pushed the she-goat to kill its anomaly,'' he said to his boy, taking him into his arms in a rare and meaningful embrace. ''For Nature death is a way to bring on change, and change is necessary if we don't want to continue as we are. To continue as we are,'' said this man who was no stranger to other men's cruelty, ''is not possible.'' He shook his head. ''Just not possible.''

Boyd tried to envisage the moment of tenderness between Gabriel and his father, and tried to remember if he had ever shared such a moment with his own father.

''Gaby grew to young manhood, as they say,'' continued Denis. He was solemn and burdened, keenly aware of the sun that stooped low to shrivel streams and harvests, of rains that could uproot the mountain slope and send it down into the valley plain, burying vines and crops; of sudden freezes that choked the sap in the roots, making them as brittle as the fissured face of the upper gorges. He found himself thinking often of the lame kid, and the complicated desires that troubled his sleep as he reached adolescence. He took a girlfriend, and for a while their games in the fields promised a distraction from an existence as settled as the dust on a country road.

On a certain summer day, one heady with promise and future, sun splattered and so indolent even the bumble bees were too heat and pollen saturated to lumber from daisy to dandelion, a film crew descended from the capital to do a three-minute filler on a recent hail storm that had flattened the year's wheat crop. Willing to take advantage of the excitement caused by the shooting, a minor assistant saw to it that Gabriel was filmed holding up one of the balls of hail the boy had preserved in the underground grange. Later, in a ravaged orchard out of sight of the filming, the man and boy exchanged addresses. Deciding to push his luck, the man placed a hand firmly over the boy's crotch, prepared to jump away should the muscled lad prove obstinate. Gabriel's reaction was surprise, followed by trembling acquiescence. The man quenched himself at the source at the lad's hips, while Gabriel, deeply moved, felt his heart swell with yearning for something beyond the mountain summits that towered about him like the bars of an insurmountable prison. ''Gaby didn't go into all that much detail, of course,'' said Denis, ''but I know because all boys go through about the same shared experiences.'' Now Gaby had the key to his escape, he reminded himself as he walked back to his home patting the address safely tucked away in his jeans. If he could please a film director--as the assistant had claimed to be--and be chosen for an interview and special favors, his future seemed limitless. The boy had never read Zola, but in his dreams he was of the lineage of Nana, one who would leave hearth and homeland for the demimonde of shadows and signs, and the fulfillment of his most inner ambition: to inspire love.

Boyd gave a rollicking laugh and shifted his position on the cockpit locker, stirred by the confession that all boys go through the same experiences. He wondered if part of the story was being tailored for him. Denis smiled and continued on, faithful to the bare bones of what he knew of Gabriel's life.

Three months later Gaby found himself on the Grands Boulevards, the assistant's address sticking from his large farm-boy's hand like a lottery ticket. Through restless crowds of Saturday strollers he passed shops and shooting stands, wheels of fortune and vociferous vendors of rubbish, seeking the *porte-cochère* of his friend. He stopped at the game stands in an open arcade, mesmerized by the pinball machines. A well-dressed man in large sunglasses stepped through a gang of black-jacketed pinball players to ask Gabriel if he might assist the boy. Gabriel found himself the possessor of unsuspected reserves of composure, and the kind of arrogance known to a merchant, the holder of a coveted object. He declined to accompany the man beyond the Boulevards, but in front of the Opera Comique he accepted the gift of a ticket to the night's ballet in exchange for the promise to meet the man after the performance. He slipped the ornate *billet* into his wallet, tucking the assistant's address into the small-change pocket of his trousers.

The rendezvous after the performance was at the café across from the theater. Filled with expectation, the boy was the first to cross the square, the paving stones black and glistening after a brief shower, and settle at the bar behind a beer. Only when the café was overflowing with pre-soupé patrons and the boy was certain he had been stood up, did the man, still wearing the sunglasses, arrive. He ordered a strong drink for them both and asked Gabriel's opinion of the ballet. The boy enthusiastically described the dances that had pleased him, especially a number called the Cadets' Ball. The man, amused, asked the boy for his program. Opening it to the center he pointed to a picture of himself, taken years earlier. It was he, the general of the cadets.

Outside the café the man and boy strolled through the warm August night, the man speaking of his work, the boy listening, both occasionally brushing shoulders, an intimacy Gabriel found natural as the man spun out his life story, one part of his mind seeking the words to seduce the lad, another inventing an excuse to cancel an appointment with one of his effeminate dancers should Gabriel return to his apartment, and still another part on the next day's morning rehearsal. ''I find you very attractive,'' the man said. ''Exactly the kind of person I would like to travel with. Each year I go to Capri, and never alone.'' The images that invaded the boy's mind, romantic shirts and tailored trousers, hotels overlooking sea and azure sky, skin bronzed elsewhere than the arms and neck, room service in soft beds of silk sheets catered by liveried servants. Feeling the boy waver, the man removed his dark glasses. Immediately, in a fashion so comic the lad laughed aloud, the midnight passersby, especially old women, stopped to point to the performer, lowering their voices to mere murmurs when their eyes fell on the adolescent accompanying him.

The man's apartment consisted of two small rooms in a good quarter of the city, but the building itself was run-down. Gabriel could not guess at the future awaiting him, but as he climbed the sagging steps he promised himself to be at the height of whatever the man could reasonably expect. Behind drawn drapes of thick velvet, smelling of dust and the sweet, sickly odor of cheap sent, the man approached Gabriel, admiring the boy's belt, country made, wide with a bronze buckle, and trousers that rain and wind had melded over muscle and sinew. As

Gabriel took over his own undressing the man turned to his wardrobe, confiding to the boy the details of the dress he was having prepared for himself on the occasion of a masked ball. The world of lace and sequins, a mystery to Gabriel, had the effect of a bad dream, and the man's movements as he placed his clothes on their hangars were as dandyish and graceful as they were androgynous. In bed the lad was impotent, the man demanding and egocentric. When, later, the boy gazed at the sleeping figure, he saw the head pushed into a pillow, the hairpiece turned up at the edge, showing its white band. The man snorted like a warthog, and the enclosed room stunk like a sty. The boy wept in disgust and humiliation. He rose and dressed in the dark, his eyes filled with tears he did nothing to wipe away. At Austerlitz he caught the train back home.

"And there he lived happily ever after," laughed Denis.

"Oh, come ON. What happened to him, and he really told you all *that*!"

"Some. I think he was trying to save me from going through a similar experience. And I might have, too, had I not the image of that room always in mind. God, can you imagine the stench? And then, there's something about me that's always attracted the kind of people who need comfort like a pig needs to lull around in mud."

"Jesus…" whispered Boyd, dropping his head.

"For God's sake, not you. You're just not sorted out yet. I guess some of us are late bloomers in that sort of stuff." He didn't make clear *what* sort of stuff.

"And Gabriel, he married or what?"

"Gaby married his first and only girlfriend. She was undemanding and with little effort on his part he managed to content her with two sons. As they grew through childhood the boys became use to their father's ways, but they were never able to understand why, on fresh April days when the grass was knee-high and glistening, he would scour the rocky meadows, ferreting out newborn lame kids whose necks he would throttle."

"You're shitting me!"

"No, I'm not. Maybe he felt his problems originated by his being so tenderhearted as a boy. And one more thing that's strange. I know his sons well. They're still small, but I'll bet you all you want neither will ever marry."

.

A few nights later they went to a taverna with the new arrival, now habitual for them, a woman who seemed star struck by the wonderful setting: the outdoor terrace bathed in lamp light; the competent servers in white shirts and black trousers, darting in and out of the tables and chairs, rapid in filling orders, an ear open for requests of more bread and beer, an invitation into the kitchen to chose their food; and the gently bobbing Swan, at rest in the center of the golden light of the moon that cut a shimmering tract across the black sea. Didier was at his most charming, more bright eyed and bushy tailed than the boy had seen him, laughing and smiling with the girl, a complete gentleman to Boyd, pleasantly kidding around with Denis. He hadn't used the world plethora all night.

Back on the boat they all turned in, but Boyd, on the deck as usual, couldn't fall asleep. The remedy was valium, 5 mg pills that would push him over to the other side, painlessly. He lay on the deck for an hour, looking at the moon and sea, aware of the placid tugging of the Swan against the anchor chain, before deciding to fetch one. He got up and slipped on his shorts in deference to the woman in bed inside. He eased himself quietly down the entry stairs. He knew he'd have to turn on the overhead cabin light for the second necessary to spot his toilet bag. As he did so he caught Denis leaning against the doorway between the main cabin and prow cabin, shielding his sex with his hand, the woman kneeling at his feet, naked, Didier sitting up on the cabin cot, naked too, a blanket thrown quickly over his midsection. All at once the boy felt overdressed. ''I'm sorry,'' he muttered, switching off the light and digging out the pills in the dark from his bag. ''I couldn't sleep.'' No one said a word and he considered no further explanation necessary. He went back up to his prow bedding, inches above the head of Denis who had perhaps already put his cock back between the red lips. He wondered why he hadn't been invited. If what Denis had said about his being ''just a little confused, but basically 'normal' '', this would have been an occasion to reduce the confusion by reinforcing the 'normal' aspect. Unless Denis didn't believe what he'd said. Or perhaps it was Didier's decision. Yet Boyd felt lighter all of the sudden. He was happy that Denis was getting his, after being so good to Boyd. Thanks to the valium he fell asleep in a better mood than he had been for some time. What did he care about Didier's frowns? He'd looked pretty silly covering up like an adolescent caught playing with himself by his mother. When sleep came, he had a grin on his lips.

CHAPTER THIRTY-SIX

The Swan navigated from island to island, some so arid the parched shrubs fought for survival with an inspiring tenacity; from mooring to mooring, where the sea was of such an emerald beauty that the shipmates plunged in before the anchor touched bottom; from port to port, all with their multicolored fishing boats, quivering with pleasure beneath the radiant sun; a profusion of sights that awoke the boys' hearts to undreamed-of splendors. Happily Boyd remained blissfully ignorant of the potentially devastating winds such as the dreaded *meltemi*, capable of drawing their vessel into the depths in the wink of an eye. He lived day by day in the way that was so natural for Denis, so unknown to him.

All that was superb in Greece was united in the small port of Levkas. Access was through a sea channel several miles in length, bordered on each side by cliffs in some spots, and cedars, poplars and weeping willows on the low banks of others. Boyd could picture in his mind an arm of the Mississippi, lush and overgrown, over which he and Denis drifted like Huck and Tom. The longer they sailed up the channel the greater the glee in both boys, both asking Didier when it would end, and both not wanting it ever to end. At its extremity was a town built around a harbor that resembled a small St. Tropez, boutiques alternating with taverns, each inch of the quays taken up by yachts or fishing boats. Through lack of space the Swan dropped anchor in the middle, and immediately the boys plunged into the royal-blue waters.

At nightfall they went together to an outdoor taverna at the end of a side street, away from the harbor, less taken over by the tourists than most. Didier and Boyd kidded Denis that he wouldn't have far to swim to join the Swan in the morning. The friendly proprietor led them into the kitchen and in detail suggested what they could order. Ice-cold beers were ready when they returned to the table, and by the time the food arrived they had all finished several glasses. They were feeling good, Boyd was relaxed, Didier seemed to look at him with a benign openness, and Denis was true to his nature, giving the girls the once over while stuffing himself with bread dipped in mustard until the food arrived, talking easily with Didier as Boyd listened, Boyd realizing that throughout the whole world, this was the place he wanted to be.

''You know what I caught this guy doing this morning?'' Didier suddenly asked Denis while smiling at Boyd, his eyes beginning to glaze. ''He was watching me *shave*.''

''Your daddy never showed you how to shave?'' grinned Denis, turning his black, disinterested eyes on Boyd, just keeping the talk rolling.

''Dad was rarely home. He went to work pretty early and came back late. So no, I guess I never saw how to shave.''

''Well, you're lucky in a sense. My dad hit me when I used his razor. 'Course, I was only ten,'' laughed Denis, ''but when the time came I'd seen him do it enough so I didn't need any pointers. I'd seen all my friends do it too, *and other things I shall not mention in unmixed company!*''

''And then you're somewhat monastic ... sort of reserved....'' began Didier, his attention leaving Boyd to eye the pork and fries being placed in front of each of them. They seldom had meat, which as expensive, and never fish which was prohibitive in cost. But the beauty of crossing through the channel had loosened them up, making this a special occasion, one that they would remember later as truly exceptional. ''You never piss with us when we pull up at the roadside. We talked about that.''

''We didn't *talk* about it, it just came up once,'' said Denis to Didier.

''Come on, guys, I don't mind my sharing my experiences, but you guys start by sharing your blow jobs'', he said remembering the girl on her knees before Denis.

Denis nearly choked on his beer, but came up laughing. ''I told you he wouldn't forgive that,'' he said to Didier, spewing him.

Boyd got out of being cornered as he'd always done, by keeping a step ahead of those who would push him under, just as he'd done with the shrink during the Peace Corps vetting. But that night nothing could touch him because he'd never felt better, or as close to being adopted by those he admired and loved. The fellowship and beer had chased the evil into hiding. But he knew that sooner or later the old fears and uncertainties would resurface, turning him against those who were, at the moment, the most important beings in his life, who *were* his life.

.

The next afternoon Didier was at the helm as the Swan raced ahead in a nice breeze. Boyd and Denis had finished their exercises on the prow, had doused away the sweat with water they'd hauled up from the sea in buckets at the end of a rope. At the moment they were on the deck, leaning back on their arms, talking about the theocracy that held sway over the place where the American had been born. Boyd watched the drops of water that covered Denis's bronzed skin, luminous pearls that trickled over the naturally oiled surface of his imposing pectorals, descending to the V of his lower belly where they disappeared among the thick black hairs.

''It didn't have only its bad parts,'' the boy said, replying to Denis's observation about feeling claustrophobic under such conditions. ''They took care of their own. No one went hungry who was a member of the church, and because everyone was a member they looked out for each other. No drugs and things like that.''

''And women *à volonté* so I've heard.'' Denis's face was pointed upwards towards the sun, his eyes closed, his legs stretched out, his sex, astonishingly thick, lazing on balls at rest on the naked teck.

''That was abandoned years ago. In fact, not only are you limited to one wife today, boys and girls alike are supposed to marry virgin.''

''I presume you marry young.''

''*They* marry young. I'm no longer a part of all that. But yeah, they do often marry young. There were other good parts. If you needed help or advice, there was someone to turn to.''

''I can just guess which kind. No petting and keep it in your pants. Panaceas like that. Some advice. It's amazing the running you've done when you think about it," mused Denis. "Left your whadyacallit? State? Then your country, your religion…"

"And finally Paris for a place on this boat next to a son-of-a-bitch who believes in cutting people down." There was so much he wanted to say to this boy, but how could he reveal himself when there was a possibility of his naivety being betrayed, or his sincerity being mocked, or his confidence being abused? Still, what greater happiness than a friend to whom one could open his heart to intimate things, and exchange rare and unexpected thoughts.

"The only thing I ever cut down was the old maid who seduced me, and that was to read the rings of her leg."

"For the moment I'm doing pretty well where I am, if you want to know the truth," said Boyd, coming to the realization that it really *was* the truth.

"Until you run out of running space. What'll you do when there's only yourself left, 'cause going the way you're going I don't see marriage in the future. You turn your back on everyone."

"I don't turn away from you…"

"No one who's come on this boat merits any form of praise in your eyes. You judge and you reject."

"I didn't reject you…"

"Who knows that inner nerve I've been able to stir. But there won't always be someone like me around. What'll you do then? Continue to lose yourself in books? And then for how long? For how much longer will you choose life over death?"

"Jesus H. Christ, you go whole hog to make a point," said Boyd, bordering on tears. "Live for the moment, fuck your tail off, take life a step at a time. Not worry. Let *slide.* That's your philosophy."

"You've got to go out to people; it's only through people you'll find yourself."

"I've been through people, for Christ's sake. I was in school, you know. I did go through the university. I had friends there and we *talked.* And believe me, we *talked and talked and talked.* I've been there, done that, as the guys your age say. Why don't people get off my back? Why can't I be myself? Out of all the *billions* of people on earth, why can't I go my way?"

"Your way is straight into the wall. You're cutting yourself off. The palliative of books and other second-hand experience won't last eternally. You obstinately refuse to open up to people."

He was obstinate like de Gaulle was obstinate in London, because he didn't have a choice. To give up, even just an inch, would be a sign of weakness. When he was fifteen his father had offered him an old Ford he'd exchanged for a box of tools. Boyd used it for trips into the mountains where he took his scouts. When his father forbade the trips, pretexting the bad roads were ruining the shock absorbers, the boy never stepped foot in the car again. Without knowing it at the time, the act was his first shot towards liberating himself from the man's oppression, and it taught him a lesson on deliverance he was determined never to forget, a determination seconded by his letter of protest to Bud.

''I've opened up enough to be on this goddamned boat, you know. That's second-hand experience?''

''No,'' confirmed Denis. ''There you chose right. Now, if you opened yourself up a bit more you'll be choosing right again.''

''How do you *know* that, for Christ's sake? How can you be so *goddamned fucking* sure?''

''That's the hallmark of us brainless athletes. We haven't the intellectual equipment to *not* be sure.''

And then Denis did something so wonderful, so engaging that Boyd could but look on in rapture, all at once certain that he *was* right. He climbed onto the prow balcony, stretching upward to his full height, one hand holding onto the stay, the other stretched out in the shape of an L like a circus acrobat taking a bow, smiling, naked, of such perfection that Didier, from the cockpit, clapped and hurrahed. Optimism flooded the boy. It was true, as the poet said, that any price was worth paying for a moment of such perfect beauty. He felt that if he could have Denis's image always in mind, he could surmount the worse that would eventually come his way. Leaning back on his arms he looked up, laughing at this Hermes of times past, the wind playing through his black wavy hair, the mysterious flicker of a knowing smile, this Garbo of the modern age. As the prow of the Swan shifted into the path of the sun, Denis's head was hallowed in a circle of light from which his teeth shone, bringing to memory in Boyd's mind a similar smile, but so long ago it flickered from thought as quickly as he flickered a tear of happiness from his eye. He found himself wishing with all his heart and soul that this moment could go on and on and on … and on … forever.

CHAPTER THIRTY-SEVEN

They sailed to Crete. Passengers came and went, never more than one or two at a time. Each of the boys took on a role unique to him, sometimes working in concert, sometimes in controlled competition. Denis was the boat's young man, a charmer, often an egoist but more often generous, he squired the girls and bettered Wilde's definition of perfect social tact by wooing the men as well as the women. And it worked. In all the weeks on the Swan, he made not a single enemy. Yet at times Boyd's mind harbored back to a comment made by Claudine, the seal who lay in the cockpit begging one and all to douse her with water. She had said things that Boyd found hit the target as far as he was concerned, and so when she mentioned that in Denis was a well of sorrow that he disguised with a nonchalant amiability, he did not dismiss the observation out of hand. And it did happen, though rarely, that Denis had a faraway look that presaged some preoccupation outside the bounds of the Swan, leading the boy to wonder if their entente was partially due to an inner torment they shared.

Didier was the Swan's final authority. His word was law, but a law rarely applied, Boyd thought, because he favored Denis too much to ever come down on him harshly, and he was rarely harsh with Boyd either, perhaps because he was chary of the boy's not always predictable reactions. He was charming in a more reserved way than Denis, but everything he did was undercut by an innate pessimism that gave a troubled cast to his eyes. He lacked confidence in his fellow beings, the foremost of which, Boyd would swear, was Boyd himself. Didier could never do anything fully: never fully smile, never be fully at ease, never fully be himself. Perhaps in his job as an insurance claims expert he had heard too many lies and been caught up in too many swindles to have faith in others. He rarely connected with the men, and fell all over women to an extent that was comic to Denis, absurd to Boyd.

Boyd wished he could combine in himself the better parts of the other two. He was tired of lacking self-assurance, of always questioning his acts and motives, of being totally wrapped up in himself. He made no effort to be of service to either sex. The men sensed he had a natural chip on his shoulder; the women imagined he was playing hard to get. Didier was sure that Boyd's belief in himself was so tenuous he couldn't permit himself the luxury of giving even an inch. The boy was approachable, but only by those who would do the impossible to overcome the firewall he put up, a wall he wanted as impregnable as that which encircled the Guadeloupian. But once the wall was cleared, he collapsed with gratitude before the victor. Didier never learned what Denis had done to win the boy over, but now Boyd ate from his hand. Yet the boy's perplexity was such that the hand he licked today, he could as well bite tomorrow. That was Boyd. Preferring books to people, the vicarious to reality, sublimation to truth.

.

From the north they entered the safe, natural harbor at Kissamos, enclosed by hills where, on the steep summit of one, nestled a village of whitewashed houses and twisted cobblestone passageways. They anchored in crystalline bluish-green waters in the center of the harbor, among a flotilla of beautiful yachts, most flying the Italian pavilion. As they were leaving the next day to pick up someone in Chania, both boys chose to stay on the boat and admire the setting from there, while Didier and still another woman passenger took the tender to visit the town where they'd lunch.

Lying out in the cockpit, their backs against the partition separating the cockpit from the cabin, both dressed in black running shorts belonging to Denis, they sipped tea Boyd had prepared. Denis had convinced him to down litters of it during the day ''to keep the tubes open.'' He could have said the same thing about the need to sow his oats. A week had gone by without a girl and the young man could hardly stay in place. Luckily there was a Club Med in Chania where he was sure to ease off some of the pressure. He never inquired what Boyd did for relief, merely saying once, ''Old guys like you and Didier have forgotten what it's like to go without pussy.'' Now Boyd was kidding him about taking a good stock of rubbers to the Club. ''I never go in without a safety net,'' was the way Denis answered.

''Yeah, a guy needs protection, like a plastic jock in karate class. Those are pretty sensitive places,'' said Boyd, whose only experience with rubbers was the ones he'd filled with water as a kid.

''The net's for the girl, not me,'' frowned Denis. His face was in a corner of shadow, the eyes stern and sad at the same time, the skin taking on the hue of acajou. Boyd had kidded him about skin cancer, to which he'd replied that he'd never be around that long. Boyd had the same impression that he too would not make old bones, as the French said, but Didier assured both boys that that was the way all young people felt, and with age would come a kind of serenity. This piece of wisdom, coming from someone with hardly a gray hair, made the boys break up with laughter.

As Didier was notoriously close to his money, they thought he might make it back to the boat for lunch after all. When one o'clock came Boyd opened a can of cassoulet to which he added a can of corn and a package of dehydrated tomato soup, a mixture more favored by the boys than caviar, and only less so than lobster. They regained their places in the cockpit, giant bottles of the Greek beer Hellas in one hand, their bowls of the hot concoction in the other.

''I had a dream last night. I was wondering if you could help me decipher it,'' asked Boyd.

''At least you didn't wake up shouting,'' said Denis, his fingers searching out pieces of pork, so used to Boyd that he didn't mind making a mess. There was stew on his chin and the beer made him belch, which he deliberately amplified.

''What would the woman think of your behavior?'' asked Boyd. The more randy Denis became, the greater was his tendency to vulgarity. Boyd had tried to ape him at first, but couldn't duplicate even the simplest of gestures, like how to spit.

''Didier must really need the dough...'' said Denis. The woman with Didier was of a very certain age, said the French of those over the hill, and was the only crewmember, ever, vaccinated against the charms of the tennis man. ''Or incredibly randy.''

''Doesn't he meet all these broads in Paris before setting off?'' asked Boyd.

''Not all. A lot of people call once he's gone and his wife--soon to be ex-wife--makes the arrangements for him.''

''She probably thought this Claudine would be suitable punishment,'' said Boyd. ''Really, why marry if it ends up in divorce? Unless you want kids. Do you want kids?''

''You don't need to marry to have kids, asshole. So what about your dream?''

''Okay. So it's not the first time I've had it. It begins with an old gentleman stepping off the street into a provincial real-estate agent. The receptionist gives him to de Roquette….''

''I don't much care for stories about French royalty.''

''No, I *knew* de Roquette. I worked at Crédit Lyonnais once and he was the guy responsible for the classes, setting them up and stuff. In the dream he had the same watery blue eyes, sort of milky with age.''

Some parts of the story Boyd recounted orally to Denis, others, the details, were pictured in his mind only, as he didn't possess the erudite vocabulary to put everything into French.

De Roquette stood to indicate a seat in front of his mahogany desk, leaving his hand obeisantly ready should the gentleman choose to take it up. His smile, stilted, was encompassed by the perpetual reddish flush of his cheeks, stigmata of a vinous predisposition. The prospect of a good sale evaporated when the gentleman said he had come down from Paris in search of ''a weekend cabin'' as he put it, as if his wish was to grow a *potager* like a vulgar pensioner. Near a lake with perhaps ducks, the gentleman specified, forcing de Roquette into an unusual moment of reflection. A French hunter would have known there was no shooting allowed here, to which the man added that it was the proximity which concerned him, the ambiance to be precise, not the wish, God forbid, to harm the birds. De Roquette produced an album of weekend houses the gentleman scanned through while de Roquette considered the man's dress, a sports coat, tie and tailored trousers much too young for him, as were, de Roquette admitted to himself, his own, as well as teeth too new for the withered mouth. The house he chose was in the last album. There was one room, wood siding and tarpaper roof. The price of eight million old francs was agreed on. The agent's commission would barely pay a month of office lighting.

The gentleman produced a French identity card showing an American origin. De Roquette had dealt with British poor who had opted for dual nationality to save on administrative red tape, but Americans were quite unknown. When de Roquette complimented the gentleman on his beautiful country, he was told that it probably was, if one could discount violence, drugs, poverty and the profit motive for which countless young men had given their lives during horrendous wars so their peers could enjoy cars, beer, after-game riots, peace today if it served their interests, war tomorrow if it caught their fancy.

De Roquette nodded while filling in the forms, his own jealousy of the land that had cuffed the General and supplanted his buddies in Asia as bilious as the gentleman's. De Roquette could not help thinking with bitter assurance that when the next world conflict came the gentleman would be on the first Liberty ship back to his fortified country; that when the franc caught cold he would flee to prosperous America; that when France sank in richness to the level of an African homestead he would regain his home. Home. De Roquette knew that for an American France would never be home. The paperwork finished, de Roquette rose and, with the aid of a walking stick, showed the gentleman out, informing him that he would drop by in a few days with the final papers for the gentleman to sign.

Back in Paris, at the Samaritaine Department Store, the gentleman wandered through aisles emptied of clients by an American dollar that had depleted France of its capital. In the basement he found the wrought-iron coal stove still in vogue in cold, remote regions like Auvergne. He remembered how its splayed feet had eaten into the gray linoleum floor around which he, just a child, had mopped a thousand times, drawing lines and circles through the coal dust. On the fourth floor he bought two spirit lamps. Nearby were the beds. He bought a set of superimposed bunks.

On the third floor he stopped at the medicine chests. His face appeared in the mirror, and as he stepped back in disgust, the trapped reflection copied itself a thousand times, each a diminishing miniature of the one before. It was his mother's raven hair that his tiny baby fingers had caressed, endless wavy strands, long, silken and silver at the roots. It was her teeth that she prided herself on never removing, just as no living being had ever seen his. It was her age, her flabby stomach with its upsets and her bad heart. From his father he bore the deformations of blind anger and raging strength: his ears standing out where he had grappled them in fits of fury, tugging the boy right and left like a disobedient dog by the collar. His broken nose, slapped by fists deadened by alcohol as the boy stood up for her, the end bulbous from the clamped vice of his father's fingers as he was pulled to where he was to go, words being of scant value in his home. For two million old francs of purchases the Samaritaine delivered anywhere in the *métropole*. The gentleman gave his address and a date for delivery was arrived at after haggling. He left the store and stepped into the cold sun. He thought of his mother, his one permanence gone too soon.

The cabin sat on a plain of wind-flattened grass that bordered a tiny lake of cold, ripply water, naked of vegetation except for a few scattered tufts of stunted reeds. A gravel drive broke off from the expressway a dozen kilometers up and meandered through the plain, as lifeless as the shallow lake and bent salt grass, harboring an occasional snipe that laid it gray eggs in the like-colored pebbles of the road. Inside the cabin the gentleman was turning down the blankets on the top bunk. He wore blue jeans and a checkered hunting shirt. The Samaritaine delivery had arrived that morning. The men had climbed down from the truck cabin, puffing as if they had carried the merchandise on their backs from Paris. On the dining table the gentleman had put out a good tip in clear view. Reassured, the men pitched in with the unloading of the boxes and positioning of the old stove. Once they had set it down against the wall opposite the bunks they were truly puffing and sweating. One of them was as old as the gentleman, wrinkled and emaciated. His flimsy shirt shook from the beating of a muscular heart. He would have gladly exchanged the *pourboire* for a beer and a place to sit, but the gentleman sent them away with their rapine and comedian antics. Later, when he himself tried to budge the stove, he understood the old man's exhaustion, and felt a pang of guilt. ''If we knew how much people suffered,'' a childhood teacher had once said to her class, ''we would never be mean to anyone.'' Childhood. Everything seemed to date back to that primal and obscure time when, as in a Greek tragedy, all the essentials had already taken place, offstage.

The stove, a table, the medicine chest, the bunks and a sink with running cold water were all of the furnishings. He put town-bought vegetables in a carton outside in the winter air where a stack of log chips and coal had already been set in. He kept his back to the lake, avoiding it like a bad memory. So lost to thought was he that he did not hear the leather shoes advance over the loose pebbles. The last time he had gone out on the lake a storm had blown up. He and his father had found themselves off the shore opposite the rented cabin, the hot, blazing sun replaced by anvil-high storm clouds amassing over the peaked, rocky summits of the Uintas. Pine tree trunks that had cast their placid reflections on the clear waters shook under the assault of the descending winds, their shadows disappearing into the gray mud whipped up from the lakebed. The previous week three boats had been caught in the open under similar circumstances. Two that had chosen to cross the lake had gone down with no survivors. The third had put into the nearest shore until the blow up had subsided. That's what the boy now asked his father to do. But the man, desensitized by drink, told his son to pull up the rock anchor while he started the outboard. The motor refused to catch and the boat was blown towards the rocky shore with its boulders, pines and battered logs that bobbed along the surface. The wind had turned cold and the boy put on every scrap of clothing he had brought out. His eyes never left the surging waters. At the first sign of land underfoot he was determined to jump in and wade ashore. Too bad if he received a beating afterwards. Too bad if his father looked at him in silent disgust. He had plans, he told himself; no drunk would play God with what was his.

It was just as he spotted a submerged tangle of pine roots that the motor caught. His skin flushed with fear and the shame of the fear. His father pointed the bow out to the open water and their encampment, half a mile across the lake. The boy pleaded with him to at least follow the bank around. Father studied Son with glazed eyes, disdainful and as crazed as an enraged bull's. The boat bounced up and over wave after wave, the tiny motor sputtering and choking. Now fully terrorized, the boy stared disbelievingly at his father who began to sing a mirthless ballad, his eyes leaden and unsteady. To underline the boy's cowardliness, the man fell to his knees facing the gunwale, his fly level with the rim, and urinated overboard, rocking the boat and screaming the inane tune to the unleashed fury over which they pitched and tossed like a dispassionate cork.

Once across, the boy ran into the surrounding red clay lowlands and buried himself in the crevasse of a flash-flood gully. Too furious even to cry, he ranted against his fate: deprived too soon of the love of a mother, forced to submit to the whims of a drunken wreck and, worst of all, condemned to endure the immutable barrier of time between now and the moment he would seize his freedom like a slave, never again to return to his shackles.

''There hadn't been a thimbleful of tenderness in that world,'' he said aloud in still-fresh rage, turning back to the cabin.

''Oh yes, there's always at least one moment of tenderness,'' said de Roquette coming up from behind. ''Always at least *one* moment of tenderness.''

''Fool!'' muttered the gentleman, of himself or de Roqutte was uncertain.

De Roquette shook the gentleman's hand. I need a few signatures he smiled, not waiting to be invited inside. He planted his cane into the ground, opened the upper handle that converted into a seat, and sat down on it, happily aware of the stir his little maneuver always caused. De Roquette had learned that eccentricity went as well with the old as jeans the young. After the signing, the gentleman saw the agent back to his car. De Roquette said he'd return in a couple of weeks with the deed.

That evening turned very cold. The gentleman filled the stove with coal before undressing and slipping under the covers of the upper bunk. He could hear the ducks on the lake. He fell asleep and in his dreams he remembered back to the afternoon when as a boy he had discovered the nude playing cards in the cabin medicine chest...

''...his fathers?'' asked Denis, taking another swig of beer.

''Yeah. They ... they excited him.''

''The old guy?''

''No, me. I'd discovered them. That part of the dream is true. I'd really found them.''

''And you had a wank?'' asked Denis in English.

''That's British,'' laughed the boy. ''But ... yeah.'' His jeans around his ankles, spilling his seed over the warped planks that formed the cabin floor. He had hurt himself, his hand calloused from the work his father forced him to do. Pulling and jerking, the mounting feeling so wonderful, so *compelling* he couldn't stop, even with his knees scarcely holding him up, even with the seed spouting up and out, a hemorrhage he caught with his fingers. So dirty, so *beautiful*. A source of power of which he himself was the origin.

What followed was inexorable. With nascent adolescence his waist slimmed, his chest and limbs grew strong and indefatigable. *He* became the master of his mind and body, a body so *potent*.

''And that's where the dream stops. Or at least ... it's kind of embarrassing...''

''What can be embarrassing after that?'' guffawed Denis.

''Well, the boy in the upper bunk had erected very hard...''

''You mean *you*.''

''Yeah, the boy was definitely me. The cabin and all, I knew all that. My father had worked at a Duck Club, and I'd helped him from the age of eight. But I can't remember what took place next. Except I know that sometime later, like weeks later, de Roquette returned to the cabin. The door was locked but the window shutters had been left open. Looking inside he knew ... I don't know how, perhaps from he too-still air above the inert form on the upper bunk ... that the gentleman had indeed returned home.''

''You mean he was dead?''

''I suppose, yeah.''

''It was no longer you?''

''No, the old guy *can't* have anything to do with me.''

''I think the part about the old man is your fear of aging. And the rest, well, we've all got devils we have to exorcise. Maybe you've got a few more than others, or you're too sensitive about what happened during your youth...''

''For Christ's sake, I'm only twenty-two!'' Boyd had lied so often about his age that at times he truly forgot he was twenty-six.

''Yeah, but that's a pivotal age, after which all is downhill. Take me, I'm thinking about checking out way before then.''

''Oh FUCK YOU!'' laughed Boyd. ''Thirty, okay....''

''Seriously,'' said Denis, preparing for another swim. ''In a lot of sports you face retirement about then.'' He changed the subject because he couldn't help this boy more than he had already. He had given him advice, but one day he'd have to make it on his own, or go under like the majority who chose the path of least resistance. Yet he turned back to try once again. ''Listen dork. I've told you in a dozen different ways. Your responsibility is to live. It's not necessary to amass money, to worry, to be fearful, to appease others, it's to live a life that's all too short for us all. So get off your butt and experience as much as you can till curtain call.''

''Everyone's telling me to live life….''

''Then listen up, numbnuts.''

''Keep close to the Swan,'' said Boyd, but Denis had already plunged over the side.

.

The next day, with the dawn just rising, they entered the harbor of Rhodes, a port protected by a sea wall and crammed with yachts, the whole dominated by a hill culminating in a crenellated castle of stupendous size and beauty, the town, parks and market at its foot. Once anchored, the only way to get ashore was to go aboard the boat anchored behind them, and then the boat tied up to the dock behind that one. It was crazy. On the outside of the harbor there were anchorages in water three yards deep from which they could reenter the port with the tender. The water there was as crystalline as a mountain stream, whereas that in the port was inky black. Boyd had a verbal fight with Didier, trying to persuade him to go outside, but the man obstinately refused, without explanation.

The boys visited the harbor and lively market that skirted the base of the walled fortification. In the days that followed they shared a routine of morning jogging along the ramparts, breakfast at one taverna, lunch at another and dinner at a third. There were girls galore, those on boats in the port and others that came in by charters to the sandy beaches on the opposite side of the promontory on which the castle stood. Denis and Didier turned the horseshoe-shaped life preserver upside down when they were using the interior of the Swan for visits, which was often. Then Boyd would have to fend for himself until the horseshoe was put right-side up. He didn't mind. He was happy for the other two. All he wanted was some leftovers thrown his way; a kind word, and his inclusion in what the boys did when they weren't entertaining.

During one of his solitary strolls he found himself in the port Men's. He was surprised by a Greek lad who came rushing up to Boyd's side at the urinal, and had just the time to unpack his stubby instrument when what Boyd supposed was a priest came hurrying in, clearly pursuing the lad. The priest stared at the kid's member and began hiking his robe, but the boy ran out, zipping up as he went. The priest left too, continuing the chase. Following that *bizarrerie* two crewmen from off neighboring boats drew up to the urinal across from Boyd. Like him, they were shirtless in heat that rivaled Hades. Pleased with what they saw, they headed for a cubicle. Passing behind Boyd one gave him an unchaste tap on his butt, and with his head suggested he come along. Boyd looked away, but stayed until they came back out. This time the same man gave him a firm and highly friendly caress on one levis-clad cheek. Boyd tried to hit the offending hand that the man, with the reflex of an athlete, evaded. ''Oh! Oh!'' he chuckled, and then placed an arm over the shoulder of his companion, pushing him outside into the blinding Greek light. ''Dirty queers,'' murmured the boy, buttoning up. Curious, he went into the cubicle. The amount of semen on the floor was unbelievable. They'd obviously been at sea even longer than Boyd.

The next day events happened fast, although when Boyd thought back to them later, again and again, they unwound in slow motion, image by image, the last of which, that of Denis, would be engraved on his mind all the time he had left to live. Two new passengers had embarked, a good-looking boy and his pretty girlfriend. While they stowed their gear in the places Didier had freed for them, Boyd went wandering into the market. Denis had gone off somewhere mysterious, perhaps back to the Club Med. Boyd was about to return to the Swan when he saw the boy making his way quickly through the market only a few yards away, dressed in a corduroy sports jacket. Boyd didn't even know Denis had brought a jacket. He decided not to call out. He'd not be a pain in the ass for once. Anyway, he'd see him that night or the next morning.

But he didn't see him again. Then or ever. The last image was at the market, the broad back, the sky-blue jeans, the boots and their warn heels, the flailing tails of the sports coat, walking away and out of his life.

Back on the Swan Didier said they were pushing off. Imagining that Denis had returned by another path, and was in the cabin changing or talking with the new arrivals, he joined Didier in the cockpit to help out with the necessary maneuvers which were legend in the packed port. The new guy, still in street shirt and tie, came up to lend a hand. Soon they'd cleared the walls and sailed through the opening where the statue of the Seventh Marvel of the World had stood. Didier gave the order to hoist the sails, that filled immediately thanks to a fair breeze. The air was far cooler than within the port, the sky blue, without a blemish, except for a jet passing far, far overhead, trailing a long white streak, like that of a rocket.

''That's probably Denis,'' said Didier, tightening the halyard.

It took a few second for the boy to understand. He couldn't bring himself to ask Didier why Denis would be in a jet overhead. He wouldn't admit he hadn't known, that he hadn't been told by his friend, that the person to whom he'd said, I love you, had abandoned him. From the cockpit he examined the interior of the cabin, looking again and again, searching the same places over and over as one does with the loss of keys. Except for the girl, it was empty. He gazed at the plane and raised his hand in a wave. In his mind's eye he saw the boy, saw what they'd shared. His chin began to quiver, his eyes to water. Then a sob broke surface, and then he was wailing, his body wracked by spasms. He fell to his knees in the cockpit, his head bent into his hands, and sobbed because his world had come to an end. He fell over onto his shoulder and cried out, No, no, noooooooooooooooooooooooo.

When Didier couldn't bring him around, when the boy continued screaming and kicking, the man became fearful for his mental health, and not knowing what else to do, he turned the boat around and headed back to the port. By the time they entered, Boyd had fallen into silence. They put him to bed with the valium he demanded.

The next day Boyd picked an argument with Didier about having anchored in the filth of the port. The bad boy had returned with a vengeance. He was sick of Didier's dictates, he yelled at the Captain in front of the boat's guests. Sick of taking a back seat. From now on he wouldn't take a back seat for anyone. ''I will not roll over and take it up the ass,'' he screamed at one point, his voice croaking from the shouting. He went into the cabin and packed his bag, declaring nonstop that Didier would have to find someone else to do his steering, and his fucking translations, and the red tape. The boy and girl went off hurriedly to do some shopping. Didier remained in the cockpit, watching through the door while Boyd ranted and raged and packed. He said to the boy as he left the Swan, perhaps in an effort to get him to cool down and come to his senses, perhaps through stupidity, ''The least you could do is help clean the boat before you leave.'' To which Boyd screamed back NOT IN THIS SHIT!

An hour later he too was flying over Rhodes, the rage coalesced within his heart, the stops to his fury pulled, the treachery searing the remnants of compassion from his brain in a kind of lobotomy. As a child he had saved himself by retreating into his inner being, feeding from what he had accumulated of life like an animal going into hibernation. So it would be again. He would ferret out inaccessible reaches where he would try to bring reason to the chaos throbbing at his temples. He would retreat to where he had once been happy, and in that element play dead until he had licked his wounds and found a reason to go on, if reason there was.

CHAPTER THIRTY-EIGHT

Yves Brun

Boyd knew he had no gift for navigation, but whatever he did know he had picked up at La Ciotat, where he bought the *Denis*. Skilled or not, gifted or not, too much water had flowed under the bridge since the drowning of Laurent, three years before, followed by the death of Frédéric and the loss of Denis, for him to care what the blond or anyone else thought. For them all, he had but one warning, that of Tiberius: If they don't like me, at least let them fear me.

He loved La Ciotat. Arriving there by train, his conscience was clear. He knew he had suffered losses, losses that had undermined his mental and emotional stability, but as yet there had been no corpses for which he was responsible, no deaths to obstruct the future left to him. At the La Ciotat waterfront he saw the For Sale sign on the small 24-footer. Called the *Goldfish,* he rebaptized it immediately. Unlike Didier's Swan, no boat of his would go unnamed. He loved La Ciotat, and he liked its Harbormaster whom he called Richard the Fat to distinguish him from the port's single guardian, another Richard, he called Richard the Beau. Richard the Fat was the kind who would cut himself into pieces, as the French said, to be of help. His simple way of dealing with people made it easy for a person as timid as Boyd to go to him with his problems, the first of which was finding someone who could give him sailing lessons. Because of the friction between himself and Didier, his passage on the Swan had not been sufficient to make a sailor out of him, and his aspiration to perfect his skills had taken second place to his desire to become good friends with Denis.

There were no uniforms at La Ciotat, as were worn by the Harbor Master and employees in most other Riviera ports. Richard the Fat ran around in dark trousers with a white shirt only partially tucked in. Richard the Beau wore loose gym shorts, red and soiled, and a t-shirt when he wasn't bare chested. He was short and well built, with long black hair and rapid black eyes surmounted by the longest lashes Boyd had seen on a boy. La Ciotat was middle class, the kind that was rapidly disappearing in favor of richer, snobbier ports like neighboring Port Beausoleil. It was municipal, and therefore cheap. For that reason the moorings were rare. Newcomers didn't have a prayer unless they knew someone who could pull the right strings. In Boyd's case the someone was the Aid to the Mayor--who happened also to be the owner of the *Goldfish.*

During the day the port was all family, mom, dad and the kids anchoring offshore for lunch. Early evening, when the family was at home for dinner in front of the 8 o'clock news, called the Grand Mass in France because it was attended with religious staunchness, the--did a couple of hours of after-school sailing, followed by showers in the nude at the end of a hose, and concomitant water fights. Boyd did no sailing because the winds around La Ciotat were often sudden and extremely violent, the boy so restricted by the level of his knowledge that he had to content himself with watching the others go out for the day. But he did a lot of walking. Shirtless, dressed in levis torn at the knees, he wandered the length of the mile-long beach, stopping at the volleyball field midway, at times to use the urinal behind a four-foot high wall, low enough to permit the boys to simultaneously piss and watch the matches. Boyd was often surprised by the French nonchalance in sexual matter. He had recently seen a boy take a leak against a tree, his free hand--to Boyd's utter amazement--around the waist of a girlfriend. He mentioned it to someone in the port who answered, ''Yeah, it's terrible. But sometimes there's no other place, even though we know it may damage the tree.''

The town of La Ciotat was small and busy, the narrow, winding streets full of people, where it was good to live thanks to the ship chandlery, run by an amiable old lady, a restaurant where Boyd could take out pizzas, a shop that sold wonderful roasted chickens he devoured on the *Denis*, the name he naturally chose for the boat, and a baker who made bread and pastries worthy of Gault et Millot. The boy would have gladly remained there for life if his boat hadn't been darkened one afternoon by the arrival of a small portly man in his eighties, dressed in spanking-clean white Lacoste tennis shirt and shorts. Boyd was in the cabin when the sun was blocked out by the stubby figure leaning over the roof. He raised his head to see who it was, hoping for a second it was Richard the Beau who occasionally dropped by for coffee. ''I'm Yves Brun,'' the old gentleman said in a diffident but strong voice. ''Richard said you needed sailing lessons.'' ''Richard?'' Boyd was still thinking of the Beau. ''The Harbormaster....'' ''Oh, sure, would you like to come aboard?'' Boyd remembered the request for help he'd made weeks before. He could barely keep from laughing. He would give the old man coffee and cake to please Richard, and then away he'd go.

As the coffee water heated up Yves toured the vessel. He talked nonstop: his regattas, Atlantic crossings, trips to Turkey, interspersed with comments and questions, ''your shrouds are loose here, we've got to tighten up the windlass, where's the hold pump?, where's the security raft?, this halyard is worn, how are your sails?, in what shape's the motor?'' Boyd turned off the water and took out a pad to take down notes. The guy was a gold mine, and because Boyd had decided that this would be his first and last visit, he knew he'd better make good use of it. The man placed himself at the foot of the mast and craned to see if it was straight. The effort produced a moment of vertigo. He might have lost his balance had Boyd not been there to steady him. Pushing the boy away, he grumbled, ''I climb up the mast twice a year. When I can't do that any longer, I'll know it's time to stop sailing.'' He gazed around once again and said, ''Come on, let's go out.'' ''I've put on coffee…'', Boyd began to say, which earned him a withering look that said: That coffee stuff's good enough for girls, okay?

Outside the wind was quite strong. Yves cut the motor and sat back in the cockpit telling him he'd better get the sails up before they went onto the rocks. He lit a Havana and blew wisps of smoke, immediately swept away by the gusts. Boyd dug them up in the locker under his bed and pulled them into the cockpit and then onto the prow. While he studied the jib to determine where to attach the halyard, he asked Yves if the *Denis* was the smallest boat he'd even been on. ''I've crossed the Atlantic on a 6 meter 50 during the Mini Transat Course. This is what? A 7.60?'' ''Right on,'' puffed the boy, one eye on the halyards deployed around the mast, another on the sail rings that served for *something*, a third on the approaching shore coming up very fast. ''Jesus H. Christ,'' shouted Yves into the wind. ''I'll be back tomorrow and you'd better have your show together,'' he pouted, leaning over and starting up the motor. ''I'm caught a little short, it's true,'' Boyd panted, thanking God for the sound of the engine, ''but I have been on a boat before, in fact we went to Rhodes…'' ''Where were you during the trip, in the cabin sleeping off a binge!'' ''And I do have books, a good library in fact…'' ''Then for Christ's sake, MAKE USE OF 'EM!'' Back at the pier Yves was let off, although in a moment of confusion Boyd badly maneuvered the boat as they reached the quay, nearly dropping the old man into the drink as his foot reached out for the dock. ''Jesus H!'' he heard him say, making his way up the quay to the *Capitainerie*, stooped, heavy in the waist, the smoke trailing through what as left of his white hair.

Boyd had his work cut out for him, but by the next afternoon when Yves returned the sails were in place. ''Now, we need ropes in the prow and the stern in case we run into trouble. Keep the boat hook at hand. Is the anchor in easy reach should we be forced to drop it in an emergency?'' Drop it…? The man went on, indicating a dozen other necessities before giving the boy permission to leave the port. ''You'd be well advised to look right and left,'' Yves said as they rounded the quay, sitting in the cockpit lighting a cigar. ''Can you imagine the reputation you'd have if you ran aground on someone's deck?'' Outside, Boyd put up the sails under the older man's instructions. ''Not starboard, PORT! Can't you feel where the wind's coming from for Christ's sake? And don't steer in spurts like that. Move the tiller smoothly and only when you *have* to move it. Normally it'll take care of itself when the sails are properly taut. And take your eye off the wind arrow. FEEL where the wind's coming from. Wet a finger and stick it in the air if you don't have any nerve endings in your face.'' Yves rained down instructions, making

Boyd hop from stem to stern, while he sat placidly smoking. The boy's confidence in the old man grew to unknown heights when the boat began to sail along smoothly. He had a hard time steering because the sails hadn't as yet been set just right, but he knew he was on course. ''We'll have to do something about the windlass. I noticed yesterday it's loose,'' observed Yves Brun.

The next day Boyd cycled to Yves' home in the hills above La Ciotat. The old man had built the place himself. He didn't bother showing the kid around. They went straight to the grange converted into a workshop, and set to straightening the windlass. Boyd found out that Yves had been an engineer and married. He was not a loquacious man, and only found conversation easy when talking about former sailing trips. Back on the boy's boat he guided Boyd carefully through the steps of what he had to do. There was no discussion. From the determined tone of his voice the boy knew there would be no alternative way of doing things.

They went out daily. A favorite place for Yves was the Iles du Vent, infamous nudist islands which, to Boyd's displeasure, they never sailed near enough to get any kind of view through the binoculars. On one of the totally uninhabited islands there were the remnants of a cement pier they often tied up to to give the boy docking practice. Boyd always prepared a simple lunch, usually a chicken from the La Ciotat shop, and Yves insisted on bread to mop up the sauce. He also demanded wine, but the boy told him if he wanted any he'd have to bring it himself. Every time they went out Yves would work up a sweat about the missing wine, although he never brought any from the cellar Boyd had seen at his home. He seemed to be waiting for the boy to capitulate, as the boy invariably did, except in this. Boyd refused to even go into why he would have no alcohol onboard. ''For the love of Christ, you can't live in France if you have no feeling for wine and cheese. Do you at least like cheese?'' Boyd assured him he did, although he rarely came with any of that either. ''It's as if you're trying to starve yourself from the pleasures of the world. No wine, no cheese, and you won't touch the bread…''

Boyd grew attached to the old man. He went out of his way to make himself useful. He rode to Yves' house to bring him his morning paper at breakfast time, until Yves forbade him to make the long trip. He mailed to Paris for Havanas but when he offered them, the old man went red with rage. ''You're doing too much. I know you appreciate my helping you, but just going out on the water is more than enough for me.'' Boyd often rode past his house, hoping the man would be out in his garden, and invite him in. But except for the reparation of the windlass, there were no more invitations. Boyd studied his books on sailing and flooded Yves with questions as proof of his interest. With every question answered came an anecdote taken from a previous trip Yves had made. A question about the mast would call forth a story about a demasting, and when Boyd asked about ways to fight seasickness, he thought the tales of vomiting would never end. Occasionally Yves would ask him if he could bring along someone on their sailing trips to the islands. Sometimes it was a neighbor girl or some other girl Yves knew from the shops in La Ciotat, bait for Boyd, he suspected. Sometimes boys were invited, boys Yves knew from ship chandleries or those who occasionally made deliveries to his home. Boyd was jealous of them all. With Yves he would chatter away like a magpie, in the presence of Yves' guests he clammed up, even showing hostility once or twice when the guest appeared a bit too friendly with the old man.

They had known each other for over a month when, sailing side by side, the boy at the tiller, he learned Yves had a son. ''Just like you, his head in books and afraid of his shadow.'' The comment hurt him deeply because it was so close to the truth. ''Never had his feet on the ground. Even as a boy all was books and imagination. He lived in his head. And as I was away on business or off sailing during my holidays, I couldn't bring him back down to earth.'' ''And his mother?'' ''They were two of a kind. But women can dream, a man has to make his way through life. He's *got* to be solid if he's to be depended on.'' Boyd knew his wife had been dead for a long time. ''Where's your son now?'' ''I made him become an engineer. I told him he could dream away his life if he wanted to, but first he'd have to have a good job if he wanted to marry....'' The word ''marry'' chocked him up as audibly as if he'd caught a bone in his throat. ''And your father?'' asked Yves of Boyd. ''He must be well off if his son is foot-free wandering about Europe.'' ''He has his own construction company. We had a little falling out so I went away, time enough for us both to cool down.'' ''That may not be a bad idea,'' the old man observed. Of course, they were both lying through their teeth.

As time went by, and Boyd became more sure of himself, he started to resent Yves' yelling or mocking. Yves could never just tell him what had to be done. He had to shout it. On the boat out in the Mediterranean this was no problem. The boy sincerely liked him more and more, and was even waking up in cold sweats in the middle of nightmares centered on the old man's death. Yves was giving him confidence in himself, breaking through to the tip of the emotional iceberg that made up the boy's façade. Perhaps, one day, he would even help him understand the immense black zones under the surface, zones which at times terrified the boy. He had become a life buoy indispensable to his survival. But Boyd resented the yelling, especially when they had guests, or in the port in front of other yachtsmen. At first he had played the dutiful son, bowing his head when chewed out before others. Now he felt that things should be gradually put on an equal footing, perhaps not exactly equal, perhaps more of a lopsided partnership.

The derision was worse still. For Yves the boy could do nothing right. He had to be shown even the simplest of things. He had no real physical agility or finely tuned muscular coordination. Yves felt that it wasn't enough to just tell him what had to be done, what was needed was a shock capable of putting him on the right track, even if it meant taunting him. For the boy the taunting was just so much groundless humiliation. He couldn't understand why his genuine efforts at improvement were not recognized, why the old man had to put in the knife and then turn it. Yves would physically wrench a hammer, say, from his hands, mumbling about the boy's mongoloid reflexes. He would shake his head when Boyd had problems adjusting the sails to perfection, assuring him he would never have the natural gifts needed to make even an *incompetent* sailor. Handing Yves a can opener one day Boyd confessed, "This is the third one I had to buy. The first two didn't work." He immediately regretted the comment. "So why didn't you change the brand after the first one broke? You have to be goddamned stupid to buy three of something that doesn't function." Yves never left him a way out. There was no way he could save face. It was not enough to show him he was wrong, his nose had to be rubbed in it. Yet like a puppy, the more Yves seemed hard on him, the more Boyd was drawn to him, because like a puppy, he needed Yves' approval: he needed to emulate this man who could make *him* a man.

Sometimes Yves would not be free to go out. Boyd suspected he had health problems. He knew he suffered from asthma, and he feared perhaps from other, graver things. Why does he have to be so old? he repeated to himself over and over. Why couldn't we have met sooner? To prove his willingness to improve, and to keep in some kind of contact, Boyd would go out by himself, even when the wind was very strong. He would call Yves and ask if it was okay for him to sail on a particular day. Yves would ask about the weather. Even in a Force 5 Yves would not hesitate to send the boy outside, and the boy never doubted an instant his sailing capacity, once he had received Yves' go-ahead. On one occasion he took Richard the Beau with him. Richard knew nothing about sailing, and it became clear to him very fast that Boyd knew only slightly more. The wind was very strong that day. Leaving the port the boat just missed grounding on a field of shoals, and the more Boyd tried to show off his new skills to his friend, the more Richard cringed in the corner of the cockpit, until he asked to be taken back. Another time Boyd went to a neighboring port, Les Lecques, just to practice berthing his boat in an unfamiliar place. His anxiety was so high he had to piss ten times in the twenty minutes it took to get there, but the procedure was a success. Anyway, he knew it would be because Yves Brun had assured him as much by phone.

One afternoon he ruthlessly barged in on Yves on some pretext. As it was a hot August day, the old man invited him into the kitchen for a drink of water. The window above the sink looked onto a swimming pool. When he asked if it was heated, the old man took him out to explain the system of black tubing warmed by the sun he had invented and built, as he had the pool, and as he had, the boy knew, the house. Yves said the boy could take a swim, but only after Boyd had worked up the courage to ask. Yves set a condition though, that Boyd wear a swimming suit. As luck would have it, he had one on under his jeans. After a few laps Yves came out to join him, for the first time without his usual Lacoste polo. A scar descended from his clavicle to his navel, just like Phil Navarre's. ''Christ, what caused that!'' questioned the boy. *Nothing*, was the swift and final answer.

One rainy afternoon Boyd was surprised by Yves' visit. The boy was tying up the ends of rope to keep them from uncoiling, as Yves had shown him. The old man made his way down the gangway into the cockpit with difficulty. The boy was beginning to wonder if the reason for Yves' dourness and bad temper was his great age, a phenomenon which seemed natural to the boy, perhaps because he was so distanced from it, less so to the man who faced it daily. ''What a whorehouse!'' he grumbled as he entered the cabin, the French expression for a mess. ''I hadn't been expecting you, Yves,'' grumbled Boyd back, tired of being barked at. ''If you're unhappy with life in general, why take it out on me in particular?'', Boyd continued mercilessly, pushing his advantage, another lesson he had picked up from the old man. ''It's easy for you to talk,'' replied Yves. ''Armed by your youth, what do you have to fear? I haven't even been up the mast once this year and the season's nearly over.'' ''Thanks for the insight into what's awaiting me,'' said the boy snidely. ''Don't bait me, son. I can complain because I've had to fight for everything I've ever had. I didn't get it sitting on my butt on a boat fiddling around with a bunch of ropes.''

''For your information I started work when I was eight with my father. By the time I was fourteen I was earning a salary. I've worked every day of my life. The difference between me and other boys is that when they were sixteen they bought cars, I went to the university. I work NOW. This is just my vacation, for Christ's sake.''

''And I went through a WAR for Christ's sake.''

''Sorry about that but I wasn't around then.''

''My dad was killed in the war, and from then on I had to fend for myself.''

''*My dad was an alcoholic*,'' shouted Boyd. ''And I wish for fucking sake *he'd* been killed?'' The rage shocked the boy and surprised Yves who suddenly began to understand certain things. ''My first memory was my mother pulling me from bar to bar looking for him. I can still remember the beery smell of those bars, the cowboy music and the men curiously watching the woman and her little kid of four. And when he came home it was to beat her and then me if I tried to stand up for her. See this nose, that was his work.'' Boyd looked out of the cabin window. Rain was pouring down, sending waves over the plexiglas. He had begun to cry, to Yves' deep embarrassment. ''And then coming home from somewhere he killed her. Drunkin' driving, it's called. It finally sobered him up. But by then I was eighteen and GONE!''

Boyd sat across from the old man. He would have given anything for Yves to hold him, but he couldn't ask.

''How did he keep up his company ... drinking....''

''There as no company. My father was a day laborer...''

''Why did you...''

''Because this is France. Because you have no respect for people who work with their hands. God knows America's got its problems, and because of them I'm content to spend the rest of my life here, but working one's way up from nothing to something, isn't one of them. I didn't want you to write me off before you even knew me.''

''I understand why you never have anything to drink here, but now we could make an exception. Just this one time. I'll go get us something.''

Boyd took out a bottle of gift-wrapped wine. ''It was for when I left at the end of summer,'' he said, passing it to Yves.

''This is a very good vintage,'' smiled Yves, opening the package.

''Don't be too nice,'' laughed the boy wiping his eyes. ''I'm not used to it. Anyway, I don't know wines as you do, this one just cost a lot, that's how I picked it out.''

And then Yves told Boyd about his boy. ''I had been away a lot and he was more or less brought up by his mother. She filled his head with 'culture', as if he didn't get enough of that already in school. Our home was turned into a goddamn fortress, the two of them left to their books as if they were the lone survivors of some goddamn earthly catastrophe. I tried to shape him up when I was there. He never wanted to go out fishing or grouse shooting, I had to force him. What's the purpose of a father if not to shape his boy into an oak strong enough to face the challenges of this life, not all of which are pleasant, far from it! As I told you, he became an engineer--he was really a brilliant student, but he dabbled in writing and painting, 'searching for himself', as she put it. We grew pretty much apart. He took up with some girl I never met and they lived in a studio at St. Cyr that I paid for, along with the rest.''

He paused a long moment. The story of his son was parallel to Boyd's own. During the disputes between his parents Boyd would put balls of wax in his ears, as he had read in the *Odyssey*, allowing him a complete withdrawal into himself. His father too had obliged him to wake at three and sit through the cold and snow waiting for ducks, for deer or fish to bite, warming himself with his bottle of whisky. The only time he had seen him smile was when passing around the bottle if companions were present. The only tenderness he had ever shown him was when they had slept in the cabin by the lake, in front of the big iron stove, when....

''Yes, he was like you...'' continued the old man, and again broke off to fill his glass, half of which he immediately drained.

Yves knew he should never have come to give Boyd lessons. He was drawn naturally to the port, to any port, and when Richard brought up the boy who was going to kill himself if someone didn't help him out, he had imagined two or three outings, just some water under his feet before hanging up his slicker indefinitely. It was only now that he realized he had been drawn to the boy because he had something of his Christian. But he had now gone as far as he could. Boyd would have to find a younger role model, someone who was as far from death was he himself was close. It wouldn't be for years and years before the boy would feel the first stiffening in his legs, the first shyness of taking a false step, the first wariness of his balance. Then the loosening of the skin, and all the rest. Boyd could never understand something like that, and in reality there was no way Yves could put it into words ... and then, to what good? Let the boy live his vitality without the knowledge of the lead dormant in his young limbs. Because Yves could no longer keep up, he had only to fall back. Cleanly and definitely. Yet before withdrawing he would explain the reasons for his comportment, the cause of his sadness, and why he could nevermore laugh and be good--albeit aging--company.

''Like you he had to have his cocky independence even though at his age he needed me more than a boy normally does his father, because he had really never had me as a father.'' He paused, his throat constricted by the confession of remiss he had always harbored like a lurking virus, but only now--when all was lost--dared face. ''Like you. Like you, it would seem. Okay, that was my fault and it's the weight I have to carry forever. I loved that kid and I wanted him armed like a man. I had to wait for him to come to me, to acknowledge his need. How could he change, if not?''

''But why couldn't he just go on with his painting or whatever?''

''Because this isn't America, boy. You don't begin sweeping a bank here, and end up president of that bank twenty years later. Here you need diplomas. No one's going to put bread in your mouth if you don't do it yourself. I've been over there. I know you can mess around before settling down and founding a family. Not here. The few jobs that exist here have to be won and then kept. He was an engineer, at least he would always have that.''

''He wouldn't take the first step?''

''I guess he thought *I* would.'' The old man hesitated. ''Really, I don't know what he thought. There was a kind of competition. He'd prove he could make it without me. He stopped taking my money, and if his mother hadn't been there to give it to him in little gifts--he never imagined *I* had anything to do with it--he would have wound up in a Salvation Army dormitory. When she died I guess he didn't know where to turn anymore. He started telephoning me. He accused me of letting him down, of not respecting him nor the things he needed to make life worth living. He repeated a lot, Life's not worth living now Mamma's gone. There had been at least that, he'd say. Mamma who felt for him, who understood him. He ended up crying ''Why didn't you come to me when I needed you? Where were you, Papa, where were you all those years you should have been by my side?'' As furtively as he could, Yves dabbed his reddened eyes with his sleeve.

Suddenly Boyd sensed where the conversation was going. Throughout his life he had wished and even plotted for the deaths of those he hated. He knew what thoughts of that kind meant in psychiatry. He knew what his subconscious was constantly telling him. The story of Yves' son was coming too close. He wanted to escape the presence of the old man. He wanted to run as he had so often before, from jobs, from his city and country. From friends who let him down, as he so feared Yves would let him down. But here he was in a boat at the very edge of France. There was literally nowhere else to run. Nowhere else.

''I told him I would help him, but he knew I wouldn't. Physically I'd be by his side, but he knew I'd have him working and then we'd be sailing and there'd be grandchildren…''

''Your life, not his…''

''That *is* life! You've got to know, that's what life *is*. It's not running out on your family and taking up whims and not *contributing*. He *had* to see it my way if he was to survive.''

''But that's so…''

Yves made a dismissive gesture with his hand. ''And then he called me and for pure spite,'' he forged on, his energy running out like a wound-down clock, ''he said I was the cause of all his ills and if he was nothing it's because I wouldn't let him be what he was, what he wanted to be. He said he wouldn't go on like that. He wouldn't anymore.''

Boyd started shaking his head. He didn't want Yves to continue. The story cut too close, as if Yves were reading in the cards of the *future*, not the past.

''He had a gun, he said, and when he hung up he'd use it. Then the line went dead. I knew the local head of the gendarmerie. We'd sailed a lot together, he and his sons…. I rang him and he went out and … and you can guess the rest.'' The rain continued over the Plexiglas as Yves lowered his head over his lap, a fat old man stuffed in a snow-white Lacoste polo with a smiling green crocodile.

.

Boyd wasn't alarmed when Yves showed no sign of life during the last week of his vacation. There was a mute understanding that they would let things cool down until the following summer, at least that was what the boy had imagined. But the autumn and winter months were long. At the end of December he rang Yves to wish him a happy Christmas. He got the answering machine, on which he left a cheery message. The second time he left his own number, knowing Yves had it already, but what if it had been mislaid or something? Anyway, given the difference in age, he felt no compunction about calling back again and again. He sent a Christmas card, and much later a card for Easter. He sent cigars, too, again the best Havanas. He sent a can of caviar. If Yves liked expensive cigars, perhaps he would be fond of caviar. Anyway, he had an Iranian girl student who had offered it to him for his Christmas.

Due to a lack of classrooms needed to give the baccalaureate exams, his were requisitioned, permitting him to leave early for the summer holidays, He arrived in La Ciotat by train during the first week of June. He immediately checked out the *Denis*, and then rode his bike to Yves' house. He caught the old man in his garden, trimming the hedge. The winter hadn't been good to him. He looked much more fatigued, clipping the unsightly branches in a methodical but robotic way, hands and arms uncoordinated. He won't climb to the top of the mast this year either, thought the boy. Yves was not pleased to have Boyd see him that way. The boy was invited in for coffee, gruffly, the old man meticulously setting out the table as one would for a passing priest perhaps, not a friend with whom one had shared intimate experiences. Yves remembered too well and too freshly the past which seemed still so recent. How could the boy before him know what a handsome lad he had been, and how cocky, and how he'd strode across the stage of life *full of life*? He did not want the boy to see him diminished, he did not want to be seen by anyone any longer. He was old, said the lead in his legs, he was old, his prick reminded him when he waited for it to piss, and waited and waited. He was old said the pinched muscles at his throat and the webbed skin of his body. He was old, even he had to admit, even though within he knew he was younger and more experienced and more *daring* than the boy seated across from him. He was old now and he wanted to take that age with him to a watery grave, unseen and unseeing. Throughout all his life he had wondered if he would know when the time had come. That time was now, and he knew it immediately: It was when he no longer wished to see his reflection in the eyes of the one he loved.

None of this Boyd sensed. And so it was natural for him to invite Yves to the *Denis*, hoping to get things back to normal between them, hoping to sail and learn and share with this man who would be his touchstone to manhood. And surprisingly, Yves agreed. He clearly saw he would not rid himself of the boy in any other way.

They left the next morning before sunup. The port was asleep at that hour, completely abandoned by the yachtsmen who wouldn't show up in mass until well into July. The sea was rough and cold. They donned slickers and headed for the Iles du Vent, today well named. Yves had hardly said two words since entering the cockpit. Then suddenly he began to shout at the boy. "For Christ's sake, look how you harden those sails! Haven't you remembered any goddamned thing you learned last summer, if 'learned' can be applied to what goes on in your head! DON'T LOOK UP AT THAT ARROW. CAN'T YOU *SENSE* WHERE THE WIND'S COMING FROM, FOR CHIRST'S SAKE! And STOP pulling on that tiller in fits and starts. Oh let me do it!" he cried out disgustedly, jerking the tiller out of the boy's hands, the first time he'd *ever* taken physical command of the boat. "No good even trying to be literate with an ass like you."

"I thought everything was ready…"

"Pretentious little shit. Go forward before I kick your ass in."

He did as told, feeling an inner rage rising to his throat, cutting off the air. He knew it and what it meant. He knew it mustn't take control of him, as when it had exploded before, forcing him to scratch Phil Navarre's face, to tell Didier to go to hell, to…. Other images tried to break surface, but were repulsed. All his life he had curbed the rage, turning back the imminent chaos. All his life he had been the good boy, doing what he was told, *always* conforming, always hiding the rage, now abandoned by this man he loved. Again. He couldn't be abandoned again. This was his last chance. He *knew* Yves was all that was left to him. He must hang on for his life, literally for his life. But Yves wouldn't have it that way. The more he had Boyd running to the prow to check the sails, the inclination of the mast, the tension of the shrouds, the this and the that, the more Boyd tried to explain he was doing his best. At the same time he was glad to be out of the cockpit, away from where Yves could grab something out of his hands, making of him too much of a fool to even bother with.

But Yves made him return. "Come here. I'll do it myself, for Christ's sake. For the love of God, what did I get myself mixed up in. COME HERE, I SAID. COME HERE AND LET A *MAN* DO IT."

Boyd swung into the cockpit beside him, hurtling his body against the old man's. His voice was calm. "You know, Yves, you don't have to call me a useless asshole. After all, I'm not your son."

"THAT'S IT! TAKE ME TO THAT QUAY AND LET ME OFF. I'LL SIGNAL A PASSING BOAT TO TAKE ME BACK."

It was the quay where they had tied up a dozen times. The wind was blowing from the land, which minimized the danger of the boat smashing itself against the cement surface.

The tide was low, the distance from the cockpit to the top of the quay a good foot. Yves would have to jump it. The old man lowered the fenders as they approached. "Don't bother tying up. Just let me off and get away." Wordless Boyd did as told. The boat leaned into the quay, bobbing in the swell. The old man put a foot up but an inch short, and the irreparable took place. So strong was the wind Boyd didn't hear the entry of the body into the water, and that despite the fact that it was heavy by its weight, and heavier still by the leaden shroud it had cast over those who had touched the man's life, smothering them beneath its mass: the son he had tyrannized, a wife dying of sorrow at the loss of her son, and now Boyd, to whom remained as much feeling as a corpse.

He headed back to La Ciotat. He drew in the sails and gunned the motor as fast as it would go. A cold, spitting rain began to strike against his face. He closed the collar but left his hair in the whipping wind. He knew he wouldn't stop crying until he had somehow erased the words from his memory. Halfway back he began to tremble so badly he had to drop the tiller and enter the cabin for some valium. Two pills, and then a third. In the port it was still very early. He tied up and went back into the cabin where he collapsed on the floor, his knees into his chest. He slept until the next afternoon. During the days that followed there wasn't a word of Yves' disappearance. A week later he left for Italy via Port Beausoleil, where his life came full circle.

BOOK IV

CHAPTER THIRTY-NINE

Welcome to the Zoo

"He's lost control," the black-haired boy standing at the foot of the three-story *Capitainerie* scoffed into his hand-held VHF. "He's drifting down between Quays 3 and 4." His blond colleague pulled up on his bike to watch Boyd's fruitless attempts to maneuver the boat. He gave a disgusted grimace before riding off with a smooth pedal thrust, leaving Boyd to cope by himself with a motor that wouldn't start. Boyd looked up in time to catch the squared-off chest silhouetted through a t-shirt where a circular insignia declared: *Port Beausoleil À Votre Service*. The black-haired boy was similarly trim and "tautly-muscled", *bien dessiné*, as the French said of those with firm Spartan chests and hard abdominals, nothing superfluous, just functional simplicity. This Boyd had first noticed upon entering the port. Sidling up to the Reception Dock at the helm of his boat, the one with black-hair had indicated, with a combination of shouts and apathetic gestures, the place where Boyd was to berth. The indifference of the two boys reassured him. He didn't want to attract attention by pointing out that he had been having trouble with his motor since leaving his homeport, La Ciotat, a few weeks back. He had anchored offshore since then, avoiding ports where his description might have been broadcast. What would he have done, he wondered, if he had spotted one of the youths transmitting his characteristics into the VHF: "He's about my age, around 6 feet, thin, sturdy." The fear of being discovered had had its consequences on his body. Since his precipitous departure he had been pissing urine as black as ink. A part of him was persuaded the phenomenon resulted from the mental shock and sudden physical fatigue pursuant of his last encounter with Yves Brun, but because there were no accompanying symptoms, no pain or weakness, he'd decided to let his body work the toxin out. Yet the inner fear that the problem was a harbinger of something more fearful obscured his thinking. Luckily there was no wind. He could advance the boat by sculling the rudder until someone threw him a line.

A diver passing in an inflatable Zodiac summed up what was going on with a practiced glance: an inexperienced kid whose motor was having kittens, facing off against the two pricks working as smart-ass summer guardians, neither of which would drop his pud long enough to offer a hand. He told Boyd to throw him a line, *easy*, without killing them both, and pulled the boat into the berth indicated by the scowling blond adolescent on his bike, back as soon as he saw port troublemaker drawing up in his Zodiac.

''What the hell,'' the diver guffawed in a high-pitched voice, an outburst that nearly toppled the boy-guardian from his saddle. ''A lot of guys who don't know as much as you--and you know *shit*--'' he mumbled in an aside, "are out with whole families. He's only got himself to drown, so where's the problem?''

After attaching the boat Boyd went to the *Capitainerie* to fill out the appropriate *fiche*. Behind the counter stood a small, thin man, nearly a midget, a Corsican, Boyd found out later, named Grimaldi, ''the same as the royals in Monaco.'' Someone had written that the Corsican was a combination of the worst of the French and the Italians. Gruff, snide, Grimaldi had, in addition, the Napoleonic complex of small men. Dressed in summer whites with gold braid on his shoulders and hat, it took all of Boyd's patience to win a grudging *au-revoir* and key to the showers.

At the entrance to the sanitary block were two doors in slightly receded alcoves. In front of the one marked *HOMMES* a young girl, her skirt lifted up above her belly, was fingering her pussy delicately, kneading a pearly extract between the tips of her fingers. She hurredly dropped the skirt as Boyd approached. Inside, a half-dozen boys, mostly in undershorts, some the old-fashioned kind that rose as high as the navel and descended in an ample pouch, were waiting for the two shower cubicles to be freed. They were all speaking Italian, a surprise to Boyd who was as yet unaware that Port Beausoleil, at the farthest eastern extension of France, was a kind of nautical dormitory for the rich of Turin. He went to the washbasins, the only free one facing the end of a row of urinals. In the mirror he saw a boy pissing, his cock, blood heavy, filling his hand. Outside, the girl's voice called ''*Mario, sei prontó*?'' in a nagging squeal. The boy shook his cock while turning his head to the door. ''*Arrivo!*''

Boyd turned in early. The incessant images from La Ciotat, the dread of being caught and tried and locked away, and the uncertainty over the black urine, caused him to writhe, his body entrapped in the sweat-soaked sheets, his mouth as dry as a desert. He tried to find solace in memories of Laurent, dead for nearly four years. Finally he took shelter in fantasies involving the boy and girl at the showers. He fell asleep in the moisture of his briefs, calmed by the spurts that seemed to empty the body of poisonous worry.

His motor turned over the first time the next morning, permitting him to leave the port at dawn. But just outside, the halyard to the mainsail broke, sending the sail crashing onto the boom. He returned to the port for repairs, escaping the mockery of the two young guards who hadn't as yet come on duty. At ten the repairs were finished, but as he never set sail except at daybreak--the better to get away without prying, judgmental eyes--he decided to go to the hospital in Menton, the nearest town to Port Beausoleil, to see what was wrong with him.

He was admitted to the *Urgences*. He had brought along a bottle of his urine, and for the next hour he sat shirtless on a gurney, while through the small porthole in the door of the examination room he saw the intern he had given the sample to go back and forth, showing it to everyone he crossed. Doctors and nurses dropped by behind the door to look in and study the boy who pissed ink. He was given a bed in one of the upper floors, and for the next two weeks the hospital was his home.

The hospital doctor, Saramago, put in two or three appearances during his stay. As far as Boyd could tell, the reason his urine was black was never discovered. He went through dozens of blood tests and had dozens of x-rays and ''ultra-sounds'', but nothing turned up. As he felt perfectly well, he left the hospital for most of the day, often leaving in levi's and sandals, shirtless, on the bike he had brought from La Ciotat. His destination was invariably the port, Quay 3, where he potted around for the day on his boat, the *Denis*. The interns and nurses, frowning down at him from the balconies as he rode away, made it clear they did not approve of his mistaking the hospital for a hotel. Word got back to Doctor Saramago who came charging into his room one day and warned ominously that ''Whatever you have, it won't be cured with an aspirin.'' Nothing more was needed to convince the boy that he had cancer. For days afterward he wandered around in a daze wondering what was going to become of him now.

The only person he could turn to now was Denis, whose phone number he'd carried for over two years in his wallet, on the flip side of his photo of the *Swan*.

CHAPTER FORTY

And the Monkey House

At the Menton Hospital Boyd asked an intern who knew the Harbormaster of Port Beausoleil to call and ask if a permanent berth could be found for his boat. Boyd knew there were no spaces available, and this worried him should he be forced to stay in Menton for prolonged treatment. The Harbormaster, Mr. Rimini, gave the boy a ring to let him know that a place would be reserved for him. Then late one night Boyd felt that something terribly wrong was going on in his lower abdomen. He rang for the night intern but no one answered the call. He went to the bathroom where this time pissing caused excruciating pain. He returned to his bed in a deep sweat, too tired to ring for help. Yet from that night onwards the urine turned from black to blood red, then to pink, and finally back to normal.

On the last day of his hospitalization Doctor Saramago came by for a surprisingly cordial visit. He suggested to Boyd that he become an outpatient at a nearby clinic. ''I've asked a specialist from the clinic to drop in this morning to see you.'' The urologist who showed up that afternoon told Boyd that since they had not found the cause of his problem, he should undergo more tests. The urologist was surprisingly personable and looked only slightly older than the boy himself. Boyd was flushed to find himself at last talking to someone human. During his rare visits, Saramago had stayed only a few grudging seconds. ''Do you think I hurt myself doing physical exercises?'' asked the boy. ''Or perhaps I strained something, like when I pulled up the anchor, or an orgasm that was too intense?'' The specialist laughed and said the new tests would tell.

Back at the port Grimaldi, his shoulders just visible behind the counter, chuckled at Boyd's innocence. The boy and the man had grown friendly, proof of something Boyd had observed before, that the gruffest people were often the most vulnerable to a little consideration. ''Doctor Saramago works at the hospital. He only has to pop his head through the door of a room to earn a pile. That's how the French Social Security wastes our money. He *owns* half of the clinic he wants to send you to. At the hospital Saramago milked you and the welfare system. Now you're being sent on to the clinic where he'll continue the fleecing.'' Boyd cancelled his appointment with the specialist and sent off a letter of complaint to the Social Security, detailing the extortion to which he believed he had been a victim. Anyway, he wasn't too worried about his health. He was certain he had passed a stone the night he had urinated in pain.

At the quay a new boat had drawn up aside his, the *Bonità*. Inside was another tiny Italian--if one counted, as Boyd did, Grimaldi and other Corsicans as Italian--mostly bald, with what remained of his hair pulled back into a pony tail, seized by an elastic. Stocky, bordering on fat, loud, vulgar, accompanied by a servant-wife, statuesque as were most of the female trophies sported by rich Italians. They had a boy, spoiled, cringing, his eyes blackened, perhaps through lack of sleep, hoped Boyd, as he fought to repress the vague remnants of his own beatings. They invited him to their boat for lunch, where they talked money in excellent French. Dino, a former optician looking sixty-five but in his early fifties, described how he had put his savings into ghetto apartments, thanks to which he was able to retire. He and his wife were back from a cruise to Capri where Dino had done everything possible to fuck the Italian ports, as he put it himself, out of their ridiculously steep tariffs. ''We stayed off the pier at Ravenna all day. The Harbormaster wanted 50,000 lire and I offered 10,000. I told him it was better than nothing, and that we'd leave if he didn't lower the price. All day we argued. Finally, at nightfall, I squashed up 50,000 lire in notes and threw them onto the pier so we could moor, shower and go out for dinner.'' ''What was the Harbormaster's reaction?'' ''He was happy. He'd won.'' It was a game, Italians screwing Italians.

On the boat on the other side of the *Denis* was a family of three, the Italian husband short, albeit a head taller than Dino, muscular, his thinning hair colored black, Boyd learned, when he surprised the man crouching in his cockpit dyeing the remains of the hair on his head, as well as the matted mangrove on his chest and impressive pubic bush, his swimsuit pulled down under his *service trois pièces*, other words the French had for the male genitalia. All three spoke only Italian

His wife was a looker whom all the boys in the port found as desirable as the daughter. She sunbathed on the front deck of their sailboat, topless, her deflated breasts like twin udders. Her daughter also lay out topless, her knockers silicon-sized but without the silicon, wet-dream fantasies that kept the boys circulating around the boat on bikes quayside, in tenders and other inflatables from the water. Men dropped by to chew the rag with the husband, Aldo, as foreplay to rapping up the girls. Aldo had a deep testicular voice at those moments, as he affected to be oblivious to the reason for the visits.

The boys preferred the mother but only laid, as far as Boyd knew, the daughter. As Italians never slept before three in the morning, Boyd, whose nightmares left him little rest, often woke up to see the daughter wondering up and down the quay at the side of a youngster her age, talking and taking in the cool night, while Boyd pissed in the washbasin of his cabin, satisfied with the liquid as clear as bottled water. He took to going on early-morning drives across the border with Aldo to Ventimiglia for a cappuccino. The girls slept in late and later went to the Narval Café for morning coffee.

He became acquainted with the woman on the *Bonità*. As he had a habit of transforming Italian names into a French proximity, she became Francine. Their conversations consisted of her trying to maneuver him into bed, and his countermeasures that were basically reminders that she had a husband and son. She often took her boy to a nearby park where she freed him to play by himself in the sand. ''It's terrible making love to an older man,'' she complained, eyeing Boyd's buttocks through the weathered levi's. ''Can you imagine being in bed with him under the sheets?'' ''Maybe you shouldn't have put him there,'' he replied mercilessly. He had to be merciless because she was capable of hiking up her skirt for him in some corner of the playground, and to hell with the preliminaries--the ''petting'' or the getting her ''hot and bothered'' that had been so severely abjured by Mormon seminary counselors like the bloodless Ichabod Crane.

She told him that to get a berth in the port they had had to pay Rimini a bribe, via Bernard, one of the guardians, of five hundred francs. Bernard was a bearded redneck with the brain of a Neanderthal, hooded bushy eyebrows and a stomach that spilled over his belted trousers, a sight that sickened the boy. A mean son-of-a-bitch from Brittany, used to harsh weather and harder times, a submariner who had been forced into early retirement for minor disobedience. Boyd hoped the accusations against Harbormaster Rimini were untrue because he liked the man. Short with narrow shoulders and bowed legs, the center of gravity at the ballooning midsection, the whole in impeccable whites cut by a master tailor to give the aura of comeliness, Rimini had found a place in Boyd's heart the day Boyd, at the *Capitainerie* window, saw him help Jean-Loup, the garbage boy, empty and clean the garbage cans Jean-Loup had collected on his morning rounds. ''Isn't that sad!'' tut-tutted Grimaldi at the sight of Harbormaster Rimini in rubber boots and rubber gloves, up to his elbows in rubbish. ''I kind of admire him,'' Boyd had said. ''It's a very democratic, American way of doing things.'' Grimaldi let out sour air. ''No one in France would respect someone in Rimini's position up to his elbows in crap.'' Rimini also inspected the toilets, Boyd knew, which turned Grimaldi's stomach but won the Harbormaster immense favor with the yachtsmen, who could count on clean facilities thanks to the inspections. Rimini circulated around the port mornings and afternoons, weekdays and weekends, assuring himself that things were shipshape, and offered a helping hand when one was needed. He spoke fluent Italian, bowed to every yachtsman, and kissed the hand, with admirable naturalness, of every yachtsman's wife.

So it was that Boyd went to find Harbormaster Rimini to inform him that the *Bonità* was telling whoever would listen that he had taken baksheesh, the word favored in the French Southeast. As the Harbormaster was out, Boyd descended to the guardians' room to fill in Grimaldi. Boyd had had the opportunity to see Rimini and Grimaldi work together, and had imagined they were close friends. He had chalked up Grimaldi's disdain for what Grimaldi considered Rimini's obsequiousness as Corsican distaste for ass-licking, a subject on which the Corsicans were hypersensitive. In their own mafia-ridden society they were obliged to treat everyone with respect, as one could never know who was potentially dangerous. To Boyd's surprise, Grimaldi doubled over in laughter. ''Everyone knows Rimini's on the take,'' he sneered. ''Listen, Rimini appropriates for himself anything that's not nailed down. He goes through the *garbage cans* in the mornings before the port awakens in search of something of value. He even puts his name on pieces of discarded wood, for God's sake. He puts his *name* on it, and then sends the guardians to collect the stuff or asks Jean-Loup to bring it in.'' Boyd, an early riser, had observed this for himself, but had assumed it was the reflex of those who had lived through the rigors of the War, feeling they needed to hoard whatever was available, just in case. ''Forget about the five hundred francs. You have no idea of the shit you'll be in if you don't.'' Grimaldi had other advice for the youth. ''Never marry an intelligent woman,'' he said, assuring the boy with a nod that *he* had escaped such a fatality. ''The man's got to rule, and an intelligent woman can only be an obstacle.'' He had similar views concerning the Arabs. ''In Corsica Arabs still walk with their heads down and their eyes directed at the ground. It's because it's not like that here on the mainland that we're having problems.''

Following his disclosure to Grimaldi, the guardian Bernard took to riding his bike up and down the quay where Boyd was berthed, as if the protection of the boats there had become a fixation. He would stop directly in front of the boy's cockpit, smoke a cigarette while studiously looking away from Boyd, and then flick the cigarette over his shoulder, into the cockpit. When Boyd asked him to be more careful, the guardian looked at the boy with a kind of death stare, and rode away without a word. Boyd brought up the subject with Grimaldi. ''Bernard took the *Bonità* money in Rimini's name but either didn't give it to him or only gave him part of it. As you asked me to do, I told Rimini your story about the *Bonità*'s ratting on him for taking the fix, and he probably had words with Bernard. I don't know what went down exactly, but as I said, watch out for Bernard. He'll fuck you over if he gets the chance.''

''That fat ass! He can't even see his dick when he pisses!'', was all Boyd could retort.

Grimaldi wanted to liquidate all his holdings in France before retiring to Corsica in a few months. His wife Thérèse agreed to move to Corsica, but only for six months of the year. She felt instinctively that although she counted for little in Menton, the moment she stepped foot on the island she would be confined to the walled city and its lot of domestic chores as were most of the women of Grimaldi's generation, where in rank a woman came after a jeep and rifle. Since the cottage, and especially their apartment in Menton, were in both their names, Grimaldi was walking on eggs for certainly the first time in their married life, as her signature, under French law, was obligatory.

The *Bonità* moved to a new emplacement, to Boyd's relief. Dino's behavior towards his son was insufferable. He ordered him to shut up when the boy made the merest noise, obliging him to sit still during discussions between ''adults'', informing Boyd in his son's presence: ''We never planned on having children. I wanted a retirement free of millstones so we could sail to any place on the spur of the moment. He came along through some accident of Francine's, and we're stuck with him.'' Boyd didn't want to pursue the discussion in Boy's presence--that was Dino and Francine's nickname for him: Boy--so he never learned why an abortion hadn't been performed. Although shy, and as nearly erased in her husband's presence as Thérèse in front of Grimaldi, when they were alone Francine was anything but reserved. Her conversation was intelligent and her intentions unrelenting. Often he kidded with her about a possible boating accident Dino could fall victim to, freeing Francine to follow her instincts. He had met several of Dino's friends, fat, balding Italians with pouting, childish wives, Philistines who neither read nor carried on a conversation that wasn't based on the price of goods, and the restaurants where they had dined or would dine. There were other friends Francine seemed to have imposed on Dino as she had imposed Boyd. Boyd never found out why Dino put up with the men she invited aboard--or rather boys, for such was her taste--tall black-haired Adonises with resonant, virile Italian voices, who knew how to banter with a woman in a way so pleasant it was no wonder Italian girls felt they had diamonds in the place of their cherries. Assured of the attention they aroused, the girls paraded as if on continual presentation, *à l'italienne*, chest and buttocks thrust out, in provocative oscillation. Once he had heard an Italian mother scold her six-year-old son: "Why don't you look at the *donnas*? You must look at them when they pass!" She stopped just short of calling him a queer. Young girls, those without approved beaux, were forced to toe the line if they didn't want their adored brothers to give them a fat lip when they stepped out of line. Once married, they were relegated to the kitchen where an excess of food and repeated childbearing left them spread out over two chairs, while their aging husbands escaped the conjugal hearth on the arm of "fresh flesh," young girls paid to find them ever manly. Who cared now if their wives' hair reeked of olive oil, or if the odor of sour milk seeped through their pores, or the fustiness of garlic soaked through the matted tufts under their armpits? Even then the women strutted forth, in their mind's eye as desirable as the divine Garbo. One of Francine's favorites was Claudio. He invariably turned up in a three-piece suit of Armani-looking quality, an overcoat from the cover of Vogue, and polished-to-perfection loafers. He was pale, so handsome Boyd had to force himself not to stare, a *je-ne-sais-quoi* resemblance to Boy who was then age five to Mario's 23. Francine treated him as she did Boyd in the presence of Dino, a kind of courteous distancing, a sister's dutiful respect of his maleness.

.

One day his neighbor Aldo invited him to Ventimiglia to look for whores. Aldo was so excited he dribbled spittle from the corners of his mouth. Boyd knew he "worked" the cafés and markets, chatting up salesgirls, while his wife Roseland and their daughter were off at the Narval to be made a fuss over by the servers, cheap Italian labor from across the border. Boyd had accompanied them once. Perhaps considered a potential rival, he got an unselfconscious toe-to-head examination from the waiters, who appeared dead serious about their "courting" of the two women. He had seen the Italians often enough in the showers to imagine their cocks, too big and thick when hard to be pulled through their flies, gently swaying while their owners lowered their trousers, preparatory to propping the girl up against the door of the café john, ready to discharge in a minimum of strokes. Too bad if the girl didn't get much out of the quick plugging, they'd have the compensating surprise, as the girl in front of the showers, of watching what dribbled out later in uncanny abundance. Because the salty air filled Boyd's mind with such salacious thoughts, he had agreed to ride off with Aldo. In Ventimiglia the man did the negotiating from his car window, but the prostitutes were too sordid for even Aldo's wants, and the price, it seemed to the boy, sky high for the rundown border town. Back at the quay, Aldo, aroused from cruising the whores, went in search of his wife. Twenty minutes later their boat left the port, something it did only when he needed a quiet place to hump undisturbed. The daughter was left alone on the quay, but never for long.

Francine dropped by his boat later that afternoon. Shirtless and in low-slung jeans, he leaped onto the quay to greet her. Aldo and Roseland looked on benevolently from their boat, while on the other side of the quay, facing their cockpits, a Swiss couple on their immense motor yacht, and a German couple on an even bigger yacht, did their best to ignore Aldo and Boyd's tiny vessels as they would a mess a dog had inadvertently shat in front of their boarding ladders. The Swiss were retired, the Germans had made their fortune by opening up tennis courts first in Munich and then throughout Germany. The Swiss watered the plants and flowers on their balcony with Evian, to the disgust of the non-Swiss. The Swiss owner was nail thin and wiry, displacing himself in jerky twitches. His wife was the pack animal of the two, carrying suitcases and provisions. Boyd had watched them spend a whole day cleaning their folding aluminum bikes, the seats of which were protected by plastic supermarket bags, with *toothbrushes*. The German gentleman had just taken up underwater diving. He was robust, in his fifties, his wife the same age, but still attractive thanks to liftings and daily aerobics.

For the benefit of Aldo and Roseland, Boyd welcomed Francine with kisses to the cheeks and a hug. He could see her husband and Boy waiting at the end of the quay. Boyd had made clear his revulsion of the obnoxious old fool who now hung back while Francine came onto the quay to do the hellos from them both. Boyd suspected the son-of-a-bitch wanted his wife to keep up contact because he imagined Boyd had entrée to the *Capitainerie*. In the presence of her husband and Boyd's neighbors, Francine shied away from a display of affection. For the same reasons, Boyd felt secure enough to press his body into hers. "If there's one thing you learn with age," he said inanely to his audience, "it's to exploit your aces. Mine are my accent which Francine just *adores*, and my abdominals she can't get enough of." And it was true that she was constantly looking down at the squared-off stomach and the fine line of black hairs between navel and brief tops. Francine went red, pecked him on the cheek, shrugged and called out to Roseland and Aldo, *E pazzo!*, then hurried back to her waiting husband who made a slight wave to Boyd that he didn't bother to return. Boyd marveled at his show of good humor, while inside he shook with fear. Two months had gone by since the incident, and no one had come to lead him away in handcuffs. Had the cops done their job, at the very least they would have interviewed those who had last seen Yves Brun alive.

.

On Quay 4, facing the prow of the *Denis*, was a big sailboat occupied by an old man who lived amidst a harem of female cousins, sisters, wives, mistresses--Boyd could only guess. What was grating for the boy was the man's voice, so loud and retchingly hollow it seemed to come from the inner reaches of colossal testicles. Next to this boat was a fairly big motor yacht, the *Kitty*, skippered by still another pappy. It was on the *Kitty* that the Italians assembled until they became so numerous they set up tables on the quay, to which each brought his contribution. The racket invariably began when the hostess of the *Kitty* greeted her friends with an incredibly high-pitched bellowing, ''*Buongiorno, Giovanni!*'', ''*Buongiorno, Fulvia!*'', and when the arrivals became to numerous to name singly, ''*Buongiorno TUTTI!*'' All night they same ''*Buongiorno TUTTI!*'' Despite the late partying, the owner of the *Kitty*, as Boyd, was an early riser, and often wandered the quay before sunup, while the port slept on. He had the habit of pissing against the garbage can at the foot of his boat, while at the same time taking swigs from a hip flask he carried with him everywhere.

Since Boyd couldn't sleep, he decided to leave the port before sunset and anchor several yards from the coastline. He was angry with himself for not having thought of the idea before. There, he tried to contain the rancor eating away at his heart. He grieved over all the evil done to him during his life, except the first years, the details of which were expunged as from a lobotomy. He vaguely remembered how the child he had been had turned into himself, terrorized by the iron fist of his father, rejected by his pairs at school because he couldn't fit in, a child who sought the shelter of his mother's flank in the warmth of her bed, where she installed him mornings as soon as his father left for work. He racked his brains to remember the reasons for his difference. He brooded over the torments he was going through even now, the noise made by the old fool and his English pussy, the dishonesty of Rimini, the butts thrown into his cockpit by that bearded shithead Bernard. Beyond his own suffering, he extended his hatred to Dino who abused his boy, and to Dino's wife who did nothing to restrain the abuse. Yet he knew too that in order to redeem himself for the injustice he had committed against Yves Brun and for the tragic end of Frédéric, he would have to accept, without sniveling, the injustices of others, even if they continued throughout all the years he was still destined to live. That thought--that another could never do so much harm to him as he had done to himself and to others--immediately calmed him. Yet later, the moment he forgot the debt he owned to those he had hurt, his brain, with a life of its own, returned to the wrongs he had suffered and was suffering again, wiping away, like a fairy with her wand, the memory of his own crimes, replacing it by fresh thoughts of hatred and revenge.

Yet the tranquility of the anchorage, and the setting of monumental beauty that surrounded him, brought moments of peace. The mountains of the Southern Alps encircled the boat to the north, holding in its lap, on the slopes along the seafront, a few original white Victorian mansions encompassed by gardens and parks of cypress, palms and poplars. To the east rose the jagged cliffs of Italy, and to the west a promontory carrying the town of Menton, early Italian, a palette of ochres, beiges and pale reds. Nothing so lovely as Menton had been built in centuries, the boy thought, watching it turn to gold each night as the sun set behind its churches and chapels. And beyond that, the promontory of Cap Martin. The more the Italians made themselves obnoxious, the more their motorboats bullied the sailboats by making them flounder in their wakes, the more they let their dogs run around to piss and crap where they wished, the more Boyd thought the seizure of Menton by the French from the Genoese Grimaldi family was a just recompense. At anchor 200 yards offshore, beyond the buoys that marked the limits of the stretch reserved for swimmers, Boyd spent his time reading, resolute on keeping out of further trouble.

.

As Boyd left the port during the evenings, he took to showering in the early afternoons when the sun was still hot and the shower stalls were as cool as oases. The doors were made of slanted slats, permitting those within to see out, yet impossible for those outside to see in. One afternoon, through the slats, Boyd saw Thierry, a boy who hired himself out for miscellaneous jobs around the port, came in to wash grease-stained hands. His thinning hair, long and scraggly, fell to his shoulders. It was rumored he had been busted for drug usage. His eyes, blood-specked and watery, were reminiscent of an alcoholic's. He often spent an entire day cleaning a boat with a thoroughness that even surpassed the Swiss and their toothbrushes. He also habitually showered for an hour at a time, scouring every nook and cranny. That afternoon he was at the washbasin when Claude entered. Claude had an electronics shop on the port that he ran with Jean, his brother, and his mother, a tall, thin woman with black hair and dark features, nicknamed Vahinée because she had lived in Tahiti, the birthplace of her sons. Claude got around on a fuming, stinky red Vespa. The brothers were so different Boyd questioned their parentage. Jean was as tall as Claude, but where Claude was extremely handsome, with curly black hair and eyes of such intense blue that one was uncomfortable looking into them, Jean was blond and crew cut, as pale as Claude was swarthy.

Claude pulled up to the urinal. The jerking of his elbow left little doubt as to what he was doing, a movement that Thierry caught sight of. "Hey, Claude," rang out Thierry's voice from the washbasin, "Wha' ya' doin'?" "Jackin' off!" came back the response, which bent Thierry over in glee. Then Claude turned sideways to show a rod that made Boyd gasp. For a split second the boy's mind raced back to the preceding summer when he had booked passage on a sailing boat headed for Rhodes. One of his companions was a remarkably good-looking kid who took to sailing in the nude. At one stop they had picked up a schoolmarmish woman who was at the wheel the first afternoon of her arrival when the boy, who had been catching up on his sleep, made his way from the cabin up the steps to the cockpit. Her gasp at seeing his partially deployed member, warm from the sleeping sack, was so audible that Boyd, sitting on the roof in the shade of the mainsail, had swerved to see what was wrong. This time it was his turn to show surprise, because he had never seen anything to match it. "Jesus!" guffawed Thierry. "You really are!" "Go to the Club quay," laughed Claude, turning back to the urinal. "You'll understand." "Show me," said Thierry. Obligingly, Claude buttoned up and they left. Boyd dried himself and followed.

The Club quay, officially Quay 1, was nicknamed after the restaurant there, the Club House. At the moment it resembled the Champs-Élysées at its busiest. Cars were driving past, male yachtsmen were strolling up and down the roadway in front of the Club, and at the Club's windows every male face was turned to a small sailing boat where two entirely naked, very young girls, small breasted and downy cunted, were sunbathing. Inexplicably, the port, known to be "familial", had a ruling that one could go attired as he or she pleased when on his or her boat. Often the guardian Marc said how embarrassed he was, especially around the immodest Germans, to find them naked when he had to go aboard on official business. The girls moved about in detached abandon, with a certain elegance, reminding Boyd of young Isadora Duncans. This, and all of the other bizarre goings-on in the port, made Boyd think he was in the Monkey House of a zoo.

The *buongiorno-TUTTI*s, his moniker for the Italians on Quay 4, bought a dog, a stiff-limbed fox terrier that hobbled around as maladroitly as its owner, so different from sleek, adventurous Scot. But like Scot, it barked. At the foot of the gangplank it gathered at the feet of the old Italian and the English bitch and barked, obliging the boy to put down his book, while the two carried on conversations with their friends, oblivious to the noise. Worse still was when the dog stopped barking. Suspended, the boy wondered if he could resume his reading. He waited. Finally he reached out his hand, lifted the book in hopes of … and the barking resumed. If it had gone on for an hour he could have done other things. But it went on and then stopped. And then went on and on and on. Finally, after days of putting up with the problem, and seeing that the Italian neighbors did nothing, he decided to go over and talk with the owner. He had long learned that with the Italians it was live and let live. A neighbor could do anything he wished so long as he let *his* neighbor do anything *he* wished. He found the old man standing to the side of his garbage can, buttoning up his fly, a puddle of urine at his feet. ''Your dog makes much too much noise, sir. It's highly disturbing. Would you please try to keep it down?'' The old man shrugged disdainfully and started up the gangway. Boyd, having used up all the Italian he knew, shook his head and started back down the quay, thinking You can't say anything to these arrogant assholes. Unfortunately, halfway up the gangway the Italian turned and said to Boyd, with an unctuous pretension that made the boy see red, ''You know how to speak French?' ''Yeah, I speak French,'' the boy rejoined, ''and you have no right to disturb your neighbors, you have no right to disturb *me*,'' he bellowed in fluent French. The old man stepped down to the quay, his razor-thin lips elongated in a ragged clam-like grin. ''Do you know who I am?'' he asked suavely. Sure, thought Boyd, you're an old fool who'll soon be dead and it'll be good riddance. ''Yeah,'' smirked the boy, coming up to within inches of the withered face, ''you're the gentleman with the pretty red BMW convertible.'' Both Boyd and the Italian had the same instantaneous vision of slashed tires and scratched paint. ''When I finish with you you won't dare threaten me or my dog,'' the old man sputtered. He again grinned, the parchment at the corners of his lips drawing back into chaotic folds. Boyd, sickened by the mocking and by the reeking, whisky-sour breath, made a gesture to seize him by the collar of his shirt. The smug smile vanished and the old man stepped back in panic, while from the balcony of his boat came a screech. The English bitch was flailing the air with her clutched fists as if wanting to come to blows with Boyd, but when the boy turned his gaze on her she quailed in retreat. The old man, trembling, staggered up the gangplank and yelled, ''This will not go unreported!'' From the table on his balcony he took up his VHF to call Rimini. Boyd made his way to his boat.

When Rimini came by an hour later Boyd had worked out his defense. He told Rimini about the noise, the arrogance of the Italians to whom one could say nothing. How he had put up with the nuisance for *days* already. The parties into the night. The lack of sleep. The essential points jumbled together, stated in a controlled, calm voice, remembering that Rimini was himself of Italian origin. "I've spent months in Italy," he continued. "I think the Italians are a *wonderful* people, but those here think they can get away with murder." Rimini frowned. Boyd had never seen him frown. Rimini was unhappy. *No one* had seen him unhappy. The boy was certain he was about to be ordered out of the port when the German, who had been quietly observing the scene from the terrace of his yacht, came to his rescue, seconding every point. Far richer than the Italian bastard, as well as the natural representative of the Germans *and* the Swiss, Rimini was obliged to listen to him and to agree that, indeed, the continuous barking of a dog was indeed unnerving. A stalemate developed. From the corner of his eye Boyd could see the Italian turd on the other quay, braced up by his English slut and spurred on by the neighbor with the bellowing testicular voice and other assorted hangers-on who had come by to see what the ruckus was about. And on Boyd's quay, Aldo and Roseland silent in their cockpit but nodding favorably in the boy's direction each time Rimini looked their way, the rich German now standing at the boy's side, a hand on his shoulder, his attractive wife observing stone-like from the balcony of their spic-and-span yacht--the Italian's boat a mere *tender* in comparison, the Swiss on *their* balcony, in front of cups of morning coffee and honey cake, surrounded by their Evian-nurtured flowers. "He said you tried to strike him," muttered Rimini, his voice no less severe. "Mister Rimini, I'm a professor, I'm not a crook," he answered, unhesitatingly serving up a variant on Nixon's famous declaration, sensing that like Nixon he too would be shown the door. But no final decision came because, as the French saying goes, Rimini found it urgent to do nothing. Rimini let him off with a vague warning, bowed to his audience, and returned to the *Capitainerie*.

.

Boyd came across Claude working on a sailboat, some brand-new electrical equipment in his hand. The French boy glanced up, his face haloed by the forest of black curls, the eyes a royal blue in the shade of the tarp stretched over the boom. Boyd, just to get Claude's attention, recounted the story of the baksheesh the *Bonità* had been obliged to shell out. Claude just smiled and advised him not believe everything he heard. And anyway, if things should be cleaned up, the cleaning should start with the politicians. What was a little baksheesh at the level of a Harbormaster? Why did the little guys like the Harbormaster get hooked while the big fish got away? What was needed was a revolution better than the one on the 14th of July they'd just celebrated. This time heads would *really* roll. No hesitating this time. "If I had a fucking Uzi I'd align them all against a wall and mow them down", said Claude sternly, an imaginary machinegun in his hands that he directed right to left, left to right. "I'd cut through the fuckers to the very last." Then he turned to continue his work, leaving the boy to slip away without even a nod of goodbye. What a prick, Boyd muttered to himself as he went towards the *Denis,* what a negative bastard, an inner rage equal to Boyd's own.

Rimini was back the next day, having found a way to con the boy. He took off his braided cap, bowed slightly, and with a huge smile engaged Boyd in conversation. Chuckling he said, "When the hospital called about your boat and I rang back to tell you there was a place free, I had imagined you were an old man on his death bed. As you know, we're fully filled up. We don't even keep a waiting list anymore." "I know, Harbormaster Rimini," said the boy contritely, "and I hope I'll be able to show you my gratitude soon." This was the key phrase for some form of baksheesh Boyd now conceded he would have to fork over. He hoped he could put it off until Christmas when it would seem less dishonest. Rimini put a fatherly hand on his shoulder, put his braided cap in place and ambled away. The young man was awed by the deft performance, one that made it clear that he too, for all his youth, would have to grease his ass in preparation for being screwed, just like all the other small fry in the port.

.

Grimaldi came to Boyd's boat a few days later, a rarity, as Rimini's Aides, Grimaldi and Genet, nearly never went onto the quays. That job was reserved for the guardians in whose ranks the two Aides had spent years. The guardians cycled around the port, season in, season out, making certain the boats were correctly moored, looking out for possible theft, stopping the yachtsmen from wasting water by washing their cars, keeping out Menton fishermen whose line or hooks inevitably entwined propellers or implanted themselves in mooring ropes, cutting into the yachtsmen's fingers when they hauled them in. Once a guardian was named an Aide, he did not stray from the *Capitainerie* with its swirling fan in summer and winter radiator.

"What a surprise!" yelled out Boyd, trying to mask his jitters. "It's about time one of the Aides found out what's *really* going on in this port. And it never hurts to do a little PR with the yachtsmen." He finished kissing ass, hoping Grimaldi hadn't detected the note of uncertainty in his voice as he tried to figure out why he had come by. Instinctively, he looked over the Aide's shoulder to see if he were leading the way for the cops. Two months had passed since the disappearance of Yves Brun and no one had shown up to put him in cuffs. At the very least they should have come to ask him when he had last seen Yves alive.

"Thérèse thought you might like to drop by for lunch tomorrow. I'm off until 2:00."

"Of course, great. I'll bring the dessert."

"Around 11:00 if you want. That way we'll have time for a drink and a walk around the garden."

''Jean you sawed-off little prick,'' came a voice up the main channel. Grimaldi winced. A rubber dinghy drew against Boyd's boat with a heavy thud that made the boy cringe for the damage to its polish. ''You're as rare as a virgin, outside your nesting grounds.'' The accent was South of France, not unlike singsong Louisiana Cajun. The occupant studied Boyd. ''I thought I'd stretch my legs,'' muttered Grimaldi, looking suddenly even tinier in his whites. He put back the gold-braided admiral's hat he'd taken off, preparatory to leaving. ''That's some accent you've got there,'' laughed Boyd. ''You should talk,'' retorted the man dryly but pleasantly. When Boyd was nervous his accent thickened. That, coupled with the occasional difficulty he had using his jaw following his accident at the Gaillards', could at times make his speech incomprehensible. ''No, really, I'd give anything to have it,'' insisted the boy. ''In that case you have to be born a Blackfoot,'' said the man. Boyd looked at Grimaldi, pretending puzzlement, his way of getting the spotlight off himself. ''A Blackfoot's the name for the French born in Algeria,'' smirked Grimaldi. ''They had to leave during Algeria's Independence and most of them put down roots on the coast here or in Corsica.''

''Ah, Corsicans,'' spat the man, knowing Jean was one.

''At least in Corsica the Arabs walk around facing the ground,'' sputtered Grimaldi, repeating what seemed to be, for him, the island's chief quality. ''That's more than can be said for them here.''

''They're pretty tame in these parts too,'' said the man, unsmiling. Then to Boyd: ''Anything to drink?''

''To drink...'' repeated the boy stupidly.

''For God's sake, who is this kid?'' asked the man of Grimaldi. ''He doesn't have anything to offer to drink. Does he fuck?''

Boyd couldn't believe his ears.

''He doesn't drink,'' sneered Grimaldi, sharing the man's disgust.

''So if he doesn't drink, does he fuck? Every time I come by this boat he's always alone. No girl.'' Boyd remembered. This was the guy who had towed him to his berth when he first came to the port.

''Well, there's no possibility he'll ever have your reputation,'' said Grimaldi with a trace of a smile.

''Do Blackfeet have anything in particular, outside their accent?'' asked the boy, hoping the man would drop the subject of fucking.

''Yeah. You know what they say 'bout us? We're buried in a coffin with a hole in the top. You know what for? For our cock, 'cause it's *always* stiff.''

When the man had left Boyd turned to Grimaldi, raising an eyebrow in interrogation. ''He's a baker,'' said the Aide. ''Name's Michel. He's currently going with a *black* girl.''

''Does he have a wife or something?''

"Wife and two kids."

"What does she think about the girl?"

"Doesn't know, does she?"

Showering that afternoon, who should enter but Michel and a diving friend, both just back from underwater fishing. Michel was singing and hooting. Despite the noise of running water coming from the boy's stall, he grabbed hold of the door and pulled it open. "Haw haw," the baker bellowed, "so that's what's been stretching out the cunts in this port. Leave some for little guys like us to plug," laughed the baker, releasing the door for Boyd to close. Through the slats Boyd saw the two men strip. Michel looked more American than French. Of medium height with a blond crew-cut, he resembled a hefty college football freshman, except for the additional fifteen years which scarcely showed. His ass was puckered and dimpled with cellulose, a Delacroix wet dream had he been a woman and born in the voluptuous sensuality of the preceding century. The boy retreated as the man again came and pulled open the door, with such force it nearly shattered. "Look at this," he said. He went over to the washbasins under which he had kicked a hug rubberized diving sack. His froggy ass pointed at Boyd, he reaching in and took out a bronze compass, the ancient kind Boyd had seen in pictures. The boy whistled his admiration. Michel's friend, Alain, came out of the adjoining shower stall, a good compact body with matted hair highlighting the pectorals. "Know where I got it? You'd never guess. Know the Pointe du Raz? Well, one of those big motorboats sank there just a few hours ago and it was already swarming with divers." Boyd knew the place, in Italian waters, less than a mile from Menton. "They were salvaging everything"--he meant stealing--"and this had been overlooked. A beaut no?"

"A boat from here?" Boyd asked.

"Yeah. *Flipper.* The Italian divers said the motors had clogged up and the boat went onto the rocks. Who would have believed there were things like this aboard?"

As Michel replaced the compass in the sack he yelled in Boyd's direction, "At your age I *never* showered alone. I always had a 'little friend'," 'little friend' being the French equivalent of mistress.

"Well, I see you've got *your* 'little friend'," answered Boyd, leaning out of the shower and looking at Alain. In the masculine gender 'little friend' also meant catamite. "Yeah," cried out Michel, waltzing towards Alain. "My 'little friend'. And if he turns his back on me in the shower this little friend's going to get FUCKED." Boyd closed the door as Michel continued parading around Alain, enacting what Boyd supposed *he* supposed was a mating dance between queens.

.

The local ship chandlery, Thalassa, was run by a svelte jeans-clad woman in her mid-thirties, Colette. A former teacher, she had given up her job to sail off to Trinidad with an Italian, Marcello. They had returned to open the shop that they put in Colette's name thanks to the Italian aversion to declaring anything to the tax inspector. When they eventually split up, Colette kept the shop while in retribution Marcello opened his own ship chandlery a few stores down. It was at Marcello's that Boyd had first entered on arrival in the port, but due to his torn levi's--his knees and part of his butt slightly exposed--he was made to feel unwelcome. For the Italians, Boyd felt, all was surface show. Like the blacks he had known in his home state, they had the showiest cars and wives and clothes, even if they lived in hovels. Of course, no one in Port Beausoleil lived in a hovel. But that was the mentality, and that was why Boyd was sent packing. Colette had seen through the packaging to the potential client. She opened him an account from which he drew freely. Leaving her shop on that first visit, he had caught sight of her running to the window to look his way as he mounted his bike in order to catch sight of a little bare skin and briefs, no doubt about that, Boyd smiled to himself as he rode away.

Another day, as he entered Thalassa, he was stopped by a dog that came barking around his legs. "Charlie!" came a harsh no-nonsense snarl from inside. The dog immediately turned away and pranced into the shop where the boy discovered a bull-sized gray-haired man with a welding torch putting up shelves. Colette was trying to give him instructions but he interrupted in the same harsh tone he used with his dog. "Don't break my balls, Colette. Go back to something you know how to do, like sewing up hems." The boy was aghast and Colette clearly embarrassed. Later, when he asked people who the miscreant was, the response was inevitably, "That's Guy. He does odd jobs around the port and he's not to be messed with." From then on the boy and the man often crossed paths, both staring straight ahead, Guy looking evil and determined, his dog always on a leash to which the man would at times give a stern yank if the dog tried to outdistance him. Later still, when Guy referred to the boy to someone in the port, he called him *le fada*, the crazy one. There was no rational justification, just something the man had observed in Boyd's eyes that first time in Thalassa.

On Saturday Michel motored by in his dinghy, dressed in smart tan shorts and a green Lacoste polo. At his side was his African beauty from Cape Town. She had been a professional dancer in Monte Carlo, where Michel had picked her up. Very politely he introduced the girl to the American. "Speak English to her," he asked. "You'll see how she replies." The boy said he was pleased to meet her. "I am too," she answered. "You see? She speaks! And you wouldn't *believe* what she can do in bed!" cried out the baker, grinning evilly at the girl who didn't seem to catch every word of his southern French accent. Then he went off singing at the top of his lungs, which was for Michel, all things considered, his calm mode.

The following day Michel came by wearing the same shorts and a royal-blue Lacoste polo. He introduced the boy to his wife and two children, a cute girl of perhaps eight and a good-looking lad of thirteen. Their mother resembled the French ballet dancer Zizzi Jean-Maire, *very* petite, jet-black hair. Boyd had picked up somewhere that she was a good deal older than her husband, perhaps ten years. Michel was in his "little slippers", as the French expression goes: voice scarcely more than a whisper, modest smiles, the archetypical proud father figure, surveying his prodigy in a way that broke the boy's heart. Once Michel had said, in response to an enquiry by Boyd, that his wife knew nothing about his private life. Yet by the way she surveyed her husband, through eyes far shrewder than his own, Boyd wondered whom the baker thought he was kidding.

.

Boyd went to the Grimaldis by bike as he had been invited to, cycling high into the hills above Port Beausoleil. He wanted to learn as much as he could about Rimini who had the power to either keep him in the port or to exclude him. The country house turned out to be a converted garden shed that Grimaldi had slightly enlarged against French law, making it into an inhabitable cottage with a couch that filled half of the single room and converted into a bed. A tiny kitchen with a dinning table was crammed into what was left of the room. Around the cottage Grimaldi and his wife Thérèse had planted a vegetable garden and flowers. A narrow dirt path led down to the cottage, and when Boyd arrived he was dripping sweat from the hard climb up the main road and the deep descent that forced him to carry his bike on his shoulder. Over a lunch of garden tomatoes, salad and meat impossible to chew, Grimaldi, toothless, sneering, eating with his hands as primitively as though he were eating with his feet, divulged years of scuttlebutt into the boy's virgin ears.

Boyd knew--or at least it seemed obvious to him--that Rimini could make money simply by assigning berths to rich Italians who had acquired motorboats and needed to hide them from the scrutiny of the Italian Revenue Service. "Have you thought about the number of boats in the port?" asked Grimaldi rhetorically. "Maybe there are a thousand boats, say, but only 900 are declared." "There's no control!" asked the boy. "There's control, perhaps, but perhaps the controllers are part of the inaccurate counting. Or perhaps the Director gives the Harbormaster his head." This was the first time Boyd had heard of a "Director," but for the moment it was Rimini who held his fate in his hands, not some person so illusive and invisible Boyd had never seen or heard of him.

"And then the boats that pass through. Some yachtsmen are satisfied to plunk down their money and leave. Why give a receipt if they're in a hurry? And the supplies. The Harbormaster decides who buys what for the maintenance of the quays, where the uniforms are bought, the purchasing, in fact, of thousands of things from rolls of bum paper to the bread served in the Club House, provided by your friend Michel."

His wife Thérèse's protests that he was talking too much just spurned Grimaldi on. The boy learned later that the apartment in Menton had been sold. Grimaldi had somehow succeeded in extorting her signature, and henceforth could be heedless of her wishes. "Or you want to change places. Out to the end of a quay, for example, where you have room to stretch, even have your tender there beside you. Or you only want small boats next to yours so your hull doesn't get marked up. Or during the summer, when your neighbor is away, you don't want the port to direct passing yachts to the empty berth because of the noisy transients you have to put up with, and the damage they can do going in and out of the berth, especially women with a boathook in hand that'll scratch up a paint job!" "So you could conceivably pay a supplement to have the neighboring berth remain empty," said the boy, adding, "What could be more natural?" "A *big* supplement," jeered the Aide. "The moment that Rimini lifts his cap and bows real low, it isn't for peanuts!" Neither one noticed when Thérèse rose, disgusted, and left the table. Grimaldi sneered through his nose, his face inches from the plate. "Rimini will steal anything not nailed down, it's as simple as that," he said, repeating what he had told to the boy before. "If you have anything worth anything, put it in the bank. If you want to be on his good side, give him no matter what. For example! Agelli of the *Never Say Never*. A bigwig wheeler-dealer in oil. Super rich. At Christmas Rimini came to his boat to put on his usual show, genuflexion and *Buona Nativa, Buona Nativa*! From his Gucci overcoat Agelli took out a Marché-U supermarket sac that he handed over to him. Inside was a pair of *socks*! You think Rimini complained? Nothing, *nothing* is miserable enough to be unworthy of him. Nothing."

.

"We'll be leaving soon for Turkey. Dino wants me to ask you to come along and give lessons to Boy," said Francine, standing on the quay in front of the *Denis*. She pulled the child's hand, trying to draw his attention from his feet. "Would you like to learn English?" she asked him. There was no silly smirking or coy twisting around his mother's legs as with other children. The kid never reacted to any stimulus. In the park he'd sit unmoving on the bench, or stand unmoving on the periphery of the playground, wherever she abandoned him. Today they had him dressed, like a manikin, in wrap-around sunglasses and a cowboy suit. Boyd shook his head, "The fucking son-of-a-bitch," he murmured in

English, in a low growl, thinking of Dino. "*Come*?" she asked. Boyd had had the shit beat out of him at that age, but had kept alive a coal of inner life. Sure, he knew, he had had to retreat within himself to find the substance to live off, becoming an *introvert* as the French put it. He'd learned, young, to count on no one but himself, but at least he'd had *himself* to count on. It was a dog-eat-dog world, he had found out perhaps earlier than most, but that was one useful lesson. Dog was too mild. *Wolf* was more accurate. Packs of wolves, and only the fittest would survive, only the most intelligent, the most clever. But this kid didn't even have a chance anymore. He was cerebrally dead. "The fucking cocksucker!" For a split-second Boyd saw himself shooting the scumbag Dino in his elbows, and then his knees, and then...

"*Come*?"

"Nothing. Of course I wouldn't be found dead on the same boat with your husband", he continued in French. "We'd be at each other's throats in an hour." Let the kid's father rot with cancer, what else could be done? He couldn't top them all off. He'd like to, but he couldn't. They saw Dino stride into view at the end of the quay. She took flight with Boy.

.

To the south of Boyd's boat was a quay that ran alongside the dike, the berth of very long and luxurious sailing yachts and big motorboats. Between the dike and the boats was a narrow stretch of asphalt for the owners' cars. The high wall of the dike opposite the boats was faced with smooth cement, while the side facing the sea was a talus of giant boulders. The top of the dike was flat. There, every afternoon, in full view of the entire port, strode Buchenwald, Boyd's term for the tall skeletal woman with long hair and gigantic silicon breasts. Her skin resembled crumbling papyrus clinging to her bones, and her ass was shriveled up like a chimpanzee's. What's more, she was totally nude.

Before Boyd had become aware of the creature's existence the very first time, he had remarked the symptoms. The Swiss suddenly frozen on their balcony, coffee cups and cloth napkins in hand, the Germans shaking their heads, their son's mouth unhinged, yachtsmen passing through the channel suddenly staring at the top of the dike, leaving their ship to wander dangerously close to Boyd's. He had followed their line of vision only once. Afterwards when he noticed the warning signs he turned his head away. The thing seemed to cast a spell over Aldo who would stare at it until it disappeared. Roseland would wonder aloud, "Could she possibly find herself still attractive?"

At that moment he sensed she was turning her wizened cadaver towards him. Since her arrival she had made a point of stopping directly opposite his boat, at perhaps the distance of 200 yards, and stare at him while he went about his reading or did the day's chores.

"She's banged everyone here in years past," said Jean-Loup, the garbage boy who wouldn't stop staring at her, to Boyd's disgust and puzzlement. "She a Kraut," he added, "and like all the Krauts she's a pervert." Jean-Loup had often spoken about the propositions the Germans of both sexes made to him, invitations to take part in their fucking. Naturally, Boyd thought of Reiner and the German industrialist. "Just wants to get banged, that's all she's looking for."

.

Michel came by in his Zodiac later in the afternoon. Boyd sat on the roof of the *Denis*, welcoming a few minutes of entertainment. "I'm thinking about buying a boat, live on it like you do. Maybe the *Giola* if it's up for sale, now that Julie is getting on well again with Guy." Guy, Boyd remembered, was the creep with the dog, Charlie, who had been loud-mouthing Colette in Thalassa. Julie, Michel explained, had been Guy's mistress for a number of years until they broke up. "Who could remain with a vulgar nonentity like him?" asked the boy. "Anyway," continued Michel, "she bought the boat when Guy kicked her off his and now that they're back together, who knows, it might be up for grabs." Michel explained that in commerce you had to have a "feeling" for when the right time to strike was at hand. "My daddy used to say, 'A pigeon rises every morning, and a pear falls every night'." Both pigeon and pear meant fool in French argot. Julie had often let Michel stay on the boat when he needed a place to bring a girl, so he knew it well. "You saw the new 'chosen-one'," he said, meaning his South African girl, his southern accent and the Donald Duck pitch of his voice invariably sending the boy into stitches. "It's for her."

"And your wife never says anything?" asked the boy. Michel chewed on this and then answered, "I don't think she knows."

"You mean your own wife doesn't know what everyone else in all of Menton knows!" He mauled over this too for a moment: "Maybe she does," he admitted reluctantly. "But so what? She's got my name, the business, money. She knows I kill myself at the yoke. If she ever left me I'd have a replacement in the house inside a week."

"The South African?"

"Yeah. I can't live without a woman. I keep my wife because of the kids and because she accepts more or less what I do and because I like my clothes cleaned and my dinner ready when I return home."

"And the South African can do all that?"

"She hasn't so far, but she can be trained. I've got her working behind the counter at the moment in the shop."

"'She's *working* in your tea shop, alongside your wife!"

"Listen, she'd never make a scene. She knows what she'd lose if we divorced. She even told me once, 'I'll never find another man like you', she said. But what do you want, a man's got to follow his instincts. Really, life's too short. You know, sometimes I feel I'm a hundred years old, I've done so much. Just this morning I finished my bread at three. Then I went off hunting at my property outside St. Agnes. Then I went mountain climbing with some guys I know, and now I'm off spearfishing. I never stop. You stop you're dead. Life's short and it goes by fast,'' he said as he turned over the motor. ''You, too, should shack up with someone. It's not good living so alone.'' He left, giving the boy a slight wave of the hand.

Boyd was certain Michel felt sorry for him, always on the deck of his boat reading, whether in the port or outside at anchor. He had read once that getting lost in books indicated the desire to return to the womb. He thought it could just be true in his case, but still the same question was posed, How to get back … without *suffering*?

He'd never married because he'd seen what marriage could do to two people, he thought. He was happy to live the life of a boy, without strings, free. When he wanted to go right, he went right. When he wanted to go left, he went left. And besides, there was a certain safety in fleeting relationships in which there was little intimacy except sexually, and small risk of being questioned, little danger of having his self-image contested, an image he had erected stone by stone, like a fortification, throughout all the years of his childhood.

He'd never married because he knew that his father had implanted a gene in his DNA that would push him, sooner or later, to beat his own son, just as, for generation and generation, that was the way to break in a boy, that and getting drunk, screwing pussy, hunting and driving at breakneck speed.

And then, he thought to himself as he lay out over the deck of his boat, his mind jumping from one subject to another like the worn needle on a badly warped record, there was the slippery soil, the clods of slimy mud you couldn't get a foothold on. How could one consider marriage or settling down with so much impermanence in the world? If he didn't have himself to count on, who would even throw him as much as a bone? *For Christ's sake*, he admitted, *you needed a foothold to be able to climb through this fucking life, one notch at a time*. And a foothold, even just one, he didn't have.

His instinct made him suspect that there were other sources of his pain, sources at the center of his being, an arid land as empty as a desert, where cries go unheard and thirst unquenched. It was a solitude of horizons without limit, that no amount of care could bring to fruition because under the sterile and shifting sands there were but more sterile and shifting sands. It was a life of an occasional spring drizzle which worked a momentary miracle, and then an eternity of stultifying waste in a region beyond the scope of human reach. The core of the desolation was a feeling that gnawed at him, bringing suffering every moment of every day, anchored onto his heart like an entrenched parasite: it was the feeling of *loss*.

.

At the end of summer Boyd regained Paris where he resumed his classes, but not for long. At the end of the autumn semester, at the beginning of December, he exchanged the calm and security of the university against a flight back to the airport of Nice-Côte d'Azur.

As Christmas neared the other boats began to fill up. First the Swiss, then the Germans with a dog but without their son who would be by on the 25th with a new girlfriend. The Swiss offered Boyd a box of chocolates because "every time you pass our boat you smile at us." Aldo and Roseland showed up overdressed for the mild Menton winter, but offering Roseland an occasion to show off her new fur coat, bought thanks to the economies made by not paying their income tax, bragged Aldo. Their daughter was away with a recent conquest, a boy neither parent could stomach. Whenever Aldo mentioned him, he'd mine the act of throwing up; Roseland would squeeze her eyes shut and ruffle up her face as if biting into a lemon. When Boyd pursued the subject, Aldo admitted that the boy's sin was to have told their daughter that Aldo had the intelligence of a baboon and Roseland the nature of an orangutan in heat.

The nights were at last calm. Sitting cross-legged on the prow of the boat one evening, Boyd gazed at the promontory that held the floodlit old city of Menton, its church, chapels and three-story houses, all in ochres and pastels. He marveled at the peace and tranquility of the port, a haven without noise and chaos.

The next morning, as the zoo awoke, he learned that only the tomb could offer a veritable haven of peace. Jean-Loup showed up to empty the garbage can. Approaching Boyd's end of the quay where the wealthiest occupants of the port resided, he yelled out, "So let's see what the fat asses had for dinner last night." He then pulled out the garbage sack from its metal holder, glanced in at the champagne bottles and wrappings from the best gourmet shops in Menton, Cap Martin and Monte Carlo, and then, still grumbling insults, he swung the sack into his little cart. But before pushing off he lit up a cigarette and, with his free hand, flipped the hinged lid of the can up and down, making it crash like a cymbal. Only with the arrival of Harbormaster Rimini did the noise cease. Rimini was making his rounds, accompanied by a newcomer, a young man nearly lying over his bike, his arms folded across the handlebars. He oozed feline grace. He was dressed in spotlessly clean and faultlessly ironed navy-blue military slacks and wore an aviator's jacket with a tie at the neck. His pilot's cap shadowed a sharply sculptured nose, blue eyes, thin lips and cleft chin, around 35 Boyd estimated.

On the excuse of having lost the key to the showers, Boyd went to see Grimaldi.

''That's Rimini's replacement,'' came the sour grin, always content to share what he knew, and at the same time poison the well for others. ''Can you imagine, a *helmsman* running this place.''

''What's that exactly?''

''He steered boats. In the navy.''

''I didn't know they were searching for someone to replace Rimini.''

''I told you that like me he was up for retirement. The problem is, and this is between the two of us, the problem is Rimini doesn't want to give up the job just now. The Director made him find a replacement, but you'll see, he'll drag his heels. The helmsman isn't in yet.''

For a second Boyd wondered who this mysterious Director was, but his mind was still on the newcomer. ''There were a lot of postulants?''

''Yeah, but the new guy came along with a dish and Rimini fell all over himself making her at home in *his* port.'' Grimaldi laughed and sneered in unison. ''*She* was the one who got the job is what it comes down to.''

''What's the new guy's name?''

''Ariosto.''

''An Italian!''

''He can't speak a word of Italian, which'll be a big help around here,'' said Grimaldi, shaking his head. ''He's from Corsica.''

''Another!'' shouted Boyd, earning a black look from Grimaldi.

''The makings of a real mafia,'' decided Grimaldi, at home with the idea, ''except that Ariosto was brought up in Grasse, so he doesn't count as a Corsican Corsican. He's one of those expatriates. Once they're gone from the island, they're deader than dead.'' Wasn't that true of Grimaldi? the boy wondered.

''He doesn't have family in Corsica?''

''Sure, in Bastia. His sister lives down the street from my mother. *She's* Corsican.'' Grimaldi's mother was one of the reasons Thérèse didn't want to return to Bastia, where she would have to take care of the old woman who was totally disabled--*grabataire* in French, a horrible word which always brought to the boy's mind the image of someone hauling himself over gravel. During their vacations on the island Grimaldi would go off to the cafés with his male friends while Thérèse spent her days and nights at the side of Madame Grimaldi-*mère*.''

While in the *Capitainerie* Boyd made plans for his boat to be put in dry dock so he could apply the yearly anti-fouling, the painting of the submerged part of the boat with a chemical substance that protected it from marine plants and animals. ''Can you start tomorrow?'' asked Grimaldi. ''Sure,'' Boyd answered irrationally. He had never done the job before or seen it done, and had as yet no idea of the necessary preparations. He had noticed a list of boats chalked up on the blackboard, and had assumed he'd be placed at the end of it, giving him time to document himself. Instead, Grimaldi wrote in *Denis* at the top of the list. ''Tomorrow morning at 6:00.'' Grimaldi glanced at the nearby schedule. ''Bernard.'' ''Do I have to have him?'' pouted the boy. ''He's on duty tomorrow morning and he's the expert with the crane,'' Grimaldi replied dryly.

At 5:30 Boyd docked the *Denis* alongside the reparations quay, just under the crane, at the foot of the *Capitainerie*. Sharply at 6:00 the bearded Bernard came striding out. He passed two wide straps to Boyd who was on his boat, one strap the boy passed around the prow, the other around the stern. Bernard attached them to the crane cable hook, jumped in the crane cabin and lifted the *Denis* out of the water, placing it with the care of an egg on the dock. The guardian's attitude was all business. He was in command and Boyd did as told. He climbed down from the crane and shored up the boat with logs so that it rested snugly on its keel. He gave Boyd a ladder that the boy could use to climb aboard, and Boyd gave him an envelope with the 200 francs Grimaldi told him was his insurance against accidents during the maneuvers. Alas, accidents there had been. Where the straps had been placed he found scratch marks on the white hull. Claude, the electrician, came by on his red Vespa while Boyd was examining them. ''If the asshole had rinsed the straps before using them, this wouldn't have happened.''

''Rinsed the...'' murmured the boy.

''The impurities. Shit like grains of sand.'' He rode off shaking his head, leaving the boy standing there pale.

After leaving Grimaldi the afternoon before, Boyd had stopped at Thalassa and bought a book on how to do the anti-fouling, a scraper, sandpaper, brushes, a mask to prevent him from inhaling the poisonous dust, and plastic gloves. But once out of the water it was immediately obvious that more than a little sanding and painting were required. It was evident the boat hadn't been scraped clean in years. A growth of plants and shelled sea life covered the hull, in some places an inch or two thick. Following the book's instructions, he bought a scraper and metal brush, and spent the day hacking away at the fauna and flora stuck to the surface as if welded there. That night when he went to the showers he was covered with filth from hair to feet, with the exception of the circle around his nose and mouth where he had worn the mask. His hands looked as if he'd fallen on them from a speeding motorcycle, so cut up and scratched they appeared mangled. In bed back on the boat he missed the gentle movement of the sea that normally cradled him to sleep, but his eyes nonetheless closed the moment his head hit the sack, as exhausted as he'd been on the *Swan* heading for Bonifacio.

The next morning he finished scraping the keel and by noon had finished sanding down the old anti-fouling. He applied the sky-blue anti-fouling paint to the keel and parts of the hull that would be submerged. The *Denis* began to look presentable.

The following day he turned to the scratch marks on the hull, a far more difficult business, perhaps beyond his competence. Luckily Claude came by to offer pointers. Boyd was in the midst of this delicate reparation work when the cause of his problems, Bernard, rode up. "I could never do that kind of job because I don't have a queer's dainty fingers." Rimini and the future Harbormaster Ariosto chose that moment to come by on their bikes. The day had turned warm and the newcomer was dressed in a navy-blue shirt and sweater, the tie showing over the top of the crew collar. "Why do I have to put up with a Neanderthal like this?" Boyd asked Rimini, pointing to Bernard. The boy made a barely discernible pause to take in air. "Look at how this redneck lout messed up my boat when he took it out of the water. Didn't even have sense enough to rinse the straps, for Christ's sake. I know these guys get a miserable salary, but is that a reason to scrape the bottom of the barrel when you do your hiring?" Boyd tried to back away from the flash point, the one after which he would lose all control. He was red and hyperventilating. "Look at him, that fat gut spilling over the handlebars like an overturned trashcan! And that's not the worse," he continued, despite the expression of incredulity on Rimini's apoplectic face, as bloated as a bullfrog's. "He has a *son*! What chance does a kid have in a world with an illiterate peasant like this!"

Ariosto looked amazed. Surely Rimini would have to stick up for "his men" in front of the newcomer, and as Boyd began to cool down he prepared for the worse. But it was the unexpected that happened. Rimini heard a noise only his ears seemed to have been trained to hear. He looked behind him. At first the boy thought he was interrogating Ariosto with a glance before taking the decision to expulse the *Denis*. But it wasn't at Ariosto that he was looking, it was more upward, over the future Harbormaster's head. Boyd followed his line of vision, but was an instant too late. Someone had been observing the dispute from the third-floor terrace encircling the *Capitainerie*. Boyd saw a sliding door close behind a figure that disappeared into the interior shadows. "I'd better have an explanation for all this," ordered Rimini, his attention again on the boy. "You'll have that explanation, Harbormaster," said Boyd, now in command of himself. "In writing. And there'll be other things in that explanation. There'll be how this clown is a danger to this port, and if he's kept on," he threatened, "you'll be held judicially responsible. Now if you'll please excuse me," he concluded with as much politeness as he could muster, knowing he'd used up more than his nine lives, "I'll get back to repairing the mess made by this cretin." As with Sylvie in the car heading for Rome, Bernard should never have accused him of being queer.

Bernard, the cretin in question, stood stiffly at the side of Rimini and Ariosto, head bowed, absorbing blow after blow without turning a hair, waiting for the moment he'd have the little bastard's skin.

.

An hour later, while Boyd was finishing up the masking of the scrape marks, Michel came by in his Zodiac with Alain and a couple of kids a bit younger than Boyd, all four dressed in black diving gear. ''We're going out fishing,'' Michel declared as he motored past. ''I'm going to show these young cocklings how to catch more than pussy. They *know* how to catch *pussy*. In this day and age they're *born* knowing how to catch pussy. What's hard is catching *fish.* ''

''Well, I hope they'll listen to an old guy like you,'' shouted Boyd, tickled to see the baker after the tension caused by his outburst.

''They'll listen. For them I'm GOD!''

That afternoon Boyd asked for the boat to be lifted so he could remove the supporting logs, and sand down and paint where they'd propped up the *Denis*. Due to the weekly change in the duty roster, the guardian that afternoon was again Bernard. Boyd rinsed the straps thoroughly with water before placing them around the hull, and just to make sure there would be no more scratches, he put towels between the hull and straps to act as a soft buffer. Bernard smirked while this was going on, to the boy's total indifference. He had gone through too much to have any feeling of any kind for the guardian. In fact, he would have jumped for joy had someone slit the bastard's throat, just so he could see how much blood was in the fat sow. Once the boat was raised, the keel hovering a couple of inches over the ground, and the logs removed, Boyd got to work cleaning and painting the previously inaccessible spots. The painting done, Bernard began maneuvering the boat with the intention of lowering it into the water.

''No you don't!'' Boyd cried out. ''They need eight hours to dry.''

''That's what you think,'' Bernard declared, beside himself, as he continued to move the boat out from the quay. ''You can't tie up the crane for eight hours,'' he added legitimately.

''If that boat touches water I'll go to the Third Floor,'' said Boyd, making a move towards the *Capitainerie*. The result was electrifying. Bernard swung the boat back over the quay, two inches above the ground, made sure the crane arm was locked in place, descended the ladder from the control post, and hurried away to do other business. Boyd glanced up to the Third Floor. There was nothing visible, just the solid walls of glass and terrace, hiding what magic, he wondered, while trying to detect the slightest sign of movement.

.

The next day, back at his usual berth, the apprehension that Boyd felt was given substance. Bernard went out on the launch into the channel with the port diver, Pierre. Some of the chains that connected the prows of the boats to the cement moorings in the middle of the channel had become bogged down in the silt and muck. The diver tied a rope to them that he attached to the stern of the launch. Bernard, at the wheel, was to step on the gas and disengage the chains from the mud when given the order by the diver. But he never waited for an order. Time and time again he drove the launch forward before the diver was completely clear of the rope. The diver at first yelled and then screamed at Bernard to await his command. Boyd got on the VHF and told Grimaldi what was going on. ''Bernard knows what he's doing,'' said the Aide dryly, and then hung up on the boy to show who was in charge. Seconds later Pierre cried out as his leg became entwined in the rope. Boyd screamed into the VHF to send an ambulance. When he jumped back into his cockpit he saw Bernard lifting Pierre onboard the launch, his leg covered in intricate webs of blood. The launch headed to the *Capitainerie* at breakneck speed, making the surrounding ships tear at their mooring chains.

Boyd was certain this was the last of Mr. Bernard. But Rimini somehow papered things over. The diver who had done occasional work for the port was taken on fulltime. After all, he had only lost a little skin, and a permanent job was worth the loss of a pint of type O-negative. Bernard remained chastened for nearly two weeks.

.

Near the end of the Christmas vacation he found Aldo in front of his boat, kneeling beside his luggage. Roseland had already returned to Turin to be with her daughter who'd been ditched by a boyfriend. When Boyd asked him if he was glad to get back to his wife, Aldo answered, ''She's no longer young but she's there when I need a little *figa*. Speaking of which, I hope you're getting yours.'' Although Boyd didn't know the Italian word for pussy, he nonetheless laughed and saw Aldo to his car.

It was with the conundrum of *figa* in mind that he went to the showers. Different sections of France were on holiday at different times in order to prevent the ski resorts and highways from becoming overburdened by travelers at the same period of the year. The Paris schools were out at the moment, and as few Parisians preferred the French Riviera to skiing, the port was nearly empty, a far cry from the days when the Riviera had been colonized by English pensioners and vacationers during the cold season.

He went into the stall, undressed and soaped up. The shower always made him think about Claude who had gotten hard at the urinal, producing the same effect on him. He wondered if Michel the baker was still with his South African beauty. He thought too that he hadn't crossed paths with the notorious Guy and his dog Charlie, nor seen Francine. Then he heard someone enter. Mechanically he gazed through the door slats, wondering if it were perhaps Thierry or Claude or, as his imagination took over, a group of divers, boys and girls ready to strip down naked, soaping each other....

It was Bernard. As an irrational reflex, he bolted the door. The guardian had seen the boy's bike, so why come in? He watched him make his way directly to the shower door and jerk it. ''There's someone here. Can' you hear the water for Christ's sake?'' he said as huskily as he could manage. The man put his fingers through the slates and yanked the door free from the lock, child's play for a slob his size.

''What's got into you!'' shouted Boyd with as much vile scorn as he could muster.

''Grimaldi told me you wanted to know if I could see my pecker when pissing. I thought I'd give a demonstration.'' He moved to get past Bernard, who put up his arm to block the passage. The guardian's whiskered lips were trembling with fury, the man's skin livid.

''Let me get by.''

The guardian shoved him back.

''And what's this shit about my kid, who, by the way, at six, is hung about the same.'' It was true that Boyd's groin was suddenly as knotted up as the rest of him.

''What chance does he have with an imbecile like you, Bernard? That was the complaint I had. Why bring kids into the world when you don' have the brains to make more of them than manual workers?''

''The tips I get from the boats are for *him*. It's because I wanted him to be different than me that I work for the extra dough.''

''That was baksheesh, not tips. That was *graft*.'' He had him speaking. He could feel the tension lessen, and already he was mentally composing the letter of complaint that would see the asshole out of the port forever.''

''And now the Harbormaster chose two Aides over my head...''

''*That* has nothing to do with me...''

''Someone told him about the tips and shit...''

''Shit that included lighted cigarettes thrown into my cockpit...''

''He gave the preference to others because he's a queer like you. As an Aide I'd've made 1000 francs more a month.'' He began to undo his belt. ''In the navy we had our own special ways with squealers...'' His hands occupied, Boyd tried to push past him. There was no question of his hitting the man. The laws in France, so unlike those in the States, were rarely in favor of the attacker, no matter what the motivation. The man grabbed him with surprising speed by the right arm and with a blow to the chest propelled him back against the wall with such force his face was whip-lashed against the tiles. His eye was immediately blinded with blood gushing from the brow, spotting the trousers of the advancing figure. The boy thought he was standing, but as Bernard bent over he discovered his legs had buckled, and he was squatting in the corner of the shower. In fact he no longer knew where he was or what he was doing. He felt like a swimmer trying to break surface but was instinctively certain he was on the verge of drowning.

"Okay ladies," came a roaring, atrociously off-key sing-song, "drop your socks and pick up your cocks! Michel is here with a ten-inch surprise in hand." The baker, aware, as everyone else in the port, of the bad blood between the two men, instantly summed up the situation when he saw Bernard hovering over the boy. With a brusque gesture he pushed Bernard out of his way and entered the stall. He pulled the boy onto the floor outside and took out his handkerchief that he applied to the forehead. "Get a doctor!" he ordered. "*Get a doctor!*" Bernard fled from the room like a madman. Boyd, seeing him gone at last, fell into unconsciousness.

.

When he came to he was looking at the face of Jesus, one similar to that which had hung for years in his morning seminary class, the handsome bearded face encircled in radiant beams. But there was something out of place in the picture. In the background, a background not unlike the far-off greenish mountains in a da Vinci painting, were futuristic buildings in the form of pyramids, interconnected by circular glass skyways through which flowed space-age vehicles. But that still wasn't the only oddity: cradled in Jesus' arms was a helmet, either that of a motorcyclist or more probably an astronaut. The word "God..." escaped from his lips.

"Not quite. Jesus of Nazareth," came a gentle, avuncular voice from outside. He became aware that he was lying on a narrow bed in a very narrow room, scarcely larger than the bed itself. There was a doorway near the foot of the bed, emitting a blaze of radiant light. In the center of the doorway stood a tall, slim man enrobed in the brilliance.

"God!" he repeated, this time in astonishment.

"No. No. Léonard. Director of Port Beausoleil."

The figure drew closer and Boyd caught a good look at the face. Thin, smiling, craggy around the edges of the mouth, grayish-white hair combed back, an ash-colored sports coat, very white shirt and blue tie, a figure Boyd had never seen in his life--of *that* he was certain. Boyd put his hand to the side of his head. He felt a bandage, but the skin was numb.

"Doctor Caprio of the *Ghost* was kind enough to clean and stitch the wound."

"I thought Colette from Thalassa lived on the *Ghost*."

"With Doctor Caprio. In reality..." He stopped himself. In reality, the *Ghost* belonged to the doctor, Boyd learned later. "The doctor said you'll have to have the stitches removed when you return to Paris. There are only three."

"I was attacked by Bernard."

''We know. He was disappointed at not being chosen an Aide to the Harbormaster, and felt you played a role in that deception. Which was not true, that goes without saying. I had had enough complaints about Mr. Bernard to persuade me it would be more advisable to make another choice. I believe that decision has been more than vindicated. Mr. Bernard is no longer a member of the staff.''

''He tried to kill me.''

''The police can be summoned if you wish. Mr. Bernard has a wife and two very small children, and although he receives a pension from the navy, it isn't much. Mr. Delonnet...''

'Who?''

''Michel Delonnet, the yachtsman who found you. He was a witness to what happened, and Mr. Bernard has been told that if there's ever another problem, it won't be too late to bring proceedings against him. Frankly it's up to you if you want this poor man brought to justice. A police car can be here in five minutes.''

''I'll want to think it over. I can't imagine just letting him go free without punishment.'' The boy was surprised to see that only a few seconds of reflection were necessary: Police. Interrogation. Yves Brun.

''As far as the port is concerned, we've decided to release you from the payment of your berth for the coming year, as you're already paid up for this one. After all, we're partially to blame, having given employment to Mr. Bernard.''

''How long have I been here?''

''Since last night. It is now about 10:00 o'clock. Doctor Caprio said you're fit to leave when you please. I'll bring you your clothes.''

''Fuck a duck,'' Boyd said to himself when the Director had left, unable to come to grips with all the new events. But there was at least a silver lining. A year gratis. That's over 14,000 francs, for Christ's sake! He knew he was being bribed, even offered a glimpse of all the kingdoms on the earth, like the Jesus in the picture at the foot of the bed. ''Anyway,'' he murmured as he threw back his blanket, annoyed at discovering his naked body and wondering how many others--and especially Ariosto--had seen it, ''anyway, I'll never have to see Crotch Face again.''

CHAPTER FORTY-ONE

The *Kitty* and Buchenwald

Returning to the port in early June, at the end of the school year, the first sight that struck him as he came up Quay 3 was the Alfred Hitchcock profile of Bernard making his rounds along the South Quay. The boy's skin flushed, and an unpleasant tingling ran the length of his spine. He'd learned the hard way that the guardian had at least as much muscle as fat, and that he possessed a shark-sized brain bent on attack at the first scent of blood.

He decided to check out his boat before going directly to the police to lodge a complaint. It may come to nothing because he hadn't acted sooner, but the legal authorities would have to be made aware of the menace he faced. Already his mind was leafing through a list of the people who could guide him to a lawyer, with Doctor Saramago heading the candidates. Miraculously, the *Denis* was in perfect condition. More miraculous still, the deck had been recently cleaned and one of the mooring lines replaced with new cord and cushioning spring. While inspecting the interior he was interrupted by a new guardian, Christophe, who handed him a blue slip from the *Capitainerie*, at the same time wishing him a nice vacation. The message was from Mr. Léonard himself, requesting Boyd's presence when convenient for the boy. He left his luggage unopened and went to the Third Floor of the *Capitainerie*, along the deserted quay on which he was the first summer visitor.

On the Third Floor he was met by the port accountant, someone he'd never seen, a heavy-set Frenchman who introduced himself as Carl Goldoni. Affable, quick to smile, obviously willing to be helpful, slightly obsequious in the Rimini-way, he introduced the boy into the Director's office, next door to the secretary, Madame Valérie, with whom he shook hands. He never learned if Valérie was her first or family name.

The Director rose to greet him. Goldoni left immediately, nodding his head in a curtailed bow as he backed out of the office. Boyd recognized the doorway behind the Director's desk as the entrance to the bedroom where he had awoken, three months before. To the east and south the room opened onto the port through floor to ceiling bay windows. Boyd congratulated the man on the view. The Director, smiling warmly since his entrance, suddenly became serious, the inner light of his face, not unlike that of the Christ on the other side of the partition, became grave and preoccupied, the lines at the corner of the mouth deepened into gorges that ran in vertical wounds from under his eyes to his lower jaw.

''I wanted to inform you that Mr. Bernard is still among us.'' He opened his desk and extracted a paper folded in thirds. ''He's written a full confession. It's a guarantee that there will be no future difficulties. It's my experience that he's learned his lesson, and as with the Prodigal Son, his return to the flock is a harbinger of a new and more enlightened course of action towards his fellow creatures. I know his repentance is sincere. I *feel* it. And as I had the occasion of informing you, he does have a wife and children. That in itself should guarantee the exemplariness of his future conduct.''

Boyd let out an audible gasp of air.

''It's our Christian duty to alleviate suffering. The gentleman in question has not had the advantages of many of us, and so in ways is *more* deserving of our love and understanding...'' Observing the suffering *Boyd* as undergoing, he added, ''He *is* a human being...''

That was precisely what the boy doubted. But how could he show himself less humane than his host. Except for the fact, he thought, but later, once he had left the office, that it was *he* who'd had the shit knocked out of him, not Mr. Léonard.

''It goes without saying that our previous arrangements will be honored. We've taken special care of your boat, as you may have observed. And if we can do more, we hope you won't hesit...''

''I'd like to go to the Little Quay, the one made of wood.'' The Director gazed out of the window. The quay on the opposite side of the channel from Boyd's boat, the domain of Buchenwald, was the South Quay. At the end of this quay there was a prolongation of the dike to the entrance of the port where there stood the lighthouse with its white beacon. At the foot of the lighthouse was a narrow quay of thick wood planks formally called the Little South Quay. As the dike was six feet lower in this area, waves occasionally passed over it during the winter, prohibiting its use by boats. During the summer small uninhabited fishing boats and Zodiacs were stationed there. These were nonetheless in danger due to the swell from the open sea which entered the port at that place, sending the boats there crashing into each other or into the quay itself if their moorings were not constantly looked after. Worse still, what Boyd called ''house'' boats--the motor yachts with television, bathrooms and full kitchens--entered with great speed, either because they flouted the regulations, or because, during storms and high seas, their captains panicked. Occasionally a passing sailboat was sent there if the port was full up, which provided the guardians a moment of humor when, due to the constant sea swell, the occupants were inclined to vomiting, sometimes so sick, Boyd had heard, they had to be hospitalized. The quay was also used for passing sailboats with barking dogs, the guardians' revenge against the messes they made, messes the guardians had to slalom through on their bikes. Big motorboats with dogs were never exiled there. When Boyd asked Marc, the guardian, why, he was told, ''Because they give the biggest tips. Getting money out of skin-flint *sailboats* isn't worth the bother.''

As Boyd was to learn, Mr. Léonard rarely concerned himself with whys and wherefores. In the absence of the boy's reasons for such a move, he simply picked up the telephone, dialed Ariosto and *told* him that Mr. Holloway would be going to the Little South Quay, and ''Would you be so good as to facilitate the transfer.''

Ariosto's door was open for the purpose of intercepting Boyd on the way down. The Harbormaster said nothing but pointed to a chair. He spoke briefly about his family, Jean-Henri and his sister Marie, his step-children, and about Véronique, his wife, who was looking for a job; he spoke nonchalantly, as if Boyd already knew these people. The boy asked a few questions to be polite, receiving answers of bored curtness. Finally the man got down to business. From his desk he took out a folder.

"The Little South Quay is open from the 1st of July to the 31st of August. Normally we don't allow inhabitable boats there, but the Director wishes to make an exception. It's now…" He made a show of looking up the date on the desk calendar. "…the 7th of June. In three weeks a berth on the Little Quay will be readied for the arrival of the *Denis. Voilà.*" But it was not *Voilà.* For the boy it was far from *Voilà!*

"I received the impression that I'd be able to go there immediately."

"Impossible. The electricity's been cut off and the Technical Service won't put it on until the specified date."

The telephone rang. It was his wife to whom he said several words and then slammed the received down without even a goodbye. We're really among the cream of the crop, thought the boy. Immediately the phone rang again. This time Ariosto shot to attention, Yessired the caller to death, and then ran from his office up the stairs without a sign to Boyd. Moments later he flew back down at breakneck speed to the First Floor where Grimaldi and the other Aides were stationed. Boyd heard him puffing for breath and asking if the Director's report had been readied. Boyd took French leave.

On the quay across from his the *Buongiorno TUTTI*-gang was going great balls of fire. Boyd chewed at his inner lip every time he heard the bitch's full-bodied screech. But on *his* quay, through small touches, he slowly changed the manner of living. He made no bones about telling visiting boats, stopping for a night or so, that this was a quiet port. "It's written at the entry," he would say disdainfully. "NO NOISE and SPEED LIMIT 3 KNOTS." As he woke up at 4:30 every morning, he didn't hesitate to go to offending boats and bang on their gangplanks until the owner came stumbling out of his cabin, dead with fatigue, to be lectured in a strange French accent, or in a proximity of Italian, stranger still, on some wrongdoing the owner was guilty of.

The Swiss were models of perfect comportment, although at lunch one day they had guests for whom they broke out a generous number of champagne bottles. One of the visitors, a fat banker, stumbled down the gangplank and dumped the empties, that the Swiss call corpses, into the garbage can in place in front of the *Denis*. The boy jumped as they hit the cement quay upon which the inner sack reposed. When Boyd gave him a disdainful look, the man, muddled, said, "As you see, the Swiss are here!" Boyd stood and eyed him with complete contempt, something akin to the

Queen of Sheba recoiling at the sight of a dog mess. When the banker got back onboard Boyd saw him nodding and pointing towards the *Denis,* while the owners shook their heads and shrugged their shoulders. The boy had to smile to himself. He was truly David to the Goliath motorboats before him, his vessel coasting a few thousand dollars, while theirs were worth millions.

His Napoleonic commands were not infallible.

Boyd heard the boom, boom, boom of the pop music the moment the boat entered the port, despite the distance of a good mile. He repeated to himself like a Gregorian chant, *Please God, not here, not here, not here.* But the destination of the boat *was* here. Bernard pulled up on his bike, stopping at the empty space next to the *Denis,* decided to make the most of Boyd's reputation for demanding calm and quiet on his quay. The man gazed at the boy with an air of self-satisfaction as he aided the noisy sailboat and its crew of two boys and two girls into its berth.

In the days following all hell broke out. The disturbance grew so bad Aldo and Roseland returned to Turin, as Boyd and the new arrivals fought for supremacy through loudspeakers interposed between them, the ones, Italian, playing pop crap, Boyd letting go with Turandot, the loudest of his tapes. ''This is good Italian music,'' he yelled at them. ''Too bad your generation is too debased to appreciate it.'' He took to following the girls to the showers, hoping to scare them into leaving. The boys took to systematically accompanying them. As usual, Boyd left the port at night, anchored just offshore, but during the day the quay had become insupportable. Finally he was forced to go to Ariosto and complain. ''We can't stop them from playing music,'' the Harbormaster said, ''and since no one else seems bothered....'' Which was true. The Germans and Swiss had thick walls and double-pained sliding doors to filter out the noise, or the expediency of absenting themselves for long lunches and dinners at the best restaurants. ''At least let me change places,'' he pleaded. That was how he found himself at the very end of the fourth quay, the *Buongiorno-TUTTI* quay.

There, he had to watch his step, and molt into the Best Boy in the Port. The next day, leaving the ship chandlery, he heard the sound of rock music, the magnitude of which was unheard of. The Germans and Swiss, Dutch and English wondered what was going on. The Italians, ever faithful to their principle of leaving well enough alone, paid no attention to the disturbance. That'll teach my Swiss and German neighbors to be ostriches, he smiled, when he received confirmation that the racket came from his quay.

When he entered the port the next morning, he was told that the boys on the offending boat had climbed onto their mast the night before and thrown down beer cans at passersby, the cans happily empty. That threw Boyd into stitches. Not even Ariosto could overlook such behavior, and by the afternoon the boat was indeed banished.

In the meantime, Boyd had come to appreciate his new berth. Tied up at the end of the quay, he had no boats to block his view from in front or behind, and could watch ships entering and leaving the channel, a sight that was often beautiful, especially the Italian sailboats with their cargo of young people lolling in skimpy swimsuits on the teak decks. He decided to stay where he was. There were no objections from Ariosto until the day Boyd decided to wash his sails. He spread them out over the quay, using up the space in front of several boats, but careful not to infringe on the space occupied by the *Buongiorno-TUTTI* yacht, the *Kitty*. He soaped up the sails and rinsed them with floods of water. When finished, the old Italian and his dog took a walk along the still-wet quay, inspecting the water drops on the transoms of the boats on both sides, under the curious gaze of Boyd. That afternoon Ariosto sent around the guardian Marc with a note ordering the boy back to his own berth. He obeyed with grace and a renewed inner promise to bide his time.

.

The next morning Michel the baker pulled up in his Zodiac, alone, on his way spearfishing. Boyd had never seen him so down in the mouth. ''So I was there at the bottom of the stairs kissing my sweetheart goodbye when up pops my wife.''

''Let me get this straight. At the bottom of the stairs in your house, while your wife was out.''

''No, in the next room.'

''You were kissing your African queen, knowing your wife was in the *next room*? And why was she even there?''

''My wife?''

''The *girl!*''

''We'd been upstairs together. You know.''

''*In your own house* for Christ's sake?''

'''Well, and so now she wants to divorce.''

Boyd told him how sorry he was, and Michel answered that he'd been stupid, and then added something which made the boy think he was being more stupid still.

''I'll give her a vegetable stand I bought a few years ago, you know, one of those under the overpass in town. That'll bring in 7,000 francs a month if she works hard.''

''Jesus. The laws must be different in France. In America she'd get *half* of what you're worth. Minimum.''

''Ohhhaaa. She'll get the house, too...''

''And the children?''

''This is France. A working stiff doesn't have a prayer.''

"What *do* you own exactly?" Boyd loved asking this kind of question to his students, knowing the French never responded where money was concerned.

Michel, perhaps proud of what a mere laborer had been able to accomplish, decided to come clean. "There's the pastry shop but that's my working tool. Under French law she can't have that. The Tea Room. The country house. The house. A couple of studio-apartments I rent out. A few stands under the overpass...."

"Cash?"

"She doesn't know about that...."

Boyd had mixed feelings. He had liked the looks of his wife, a spunky woman who had probably taken a lot of shit over the years, if he could judge from Michel's reputation for philandering. Yet all he was prepared to give here was the home in which to raise his kids and two-square yards of cement sidewalk where she could make a living selling fruit or vegetables, provided she worked from morning till night? He had his doubts that French law would be *that* lenient on a "working stiff", or that hard on the woman.

Boyd turned the conversation to Ariosto. Michel looked disgusted. "He's been here only three months and already we have to pay through the nose. See this Zodiac. Under Rimini I had to fork over a few fish and *basta*. He let me tie it up to the prow of a friend's boat." Boyd knew this was forbidden because the tenders blocked neighboring boats from getting into and out of their berths easily. "Ariosto wants me to pay bachshish for the same privilege."

"Why don't you *rent* an emplacement?"

"Are you crazy? That would cost me *much more* than what Ariosto wants."

"So Ariosto's like Rimini."

"Not at all. We have a saying here in the South of France: Rimini ate, but he *gave* something for others to eat; Ariosto eats but he gives *nothing* in return. That's a big difference. Luckily, since I saved your ass, things have been looking up. The Director has sent the port's bread business my way. Now I supply the Club and get a reduction when I eat there. *And* I regained permission to tie up the Zodiac on Alain's boat free of charge." He motored away to the relative peace of underwater fishing.

.

Aldo and Roseland invited Boyd to the restaurant that night. The invitation was traditional before they left. As he always refused, they issued it no matter what they planned on doing. Aldo considered himself adroit in his relations with others. He never hesitated to be of service to his neighbors, and at Christmas all the guardians were given presents, his way of putting them in his pocket, an approach different from that of the Swiss who gave out much more expensive gifts as a social obligation to the less fortunate. Never for one minute did the Swiss imagine they'd need to buy assistance for a few trinkets when they could pay hard cash for what they required. That night Boyd said yes, he would be happy to accompany them. He had been unnerved by certain events of the day and he needed a change of air. Aldo did a wonderful job of covering up his surprise. The boy went into the cabin to put on clean levis and polo. The three walked along the quay together, Boyd sheepish at the way he was being examined by the Swiss and Germans, who queried the break in his routine, so immutable they all knew it by heart.

Nothing could have prepared the boy for the restaurant. To reach it they had gone through Ventimiglia, a town architecturally identical to Menton but reflecting the poverty of the corrupt, politically unstable country. The roads contained hen nests, as the French called them, potholes so big and deep that even the Italians were obliged to slow down. The town's buildings were cracked and gray, in contrast to Menton which was in constant repair. The beaches were polluted and strewn with plastic and other refuse. ''The town is poor,'' said Aldo in answer to one of the boy's comments, ''but the people are rich.'' Unlike Menton where at night the streets, clean and well lit, were empty, here the car traffic was so dense it was at a quasi-standstill. The sidewalks spilled over with people who had to walk interspersed among the cars to circulate. The passersby were well dressed. Between licks of the ice-cream cones most held, they gaily hailed their friends. ''If there's disrepair it's because the people don't pay their taxes'', Also easily confessed. ''In Italy only a fool would pay up.'' ''Okay, but look at the result!'' said Boyd, shaking his head at the decay. ''The money would just go for corruption,'' said Aldo. ''Why should I shell out *soldi* for someone else's penthouse or Ferrari?'' When Boyd didn't give a rejoinder he continued: ''The Italians are rich but smart. You can't hold it against them if they're smart.'' Boyd knew they were also hard workers, adaptable, and charming when it was in their interest. No wonder these modern Carthaginians were at home in the United States, cradle of unbridled and unruly free enterprise.

At the outskirts of Ventimiglia, between the clogged road and a railway yard full of stock cars waiting to be shunted, a bamboo wall surrounded a few tables and a small cinder-block building. They pulled off the road and drew up to the wall, getting honked at because Aldo hadn't signaled. They exited through Aldo's side, several inches from the cars that went by in clogged single file, as fast as snails.

Boyd ordered spaghetti, while the others took a full menu as the Italians do, meat, spaghetti, fish, salad, desert, coffee. Boyd had never figured out how Italians could eat so much and, in general, remain so slim. They had been greeted at the entrance by the owners, a couple who kissed and fawned over Aldo and Roseland, paying scant attention to Boyd, while the Italians already seated looked on bored, and those in the cars passing within touching distance beeped and honked and otherwise encouraged their compatriots in the other cars to advance. The meal was lugubrious but the beer relaxed the boy. It was late and he felt drowsy, yet he already knew it was one of those evenings in which a valium would be necessary if he wanted to sleep.

Early the next morning Grimaldi was surprised to see Boyd's boat *leave* the port at sunup, at the time when it usually *entered*. He anchored in a nearby cove. Stoned out of his mind on the three valiums he'd taken an hour before, he plunge into sleep, trembling so hard he had to hug himself against a pillow to try to regain a semblance of calm, so cold despite the summer mildness he had to bury himself under his blankets.

He woke at six that afternoon, the sun still high, took more pills and went back to sleep. The next morning he entered the port at 4:30, at first light, as he had done so often before. He spent the morning washing the boat inside and out, then pumped up the tender that he used to clean and wax the hull. Jean-Loup came by at 8:30 while Boyd was still in the dinghy. He hoisted himself into the cockpit and offered the boy a drink, an offer which surprised Jean-Loup as Boyd rarely went out of his way to see to his comfort.

''You who don't like noise wouldn't believe the racket yesterday. We had the police here, an ambulance, people crying up a storm, Ariosto pale as a sheet and even the port Director down from his perch on the Third Floor.'' Jean-Loup hesitated.

'Go on for Christ's sake,'' said Boyd, his throat croaking.

''Shit! If you could see yourself!''

''I'm expecting the worse. Something happened to Grimaldi or Marc or the baker?'' He hadn't the tiniest notion of how to hide his emotions.

''God no, just the old prick on the *Kitty*. Found drowned between the quay and the *Ghost* a few boats down. But there was blood on the stern transom that has everyone puzzled. They think he fell from the gangplank or was tripped up by the dog's leash and lost his balance, or maybe even the dog *pulled* him off the gangplank. All shriveled up like he was, he couldn't't've weighed much. But how did the blood get on the transom? Mystery.''

''And he's dead?'' Boyd asked stupidly.

''A cock couldn't get stiffer. I saw him on the quay half zipped in one of those black plastic jobs. So white you could see through his skin. *Ceramic* white. First dead person I've ever seen and I don' wanna see another.'' He pulled the sack from the can. ''Did you say something about a drink?''

Marc had found the body while on his rounds at 9:00. As the Italians rarely ventured out before 10:00 or later, no one had missed the proprietor of the *Kitty*. Marc called Grimaldi on the VHF for an ambulance. He told Boyd later he could tell the old guy was dead by the way he sort of hung in the water, facc down, his head and shoulders bobbing in the backwash. They found the dog on the balcony, asleep in its bed, its leash attached to the collar.

The day's events deeply marked Boyd, and formed the substance of his dreams that night. He found himself on the quay, just as the old guy, facing the transom, finished relieving himself. His face registered a fleeting look of surprise at seeing the boy so near, and vacillated between snubbing him or asking him what the fuck he was doing on *his* quay. His eyes were wary, but there was no fear, no suspicion. Boyd had never seen the man so close up and was shocked by his age, the rutted, concave jowls, emaciated and wizened, the corded throat tissues like ridges of melted wax. The weeks of having to endure the barking that the old man seemed to encourage, the shrill cries of the *Bonjourno-TUTTIs*, the tables dressed along the quay, the drinking. The chaos. But the detonator of his hatred lay elsewhere. The old man opened his mouth to demand the meaning of his presence at such an ungodly hour. In the same instant the boy was assailed by the putrid stench of the alcohol and by the vision of his mother doubled up against the kitchen wall, dodging as best she could the blows from her glass-eyed husband, while he lay on the floor, suffocated by the sobs that strangled him, his blood forming a pool on the linoleum before his eyes. His rage exploded, and in one vast propulsion of energy, as he had learned in karate, he hurtled the sack of bones against the transom. Then turning his back, he hurryed off, knowing that 6 o'clock was the changing of the guard, that none would be on their rounds until they'd had their coffee, hoping, *praying*, no one had been up so early to take a piss, as the Italians did, from their prows.

He dreamed too that he was home, on his cot, looking up at the posters of Notre Dame where Quasimodo, among the gargoyles, surveyed the mob below, in the middle of which Boyd himself had been tied to a pole, waiting to be hanged. Seeing him in danger, Quasimodo, with the aid of a rope, swooped down like an eagle on its prey and freed him from the claws of his aggressors. Back among the gargoyles, Quasimodo cried out, for all of Paris to hear, ''*Sancuarium! Sanctuarium! Sanctuarium!*''

CHAPTER FORTY-TWO

As there was no question of his remaining across from the *Kitty*, he steered his boat directly to the Little South Quay. The site was more beautiful than he had imagined. Directly in front of him to the north was the three-story *Capitainerie* with the partially snow-capped Maritime Alps as a backdrop. To the east was the open sea, visible through the entrance of the port, the lighthouse and, in the distance, more mountains, these

Italian. To the south were the shorter dike and the audible surge of the ocean. To the west was the port itself, beginning with the South Quay 200 yards away, beyond which rose Menton, and beyond Menton the serpent tail of Cap Martin, home of the Navarres and Cantons. Once installed he wasted no time waiting for the *bon vouloir* of Harbormaster Ariosto. He returned to the Third Floor to enlist the help of the charming accountant Carl Goldoni.

"Of course! Immediately!" he said when Boyd asked if the electricity could be connected. Mr. Goldoni gave him all the serious attention of someone who had just announced he was dying of terminal cancer. Frowning over the telephone, he called down to the First Floor and told the new guardian, Christophe, to send someone to do the job.

"The Harbormaster said it couldn't be done," said Boyd.

Goldoni had an engaging, ironic sort of smile which, Boyd was to learn, signified that the person or subject under discussion was too inane for additional words to cover it. As a courtesy Boyd offered him the use of his boat, should he ever wish to go out fishing or swimming. The boy was taken aback when Goldoni asked if after work at five o'clock would be convenient.

At 5:10 he showed up with, amazingly, Jean-Loup. The three went a couple of hundred yards outside the port and anchored in the place Goldoni indicated. Although in clear view of the shore, Carl--"Please, the first name, I'm not the Director"--and Jean-Loup stripped naked and jumped in. Boyd followed suit, assuming his body was now known to one and all after being knocked senseless in the shower. Later they chewed the fat sitting in the cockpit over Boyd's cokes. Carl, as fat as a blubbery seal, was only around 26, calculated the boy, and decidedly of Italian ancestry, judging from the dimensions of the virile member at the confluent of his thighs. Jean-Loup, whom Boyd had imagined far more muscular, was in better shape, but only in comparison to Goldoni.

"Why the *Denis*?" asked Carl with decidedly unFrench indiscretion, another indication of his Italian blood. "Usually boats are named after girls."

"I named it after my brother. When I left home my mother missed me so much she decided to have another kid. She was pretty old to give birth, but it was the best move for her."

"Does he ever visit you," asked the accountant, "or is he too young?"

"In reality," began the boy hesitatingly, "I never got to see him. He ... fell off a cliff during a school outing."

"God!" exclaimed Goldoni.

"They brought him back in the aisle of the school bus."

"Holy shit!" said Jean-Loup.

Anyway, Boyd had always *wanted* a brother. He often felt things would have taken a totally different turn had he not found himself alone in life.

''I trust Ariosto wasn't too angry about my taking the berth before the time indicated in the regulations,'' said Boyd, hoping the Harbormaster had pissed his pants.

''There are no regulations about that quay,'' laughed Carl. ''We always put boats there in winter till about two years ago when there was a combination of Southwest winds and high sea levels, and waves broke over the dike right into the cockpits of the boats of the Little Quay.'' Goldoni fidgeted with his cock, proof again he was more Italian than French who *never* fondled themselves in public. There was a French expression that applied, *Chase the natural, and it comes back in a gallop*, meaning that one can't alter one's innate nature.

''It was incredible,'' said Jean-Loup. ''The waves even came over the wall of the South Quay, crashing into the cars and jeeps there...''

''And sending some into the port,'' added Carl.

''You mean, into the *water*!'' asked Boyd.

''Into the transom of the ships, too,'' smirked Carl pleasantly, nodding his head at the same time. Boyd wondered how he kept from getting a hard-on with the continuing manipulation. Boyd had put his jeans back on, telling the boys it was to keep the girls from swimming over from the beach to rape him. ''What!'' Carl had exclaimed. ''We're staying naked because we *want* 'em to come and rape us!''

''The electricity in the lampposts blew out. You'd never seen such fireworks,'' continued Jean-Loup. ''Car roofs dented to the seats, the windshields bashed in or swept away. Motorcycles washed into the drink. Those flimsy plastic cockpit doors caved in, letting the waves flood into the cabins.''

''Ariosto said I might be in danger.''

Both boys guffawed. ''Not in summer.''

''Perhaps he was thinking of the boats that don't obey the speed limit,'' speculated Boyd.

Carl shrugged. ''I don't think we've had complaints, but yours is the first *inhabited* boat we've had there, I think. You'll have to ask one of the Aides.''

''D'you think I'll be able to count on them?''

''They're just waiting for their pensions,'' smirked Jean-Loup. ''If you wan' anything done, it's better to do it yourself or tip well.''

''Do you think Ariosto will be an improvement in that way over Rimini?'' asked Boyd, at ease with Carl, which was rare for him. The man's face was nearly handsome, but the folds of fat cascading over his stomach, and the wide, unnaturally white pimply ass made him wish he would dress. "After all, there was a lot of talk about baksheesh and stuff with Rimini...."

"Ariosto doesn't know fart," said Jean-Loup.

"We have our eye on what's going on now," said Carl. "Perhaps things got a little exaggerated under Rimini, but we're making sure they don't under Aroisto."

"And that other prick?" asked Boyd. "The one with the dog."

The boys shrugged. "Unknown to the regiment," said Jean-Loup.

"A dog called Charlie," added Boyd.

"Be careful, he's a friend of the Director's *and* of Jean-Loup, here present," warned Carl pleasantly.

"He's all right," admitted Jean-Loup.

"He's white trash," said Carl. "You know, Claude told me he called Claude's mother a *squaw.*"

"Good Lord, why?" asked Boyd. Carl shrugged. "Who *is* he anyway?"

"He has a boat at the foot of the *Capitainerie*, opposite where you are now. There's a bad backwash there, so we normally can't hire it out. So the Director gives him a reduction."

"What does he do for money?"

"Odd jobs. They don't pay much."

"But why's he friends with the Director?" asked Boyd. Carl shrugged again.

"And what do you see in him?" he asked Jean-Loup.

"He's all right," was the sullen answer.

.

The same saying exists in French as in English: The grass always looks greener elsewhere. By that he meant the Little Quay had its quirks. The biggest being that there was no control at all over the speed of the incoming boats. Boyd remembered that in all the time he'd spent in the *Capitainerie* with Jean Grimaldi, he'd never seen the man get on the public-address system to give any kind of warning of any nature to boats entering or leaving the port. The only exception was the blurted out, undecipherable order for entering boats to pull up to the Reception Quay where a guardian would see them to a berth.

He noticed now. He couldn't pour a cup of coffee for fear of spilling the boiling water over himself without first looking east--at the port entrance--and then west--the interior of the port--like a pedestrian at a crossing, to make certain no boats were coming or going. He also had to lengthen the mooring lines between his boat and the quay, preventing the stern from crashing into it because of the passing skunks.

The Director came down from his Third-Floor aerie for a friendly visit. He seemed to want to live and let live, as did the Italians, but with a major difference: once his attention was focused on a problem, he did what was necessary to solve it. Alas, for the boy, each visit, each solution, demanded a punishment of at least an hour of benumbing conversation.

During that day's hour, Léonard opened the boy's mind to irrevocable truths such as the irrefutable fact that all substance, animal, vegetal or mineral, formed an interlinking chain at the summit of which stood Man. He learned that if Man was evil, it was because he hadn't the wisdom to respect the Word, and that Man was so blind that the only way of bringing Him into their hearts was through a cataclysm so terrible that they would be forced to beg for God's help, which of course God would accord. "At this very moment the world is readying itself for the Second Coming of the Messiah. Man has already, within himself, that which he needs to assure his own salvation. Everything is based on respect, respect for God, for his fellow Man, as well as for all living and inanimate objects." Thanks to his years among the Mormons, the boy was immunized.

He spoke to Carl Goldoni about the Director during their second excursion on the *Denis*, this time without Jean-Loup.

"He's a genius," Carl declared. "It was he who laid out the original plans for the port. He was a well-known navigator, and then an airplane pilot and a race diver. He planned and built his house, just above the port. Modern, with a huge round bay window and every convenience. Then he up and sold it all. The house, the country house, the boats--he had two, one 36 feet and one 42--everything, the plane..." When Boyd asked why, Carl shrugged and said he'd have to ask the Director himself, although a few minutes later, under the influence of the Ricard anisette Boyd had bought because he knew Carl preferred something alcoholic, he added, "There were probably religious reasons." And later still: "Because of his sect."

Ariosto never failed to come around after one the boy's discussions with Léonard, observed with interest from his second-floor window. The boy took an evil glee in not unveiling the content of what he and the Director shared, and as Ariosto was incapable of asking a direct question, he never found out. It was clear, though, that he was curious about the boy's sexual orientation. Instead of just asking him as Jean-Loup or Michel the baker would have done, he made comments like, "People in the port think it strange that they never see anyone enter your boat, neither dog nor cat, neither friend nor foe." "Nor," added the boy, tired the man's beating around the bush, "little boys or little girls." He remembered a university friend who had stated in an all-night cramming session that sexually Boyd was neither fish nor fowl. Even Michel's "Does he fuck?" and Frédéric's "You haven't screwed since you arrived here," made him wonder why the question was of such importance. Why did they give a damn what he did with his cock? Why wouldn't they get off his back, when all he wanted was peace and *calm*. And now here he was, on this quay at the very end of the port, at the very extreme limit of France, and they still had their noses up his ass.

.

A week later the new guardian, Christophe, came down the wooden quay. The boy felt a certain admiration for him. When Christophe saw someone washing his car he would try to explain why it was not permitted. He did the same with speeders, talking to them as if they were human and not outlaws as was Boyd's reflex. Perhaps because of his ungainly bulk he did not intimidate. Now he came by to exchange a few neighborly words with the sole inhabitant of the Little Quay. The boy got him talking about his new baby and his wife, pleased with what seemed to be the unique example of normality in Port Beausoleil. Boyd recounted how Ariosto treated his wife, hanging up on her on the telephone, saying once to Boyd that if he stopped by his apartment his ''whale would make him a cup of coffee,'' supposedly because she was overweight. And Ariosto once said in passing, ''If she can't find work, it's due to the lazy mentality of the milieu she grew up in.''

''He started to say something about my wife, too,'' said Christophe, ''and I cut him off, telling him I didn't accept any reflections on my private life. I told him, 'Mr. Ariosto, I'll do the best job I can here, but my family is off-limits. I just do not want to hear any observations about what is none of the port's business.' I told him straight out.''

''That's good,'' laughed the boy, harboring the impression that the advice was for him too, and respecting Christophe the more for it, as well as the tactful way of imparting it. ''But still, you're lucky to have someone to go home to. In all my life, I've never had a meal waiting for me or had my bed turned down by anyone but myself.''

''Well, the person who's coming here won't prepare you a meal,'' said the guardian, pointing to the berth next to Boyd's, ''and he certainly won't turn down your bed, but at least he'll be company of sorts.''

Paling, Boyd asked ''*Who's coming here?*''

''I spoke with the Harbormaster a moment ago and he's just decided to send Guy for the summer. Do you know him, the fellow with the dog Charlie?''

.

Claude dropped by later with his wind board. The port let him store it at the end of the quay, three or four feet from Boyd's boat. He stripped down to his red briefs, and then turned to the job of mounting the wishbone and sail. He was as close to perfection as any boy Boyd had seen, excepting Denis. Boyd admired the muscular chest and salient abdominals, powerful thighs and briefs supporting an enviable volume. The memory of him at the urinal made the boy smile.

They exchanged a few brief words and then Claude mounted the board and let a slight southwest breeze take him gently through the mouth of the port, leaving Boyd to stare at the broad back as he pumped the sail. He thought of de Vinci's sketch of the outstretched man, the coalescing of the vital forces at the body center (15). What was the unfathomable attraction to that center, as primordial as the inexorable attraction of the planets to the burning nucleus of the sun (9).

Was it Claude who brought out Buchenwald from under her rock? A movement on the dike caught his attention, and in an instant the skeletal twigs, the lush silicon protuberances, and the puckered buttocks of a chimpanzee were etched on his retina. How he hated her for reducing to ashes the image of that broad back, replacing it with her own image, that of the perversion and disease she embodied. He hadn't noticed the fisherman, one he'd never seen before, standing on the rocks near the lighthouse a few yards from the *Denis*, a few feet from Buchenwald who was stalking the summit of the dike. Dressed in green cut-off jeans, young and handsome, his black hair reaching down to the shoulders of his black t-shirt, he had turned in profile to watch the passing of the monster. On his face was astonishment. Boyd naturally imagined he shared the disgust bordering on the nausea the boy had felt the first time he had seen the jerky displacements of the mantis-like limbs, but he was wrong. Buchenwald proceeded to the lighthouse and placed herself against the wall, appearing black against the white surface. She shut her eyes and turned her head upwards to the sun. In the place of her usual nakedness, today she wore a triangular patch of black cloth not quite covering the entirety of her privates, a portion partially drawn into the gaping slit. Abruptly, the fisherman reeled in his line. Within his jeans a cylinder extended from the root of his groin down past the pocket and protruded a good inch into view. He gathered up his pail and tackle box, oblivious to the boy, his attention divided between what he was doing and what *it* was doing. *It* languorously left the wall, aware of the fisherman who stumbled up the rocks towards her, doing nothing to hide the impact she was having on him. She quickened her step back along the dike, stopping in the center. The fisherman went up to within a few feet, perhaps as close as he dared, and from there, to Boyd's total incredulity, he cast his line into the sea, in the pretence of still fishing, his eyes magnetized by her breasts. When she resumed her indolent movement towards the steps leading down to the South Quay, he brought in the line as fast as he was capable of reeling. Buchenwald descended the stairs and hurried to her houseboat, the fisherman in pursuit.

.

A while later the port pickup drew near with Jean-Loup behind the wheel. Boyd assumed the boy had come for the garbage sack at the entrance of the quay, and was on the verge of yelling to him that it was empty when he noticed the boy had a passenger, Guy, the dog Charlie wedged in between them. Boyd nodded to Jean-Loup as he got out of the cab and came up to the entrance of the quay. Back on the *Denis* he observed the two through the plexiglas window. They had come to install a gate.

He didn't hear Claude return until one of the wooden planks squeaked. He was streaked with dried salt. Claude yelled Hi to Guy and Jean-Loup, Jean-Loup who was standing around while Guy did the work.

"Why's *he* doing that?" Boyd asked Claude.

"Guy? He works for the port part-time, pays for part of his berth, I suppose."

"You know I saw him steal some rope from a yachtsman the other day?" commented Boyd. From a distance the rope had looked like thirty yards of excellent quality mooring fiber. The owner had placed it on the electricity terminal facing his yacht and had entered his cabin for a moment, the time needed for Guy to walk up with his dog who sniffed the terminal while Guy took a look inside to make sure the owner's attention was deflected long enough for him to grab it, hoist it over his shoulder and make off on the double.

"Yeah? I saw him take a whole toilet Thierry was going to install, right from the cockpit of a boat whose owners were off having lunch at The Pirate."

That's *sick!*"

"Yeah? Why?" asked the boy, turning to face him. Or face him down. Boyd couldn't keep from smiling at those angry blue eyes in the midst of the wild black locks.

"Okay," said Boyd, "you have a sense of morality or you don't. I won't go into that, but you can't *steal* from another yachtsman. There's sort of an unwritten code about that."

"Bullshit. If those bastards are rich it's because *they* stole the money to buy their boats and Ferraris and stuff in the first place. So why not steal from them?"

"With that kind of mentality *nothing* would be safe. There'd be *chaos*. Even *you'd* be in the street with a gun to protect your belongings."

From several sources Boyd knew that Claude was less disinterested than he pretended. He charged 300 francs an hour to install material, about as much as a shrink earns, another way of screwing the rich, the boy supposed. He mounted radars and other equipment of great value. The final bill could run into thousands of francs. But he never demanded payment from those, usually the Italians, who were slow in settling up. He waited for them to come around to his shop for other things, perhaps as long as a year later. Then he'd say, pleasantly, "Don't we have a little slate we'd like to wipe clean?" If the person didn't come through then, the rising blood would darken Claude's face, and an expression of rage would contort his features. Boyd had heard that at those moments no yachtsman hesitated to fork over what he owed, just to be able to get away, many never to set foot back in the shop.

"I don't have belongings to protect. But it's true I'd be in the street. With a gun. And then," he said, aiming an invisible weapon at the invisible rich scampering away from him, he repeated what he'd told Boyd before: "Bam, bam, bam and bam."

"Ohhhh," sighed Boyd, pretending to catch on, "I've got it. You're a revolutionary."

"Damned right! I'm waiting for the revolution. But it won't be like the first one..." Boyd assumed he was thinking of 1789. "This time there'll be total annihilation." The boy's eyes were angry. Could he really believe that crap?

"And I suppose I'll be one of the first to be shot?"

"Why, what've you got?" Which as so true Boyd burst out laughing, followed by Claude.

The gate was soon finished. Had Jean-Loup been capable of doing the job, he'd have spread it out over several days. Charlie's master was not a man to waste time. His metal-gray hair was cut very close to the scalp. He was supple, belying, the boy guessed, his fifty-something age. He was not overweight but heavy in the jowls and midsection. The head had certainly been handsome in youth, and was perhaps still so, if what remained wasn't disfigured by a perpetual scowl, different from Grimaldi's in that Guy's was dangerous. Boyd was amazed by the obsequiousness of the guardians when they approached him. He reasoned it was probably a combination of the man's no-nonsense nature, his easy rapport with the guardians in general--a sort of he-man's he-man--and, if rumor could be believed, his intimacy with the Director. He thought the man would probably bring his boat to the Little Quay on the first of July, as Ariosto dictated, but even without his presence, the problems continued.

.

During the late afternoon the wind began to rise. Boyd knew his boat was particularly exposed. The guardians had spoken about The seas that would make it impossible to keep upright in the cabin, and winds capable of toppling the mast like an uprooted tree. He was upset by the coming of Guy, but otherwise the bad weather would bring calm as even the guardians would stop making their rounds. At the time the port needed them most to survey the yachtsmen's ships, they would take shelter on the First Floor. He went to the prow to do his exercises. Because of the gusts he couldn't take his towel, but as long as he could keep upright, he could undertake the first series of limbering movements that relaxed his arms and neck. He then moved into a series of sit-ups and pushups. The wind gained in force and the air smelled of the coming rain. A pure scent. Over the Alps he watched the clouds blacken--torn and swooping down at the edges where the rain had started. He had a half hour before the showers would blow into Menton, enough time to get a reasonable workout. He concentrated on the pectorals and abdominals, finding reserves of strength and resistance as his body came to life, his breathing harder but at the same time more rhythmic. He glanced at the dike behind him, savoring the absence of life, the peace that had finally descended on the ragged wisps of wind and cloud. The temperature dropped, and the new freshness stirred his naked chest, compacting the pores and contracting the muscles. He smiled for the first time that day.

Through the corner of his eye he saw a boat leave one of the inner quays and head towards the entrance of the port, over which he was now Scylla. Who had the balls to go out in this weather, he asked himself, acknowledging that although it represented only a moderate challenge for real yachtsmen from French Brittany, in the Mediterranean anything over Force 6 was considered a hurricane by the armchair sailors who preferred calm waters and the hum of the motor. It was the *Bonità*! He admitted that Dino was one of the few who knew what he as doing, but he hoped the boat would sink anyway. As it approached his prow Francine waved. Boy sat in the cockpit holding onto the lifeline as though it were an umbilical cord. Dino was at the wheel. He yelled out to Boyd as he neared: ''Why do those movements? No Italian boy would show himself off in that way. No *normal* Italian boy.'' The dwarf was dead serious.

''Listen you cocksucker,'' Boyd shouted, rising and stepping onto the balcony in one movement, grasping the stay to keep his balance. ''I do what I do so I won't look like a fat shitty runt like you!'' Dino held his hand to his ear and leaned in the direction of the boy. ''So I won't look like a runt like you, RUNT, RUNT!'' he screamed as the boat glided past. He knew there were all kinds of gestures he could use, the forked fingers indicating that the creep was cuckolded, upraising the right arm while slapping the bicep with the left hand, indicating that he could fuck himself, but Boyd was too unfamiliar with these movements to perform them instantaneously and with conviction. So he raised the middle finger and thrust it into the air, which seemed to get his point across since the dwarf's face blackened, and he needed all his wife's persuasion not to bring his boat around and come back in after the boy.

For Christ's sake, Boyd said to himself as he regained his place on the prow, they *will not* leave me be. Through his mind ran the incidents of the past days, especially those involving the *Kitty*. It then occurred to him that the greatest casualty following the loss of Philippe was the loss of his sense of humor. He no longer had a sense of humor. He shook his head in wonder. Who would have thought I'd lose my sense of humor, he muttered to the wind, and that that would be of importance?

Take Dino, he thought as he entered the cabin to sponge off the sweat. Boyd envisaged himself facing the runt. He would wait until insulted and then he'd strike out with the fingers of his right hand, the first adhering to the second to reinforce the rigidity, the third stuck to the fourth, as the Guadeloupian had shown him in Paris, the resultant mass driven into the eyes of the bastard, followed by a blow to the groin. In similar scenes involving Bernard he had seen himself opening up the belly from navel to sternum with his fish knife, freeing the shit and watching the slob shrivel up like a deflated balloon. The scenes played so real before his eyes that his breath quickened and he started jabbing the air while he took off his sweatpants. The rain had started outside, whipped up by the wind, and the quay had all but disappeared in the dark. Thunder was heard descending the slopes of the Alps, and streaks of lightening occasionally illuminated the roof porthole. As the rain was driven by the wind from the northwest, he could leave his door open for air without having water enter the cabin. He increasingly needed air as the visions continued in the film that had taken possession of his mind. He knew no one would venture out in the storm, certainly not the port pansies, all of whom had television and satellite reception.

He wet the corner of his towel and began to wash, rubbing hard over his chest and biceps, under his arms. His back turned to the doorway, his instinct, perhaps awoken by the creaking of a plank, sprung alive to a presence just beyond the limit of the light of the cabin lamp. He spun around and caught sight of the twiggy appendages, the angular arms and legs, the long razor-sharp bones of hide, the puckered skin and elongated skeletal face sheltered by a kind of incurved wing or shroud that obscured the head, *mocking his nakedness*, his circumcised sex, shriveled, *puny*. Maddened that the thing had dared come on his quay, he grabbed the windlass handle, as long and dense as a burglar's crowbar, and jumped from the cockpit and onto the quay. Whatever took place had not gone unseen. The thunder drew near and in a flash that lit up the boat, quay and lighthouse, he saw a figure on the dike, half hidden under an umbrella, but that he recognized by the dog taking shelter between the spread legs.

CHAPTER FORTY-THREE

Charlie's Master

Boyd had long suspected he would never fathom the ways of the world, and each day added to the obscure conundrum. Stretched out on the prow of the *Denis,* a cold coke in his hand, he conversed with the charming gentleman sitting on the prow of *his* boat, unnamed ''because I haven't got around to it yet,'' the gray-haired son-of-a-bitch called Guy. ''Luckily you found time to baptize Charlie,'' commented the boy. The dog, lying on the side-deck, pricked up his ears. ''I don't believe in baptism," said the man. "As for Charlie, I chose the name of the day on which he was given to me. You know in France each day is named after a saint. On that day it was St. Charles." "And the day on which you bought the boat?" asked the boy. "Can't remember. But I won't name it after a saint. Too many unsaintly things take place on it."

That was certainly true, thought the boy, as they watched the boats enter and leave the port. The sun was hot. Guy had a canvas over his boom giving him shade. Boyd preferred to roam over his deck from stern to stem unhampered by the lines extended between a tarp and the cable railing. For the past month the boy and the man had joined forces in chasing incoming boats that didn't respect the speed limit. Boyd would see them enter because he was usually up front reading. If they came on fast, he'd call out, "Be careful Guy! Incoming fire!" Usually the man hadn't the time to put away cups and dishes. In the wake of the resultant waves the boy would hear the crash of broken crockery, the shouted insults, as Guy came staggering out of the cabin, red with fury, the filthiest language imaginable on his lips. Boyd would already be on his bike, racing after the boat. As the offender came into his berth the boy would be there to shout insults until he was hoarse. This first demonstration of displeasure would be followed by Guy who would rush up on his red Vespa, and in much more purple prose *and* in Italian because the offenders were wops nine times out of ten, he would blow a gasket. The boy's antics were weird enough to amaze the foreigners, but the follow-up by Guy with his crazy-looking evil eye and build of a bull, made retreat more sensible than valor, especially as they were on holiday, so who gave a fuck? The two would return to their boats, Guy to clean up the mess, Boyd to his vigil. The boy had already learned to strap down anything movable. Guy said he refused to function in a straitjacket.

As there had never been anyone on the Little Quay, the Aides were not used to reining in felon speeders. After bawling out the boats, Boyd would climb to the First Floor to chew them out. Usually he found them reading comics or watching a portable television. He made complaints in writing to Ariosto, but the Harbormaster too proved unable to enforce the rules. Finally he had to write to the Director. God dictated his will to his dependants, and from then on there was an improvement which, coupled with the man and boy's hot pursuits, allowed them to enjoy the afternoon of cokes and conversation.

Guy was the ultimate man's man, thanks to his ability as a raconteur and hands that could do anything of a manual nature. Totally disinterested and completely lacking in curiosity, he was nonetheless aware of whatever went on in the port thanks to a good-natured smile directed at the chosen few, a smile that acted as a magnet in eliciting indiscretions. "I never ask anything, but I can't just turn away when someone has something to confide," he told the boy who sensed that behind Guy's eyes, as lifeless as a shark's, he had acquired a complete and disquieting knowledge of the baseness of human nature. He loved crosswords, but that morning *Nice Matin* was on strike, so to kill time Guy had made a list of everyone he knew who'd made love with Roseland, Aldo's wife. ''Made love and not slept with because it was usually standing up,'' he pointed out. There were sixteen names on the paper.

''I don't see yours,'' the boy said in the way of a joke.

Guy turned a playful gaze on him. His face was incredibly handsome when it wasn't scowling, handsome if one made allowances for the degradations of age, amazingly moderate in his case, but gaining ground in the flask jowls, the deterioration of the neck and, in the early morning, when he did what he could to not be seen, the dark pouches under his eyes the French called valises, apt in his case. ''Yes, me too,'' he answered after a hesitation.

''Oh God no, that Madonna!''

''A Madonna as far as you were concerned, but to no one else in this port who wasn't infirm, blind or impotent,'' he scoffed.

''But how did it happen?''

''Standing up.''

''I mean, under what circumstances. For Christ's sake, I never saw *anything!*''

''You were too busy on your escapades with her husband. There were more than just me waiting for you two to drive off to Ventimiglia for your morning cappuccino.''

''And who else?'' he asked, going over the list. ''Oh God, Carl *Goldoni!*''

''Carlo's like your Francine. Nothing too hot or too cold for our Carlo.''

''But he's married. He has two daughters.''

''Carlo married for money. His wife's family owns a quarter of Menton.''

''I can believe that. I saw her. Nondescript, wafer thin...''

''So thin you have to insert it and then jack off by shaking her up and down.''

''...with badger eyes as if she couldn't sleep for the shaking. Untidy blondish hair.'' Boyd remembered now seeing Carl wandering around the port, a consequence of his job, he had assumed. ''At least there's not Claude...''

''The electrician married the sweetest girl in Roquebrune and sometimes he comes home and doesn't even speak one word to her. Gets in black moods and she becomes as invisible as Carlo's harridan.'' The boy could see that crosswords paid off.

They spoke exclusively French, but Guy would sometimes pepper his remarks with sudden inspirations that the boy suspected were

inventions, even though Guy maintained they came from his contacts with
G.I.s during the war. '' 'Rogering' means 'the old in and out', as you
young people say today.'' This too was news to Boyd. But to Boyd nearly
everything Guy came up with was news. With time the boy became adept
at masking his incredulity.

The list continued. There was Angelo the upholsterer who had a
shop next to Thalassa, whom Boyd had assumed was gay. ''That he
doesn't have syphilis is a sign God loves fools. He works in and out of a
half-dozen boats a day and does as much for the owner's wives. Their
husbands are sent off to his boutique where Angelo's wife helps them pick
out fabrics and colors.''

''He's *married*.''

''With two of the pretties kids you ever saw.''

''No Bernard.''

''But she often fantasized about his beard grazing on her beaver.''

''Beaver!''

''That's war lingo again, laddie.'' It was true he could never go
without his morning cup of ''java'', either.

Next to dirty talk and reading sex books like the smutty SAS series
favored by Didier and Denis, it was war stories Guy liked best. And that
afternoon, cokes in hand--a gift from Guy who had a fridge--he was
recounting the arrival of the Yankees in Normandy where he'd passed the
Occupation caring for his mother. While cleaning two pistols, one dating
from the Foreign Legion that he had reported lost, the other he'd bought
off an Arab, he reminisced about Yankee jeeps, candy and cigarettes. He
said he'd started smoking at that time, around age eight, which didn't
surprise the boy as he now smoked three packs daily--and woke up with a
hack that lasted until mid-morning. Smoking normally began at around
age twelve in France, which even Guy said was *''con''*, meaning stupid in
French, as well as signifying cunt, Guy informed the boy, since cunts were
narrow like narrow-minded people. French swearwords were
anatomically opposed to their English equivalents. There were no
cocksuckers in French, only *enculés*, meaning sodomizers. Prick, in the
sense of idiot, was ass in French. These and other recondite distinctions
were amply explained by Guy, who set out to refurbish the boy's
vocabulary.

Boyd wondered if it was Guy's fondness for Americans that had
been at least partially responsible for his silence after that terrifying
night. And the night had indeed been terrifying, thunder, lightening and
rains hadn't stopped for three days, flooding huge areas in the Southeast
of France. Entire *quartiers* of Nice had to be either evacuated or
provisioned by boat. The boy hadn't left the *Denis* in all that time,
waiting, waiting, waiting for the inevitable ... which never came. The
morning after the incident Christophe had waddled along the dike,

searching in the crevasses between the rocks, until coming upon the umbrella Boyd learned later had belonged to Buchenwald. The guardian came to his boat to yell through the deafening pounding of the surge that a yachtswoman was missing, and had the boy seen anything? He also said the police had been by that morning looking around the dike, and the firemen's Zodiac was at that moment hunting for her outside the port.

The sea, whipped up by the wind that had shifted to the southwest, had furiously racked the dike that fatal night. The crest of the waves, whose spume was smitten by the gusts, swept over onto the Little Quay, ridding it of Claude's board and whatever evidence that may have lodged in the planks. Boyd commiserated with Christophe, who was forced to continue his search under a pelting, ice-cold rain. He only hoped the kindly guardian hadn't noticed his pallor, or the trembling of his hands. Four days later he saw a SAMU ambulance stopped on the shore at the level of the Customs. He learned from Ariosto that the body had been found, battered and scraped beyond recognition.

Then Guy had come with his unnamed boat, and the waiting ended. Boyd helped him tie up. The talk was stilted, since the boy's concentration was limited to the first night of the storm. As Guy never asked questions and rarely volunteered information, and as the boy was not about to ask about *that*, the subject was effectively dead. What Guy had said on arrival--which won Boyd over in his heart--was, ''I'm an old fart. I have a television and at times it's on too loud. I want you to tell me, and I'll turn in down. You understand? I'm serious when I say I'll turn it down.'' Boyd never had to say a word because the man kept the sound, and his movements, under control. He must have been warned about me, Boyd thought, full of admiration for how Guy had handled what should have been a fight to the death between them, given their dissimilar characters and ways of life.

Guy could build a motor from scratch, repair plumbing, plaster walls, tile floors, anything and everything. Besides crosswords, he liked television, walks with Charlie, low-key conversations with friends who were on his boat from early afternoon--happy hour behind a Ricard anisette--until two or three in the morning, and *women*. He liked gigantic breasts--''That's my American heritage from Normandy''--but literally anything went. At the moment he was back to going with Julie. Up at 11:00, as sluggish as a snail, curly headed forty-something, she often invited the boy for morning tea, which he accepted because he was trying to learn how to ''compose'' with people, the Harbormaster's expression used as frequently as Didier's plethora, and meaning accepting other's shit in general, consenting to be treated as a doormat in particular. Over croissants and tea, unsugared because anything caloric was banned from the boat, she recounted her and Guy's adventures which had started a decade and a half before, their trips on her boat, the *Giola*, to Corsica and

Malta. Leaning over the table, her upper body bolstered by her elbows, the boy had an uninterrupted view of spongy breasts narrowly contained by her black low-cut swimming suit. ''But he can't stay with the same person for a long time,'' she was saying that particular morning, listlessly, seeking the boy's sympathy. ''He becomes restless. That's his nature. For a while he lived on the *Giola* and all was fine. When it ended he bought this. We'll just have to see what comes of us,'' she sighed.

When alone with Boyd Guy reverted to the vocabulary he'd used in Thalassa the first time the boy had seen him. ''She broke my balls. Always nagging, always jealous, putting her nose where it didn't belong.'' The person in question was of course Julie, but it could have been any of a dozen other women. ''The only thing I regret is all the reparations I did on her boat. I installed a fridge, a heating system, an electric windlass, I rebuilt the motor...'' ''You should never regret a good deed,'' said the boy sententiously. ''My ass,'' was the ready answer.

The boy regretted the events he had triggered in Paris. He taught classes at the Finance Ministry, at the time located in army barracks dating from before the last war, and destined to be destroyed for nearly thirty years. Atypically for France, the atmosphere was as relaxed an on an American campus. He was good friends with one of his students, an accountant, a kid with a face as spongy-looking as Julie's breasts, carbuncles on his neck and, an extreme rarity for the time, a stud screwed into his tongue to make cunnilingus more exciting for girls, he explained to anyone who risked the question. When Boyd explained what he wanted in the way of tax evasion reprisals, the student said he needed just five minutes to plunge Mister Guy Desmoines into the deepest and darkest of shit. Boyd had wanted to get even for his treatment of Colette at Thalassa. But when he informed her of his vengeance, she had turned her back on him, saying, in a manner so brusque he hadn't dared return to Thalassa, that she hadn't asked him to butt in.

Boyd decided to make up for what he'd done by cleaning the dirty hull of Guy's boat. He blew up the Bombard tender and washed and waxed the surface, sweating through every poor in the August heat. In thanks, she offered him a glass of water. When her *chou-chou* arrived as fresh as a daisy from a visit with friends, *he* got a cold coke. Such was the primacy of the nearly sixty-year-old prick she was certain to profit from, to Boyd's slim-loined potential *no one* seemed to be taking advantage of.

.

Claude came by at noon everyday. He'd replaced his board and sail. He was friendly with Julie and Guy, both of whom he'd known for years. During one of his visits Boyd made light of the Director who had said something like, ''I feel there's an animosity between you and the Harbormaster. On several occasions we've had the opportunity of invoking the importance of compatible harmony between all things, animal, plant, mineral, as well as human. To achieve such harmony, I suggest you find a moment during the day to pause, just long enough to send a vibration of love to those with whom you do not feel in phase. You'll see, things will turn out for the better." The electrician's forehead buckled up, giving him the look of a young Alain Delon, tortured by life's sordidness. "I suppose your snickering suggests that you think he's crazy to imagine an interconnection between things living and dead, and that good can come from the love of one's neighbor. *Well, think about it. Why* is he crazy? In what world are we living in which the crazy guy's the one who believes in doing good and being moral?

"Okay, but … anyway, people in the know say he stole from the port to finance his sect. Talk about morality…."

"Do you want to know what the people in the know say about you behind *your* back?" His face had become so hostile that the boy's only thought was how to get him to go.

"No."

"We've become so immoral we have no scruples about scoffing at someone like Léonard. It's like in the time of the plague, when people went around naked and fucked in public because they felt all was lost. That's how we are. Raping children, snuff films, drugs, kids killed by lost bullets like in your country where it's the first cause of child mortality. Believe me, when the slate's wiped clean, guy's like you will be the first on the list." He went off, the wind so stiff his board barely touched the surface of the water.

.

At little later Boyd was on the prow, doing his afternoon exercises. Normally lasting an hour, they had stretched to an hour and a half or two hours. The events of the last few days, instead of draining him of energy, had brought a new vitality. Unlike the culmination of the act of sex, when most sought rest, he found himself the possessor of a new vitality, as if he had impregnated himself rather than spurting his seed into the four winds. His body stifled him, a constraint he strove to escape by whipping it into a sweat, despite a summer solstice that broke records as a scorcher. Usually bare-chested, he now took to wearing a sweatshirt, and then two. He could *feel* the poison circulating in his head. He had to sweat it out, he had to free himself from his body's toxins. Guy seemed intrigued by the self-inflicted punishment, and perversely encouraged Boyd to do more and more. Despite the differences in age, he was envious of the boy's body. He had ceased keeping up his own as did all the French his age or even much younger, and he wasn't one to play the fool on the prow of his boat, leaving himself open to insults from the passing vessels, most piloted by chunky Italians who could be vulgar, degenerate even, as was only possible in Italian, a language potentially far cruder than French.

Today Boyd had another reason to empty himself of toxins. He had received a letter from Mrs. Graham, Doug's mom, who had written him a letter to his Paris address that someone in Léa's family forwarded to Beausoleil.

''I'm Mrs. Graham. I was your neighbor. You may remember that I once offered you some guppies. I'm retired now but the hospital has kept me on because I work well and they appreciate that. I was here when they brought in your dad, in a pretty sad state after the amputations. He was pretty heavy and that diabetes favors, as I've seen so often here. He wanted to see you, I think to ask forgiveness, but anyway he kept repeating your name right up to the end. It was sad to see him so diminished, he who had been so hard and ornery. When he drank you'd better get out of his way, which I had to do, even when he was angry with you. You were so different than my Doug and Al. You came by when kids picked on you, preferring me because your mom just didn't like the noise and fuss that upset her. I did what I could to soothe you, I never knew a boy in such need of soothing. Your daddy never understood his son and like I said I had to keep my tongue. You may be curious about Doug. He's in the Orient with the Marines and you can count on him having a good time! You don't remember but he had some problems with the law, but thanks to our Lord he rightened himself out. You two were inseparable and so cute together. I'd like your news if you get this letter. My address is on the back of the envelope. With sincere affection my little Boyd. Alice Bernadette Graham.''

Guy came forward with a can of coke, a bottle of Ricard anisette, a pitcher of ice water and two glasses. ''That's enough, in the name of God. You've been at it all afternoon.'' Boyd was in the middle of a series of pushups. His face, soaked in perspiration, his black hair stuck to his forehead, turned towards the man. He had grown fond of Guy. He knew he was totally self-centered, perhaps from birth, perhaps from living alone, but at least he accepted the boy's difference. Boyd interrupted his movements and took the can, spurned the glass, and settled down to pass an hour chewing the fat--an expression from Guy's G.I. days.

Guy had begun drinking early that day. Boyd had never before seen his eyes so bloodshot because the boy was in his own boat at sundown, getting ready for bed, at about the time Guy and his visitors were settling down to their first aperitifs. But Saramago and Laure, the doctor's mistress, had dropped by after lunch, offering Guy and Julie an excuse to break out the Ricard. Guy was at the doctor's beck and call thanks to the constant reparations needed on the doctor's boat and at the clinic. It was the merry outbursts from their conversation that had persuaded Boyd to give up reading in favor of doing calisthenics. Now he leaned against the roof of the *Denis*, ready for Guy to recount one of his memories, a coke in the boy's hand, a Ricard in Guy's, Charlie asleep on the side-deck between them. It was perhaps because Guy wanted to convince himself that he wasn't the doctor's servant that the conversation turned to mutual ass kissing.

''I have to kiss ass enough in my work,'' Boyd said. A sudden wind had blown up and they were watching the inexperienced pilots panic as they approached the mouth of the port, between the rocks of the dike and the rocks on the north shore. Only the presence of the man and boy kept some of them from barreling through at top speed. ''I don't want to kiss ass here. I've paid to put my boat in this berth, a berth no one in the port wants, not even you...''

''You have to be crazy to stay here,'' Guy opined amicably. Guy was obliged to make the move so that his usual berth could be used for summer passage, rented out for four times what he paid.

''In coming here,'' continued the boy, ''I freed my former berth for another boat. Therefore everything they gain with me is pure profit. In that case, why brown-nose Ariosto?''

''I don't kiss ass. When I broke up with Julie I went straight to Léonard and said, 'Martial, I want to buy a twenty-seven-footer and I'll need a place to put 'er. If you have one, okay, if you don't, I won't buy 'er.' That's how I got my place in front of the *Capitainerie*.''

''You know, Guy,'' said the boy, his eye on a vessel perhaps 150 feet long that was rounding the lighthouse, leaning so far starboard the keel and one of the twin propellers broke the surface, causing a good bit of turbulence, ''if Ariosto put us together, it's because he wanted to see fireworks.''

''I know.''

''He thought we'd kill each other.''

''I know.''

''But *why*? He doesn't like me anymore because I've been such a pain about the Aides not doing their jobs, and other stuff, but why you?''

''No idea.''

''Is it because of your closeness to *Martial*?'' he laughed mockingly, having heard that Guy was the only person in the port allowed to address the Director by his first name.

''It can only be that. Ariosto is jealous of everyone.''

''He says the Director treats him like a concierge.''

''Who wouldn't? He behaves like a puppy whose messes Martial has to clean up. Martial needs someone capable of acting independently, not a guy who can't wipe his own ass. He's got enough to do without doing Ariosto's job too.''

''Do you think the Director will clean house before he retires? How can he leave the port in this fix? Look at what he's created,'' he added, turning his head from the entrance to the inner quays. ''There can't be many better ports in France. In the hands of Ariosto it'll be in ruins in three years.''

''Ariosto's small fry,'' said Guy.

''First Rimini, now Ariosto. At least, Rimini knew how to charm the Swiss and Germans. Everyone liked him. They *liked* getting screwed by him. He may have been a thief, but at least they considered him *their* thief.''

''Before Rimini left the port he had a long series of talks with Ariosto,'' said Guy. ''Initially to touch each other up a bit, then some heavy petting, before getting down to the act.''

''Which means, decoded?''

''He showed him exactly how to steal, how to register fewer boats just passing through and divvy up the difference with the Aides and guardians. How to rake off a percentage from the supplies entering or leaving the port.''

''Why would Rimini do that?''

''For *his* cut.''

''But there must be some controls. Goldoni or Léonard.''

''Goldoni's in on it. Nothing would be possible without your friend Carlo.'' It was logical, but the boy knew Guy hated Goldoni who had said that if it weren't for Léonard's backing, he would have already ejected tramps like Guy from the port.

'Poor Léonard. He probably has no idea at all of what's going on,'' commiserated Boyd.'' The boy had had enough talks with the Director to know that his philosophy was to give everyone his chance. If they did well, fine. If they didn't, fine too. He judged no one. He called it respecting one's ''free will.'' He wouldn't check up on Ariosto as he'd certainly never checked up on Rimini. All he did, and he did it every day, was tour the port on foot to make certain there were no papers and dog messes on the ground, that the quays remained free of bikes or anything that broke the sweep of his eye from where he stood at the entrance. He gave the yachtsmen what they wanted, which was a clean port where they could bring their wives and kids for a carefree afternoon. Yet he was so unassuming that Boyd had never noticed him before the incident with Bernard.

Guy shook his head. ''Boyd. Boyd. Léonard is the biggest crook of them all. The others are amateurs compared to him.'' The boy just gaped. ''Have you ever seen pictures of his country house or the house he had built in the hills above the Customs? Did you know he had an airplane and two boats and he *owned* the berths where they were moored?''

''But he sold it all...''

''When he got religion, he sold it all. But to *get* it in the first place, he had to steal it. Believe me, no one in this part of France makes that kind of money. They may *inherit* it. They may *import* it from elsewhere.

But not earn it, and certainly not *here*. The region's too poor, except for services like banks and those who cater to tourists."

"And he sold it all to make amends…"

"He sold some for his sect and salted the rest away for a rainy day. He's crazy but not *that* crazy"

"Not *crazy* crazy."

"As wacky as a loon, sonny. But not enough to refuse an envelope stuffed with bills when a contractor wants to be chosen to raise the height of the dike, which they're going to do next year. Or repair the quays, which is coming up soon too. And that's *now*. At the beginning he took graft from the entire *construction of the port*. He was in from day one. A plane's expensive to buy but more expensive to keep up. So are boats, as we both know."

"So he, Carlo, Ariosto…"

"No, he wouldn't trust Ariosto to know what's going on. He wouldn't give that prick the time of day. Léonard does his stealing on *his* level, and Ariosto does his on his petty-shit level, and never the twain shall meet."

"And Goldoni?"

"I don't know. I'd guess he has a finger in everyone's pie. At least he's…" They were interrupted by Doctyor Saramago and Laure. As usual when the doctor arrived, Guy dropped everything to be of service. Guy, too, knew on which side his bread was buttered.

Son-of-a-bitch, thought Boyd to himself. He spread out on the prow, watching the boats come and go, his mind mauling over what he'd learned. So much of it could be put to good use.

Suddenly he became aware of eyes on him. He focused on an outgoing boat of extraordinary beauty, a wood hull, teak decks and pine masts, the *Trivia*. There were two girls and four boys on board, three of which were scurrying about taking in the fenders or setting out the sails. The fourth was staring directly at Boyd. It was Eric Navarre.

CHAPTER FORTY-FOUR

Phil

The distance that separated Cap Martin from Port Beausoleil was perhaps negligible in miles, yet as impermeable as the former Berlin Wall for the inhabitants of the affluent enclave. To the West lay civilization in the form of Monaco, with its clean and crimeless streets, surveillance cameras and myriad banks, boutiques and services catering to the affluent. To the East lay Menton and its retired middle classes, a sleepy bulwark before chaotic and politically unfathomable Italy, and its hordes of illegal immigrants from every part of the globe. Cap Martians preferred the ports of Monaco for their yachts. Less bourgeois inhabitants like the Gaillards marked their difference by using Cap d'Ail. No one would voluntarily choose Port Beausoleil with the parvenu, mannerless Italians, Italians identical to the gardeners, constructors, plumbers and masons the Cap Martians employed. "Our niggers," as Phil Navarre had put it, in the same way that Americans were the niggers of super-rich Italians. Boyd had recognized the boat Eric had been sailing on as that owned by the proprietor of the Manhattan Disco, for whom making--and not wasting--money, not the prestige of a port, was the unique criteria of success.

Climbing the road leading to Cap Martin, he thought with nostalgia of the two months at the Gaillards'. There wouldn't be Fédéric, of course, but there wouldn't be Sylvie either. He'd have to contend with Marie, but if he began to use his head for once, and took advantage of his assets, then perhaps he would inveigle his way back into the lap of the family he had never ceased to love. But first he'd visit Eric Navarre to get the lay of the land. He knew Eric hated him because of Frédéric, and what had happened that night in the car at Genoa, but after four years perhaps enough water had passed under the bridge to initiate a fresh approach. He was at the end of his tether, at the very extremity of France, he reminded himself still again--should he be unable to retreat in the direction of Cap Martin, there would be nowhere else left to him. He hadn't seen the *Trivia* return, probably during his sleep. Now on the doorstep to Maître Navarre's superb house he made a silent prayer that Eric Navarre, and not Phil, would be at home.

It was Phil who opened the door and led him into the sitting room where a huge bay window opened onto the sea to the south and southwest, and Monaco to the west and northwest. Overstated Monte Carlo, he thought to himself as he sat on the sofa facing the window, where everything was sparkle, expense and disappointment, just like the royals and their children, just like the Olympic swimming pool giving onto the harbor with its magnificent yachts, scene of the yearly Monaco Grand Prix. For months Boyd had sought the occasion to swim there, only to find, when the moment came, that it was filled with *salt* water. What was more common to the coast than salt water? Yet it accurately symbolized the place, all tinsel, all fake.

On the large screen of a television lodged between the window and a wall, a corrida was beginning. Three matadors entered, on whose heels heavy-set banderilleros, as haughty as aging Don Juans, affected the struts of their masters the matadors, from whose ranks they had been excluded through lack of talent. They were followed by mounted picadors, as fat as sumos, armed with long lances. Certain matadors, such as El Cordobés, were magnificent in their bravura and bravery. The excellence of these youths was somewhat diluted by another brand of matador, has-beens who gained in weight what they had lost in agility, their ballooning stomachs and slumping buttocks made more derisible still by an accentuated barnyard rooster strut whose grotesqueness was evident to all but the most loyal aficionados, aging matrons who appreciated the Valentino-style regards and padding at the confluent of the thighs, augmented yearly in compensation of their declining virility. Boyd thought with a smile of the elderly actor who had said to Garbo, herself old, "With age my private parts are shrinking." To which the Divine replied, "If only I could say the same for mine." The four years since he had last seen a corrida, seated next to Madame, had done nothing to alter its hypnotic effect.

Phil had turned off the sound, no doubt when Boyd rang the doorbell. Corridas were forbidden on French television, except for the regional Channel 3 which had the permission to broadcast them throughout the South, where bullfighting was a tradition. There were other exceptions, televisual or not, permitted in some regions while proscribed throughout the rest of the country. Ringdoves could be massacred in the Landes but were protected elsewhere from slaughter, and in Corsica twenty-one gendarmes had been assassinated, another kind of non-regulated hunt, without a single murderer being apprehended. In the Gangster Kingdom--called the Island of Beauty in a governmental effort to sweet-talk the thugs--the law of *omertà* reduced the population--if they wished not to be shot down on their doorsteps--to an insular form of swaggering bondage, swaggering in the sense that some islanders, like lesser bullies, showed their balls by cowing the summer crop of tourists.

He accepted the orange juice Phil offered, but without the gin Phil poured liberally into his. Boyd didn't want to mix alcohol with the two valiums he had swallowed to calm his nerves before leaving the *Denis*. The visit was in itself stressing, but the boy felt ill at ease due to the sudden disappearance of Guy. He knew the man was incapable of sleeping in a bed that wasn't his own. In that he resembled his dog Charlie who spent his nights fornicating--just like his master--but invariably returned at dawn to drop onto his blanket in the cockpit. The unique time Guy had slept elsewhere was when the boat had become infested with Charlie's fleas.

Phil placed the glass on the coffee table, and then dropped onto his side of the sofa, sinking into folds hardened and stained by spilled drinks, spotted by ash and cigarette burns. He hadn't shaved. Boyd asked how he was feeling, an inescapable question as the boy, lost in his polo and corduroys, was so pale and wasted that only a hypocrite could have avoided it. The scar of his harelip--a gorge rendered more pallid by the black stubble--joined the torn skin of his chin and throat, vestiges of the

Casino thrashing. Boyd knew it continued uninterrupted from the buttoned collar to his belly. "Certainly not as well as you."

Outwardly Phil found Boyd unchanged, the same uneasy smile bent on seduction, the same voice, young and hesitant, green and nasal, unique in its high pitch and absence of resonance, an immature voice he had never succeeded in placing. But the eyes had changed, once so obsequious, now dark and lifeless. "Papa never understood why I burned the candle at both ends."

"Had you listened, you might have been spared more suffering."

"More well-worn platitudes. I'd forgotten what an inexhaustible source you are. Anyway, I did listen and that's the problem. I had seen Papa's doctor friends congratulate cancer victims on their regain of health, literally hours before they kicked off. Born liars. So to make sure they weren't giving me a load of cock and bull when they said I was okay, I listened in on the upstairs extension while Dad called around the country to specialists, untiringly repeating my symptoms and invariably obtaining the same prognosis: Irreversible heart damage. Of course, I could have tacked on a couple more years had I heeded the warnings. But can you tell me to what good? On the other hand, the hell Eric and I raised will go into the annals of Cap Martin."

The matador made several passes with the cape before directing the bull towards the edge of the arena where it was presented to the picador who, from the height of his mount, plunged the lance into its neck in an attempt to weaken and disorient the animal, stripping it of it ardor, metamorphosing a valiant, spirited beast into an agonizing wreck, too confused--aficionados said to proud or noble--to hurl out its sufferance.

"Where is your dad?"

"After mother died he retired. He's at our apartment in Paris, with somebody else he's apparently too ashamed to present to us. Anyway, he'll never introduce her to me because he knows I'll kick her ass out of here." Boyd had a faint memory of meeting Madame Navarre once or twice. He knew she had been bedridden after an automobile accident.

The banderilleros entered the arena with mincing little steps, spinning on themselves, each hand armed with a new surprise for the bull in the form of barbed sticks ornamented with ribbons. They jumped, whirled, did midair entrechats, as a prelude to plunging the banderillas into the hump of the neck, heedless of the enraged eyes of the beast, or the gaping mouth, sucking in all the air its lungs were capable of inhaling.

"And Michel Canton?" he asked, to change the subject.

"Went out in a blaze like our Frédéric, albeit without the aid of a smooth-tongued Judas beckoning him to the site of his martyrdom." It was then Phil remembered the last conversation he had had at the hospital with Boyd, the flaying of claws and Boyd's ludicrous attempts to bite with his wired-up jaw, the male nurses strapping him down and the doctor sewing up, still again, the fresh damage to Phil's face. "It's for me you've returned to Cap Martin, isn't it? You were wondering how it was you'd left your good friend Phil still breathing, after doing such a good job on Sultan and that other pigeon, Frédéric." It was an eventuality that didn't seem to intimidate Phil Navarre.

"What happened to Michel Canton?"

"What happens to all Cap Martin boys. His motorcycle came out second-best against a car, which converted Michel into a thin line of crimson 500 yards long."

"I thought he was into Porches."

"There should be a sign added to all the others along the highway, cautioning motorists to be on the lookout for irresponsible Cap Martian kids on their bikes, like the signs at deer crossings." Phil kept back tears and was obliged to hold his sides in an effort to lessen tremors that pulled against the sutures closing up his chest. He had recently had a second intervention but didn't want Boyd to know about it. He would say nothing more about Michel, a friend who had been a second brother, with whom he had shared all the firsts of life's experiences, who had lived for his buddies, and who had known as much about avarice and egoism as he had about the dark face of the moon. All the shutters of all the homes in Cap Martin were closed following the news of his passing, and remained closed until after the funeral, when Madame Canton ordered her own open.

Boyd hadn't forgotten a moment of his acquaintance with Michel Canton, as blind as a mole. He supposed he hadn't been wearing his glasses at the time. "And Alain?"

"Alain Canton married someone he knew in school, a girl you never met as she was off teaching in the islands the summer you were here. He's had two boys. Cap Martians always have sons."

"And Jean-Charles?"

"He has a bureau in Nice that he runs like a potentate, giving out orders and cracking the whip when his employees don't jump fast enough. He really fooled us. He married a divorcee who wears jeans and western-style shirts, looks twice his age, a woman he treats as an equal, pretty rare in these parts, although it's true he was never really one of us."

"I'm sorry I didn't know the Cantons better," said Boyd, picturing Michel knocking into the furniture. He thought of Alain's gauche invitation to participate in the 'festivities' in the garden, behind the parking lot. "And the Gaillards?" he asked, as casually as possible.

"The Gaillards?" Phil looked up, his face blank. "Oh, you don't know what happened after Frédéric was summoned to return home. Madame held out long enough to see Marie married to a nice Spanish kid, a boy she had known off and on since grammar school. Then her heart gave out…" He tried to swallow. "… and that as that. Mr. Gaillard's still working in his pharmaceutical company, trying to ward off bankruptcy. The honey factory went belly up, but that was expected. What else? Frédéric was interred in Madrid, did you know that? And Marie had a son she named Eric.''

''Why this obstinate hatred of me?''

''It was you who had some kind of chip on your shoulder against anyone who wasn't a Gaillard. And all those phony stories you told. You remember the one about some rich bitch who'd sent you a telegram signed only with her initials, inviting you to a bar where she offered to put you up for the summer in a hotel in Biarritz, not far from the hotel where she'd be staying with her husband during their vacation. You said you'd think about it. She gave you a ride home in her chauffeured car, and a blow job under the vigilant eyes of the driver, as a kind of down payment on what was to come.''

''And you thought, 'That poor little lying fucker...'''

''No, I thought how little I knew about the world. I thought that if I couldn't understand this young Yank, how could I hope to understand others.''

''Yeah, well, Frédéric told me about the first time you Peeping Tommed your sister...''

''Are you kidding, she was checking *me* out,'' he said, the pain cutting off an incipient laugh.

''What do the doctors say about your condition?'', Boyd asked as Phil filled his glass still again with orange juice and gin. Boyd hadn't touched his own.

''That I have as much chance as an ant in a piss bowl. That would be secondary if I could get my pecker working.''

''Aren't you under medication?''

''Sure.''

''Doesn't the alcohol aggravate it?''

''Sure, but I like a good race. This one's between delirium tremens, lung cancer and the rest...'' It was evident he was betting on the rest. ''Now that we've got it straight that it was for me you've made the trip to Cap Martin, perhaps I could find out why?''

''Wrong,'' said Boyd rising. He walked over to the bay window and stared out. ''First, I was passing through. Second, I wanted some news about the Gaillards. That's it.''

''The Gaillards were curious about you too,'' said Phil. ''After the hospital you just evaporated.''

''I guess I had a lot to live down.''

''Whatever happened to that boy who killed your son?'' some relation or other would ask the Gaillards while they took in the late afternoon sun in the folding chairs on the lawn.''

Boyd's features hardened. He wondered for how much longer he'd take it. ''You haven't told me about Sylvie,'' said Boyd, again to change the subject.

''She joined up with Serge Carrière. Now as you may know or not, and who gives a damn, the Carrières are one of the twenty richest parvenu families in France, and one of the sons is a handsome rascal named Serge who sells hot dogs and fries from a trailer on the beach to the summer tourists. Preferring the company of humble surfers, and their restricted circle of the sleek and handsome, his family told him to fuck off and be a black sheep elsewhere. The elsewhere was the beach of Hossegor. Having a taste for common crust in place of caviar, he let his hair go sun-yellow and his skin mahogany and went through all the pussy that young body could straddle, and believe me, he had one strong body. Then along comes Sylvie whose lips had caressed the masts of, let's say, a thousand ships. So one night around a beach fire, when the surfers and their groupies were encouraging each other to attain summits of ardor and endurance, he came on--literally--Sylvie. For the first time in his life he knew what it was to have his nuts pumped dry, and his brain too, I suppose, because marriage followed, and a child after that, or rather the kid and then the marriage. The parents of the young stud refused to sponsor the wedding until Alain Canton volunteered to be best man, thanks to which Serge's family made its entry into real society. Now Sylvie takes care of the household while hubby resumed some pretty heavy oat sowing.''

''Mamma Navarre never washed your mouth out with soap?''

''She always knew that most of what I said was trumped up shit. Guys who are getting theirs don't need to crow about it. With a face like mine I'd be pretty much out in the cold if it hadn't been for my brother and a great bunch of guys like the Cantons. That's why what you said, too, was so suspicious. You're a fabulist, not a doer. I'm a doer that fate condemned to become a fabulist. Your coming here was the darkest misfortune to ever hit Cap Martin. Everything you touch whither and dies.''

''I didn't have to spend two months here, I was invited. It's not as if I hadn't somewhere else to go.''

''Here you were cared for like a prince. Fed the best sole from Mr. Gaillard's fishing net. A damsel devoted to your comfort every waking hour. I even saw Madame enter your room one time with your freshly cleaned laundry, even your underpants were ironed, for the love of God.''

''Frédéric didn't share your opinion of me.''

''What Frédéric wanted was a pal to go bar crawling. You were the kind of doll a girl likes to put under glass and disrobe in the privacy of her room. A guy wouldn't go too near you because you're so full of yourself. Guys like to feel comfortable around each other. They don't like someone who's always preening and detached from the band, someone who's cut himself off from the others through a vague sentiment of superiority. And then, you were unbending. You never fell in with what the group wanted. Like those ridiculous exercises you insisted on doing on the beach every morning, showing off to a bunch of guys who didn't give a shit."

"I wasn't unbending with Frédéric."

"You had to bend because Frédéric couldn't devote himself to you fulltime. He had other friends to see to, and with friends there's a certain amount of give and take--I tell you this because I'm certain it's something you've never quite understood. You were for everything Frédéric was for, and against everything we wanted. If Jean-Charles suggested going to the Manhattan for a chicass, you'd find some pretext for having something else to do. 'Yeah, but I just remembered, Mr. Gaillard wants me to help him untangle some line' or some such crap. 'Oh, sure', we all said politely to please Frédéric, but no one was taken in. You would just not bend. What little authority you had would be lost if you gave ground, so as usual you went your way, and we went ours. And you just *loved* to suffer. I'll bet every afternoon alone on the beach, after Marie gave up accompanying you, was a kind of Garden of Gethsemane, in which you waited for the cock to crow three times so you could assure yourself over and over that you had been, were being and would always be betrayed by everyone who pretended to care for you. You wore the stigmata, one for Marie who abandoned you on the beach, one for Frédéric who preferred his buddies, one for Monsieur who obliged you to spend hours on the Zodiac, under the stifling sun, one for Madame that you suspected of being polite for the sake of her daughter. And between your ribs was a fifth, caused by Scot and Sultan, that you disposed of because you probably thought they too had turned on you on purpose."

He began to weep, silently. "Frédéric was really one of a kind. He and Michel. If you were only capable of understanding friendship you'd know what swell guys they were. Oh how I hate you and God for your indifference. For you fucking, callus, untouchability." Yet as Phil had himself said, Boyd too suffered. The loss of Frédéric, of Denis and Philippe, Yves Brun and Laurent. This boy had nothing to teach him as far as suffering went.

"And Mr. Gaillard is in Madrid?"

"He knew nothing about business. He returned a while back to tell everyone how he'd maneuvered to buy back the worthless stock of the pharmaceutical company he'd founded. The people who owned the junk had probably been unable to believe their ears. Now he's floundering in the middle of financial extinction, and like a wounded bird he's fluttering his wings and trying to rise from the dust."

"And your brother, Eric?" Finally, to the reason for his visit.

'Eric's in Corsica. He rang me from St. Florent and told me about seeing you. That's why I wasn't surprised to find you on my doorstep.''

''You didn't want to go with him?''

''My moving days are over. But he went with some good friends, one the owner of the Manhattan Disco where we've dropped a fortune over the years. They're guys who'd do him or me any favor. But, alas, they all seem to have in common a concern for my personal welfare which would prevent them from accomplishing the one thing I'm now most in need of. And because Father knows a lot of lawmen and lawyers and stuff, it would be unfair to put their futures in danger to meet my immediate needs.''

''You don't need anyone to help you pull a trigger, if it's that kind of favor you're talking about. That takes three kilos of pressure, I've read. Opening the door for a visitor takes six, I imagine, which gives you a comfortable reserve. If you're asking me to *find* the weapon, you're out of luck. Even air pistols are forbidden in France.''

''Father's study is through that door. Inside you'll find a rack with everything from a 410 to a 30/30.''

''So?''

''So I can't do it alone.''

''Christ!'' said Boyd, returning to the secure confines of the sofa. ''You remind me of a student I had at the University of Paris. He'd been accepted to E.N.A., the French Harvard, he was... You remember Mario? He was handsomer than Mario, if you can believe it, and his big problem was whether to enter E.N.A. or take a year's leave to prepare for the summer Olympics. That tells you the fantastic specimen he was. Then one day he says to me, 'I can't be alone for more than a few hours. Without my buddies, I go crazy.' You wouldn't believe the pity I felt for him. He couldn't be alone. *I've* been alone since the day my mother died. And now you can't be alone long enough to end it all. Well, tough titty. I'm no friend of yours as you've made abundantly clear, and I'm sorry you're sick. But like your friends I, too, don't want to wind up in prison either.''

''That's not possible. I'm by myself here. You dropped in without even being invited. No one knows you're here or anything about you. And I don't want you to *pull* the trigger. I just don't want to be alone when it happens.''

''*Jesus H. Christ. Why* does this sort of thing have to fall on me? You accuse me of every sin in the book, everything from an ass licker to a *murderer.* And now I'm supposed to ... help ... you ... out? One of us *is* definitely crazy.''

''You'll help me out as you helped out Scot and Sultan. Because I'll always be on your tail for what you did to Frédéric...''

''I DID NOTHING TO FRÉDÉRIC. I did nothing to Scot or Sultan either.'' He got up to leave.

"Help me Boyd. It won't cost you anything. You don' have to look. Just be with me while I go through with it. Please."

"And if you turn the son-of-a-bitch on me?"

"Listen, I don't have a choice. For me it's now or maybe never. With you gone, it would be never. And anyway, we both know you're going through more hell alive. One would have to be more of a Samaritan than me to grant you the instant release at the end of my dad's revolver."

"*You* must be going through hell to have to beg me."

"I don't want to be dragged back to that hospital and opened up another time. What's a day or a week or a few months more to me? I've lost it all, my best friends and those for whom I'm just a stone around the neck, my mother."

"There's Eric for Christ's sake. How would he feel if you followed in your mother's steps? And he *loves* you." A joy, Boyd knew, forever beyond his reach.

"Eric's well off where he is. He's already sacrificed part of his personal life for his brother, never cruising unless there was something in it for Phil, never accepting an invitation unless good-old Phil was included, never setting up house with a girl because he'd have to abandon brother Phil. I'm certain that's why he didn't wed Mary Gaillard either, although they were meant for each other since kindergarten. If Marie hooked up with the Spanish boy it's because she wanted her mother to have grandchildren before she died, and she succeeded too, just. As for me, I've had more than enough of being a ball and chain around everyone's leg. I'd have stuck it out if Mom had stuck it out, God knows *she* needed me. Or maybe even Madame Gaillard. I don't know, those sickly cow eyes could turn me to butter. But now there's no reasonable choice. Eric's left, and I want him to have his chance at a normal life."

The bull, harpooned by the banderilleros, charged the muleta. The first time Boyd had seen a matador gorged severely enough to be hauled off to the hospital, he had assumed the bull had won the right to live. Great, then, was his surprise when the wounded matador was replaced by one of his companions, who strutted into the arena like a rooster among hens, his chin thrust out in the firm intention of wrecking vengeance. Boyd was more astonished still by the encouragement of the crowd, as resolute as the matador on seeing that the bull got the ultimate chastening.

"I don't see exactly what my role is in this thing."

"In the study there's a 22 target pistol. I used to practice with it and so I know how it works."

Boyd couldn't analyze his feeling of calm. Was it due to the valium, although he had doubled the dose before without this impression of serenity, or was it that the situation seemed so conform to his conception of what the end should be, when, on the scale of survival, one weighed the for and the against? And when the outcome was so clear, as at this moment, one was perhaps lifted to a higher level of perception, where one was granted the calm needed to act. After all, what was suicide, if not the simple anticipation of the inevitable? He entered the study, weighing the alternatives in his mind. How could he be legally charged with abetting a suicide if the firearm was already there? Was he responsible for someone turning a gun against himself, before he had time to intervene? ''He told me he wanted to show me his new toy. I just brought it to him!'' And who would even know he'd been there?

The study was beautifully done in wood paneling, with books interspersed with framed photos, law degrees, rifles, and several chess sets, a room Boyd could imagine giving up his boat for. The 22 was in a thin wooden box, the form of the gun embossed on the cover. He returned to the sitting room.

''And if tomorrow what's irreparable today becomes reparable?'' He laid the case on the arm of the sofa alongside Phil. He regained his place and faced the boy.

''You can only shoot one bullet at a time,'' said Phil, dismissing the question as risible. He pushed a shell into the housing. ''French law is really something. Still, it's better than American law. If I had a real gun maybe I'd be able to take a few people with me. Although the list isn't all that long. A doctor or two and several nurses who treated me like dirt. Others were pretty good. Anyway, if I screw up, did you see how it's loaded?''

''Yeah, you don't have to be all that clever.'' Boyd began to shake. He couldn't believe what he was about to see. Yet he knew the boy was *right*. It was right and it *felt* right. Any jury that could see and hear this kid, alive but cut up like an autopsied corpse, would acquit him. Acquit him because who would want to spend the rest of his life in physical and emotional suffering? No more low blows for him. No more horrors of everyday life, children's throats slit, little girls raped and tortured, stories of sisters getting themselves fucked by their mentally disturbed brothers. ''Have you left a note or something for Eric or your father?''

The boy shook his head. He had taken out the shell to demonstrate the loading once again. But this time the bullet obstinately refused to go into place.

'Eric's going to blame himself. He went to Corsica leaving you alone,'' murmured Boyd.

''I love him and he knows it. And he knows he's not responsible because he knows me. His going away has given me the chance to free myself. That too he knows. But it would be comical if you were blamed, everyone's aware of your feelings about me, and what a vindictive piece of shit you are.''

Boyd turned away from the boy who shifted so easily from being beseeching to insulting, but whose attention, at that moment, was above all riveted to rearming his gun. The matador was giving the *estocade*, the moment the sword penetrated the *morillo* of the neck, a target the size of a fist. As repugnant as he found the killing, he was nonetheless hypnotized by what men called the moment of truth but was, for Boyd, the animal's deliverance. He felt a prickly sensation in the loins when the bull charged the matador at the moment of the sword's penetration, when man and beast were joined in the briefest of embrace, exposing the matador to the jagged horns. If the sword were deflected by the spinal column and the matador was obliged to try again, his chances of being wounded or killed approached ever closer to those of the bull. But this time the matador, amazingly quick for his corpulence, plunged the sword into the neck up to the handle, executing the animal with such exceptional fluidity that the crowd rose in acclamation. The man turned his back on the animal in a gesture of contempt, and strutted away, the gold tissue of his suit of lights tarnished with blood. But more exceptional still was the bull's reaction. Ignoring his assailant, he began to haltingly circle the arena, along the periphery, its head high. The crowd remained standing, and although the sound had been cut, Boyd knew the people were looking on in silence. What nobility, some were thinking, what courage. Human sentiments for a beast on the threshold of death, its flanks gasping like a bellows, the tongue protruding from the gaping mouth, long thick filaments of bloody saliva descending to the earth, the muzzle obstructed by snot, the buttocks caked with shit. For an animal that had only known peaceful fields of high grass, what conclusion would he have drawn from his new destiny, had he acquired the supreme intelligence of man?

''Anyway,'' said Phil, ''I'll never have to see your kisser again.'' He placed the barrel against his head. ''For me, as for you, this is the end,'' he nearly shouted, and fired. Boyd rose from the sofa, grabbing his head, his ears throbbing. It was too fast. The boy hated him too much to even share but the minimum of his last moments, just what he was absolutely obliged to. The body had been lifted by the impact and had fallen across the sofa, twitching and pumping blood through the temple. A feeling of wetness around the crotch made him plunge his hand to see if he'd been splattered. The clear liquid on his palm was urine. He closed the door behind him and straddled his bike. No matter what anyone will ever say about me again, he murmured to himself as he peddled up the lane from the compound, leaving Cap Martin for the last time, there was this one moment when I did something totally selfless, something that was finally good. (16)

BOOK V

CHAPTER FORTY-FIVE

A Dad and his Boy

He was stopped at the end of the lane leading from the Navarre compound by the police barring the route. He showed his passport, the content of which was scrupulously registered on a clipboard. When he asked what was going on, he was told ''Just routine'' by a CRS, the French SWAT.

Now they'll know I was with Phil, he fretted as he headed down the hill overlooking the sea, dark and increasingly churned up by an east wind, while to the northeast storm clouds eclipsed the Italian Alps. Entering Menton, at a crossing not far from a junior high school, a group of people was laying wreaths. He recognized the guardian Christophe and pulled up to ask him what had happened.

''One of those African dictators is in residence at Cap Martin, and in a hurry to see him his ambassador hit two kids at the crossing, killing both. He was doing 100 in a 30-mile school zone. But he said he's sorry,'' Christophe went on, squinting back tears, before driving away under the immunity of his CD plates. ''In the Southeast it's being swiped by a vehicle when you're a kid or killed on a motorcycle when you're an adolescent,'' continued the port guardian. ''I'll buy my boy a car when he grows up, if he'll promise to stay off motorcycles.'' To increase profits, sidewalks were reduced or eliminated to make room for buildings or roads, thought the boy as he continued on, sickened by the resultant sacrifice of two children. At that moment in Paris the residents of the 16th District, the wealthiest, were in the streets demonstrating again a law that would allocate more financial aid to the kids of the poor and less to those of the rich. How was such lack of civism conceivable? he wondered, shaking his head. The French debt was colossal and climbing, but who gave a damn that it would one day necessarily fall to their children to mop up? Did another animal exist that was less protective of its offspring? he asked himself, in despair and disgust.

He got back to find the Little Quay had been emptied of boats, except for the *Denis* at its place at the very end. What in the fuck's going on? he wondered. A folded and stapled blue message slip, taped to his balcony, requested his presence at his convenience in the Director's office. He went to shower first, crossing paths on his way back with Michel, behind the wheel of his bread truck. The baker looked wrung out. He returned the boy's hello with a limp wave, without stopping. So what does he expect, Boyd thought, his brain already sluggish from the two valiums he had just taken, his nervous system overloaded with the images of Phil sinking into the sofa, Christophe on the verge of crying and the African dictator, irritated by the delay of his ambassador, pacing up and down in his palatial residence. The baker. The fucker got fucked by the woman he was himself trying to fuck, he thought, showering. Yet in the long run he'd certainly be better off than the surgeon Saramago, who'd spend the rest of his life chained to someone he could no longer stand, all because he didn't want to fork over half of his property in a divorce.

As he entered the Third Floor he remarked that the lights had already been turned on due to the darkening sky. Through the bay windows he saw a black spiral of clouds rising majestic and ominous over the sea to the southeast. The Director was seated at his desk, his face partially shadowed by a lamp trained on a sheet of paper. As he sat opposite the man, he remembered Léonard's promise to loan him something that would help in his quest for the Truth. He told Léonard about passing through the crossroads, the wreaths, and the CRS stationed outside the dictator's compound to protect him from demonstrations. The man looked concerned as was his way, but reminded the boy again that he shouldn't be overly disturbed by such events.

''In other words, the world's falling apart and one should keep a clear head,'' said Boyd, whose own head felt thick and unresponsive. The last words of Phil were engraved in his brain forever: *You're totally sterile.*

''Exactly,'' he answered, as if the boy were finally piercing the obscurity. ''The lack of morality nowadays, the quest for money, the refusal to take time for reflection, means that nothing will change until there is a final cataclysm. Only then will people be *forced* to rethink their present existence, to put things into *spiritual order.*''

The conversation waxed and waned as the man gave example after example of why such a revolution was necessary, a near carbon copy of Marc the electrician's beliefs, while Boyd relived again and again the last moments with Phil. *What a vindictive piece of shit you are.*

''That is the purpose of the small group I'm a member of,'' Léonard was saying. ''We're trying to awaken as many people as we can *before* such a calamity so they can be saved *during* the calamity. But we can only help if *asked* to help. The first move *must* come from the person seeking that help. It's all a question of *free will.* Man is now complete. He has just to look within himself. I'd like you to read this.'' He handed Boyd the paper he'd been looking at. The boy's powers of concentration were such that it took what seemed hours to get through the several lines. It was the translation of a Buddhist text about an Indian god who had amassed all the secrets of the world and was looking for a safe place to hide them from desecration. He looked and looked until coming across the safest, the most inaccessible place of all, his own soul. ''So you see, we need only look within ourselves to find the answers,'' exclaimed Léonard triumphantly. ''Like invisible radio waves that we can be trained to intercept.''

When Boyd commented that the story was indeed of interest, the Director rose to make him a photocopy of the text. He came back with a paper twice the size of the original. On his face was an expression of angelic beatitude. ''I put this in the machine and look what came out! I'd been photocopying other things before you arrived, but only on the *normal* format. Things like this are happening to me *all the time*.'' He shook his head in wonder at the miracle, a script now twice the size of the original. Like Yves Brun, whose stories of sea sickness and sailboat dimastings could go on forever, Léonard then launched into examples of mysterious happenings he was daily witness to, while Boyd thought of Phil, certain he'd be implicated. *Everything you touch withers and dies.*

''...which are encouragements for us to open our hearts and reach out with our thoughts,'' concluded Léonard. Boyd remembered something Guy had mentioned. ''Once I suggested that Martial invite Commander Cousteau here for an honorary dinner. After all, Monaco, where his boat is stationed, is our neighbor, and Martial has always been a strong supporter of Cousteau's anti-pollution initiatives. And just think of the excitement of having the *Calypso* anchored outside the Port of Beausoleil. He told me he'd already tried to contact Cousteau mentally, by sending him *spiritual* thought messages that the Commander had not deigned answer, leading Martial to the conclusion that the famous explorer didn't merit such an honor.'' *How I hate you for your indifference.*

The Director paused for a long moment, studying the boy. Finding him worthy of a revelation, he took the plunge. ''The earth was discovered by a people from another planet 60,000 years ago. It was they who founded the Egyptian Dynasties. This higher intelligence is here to help us, but *only* when we make the effort to seek it out.'' The painting of Jesus in the adjoining room, holding a space helmet in one hand, the pyramids in the distance, became clear. Boyd thought of one of Kurt Vonnegut's books on similar stellar hijinks, although he was in no mood to laugh while Léonard went on about this invisible force that commonly communed with Mankind. ''In fact,'' Léonard added, ''they inhabit the bodies of many of those around us.'' There may have been the hint of something irreverent in the boy's next question--when he asked if Guy or even his dog Charlie could be possessed by these spatial body snatchers-- because Léonard signaled the end of the conversation by suddenly rising, adding that those who received the Word--and then failed to respect it-- would be the first purged. What a strange choice of verbs, Boyd thought, leaving the room. *You're nothing but scorched earth.*

Carl Goldoni beckoned him to enter his office, making a sign for him to close the door. "You look as white as a sheet," he laughed in his light-hearted way, as he tapped the arm of a chair next to his, inviting Boyd to be seated.

"You would too if you'd just learned that an interplanetary catastrophy is coming that will destroy most of humanity except the Director and his acolytes and a few hundred Martians, and I'm not talking about *Cap Martin Martians.*"

"Don't take that seriously," smiled Goldoni, who had been informed by various sources that Boyd was sticking his nose into port affairs. Why Goldoni would bother to worry himself about what Boyd thought of him or Léonard may have derived from the fact that Boyd worked at the Ministry of Finance in Paris, which was responsible for not only taxes, but was also the ministry that controlled the French Gendarmerie. Like Aldo who was nice to Boyd because he thought he had the ear of Léonard and Harbormaster Ariosto, Goldoni may have attributed powers to Boyd that could, like a lowly seedling, develop into potential danger. Boyd had even bragged about certain contacts he'd had with the sons of a couple of ministers, without revealing that they'd been basically just fleeting sexual encounters, although he did also give English lessons to a few children of politicians, one of whom tried to impress Boyd with how powerful he was by phoning directly to President Giscard d'Estaing, a call Giscard's secretary hadn't put through, pretexting that the president was in a conference, probably one of a dozen fatuous attempts she received per day.

Goldoni got right to it. "I hope you're not taking seriously any rumors of graft in this port?"

"Are you kidding? From what I've heard Ariosto is up to his ears in fraud."

Which made Carlo grin. "No. *Other* rumors...."

Boyd knew he meant Léonard and Carlo's personal involvement with Léonard, but not wanting to risk his expulsion from the port or the decision cancelling the 4,000-franc reduction on the cost of his berth, he simply answered, "You've got me stumped...."

"Okay, no problem," the accountant said in a tone that clearly inferred he didn't believe a word. Like Boyd himself, Goldoni was an artless liar. "Anyway, whatever's eating you is making you look like shit."

"It's true a lot of people here seem involved in graft..." added Boyd as a partial confession that he knew more than he was admitting, signaling to Goldoni that it was best to get off his back.

''Not me,'' cut in Carl, standing. The diversion was clearly over, the boy dismissed like a servant caught stealing. He rose, blushing, and left, for the last time, the Third Floor.

.

On the way down he found Ariosto's door--closed when he'd gone up--now open. The man had clearly learned of the boy's visit to the Director, and wanted to know what was up.

''What happened to the boats on my quay?'' Boyd asked without preliminaries.

''You want to know too much,'' said the Harbormaster, who knew so little about what went on in the port that the little he did know he kept to himself.

''Christ I'm glad I don't live in a world like yours, tiny and closed, where you take the simplest inquiry for a potential danger.''

''You're the one who lives in a narrow world. You hardly even leave your boat, reading and doing those exercises you can't even get right...'' Boyd didn't need Ariosto to tell him he should be doing more with his life than talking nonsense with Carl, Léonard or the Harbormaster, but at that moment--with images of Phil's temple gushing blood, two kids in the morgue, Léonard spouting Martian shit and Goldoni wondering how much he knew about graft in the port--he couldn't think of a single reason why he should even bother anymore.

''...while I was already in the navy at sixteen,'' pouted the Harbormaster, making him look nearly that young and, yes, Boyd had to admit, extraordinarily handsome. Like most French, Ariosto retained the innate arrogance of his people, a people who believed they were the brightest, studied the hardest, were the most logical, and that they possessed, through congenital osmosis, the greatest culture--even those who'd never opened a book or visited a museum. Like Molière's *Le Malade imaginaire*, if you're French ''all gibberish automatically becomes skilful discourse, all stupidity metamorphoses into reason.'' His disrespect for Ariosto was partially due to what he'd seen in visits to his home, where he'd slapped his whale's boy because of his low grades, telling him he wouldn't continue coughing up money for his education if this was the result. Boyd knew the little girl had been first in her class before Ariosto came on the scene. Now she was second from the bottom. In the Ariosto household Ariosto would tell her to do one thing, her mother another. The tearing back and forth reminded Boyd of his youth, which at times made him hate Ariosto as much as his own father. Boyd had once been invited to a dinner at Ariosto's home while his family was away. During the meal they watched the election of Miss France on TV, Ariosto's eyes glued to the screen where the candidates paraded half nude, a scene that evidently brought his stepdaughter to mind. ''Marie jumps between my legs and kisses and touches me. She doesn't know what she's doing but it's troubling." Ariosto had told him that at times he showed himself naked to her and Jean-Henri, as a way of teaching them that there was nothing sinful about the human body. Jean-Henri had certainly looked too hard because he went on to say, gritting his teeth, "That boy had *better* be normal."

Like Goldoni, Ariosto knew that Boyd was bad-mouthing him. "Even in bad ports the Harbormasters are better paid than me," he had once said in his defense. "I've just changed the berths of two yachtsmen who weren't satisfied where they were. For the moment I haven't received anything. Perhaps at Christmas. *Bernard* got a tip, that I saw, and I know he doesn't split it with the other guardians as he should." Boyd knew Ariosto didn't split his, either, with his men. Once in the privacy of his office he had shown Boyd a catalogue from which a rich Italian merchant, in exchange for a favor, had told him he could order whatever he pleased. He had chosen a motor scooter. "I can tell you to your face, I'll take what they give me and do what they want for it. If they give me ten thousand francs, I'll take them, if they give me a million, I'll take that too."

To which Boyd had replied, "A lot of people in the port are talking, and certain guardians are unhappy about being pointed out as thieves, when it's the 'higher ups', as one of them said, who are guilty."

"The guardians are loyal to me."

"They're loyal to their paychecks. You chose them stupid, but they might not remain that way forever." Once Ariosto had shown him a pile of curricula vitae. "You see this c.v.?" he asked, pulling one out of the stack. "This guy's perfect. Military background, so he'll wear a uniform without complaining. Presentable. Has a degree in electricity which would come in handy when dealing with the electrical problems on the quays, *and* he knows stuff about accounting." He flicked the c.v. across the table for Boyd to study. "But one of the first things you learn in life is to *never* hire someone more intelligent than you are." He shook his head, satisfied with himself, "Never."

"Where are the boats on my quay," he again demanded.

"It's not *your* quay. Half the problems we're having in this port is because you *think* it is."

"Come off it. Did Guy move his boat?"

"Mr. Desmoines seems to be having serious trouble with the Internal Revenue Service. I wouldn't be surprised if they took him for everything he's got. In any case, it's none of your business," he purred like a cat that had just disemboweled its prey, evidently happy that someone else was in greater difficulty than himself. But the news, the consequence of Boyd's intervention in Paris, hit Boyd hard. He still repeated his question: "And the other boats?"

"Today's the 1st of September. From now to the end of June no boats are allowed on the Little South Quay. *Yours* shouldn't be there. And if you didn't have special relations with the Director, it wouldn't be. And, I can add, it *won't* be there after the next violent storm blows it onto the rocks, which may be tonight if you've glanced at the barometer.''

''Those kinds of storms come in winter, not in September. I'll be moving it in a week or two, before returning to Paris.'' He suddenly realized that tomorrow, the 2nd of September, was his birthday.

''As you yourself once said to me, things are not always so black and white. A bad storm doesn't necessarily have to wait till winter to please the captain of the *Denis*. At any rate, another time we're going to have a talk about the guardians. Your offensive ways have earned you their…''

''I don't give a fuck about the guardians. If they'd done their job there'd never have been a problem. The *problem,* I've come to realize, is upstairs. For reasons of social conscience the Director won't kick ass. This is a *private* port where the clients should come first. Here they come last because you think they're too weak to unite against you. But you may be in for a surprise. Someone with the time and energy may round up the votes necessary to change the direction of this port, and then, Mister Harbormaster, your butt'll be the first trophy they'll nail to the wall.''

''That'll never happen.''

''If you're so concerned about how the guardians are treated, why don't you really *do* something about it? Every time I ask one of them why he doesn't do his job, he invariably answers that the clients tell him to fuck off.''

''When I complain to the clients about their incivilities, they call the Director and he pulls me over the coals. So what can you do?''

''Then there will be a revolution,'' said the boy at the door. ''Even Léonard knows that.''

''*Mister* Léonard.''

''Oh, God,'' he groaned, beside himself. ''We do need to be saved! From imbeciles and *doormats*.''

''And you can clean up your language if you expect to converse with me.''

''My language is a sign of my disgust,'' he shouted, turning in the stairway to face the Harbormaster. ''The disgust has made me so weary I feel a hundred years old.''

.

Strangely, he left the *Capitainerie* in good humor. The perspective of reigning terror over this band of bums--forcing Ariosto to resign, getting a friend of his at the Ministry to initiate an audit against Goldoni and Léonard--excited him. It was thusly with a smile that he glanced over at the boats tied up in front of the *Capitainerie*, wrecks deserted by, for the most part, Italian owners who couldn't or wouldn't pay the costs for their upkeep. Abandoned as the French abandoned their animals before heading off on vacation, they tossed and rolled in the strong backwash, their hulls knocking against each other for want of fenders, the sterns breaking up against the quay because no one cared enough to distance them by adjusting the bow chain. The place was sinister, and the boy was about to turn away when he spotted the boat without a name, its captain sitting in the cockpit with, quite naturally, a woman, her back to the boy. A large grin on his face, Boyd approached to say hello to Guy. But the glare in the man's eyes as he looked over the woman's shoulder, straight at the boy, brought him to a standstill, icing the blood in his veins. Recognizing the woman, Boyd remembered something Guy had once said to him. ''There are dames who love being handled like the saints they're anything but, others who get off a max by being treated like sluts. One thing's for sure, if I tell a woman she busts my balls and other related classiness, it's because she wants it. And I know she wants it because, without exception, at one moment or another, I've fucked her.'' The woman facing Guy was Colette, and it was exactly in that way he had spoken to her in Thalassa. And then came the sudden realization which made his hair stand on end. Without a shadow of a doubt she had told him who was responsible for his nightmare with the taxman.

.

He was digesting that as he passed in front of Claude's shop. The awning above the lighted bay window was shuddering under the assaults of the mounting wind. Claude was behind the counter, fidgeting with some electrical device. He looked up at Boyd, caught and held in the light as if someone had hit the pause button on a video recorder. He nodded, just perceptively, for him to enter. The boy thought the best defense would be attack.

''You tell Goldoni what I said about Léonard stealing money for his sect!''

''Why?'' he asked lymphatically. Boyd recounted his conversation with the accountant, and his talk with Léonard about the space-age Jesus.

''Did the Director tell you that there are people from another planet among us,'' asked Claude, ''that they're waiting for the Word to go into action?''

''Oh, Christ, *no*. Not you. *You* don't believe that shit. You're not telling me one's in front of me now in the form of an electrician?'' It amused Boyd to think of Claude as a kind of extraterrestrial seducer, sent to recruit women and the weak of mind into the ranks of the Martians.

Yet … the absurdity of Claude's participation into something so absurd was attenuated by the hard fact that in recent history the Solar Sect, of French and Swiss invention, had made headlines by the murders and suicides of its members, among them numerous children. In California twenty adherents of a sect had committed group suicide in order to facilitate their departure from the earth on an interplanetary spaceship, and Jim Jones, the founder of still another sect, had been responsible for the death of 900 disciples in South America. But for Christ's sake, thought the boy, this is France, home of Descartes and Sartre, where people are too educated and logical to consider such madness. For Boyd, just believing in the politics of the French Extreme Right was the limit of the intergalactic void capable of alluring a small, although growing, minority of French cretins. If the members of sects, many of whom were superbly well-educated and wealthy, could fall for such mumbo-jumbo, why not an electrician in a tiny port lost in the southeast of France?

"Did you speak to Léonard about me?" asked Boyd.

"I don't deal with the Director. I pass through Carl."

"Carl only believes in one and one making two!" said Boyd. "He believes in salvation by profit. His god is Mammon. If he's told you anything else, he's leading you around by the nose."

"You know the expression we have in French: 'Don't worry about the straw in your neighbor's eye, before taking care of the log in your own?'" queried Claude. "Before accusing others of blabbing, you'd do well to watch your own betrayal."

"Which means?"

"Guy's in the blackest, deepest shit, and it seems some stoolpigeon in the port is the cause. And Doctor Saramago. The Social Security organized a police raid all along the Côte d'Azur. Fake bills of sale. Excessive pricing. Prostheses of poor quality and sold at several times their value. And thanks to a specific complaint, the good doctor wasn't forgotten. Saramago's looking for you, to bring the accounts up to date, as Goldoni would say. But for that, he'll have to wait in line. You've done nothing but screw up since entering this port. Humiliating some, mocking others, putting your nose there where you'll regret having put it."

"Look Claude. I've had a tough day. My legs are giving out and I just can't stay around and shoot the breeze. But ... I like you personally and want to be your friend. So *please* let's let things lie. I won't put my nose in anything anymore, and everybody will leave me be." He headed for the door, expecting Claude to make a comment. It was evident that the menace inherent in his silence was the only comment he intended to make.

.

Carlo Goldoni, he sneered, hastening his step. Carl was the only normal one among them all. He was pandering to the whole lot, Boyd *y comprit,* to facilitate his making a bundle. There was no doubt that Léonard believed in the crap he preached. At least Claude played an authentic role as avenging angel. Like Boyd, he must have suffered from injustices he wanted to get even for. Maybe he had endured a reverse form of racism by the Tahitians, who didn't much care for the French who ruled them, or he had to bear the stigmata of not knowing his father, or whatever other terrible thing that had corrupted the mind housed in such a perfect body. *Just like me,* admitted Boyd out loud, heading back to the *Denis. We've both drifted into the same dead-end backwater, dumped in with the dregs of society, in this, the anus of France.*

His rattled brain shifted to de Roquette, the old show-off in the dream he'd recounted to Denis, spouting out platitudes like, *Despite everything, there's always a moment of tenderness in life, always at least one.*

He decided to go to bed. Tomorrow he'd figure out who was responsible for what, and what was to be done about it. But it was true that his time in the port had drawn to a definitive end. He'd put himself between some nasty sheets, as the French saying went, and he would now have to extract himself, and quickly.

.

The Little Quay was wet with spume from the gathering waves. As he approached the *Denis* the Custom's PT boat came roaring from its quay and headed out the entrance of the port, violently flipping the *Denis* from side to side. Not a word from the First Floor of the Capitainerie where he could clearly make out Marc's white beard. He gave the PT the finger and jumped into his cockpit and cabin. Over the VHF he yelled to the world listening in on channel 9, the channel used by all the *Capitaineries* in France, that the Aides of Port Beausoleil were an incompetent band of do-nothings waiting for their pensions. He slammed down the receiver and stormed out for a breath of air. There he came nose to nose with Christian Lescot, head of the Gendarme Customs, and six of his gang, all armed with revolvers nestled at their sides, two other Customs' officers left beside the PT, presumably to protect it from the building surge threatening to send it smashing into the quay.

"Are you enough to handle a single American?" Attack, the Guadeloupian had said. "Always attack."

"The non-respect of an official in his line of duty" began the man, his face bled white, a pallor that accentuated the carbuncles around the collar and the acne scars on his cheeks, "is heavily fined." Boyd tried to focus his thoughts. Was this idiot talking about having been given the finger?

"YOU listen," he interrupted, yelling. "There's something you don't know but I'm now going to make clear. Over the past year I've given a morning class at the Ministry of Finance, where a third of my students are from the Gendarme Customs. They have always been my best students. *Two* of them have become *intimate* friends. With one I go horse riding once a month, with the other swimming twice a week. They are going to be *very* unhappy to know there are guys like you in the Customs who do not--What's the word you used? RESPECT--the laws against speeding you're supposed to *enforce.* You may not think those poor specimens in the *Capitainerie* will testify against you, but they'll sell their children and cut the throats of their parents to keep out of the suit I'm going to bring against you and the port. Now, I'm going into my boat and I'm writing to my friends to find out who *exactly* I must contact so people like you, who speed around and then try to threaten people like me, will be revoked. That's *all*."

"He's nuts," one of the recruits murmured.

Another had a firm hold on his pistol, cuddling the holster in his palm, hefting it like a precious ingot, the thumb absently stroking the butt.

"I want to see the papers of this boat," said Lescot, his chin and mouth twitching.

"I have the right to refuse, and you the right to get a judge's order. So go ahead and get it. And I've changed my mind. I'll *call* my friends tomorrow to see what I have to do." He turned and reentered his cabin. Shaking, he went to the porthole to watch Lescot who hesitated a moment before going off to the PT where he exchanged a few words with the two men he'd stationed there, perhaps to bring them up to date. Their evident disapproval seemed to have motivated a change of heart, as Lescot made a movement to return to the *Denis*. But a stronger consideration caused him to stop, turn around, climb aboard the PT, and give orders to shove off.

Shit, shit, shit, the boy said to himself. Will it *never* end? Oh God, please, let it end. His brain was on automatic pilot, the part dealing with affect reduced to reflexes and instinct.

He took two more valiums and got into bed.

.

He fell into a deep sleep in which he found himself in a kind of courtroom. A dead mantis-shaped object was on a table in front of the tribunal, under a blanket, the elbows and knees pushing the material into strange forms and angles, a claw-like foot visible in one corner, a bloated breast protruded in another. Jean-Loup was in the jury, glaring at Boyd with hatred, yet it wasn't Boyd in the prosecution box. Another of the jurors was Yves, and there was Colette, and ... oh God ... that horrible *buongiorno-tutti* woman. Didier from the Swan was there, and Richard le Beau in his silly shorts. The oversized photocopy of the Buddhist Enigma was also on the table. He prayed there were no bad surprises behind one of the closed doors circling the courtroom, no Phil Navarre or Scot. The thing under the cover twitched, frightening the woman next to him into seizing his arm. Oh, Madame Gaillard, he said tenderly in an inaudible voice that came from watery depths, where he saw the blurred face of Laurent, Laurent who had died four years ago, day for day, as Hadrian had died four years after the passing of Antinous. He looked about for Frédéric, in vain. He looked up to the judge's tribunal, far, far overhead, where he discovered the serene face of the space-age Jesus. He was immediately invaded by a sentiment of soothing peace. What ill could possible come to him in the presence of Jesus? Then came the recognition. Jesus was Denis. Now he *knew* he was saved. Everything Léonard had said was in fact true. The face before him was without any doubt possible that of his Savior.

.

The pitching of the *Denis* brought him to consciousness. Perhaps the Custom's PT boat had reentered, perhaps it was the storm whipping up the sea and sending it into the mouth of the port. Nothing was now of importance. Like a flash of lightning he knew what he had to do. It was all at once so clear and evident. Why would he possibly wish to go on as he was, were it not for Denis? What was left for him on the surface of the earth, if not this boy?

He climbed out of his bedding and staggered into the cabin. The boat pitched and tossed with such force he had to sit on the floor to pull on his jeans and sweatshirt. Outside the rain hadn't started, but lightning flared across the Alps, and the very distant explosions of thunder could be heard over the howling of the wind. The *Denis* lurched to and fro, at times within inches of hitting the quay before the mooring line at the prow jerked it away. The boy's brain and body were groggy and heavy, as if he were in a weighted diver's suit of yesteryear. He made his way to the telephone cabin at the U-Marché on foot, too unsure of his head and reflexes to consider taking the bike. *I'll be his servant*, he said, perhaps to himself, perhaps to the raging wind. It's so clear, he marveled. *He won't be able to turn his back on someone who's there for his good.* The first drops of rain began to spot his sweatshirt.

Inside the telephone booth he pulled out his wallet and the little piece of paper he'd stuffed there three years before. He dialed and waited. The phone rang a long time. He lay his head against the cold pain of glass, over which rivulets of meandering streams descended outside. A memory from his youth came to him. He had decided to see the Great Salt Lake up close. There he discovered a flock of pink flamencos with their young. The adult flamencos had a curious way of displacing themselves, one that the boy had first taken for a tic. They would lift a foot, one at a time, and shake it. More amusing still, most of the baby flamencos would assiduously imitate their parents. Then he noticed that rings of salt had formed around the legs of those that weren't copying the others. The rings on some had become so thick that as Boyd approached, they were unable to fly away. It seemed evident to the boy that with the coming of winter, at the moment of their migration, these young were fated to freeze to death. It occurred to him that this too had become his fate. Over time he had become weighed down by the acts he had committed since leaving the hearth of his university. A ring for not understanding Philippe and for maltreating Sylvain, one for Yves Brun and Frédéric, for the old guy on the *Kitty*, his youth, his mama. Locked up within himself, without a guide when he had most needed one, he had become isolated from those who could have shown him the road to survival. At present he too was pinned down. He remembered his arrival on the Norman coast ten years before, the fresh and vivifying air of Cherbourg and, especially, the sentiment of the exquisite future awaiting him. What could he do now, except shake his head at the bewildering deviations events had taken.

"Hello!" came a voice, a woman's, clear and impatient.

"May I speak to Denis, please?"

"Denis isn't here!" Of course he wouldn't be there, thought the boy. Who'd remain in Pau when there were things going on in the world?

"Could you tell me where I can find him please?"

"Listen, it's three in the morning…"

"I know," he lied. "I just got off a boat that's in port for an hour. We shove off again at four. I may not be back for years. Could I please have a number where I can reach him?"

There was silence on the line. The rain battered against the booth with such force that he had to ask her to repeat herself when she came back on. It had sounded like He's in bed, which didn't make sense.

"He's dead! I'm sorry. I'm his sister. I'd prefer not to talk about it. Please. We want to forget."

"How? How?" he asked barely audibly, the receiver pressed into his mouth.

"A terrible illness. Please. Please." The line, too, went dead.

What had he said, *That pussy cost me everything*. What had he said about the pussy? *That's* why he never went in without a net. *Not for me*, he'd said, *it's to protect the girl.* Because for him it was over. And that's why he'd left without saying goodbye. What use was there dragging Boyd through whatever future was left to him?

He walked away from the cabin, his body whipped by rain and wind as he made his way back to the only *Denis* that would always be his. So much could have been avoided if he'd known, he thought. So much hate would have been evacuated. There would have been no reason for any of the things he'd done. He'd have helped the boy. His devotion to Denis would have given him a *direction* for Christ's sake, a reason to live.

At the end of the Little Quay the *Denis* bobbed and tossed like a mustang, *alive*. Through the plastic window the yellow light from inside beckoned. His *Denis* lived and he would enter it, warm in its shelter against the surge that pounded its hull, the rain that pelted its deck, the wind that tore at the mast. He thought of Yves and his son. He pulled himself into the cockpit and backed down the ladder into the cabin, drawing the door home behind him. Home. He undressed and toweled himself dry. There would be Frédéric and Denis, Yves and the son he'd never met, he thought, swallowing the pills a few at a time. He couldn't get over how strange life was. His greatest fear, he now recognized, had been, all along, of being abandoned. He laughed at the thought. He who wanted to be alone, had in reality feared just that, being alone. Now they were waiting to receive him. And who knows, there may be others, Doug perhaps, from the childhood he'd forgotten, and Philippe, especially Philippe. His enemies would be his friends, since he was paying the price of his redemption. He might even discover the moment of tenderness that de Roquette had promised, or come upon he who would help him become, at last, a man. He slipped between his covers, his legs drawn into his chest against the remaining chill of the rain. And, he thought, the pain. He'd been afraid of suffering pain. But he was slipping away, warm becoming warmer. He wondered if Phil would be healed and if he'd have to apologize to the man of the *Kitty*. Or would sleep, gradually enfolding him, take him to a place where he would be, forever, unseeing and unconscious?

He dreamed.

He was asleep on the top bunk in his father's hunting cabin, across from the big black stove with its flayed feet and amber light, warmth emanating from the red coals behind the mica door. On the lake a flock of ducks had settled in for the night. That afternoon he had discovered the dirty playing cards in the medicine chest. The pictures had brought on a great excitation. He smiled at the thought of his new-found power. With adolescence had come immense strength. His limbs, slim and strong, were indefatigable sources of exploits. The right of passage was in harmony with his life, secret and solitary, but with it came knowledge and decision, understanding and hope. He was the master of his mind; his body was a source of steel that would free him as surely as Prometheus shattering his chains. That body, beautiful and potent; that mind, decisive and determined. The sensation of well-being radiated from him as if it were he the center of the universe.

A movement brought him back to consciousness. The memory of the playing cards had made him erect very hard. A hand withdrew itself from the sheets. He opened his eyes. He saw his father turn away from the bunk and move back to the stove, blocking out the light and taking away the heat like a sun drawn into itself by implosion. (18)

FOOTNOTES

1) At that far more innocent time I'd never *ever* heard the words shit or fuck stated orally, not even in my high school or university locker rooms.

2) What was called the Masturbation Panic originated with Simon-André Tissot, 1728-1797, who claimed that the loss of an ounce of semen equaled the loss of forty ounces of blood, a crippling factor that could lead to the loss of eyesight, to diseases and, due to increased blood flow to the brain, insanity, consequences as damning as religious threats of Hell due to the nefarious, unnatural act of self-pollution, the mortal enemy of procreation. In the mid-1850s masturbation was blamed for the corruption of morals, as well as vile thoughts that threatened the salvation of the soul itself, accompanied by the exhaustion of the entire nervous system. Boys were ordered to do physical exercises until they dropped from fatigue, to take cold showers, and fathers were advised to tie up their sons' hands at night. Some surgeons recommended replacing the testicles of masturbators with healthy ones (which could lead to castration because the new testicles were rejected by the body, and death if the surgery was done in unclean surroundings, often the case in those times). Freud himself showed interest in the possibilities of the operation--for others, not himself. (The full life of Tissot can be found in my book *Male Self-Pleasuring*.)

3) This incident, never forgotten, led to my writing, in 2020, *YMCA Homosexual Haven*.

4) My early reading eventually led to my preferred book, *TROY*, and the life of Lorenzaccio, that I'm now working on, and will probably have for title simply *Lorenzo*.

5) It was the founding moment of my love for Greece, the origin of my books *Greek Homosexuality, SPARTA, TROY, The Sacred Band* and *Alexander and Hephaestion.*

6) I later wrote about the irresistible pull of uncircumcised boys, exemplified by Al Parker who eventually had his foreskin restored, covered in my books *All-Boy Porn Stars, Phallus* and in my X-rated *Hustlers*

7) Flynn's life is recounted in my books *The Garden of Allah* and *Tasmania.*

8) At that exact same moment, unknown to me, groups of men were fighting for gay rights, the story of which is found in my book *The Mattachine Society.*

9) A fixation that led me to write *Phallus, the History of an Obsession.*

10) See my book *Greek Homosexuality*.

11) See my book *Boarding School Homosexuality*.

12) Only years later did I learn that such clothes were inspired by San Francisco Californians, their chief representative Al Parker. Jeans, lumberjack shirts, trimmed beards and moustaches, copied by so many boys that they became known as Parker clones, Al's life related in my X-rated book *Hustler*.

13) The memory of that evening was responsible, half-a-century later, for the writing of my book *Hadrian and Antinous*.

14) For reasons the reader will discover, I've now switched from the first person to the third person, from I to Boyd. Concerning my name: my father's first name was Boyd, which was my second name. I ceased using my first name, Michael, in favor of my second name at the time of his death.

15) The picture of which I chose for the jacket of my book *Renaissance Homosexuality*.

16) The reader will naturally believe that I deliberately coincided the bull's death with Phil's, a literary gimmick. A corrida *was* on the screen at the time, although I did structure it to coincide with the moments before Phil's suicide. A part of me has always been mesmerized by bullfights, the most violent form of killing allowed today, far worse than dogfights, which my dad took to me see several times during my childhood.

17) A problem coming gradually to France where, when I arrived, not only was obesity nonexistent, the French were not even a little overweight. Images from America continue to shock, and although, today, there are advertisements aimed at helping the French lose weight, I've never ever seen a single Frenchman as hideously fat as those commonly shown in malls or on the streets of the States.

18) For judicial reasons I'll have to let the reader decide which parts of the book are true, which are exaggerated, but in one form or another, in one location or another, it all did take place, as I'm incapable of invention, invention that I find superfluous when reality is always more unexpected and damning.

Which brings me to the inevitable question, Did I or did I not try to kill myself. The answer is I did. But in one of life's incredible surprises, I survived: The original ms was over 800 pages in length that I cut back to 300 for reasons of publication. Among the 500 cut pages was the story of Julien, that everyone called Monkey because he jumped on and off the boats, never using the gangway, or if the boat was extremely high he simply shinnied up the mooring ropes.

Once he spent the whole day cleaning a huge sailboat with teak decks and cabins, showing off a fabulous set of muscles, iron-hard pecs and abs, to the owner's wife and her teenage daughter. On this particular day I was on the *Denis* reading and admiring the kid from afar. Somewhere along the line the conversation must have turned to the subject of octopuses, because he dove into the water and came up with one. He tossed it aboard and climbed up the ropes to the deck, where the girls were examining the squirming animal. As the reader may know, octopus flesh is too tough to even chew, so it has to be tenderized by beating the animal against something hard, like a stone. Julien chose the teak deck he had just cleaned and polished. The reader may also know that the animal has a supply of indelible ink. The girls' oohs and awes rapidly turned into screams of indignation, the teak definitively ruined.

Because this was Julien's carefree (and, of course, brainless) way of going about things, he steadily lost customers, which forced him to consider expatriation to an English port. In order to do that he needed to publicize himself in London papers, and as he knew not a word of the language, that's where I came in. As Julien had no hours, he dropped by shortly after my suicide attempt, in search of the publicity I had written for him. He immediately called the SAMU, the French 911.

I exiled myself to the opposite corner of France from the French Riviera, to Hossegor, the surfing capital of Europe, a summer paradise of beautiful lads. Here I've decided to dedicate what remains of my years to historical works recounting the fabulous lives of the men and boys who preferred other men and boys.

As de Roquette said, there's always at least one moment of tenderness in a parched life, and that moment for me came through my father's natural curiosity to see if I was developing normally, by checking me for what is called, today, morning wood, which reminds me of a film in which Mastroianni asks his son's mistress if his boy is a good lover; she can't believe her ears but the enquiry is nothing more than age-old concern/curiosity of a father about his son's manhood. As far as I can remember, it was the only moment he *ever* touched me.

As for the rest: The book's Port Beausoleil is a fictitious name, although there is a very real Port Beausoleil, on the Riviera, that is very close to the one in my book. Two dogs are mentioned, but I've never hurt an animal in my life. I've been unable to find my first lover, Philippe, to apologize to him, although I sent letters to every Philippe who shares his last name in Brest, and there are more than a hundred! Léa is going strong at nearly 100 and her son Bertrand, the owlish lad with thick glasses, is now a renowned French brain surgeon. I will die a virgin, heterosexually, hopefully on the *Denis*, as originally planned.